THE SUNLIT SUMMIT

THE SUNLIT SUMMIT

The life of W.H. Murray

Robin Lloyd-Jones

Foreword by Robert Macfarlane

SANDSTONEPRESS
HIGHLAND | SCOTLAND

First published in Great Britain by
Sandstone Press Ltd
PO Box 5725
One High Street
Dingwall
Ross-shire
IV15 9WJ
Scotland.

www.sandstonepress.com

Editor: Robert Davidson
Copy editor: Kate Blackadder
Technical support: David Ritchie
Index: Corey Gibson

The publisher acknowledges subsidy from
Creative Scotland towards publication of this volume.

ISBN: 978-1-908737-38-0
ISBNe: 978-1-908737-39-7

Cover design by Gravemaker + Scott, Amsterdam
Typeset by Iolaire Typesetting, Newtonmore.
Printed and bound by Ozgraf, Poland.

CONTENTS

LIST OF ILLUSTRATIONS

Black & White

1. Murray on the Cioch in Skye. Ben Humble's best-known photograph taken when there was still full daylight at 9 pm, June 1936.

2. This photo was taken on the same evening as Plate 1. Murray commented that Humble would spend hours trying to get the right shot.

3. Murray climbing in Skye with the Cioch below.

4. Murray (standing) with Rob Anderson on the Cuillin ridge, Skye. It was Anderson who drew the maps and diagrams for several of Murray's books.

5. Murray, Douglas Laidlaw (sitting) and Dr J.H.B. Bell outside the CIC Hut during the exceptionally hot summer of 1940 that was overshadowed by war.

6. Part of the first page of Murray's application to join the SMC. 'Occupation' has been left blank because, in 1945, Murray was still in the army and uncertain of his future.

7. A pre-war group outside Lagangarbh, Glencoe.

8. JMCS membership card, 1939. Murray's address on the card is his mother's house.

9. JMCS programme for 1937. The JMCS was at the centre of Murray's climbing activities and of his social life.

10. Percy Unna in 1932. Unna, a former president of the SMC, was one of the NTS' greatest benefactors and was passionate about keeping the mountains unspoiled.

11. Dr 'Jimmy' Bell who climbed frequently with Murray and whose exploits spanned the pre- and post-World War I years, linking with the newly formed JMCS and helping to keep Scottish climbing alive.

12. Tom Longstaff in the Alps, 1904. Murray greatly admired Longstaff and his uncompetitive attitude to mountaineering.

13. POWs at Chieti, Italy. Taken in 1942 at the same time as Murray was imprisoned there.

14. The first moment of freedom. A jeep of the American Ninth Army arriving at the gates of the Brunswick prison camp in Germany in the Spring of 1945.

15. 1950 Scottish Himalayan Expedition. Dotial porters carrying heavy loads at 18,000 feet to Camp 3 on Bethartoli Himal.

16. Gorges and rushing torrents sometimes gave way to calmer waters and time for contemplation.

17. Tea break during one of the many long treks through the Eastern Garhwal region of the Himalayas. Tom Weir holding up his mug.

18. The Sona glacier beneath one of the peaks of the Panch Chuli.

19. Dotial porter with the head of a goat which had been executed for a feast. Goats in this part of the Himalayas were also used as pack animals by the local people.

20. Loading a jhopa, a kind of yak, for the trek from Dunagiri to Malari. The agreed load for each jhopa was 160 pounds.

21. Camp 2 on the unsuccessful attempt to climb South Lampak Peak. Behind the tent is the 7,000-foot wall of Tirsuli. Note the evidence of a recent avalanche.

22. The Central Pinnacle at 18,000 feet on Uja Tirche. Murray, Scott, Weir and MacKinnon went on from there to make a first ascent of Uja Tirche's North Ridge (20,350 feet).

23. 'Number your red-letter days by camps, not by summits,' Tom Longstaff wrote in a letter to Murray. In camp was where expeditions could relax, enjoy their surroundings and the company.

24. Payday for the porters. Murray at the table with Scott behind.

25. Murray wearing a monk-like cape at Darmaganga. Next to him is Douglas Scott.

26. This portrait of Murray, taken in a professional studio, was used on the cover of his autobiography.

8. Murray at the entrance to the Githri Gorge on the 1950 Scottish Himalayan Expedition. One of many fine shots taken by Douglas Scott who later became a professional photographer.

9. Camp at the base of the Panch Chuli, 1950 Scottish Himalayan Expedition.

10. 1950 Scottish Himalayan Expedition. Centre row from left to right: Scott, Murray, MacKinnon. The six porters are the Dotials who stayed with them throughout the four and a half months of the expedition.

11. Lochwood on the shores of Loch Goil, which Murray bought in 1947 and lived there for the remaining 48 years of his life.

12. Murray (left) at a meeting of the CCS, Battleby House Conference Centre, Perthshire, in 1974. He is talking to Sir John Verney, at that time a Forestry Commissioner and Chairman of the Countryside Commission's English Committee.

13. Photo taken after presentation of honorary degrees by University of Strathclyde in 1991. Front (l to r): Prof. Ian Macleod, Murray, Sir Graham Hills (Vice-chancellor); back: Peter West, unknown, unknown, and Dougie Donnelly, the TV broadcaster, who was also receiving an award that day.

14. Murray with the adapted slater's hammer which he used on his pre-war ice climbs.

15. Left to right: Murray, Scott and Weir in their later years.

16. Cover of first edition of *Mountaineering in Scotland*, published in 1947.

17. Murray's *Highland Landscape*, published in 1962, continues to influence country planning reports regarding the delineation and preservation of areas of natural beauty.

18. Murray, aged 80, in his study at Lochwood, reading from his manuscript of *Mountaineering in Scotland*.

Sources of Illustrations

Black & White:
1–3   Ben Humble, courtesy of Roy Humble
4, 15–23   Douglas Scott, courtesy of Audrey Scott
5   J.E. McEwan
6, 7, 10, 11   SMC Image Archive
13, 14   Imperial War Museum
8, 9   JMCS Archives
12   Courtesy of Anne Amos
24, 25   Tom Weir, with permission of National Library of Scotland,
            courtesy of Rhona Weir
26   J. Stephens Orr
27–31   Royal Geographical Society
32   Alpine Club

Colour:
1   Robin Lloyd-Jones
2, 4, 11   Michael Cocker
Cover image, 3, 5, 7–10, 15   Douglas Scott, courtesy of Audrey Scott
6, 18   BBC and Triple Echo Films
12   John Foster
13   University of Strathclyde Library, Department of Archives &
      Special Collections
14   Ken Crocket
16   J.M. Dent & Sons Ltd.
17   National Trust for Scotland

Sketch Maps:
1–3   Sallie Lloyd-Jones

ACKNOWLEDGEMENTS

I am grateful to the Scottish Arts Council (later to become Creative Scotland) and to The Authors' Foundation (administered by the Society of Authors) for generous funding which, at various stages, has sustained the research and writing of this book over a period of four years.

I wish to acknowledge a very special debt to Robert Aitken who has been my mentor throughout the production of this biography. His knowledge of all things related to Murray is unrivalled. This he has generously shared with me, supplying me with books, documents, contacts, information and much good advice. *The Sunlit Summit* could not have been written without his help.

Special thanks are also due to Robin Campbell, The Scottish Mountaineering Club's archivist, for pointing me towards a wealth of useful material; and to Michael Cocker who made available to me the results of his own research into aspects of Murray's life, and has allowed me to make extensive use of his annotated Chronology of Murray's 1935–45 climbs.

Murray was widely respected and admired and this is reflected in the long list of people who were eager to help me celebrate his life and achievements and to offer their assistance. In particular I would like to thank Penny Aitken, Prof. Gavin Arneil, Richard Balharry, Chris Bartle, Dr Donald Bennett, Prof. Ian Boyd, Bill Brooker, Margaret Brooker, Peter Broughan, Alastair Cain, Ken Crocket, Mark Diggins, Elizabeth Dutton, Douglas Elliot, Richard Else, Diana Foreman, John Foster, Dr Abbie Garrington, Ann Gempel, Terry Gifford, Prof. David Guss, A.H. Hendry, David Hewitt, Joy Hodgkiss, Glyn Hughes, Roy Humble, Tomoko Iwata, David Jarman, Bridget Jensen, Dr Michael Jepps, Sir John Lister-Kaye, Jimmy Marshall, John Mayhew, Malcolm McNaught, Rennie McOwan, Findlay McQuarrie, Amy Miller,

Prof. Denis Mollison, Graham Moss, Charles Orr, Malcolm Payne, Jim Perrin, Tom Prentice, Dr Martin Price, John Randall, Roger Robb, Jean Rose, Marjory Roy, Des Rubens, Audrey Scott, Gordon Smith, Roger Smith, Hannah Stirling, David Stone, Suilvan Strachan, Greg Strange, Maud Tiso, Russell Turner, Dr Frances Walker, Dr Adam Watson, Rhona Weir, Felicity Windmill, Susan Wotton, Alan Zenthon, Ted Zenthon.

In my research the following organisations were especially helpful: The Alpine Club, Buckfast Abbey Archives, The Glasgow Academy, Imperial War Museum, Island Book Trust, Junior Mountaineering Club of Scotland, John Muir Trust, the Meteorological Office, Mitchell Library, The National Archives, National Library of Scotland, the National Trust for Scotland, Random House Group Archive & Library, Royal Scottish Geographical Society, Scottish Mountaineering Club, Scottish Natural Heritage, University of Strathclyde Archives, Triple Echo Films. My thanks go to the officers and staff of these organisations.

All sources of quotations or special insights have been acknowledged in the notes for each chapter. The sources of the photographs are also acknowledged. My thanks to all concerned for permission to use their work. My thanks, too, to the authors listed in the Bibliography. Not all of them are mentioned in the text, but they influenced my thinking nonetheless.

I am most grateful for the helpful comments made on the draft text by Robert Aitken, Michael Cocker, Andrew Muir, Jim and Olive Muir, Deborah Nelken, and members of the Helensburgh Writers' Workshop.

The support and encouragement of my family has been important to me during this project. This includes hours of secretarial work by my grand-daughter, Chloe da Costa, research advice from my cousin Angharad Williams, help in solving various computer problems from my niece, Julia Rardin and her son Stephen, and proof-reading and map-drawing by my wife Sallie. To the latter also goes my gratitude for her patience and understanding.

Finally, I would like to thank Robert Macfarlane for his support and for writing such an insightful Foreword to this book; and Robert Davidson, my editor at Sandstone Press, for his cheerful encouragement throughout the project.

Foreword by ROBERT MACFARLANE

The term 'essay' (*essai*), so familiar to us now, was first coined by Michel de Montaigne in 1580 to mean a short prose discussion of a particular subject. Montaigne made his noun out of the verb essayer, which in Renaissance France connoted variously *apprendre par experience* (to learn from experience) and *éprouver* (to test or undergo). Implicit in the essay form at its birth, therefore, was a sense of exploration. To 'essay' was to try but also to be tried; it involved discovery, but without clear promise of outcome.

W.H. Murray was in life, as on the page, an essayist. Mountaineer, writer, explorer, philosopher, conservationist; hob-nailed aesthete, bank-clerk mystic, secular monk, intellectual knight-errant: he was all of these things, and he was them all adventurously, for the key criterion of adventure was, in his definition, 'uncertainty of result'. He climbed as he wrote as he meditated as he lived: exhilarated by the endeavour and unsure of the conclusion. '*Que scay-je?*' was Montaigne's motto ('What do I know?') and it might also have been Murray's, for like Montaigne he understood that to establish the extent of one's knowledge is necessarily also to establish the extent of one's ignorance. Almost all of Murray's writing – not just his best-known essays – glimmer with 'the evidence of things not seen', and are devoted to those kinds of experience that can only be glimpsed or intuited, rather than seized and simply scrutinised. Into the heart of mountain literature, Murray smuggled the spirit.

His greatest essays are prose canticles in terms of pattern and beauty; they ring with fierce joy and sharp wit; and they are also (quietly, unobtrusively) attempts to express the ineffable. Several of their scenes are blazed onto my memory, and have come to influence my own mountain days: swimming in the sea-lochs of Skye, bone-tired but mind-blown; or a winter dusk on high ground, with 'the wide silent snow-fields crimsoned by the rioting sky, and ... the frozen hills under the slow moon'. Yes, Murray knew how to hear what he once called 'the world's song', and he knew how to catch something of that song in language also. Deep in an essay on Glencoe, he talks of those uncommon places where 'the natural movement of the heart' is 'upwards'. His essays are just such places – they leave you shifted, lifted.

There need never be another account of Murray's life. We have his posthumously published autobiography, and now – in the year of the centenary of Murray's birth – Robin Lloyd-Jones's subtle and wonderful biography, *The Sunlit Summit*. Taken together, these two books tell us all that needs to be known about Murray. Robin has filled in some of the many ellipses of the autobiography, but without ever compromising Murray's keen instincts for discretion and dignity. He has chosen not to write a cradle-to-grave biography, but instead to focus on those periods when Murray's 'life was lived at great intensity'. The narrative structure that results from this decision is intricate in its form and skilful in its moves: with cut-aways from Italian prison-camp to Lochaber ridge, and flash-forwards from the Alps to the Himalayas. We gain oversight of Murray's long and varied career, and we gain insight to the episodes that shaped him most.

The first of these was his discovery of the hills, which came surprisingly late in his life: Murray grew up in Glasgow as a 'confirmed pavement dweller', until in 1935, aged 22, he climbed his first Scottish mountain – the Cobbler in Arrochar – kicking steps in the snow, and slipping upwards in a pair of unsuitable shoes. The experience struck him with the power of a conversion: 'From that day I became a mountaineer.' In the five years that followed, Murray was a climbing tiger, pioneering new routes, forcing established classics under desperate conditions, and – in Robin's phrase – 'giving back to Scottish mountaineering the impetus which had been lost in the trauma of the Great War'.

Then came the World War II: Murray served in the North African desert during the months of Rommel's dominance, saw fierce fighting, and escaped death so repeatedly that it came to him to resemble fate rather than chance. He was taken prisoner at the Battle of Tobruk, and confined to a series of camps in Italy, Czechoslovakia and Germany, where he suffered severe and prolonged physical deprivation. While for most POWs, incarceration was a closing-down of life, Murray was opened up. He 'lived inside his mind amongst the mountains he loved', as Robin finely puts it, and somehow wrote much of what would be published as *Mountaineering in Scotland* (stuffing the manuscript down the front of his battledress tunic when in transit between camps, and patiently reconstructing it after the first draft was confiscated and destroyed by the Gestapo).

In the camp at Mahrisch Trubau came Murray's second conversion, when the charismatic younger officer Herbert Buck chose him as his disciple in 'the Mystic Way' and inducted him into Perennial Philosophy. Robin is especially good on this encounter, sorting rumour from fact, and demonstrating the consequences of Buck's teaching for Murray's later life, including his conservation politics. In 1961 Murray was commissioned by the National Trust for Scotland to produce a report on the Highland landscape, identifying and describing those regions which were of supreme value. With bracing boldness, he elected 'beauty' as his chief principle of evaluation, defining it as 'the perfect expression of that ideal form to which everything that is perfect of its kind approaches' – hardly the kind of language that would survive the crushing-machine of contemporary planning policy. Murray worked out his definition in part from Plato, and in part from Buck, Huxley and Perennialism. The result was his landmark book *Highland Landscape* (1962), the influence of which has been pervasive if not dramatic, and which advances Murray's deeply held conviction that wild places are good places, and that we must preserve them as aspects of what Wallace Stegner once beautifully called 'the geography of hope'.

At the centre of Murray's achievement, and therefore rightly at the centre of *The Sunlit Summit*, is *Mountaineering in Scotland*: a book 'written from the heart of the holocaust', in Murray's unforgettable phrase. The title of his most famous book has long imprisoned it. Who but a Scottish mountaineer, one wonders, would wish to read a book called *Mountaineering in Scotland?* The answer, of course, is almost anyone who picks it up. I have long wanted to see Murray understood and valued beyond the borders of 'mountain-writing', and the contexts provided here by Robin make that newly possible.

To my mind, Murray should be seen as an outlier of the Scottish Renaissance of the 1930s, and especially as familial with two other great Highland writers, Nan Shepherd (*The Grampian Quartet*) and Neil Gunn (*Highland River, Silver Darlings, The Atom of Delight*). Murray shared with both writers an engagement with mysticism (predominantly Zen Buddhism for Gunn and Shepherd; Perennialism in Murray's case), and with the transcendent experience enabled by certain kinds of landscape, particularly Scottish. The work of all three writers contains crucial moments, set in wild country, in which the consciousness of the subject is expanded to the point of dissolution, and the individual is – as Murray puts it – 'self-surrendered to the infinite'. If this is a kind of grace, it is Pelagian in nature: and searched-for and 'self-surrendered' to, rather than chance-bestowed as in Augustine. Thus Nan Shepherd 'melting' into the granite of the Cairngorms – and thus Murray, walking alone and at night, feeling 'something of the limitation of personality fall away as desires were stilled; and as I died to self and became more absorbed in the hills and sky, the more their beauty entered into me, until they seemed one with me and I with them'. At moments as these, Murray's language wavers on the brink of production and failure. Words are the only viable medium of record, and yet what is being recorded by definition exceeds language. This has long been the generative paradox of mystical literature, and for Murray – as for St John of the Cross, or Thomas Merton – it is the best way to resist an impoverishing divide between subject and object.

Not all of Murray's readers have warmed to these aspects of his work and thought: 'Bill saw an angel in every pitch,' remarked his climbing companion William Mackenzie (though, like Robin, I take this as an expression of fond bafflement, rather than a jab at ersatz mysticism). Certainly it is easy, when writing of intense spiritual experience, to lapse into a sonorous vagueness. Murray never does, and one reason is that he ballasts his visions with precise empirical detail: thus the 'fat blue spark where a boot-nail struck bare rock' as he descends Crowberry Ridge on Buachaille Etive Mor at night, or the plate-like white ice that cracks and shivers off beneath his feet as he struggles his way up Tower Ridge on Ben Nevis.

Murray's other salvation is his humour. He is a very funny writer, alert to the semi-epic, semi-silly aspects of mountaineering. I often hear hints of P.G. Wodehouse and Pooter in his prose, particularly in the mock-heroic portrayal of his friends Mackenzie, Ben Humble and

Archie MacAlpine (the last of whom, as a pyromaniac stoker of bothy fires, 'had the genius of Satan himself'). At times, reading Murray, the Highlands can feel like a high-altitude, high-risk Blandings – but with the cocktail of choice being 'Mummery's Blood' (three oxo cubes and two gill bottles of rum mixed in a pint of boiling water on a primus stove) instead of Bertie Wooster's beloved boozy battering-ram, 'The Green Swizzle' (rum, crème de menthe, lime, mint, ice, mixed in a highball on a tortoiseshell bar).

The man who emerges in this biography, then, is rich in contrast if not in contradiction: a comic mystic, a modest hero, a lover of the particular but a devotee of universalism, a fierce cleaver to principle but a believer in transcendence. Robin's own formidable range of learning ('From Coleridge to Changabang' reads the title of one chapter, and it might stand for the reach of the whole) allows him to relate the many sides of his subject: he is made vivid in his complexities, lucid in his achievements, and we understand him to be – as Robin puts it – 'not the second John Muir, [but] the first Bill Murray'.

The last lines of Murray's autobiography take the form of a retrospect that is also a prospect. He imagines himself in some high place, with life stretching away from him in the form of terrain traversed and loved: 'Looking back over a wide landscape, cloud shadows racing over the mountains, sun, wind. I know that I have known beauty.' It is a rare and moving declaration of certainty from a man who was so invested in the importance of not-knowing, and in the enlightenments of ignorance. Beauty was his final conviction: the point to which, over the course of his remarkable life, he had essayed.

Robert Macfarlane, February 2013

INTRODUCTION

To begin with the basic facts of Bill Murray's life: William Hutchison Murray was born on 18th March 1913 in Liverpool. At the age of two he was taken by his mother to live in Glasgow where he grew up, attending a private school before becoming a trainee banker. He began climbing in 1935. He and a group of friends in the Junior Mountaineering Club of Scotland were soon one of the top ranking climbing teams in Scotland, particularly when it came to winter snow and ice climbing. They gave back to Scottish mountaineering the impetus which had been lost in the trauma of the Great War. His book *Mountaineering in Scotland*, published in 1947, inspired a similar regeneration following World War II. It remains one of the great classics of mountain literature.

At the outbreak of the war he was commissioned into the Highland Light Infantry. Only a few months later he was in action in the Western Desert in a last ditch defence to slow the advance of Rommel's tanks. He was captured and spent the next three years as a prisoner-of-war, first in Italy, then in Czechoslovakia and Germany. It was during this time that he wrote the major part of *Mountaineering in Scotland*. He also used this time to study the Perennial Philosophy – based on the transcendental and mystical elements of the world's major religions – which was to guide him for the rest of his life.

After the war, Bill Murray considered entering a monastery, but finally chose to make a living as a writer. From his pen came over 20 books, embracing mountaineering, travel and exploration, conservation, history and topography, and four novels. He wrote the first serious full-length biography of Rob Roy MacGregor to appear in a hundred years, which was a landmark in the study of the man. His guidebooks to the Highlands and Islands, as well as displaying an impressive breadth of research, are amongst the most beautifully written of their kind.

In the post-war years Murray returned to climbing and, between 1950 and 1953, took part in several Himalayan explorations. He was deputy-leader of the reconnaissance expedition which established the viability of the route by which the first ascent of Everest was made. From the 1960s onwards he was heavily involved in campaigns to conserve the Scottish countryside. His book, *Highland Landscape*, commissioned by the National Trust for Scotland, identified areas of outstanding beauty that should be protected. It proved to be extremely influential. The fact that most of these areas remain relatively unspoiled today owes much to his guidance and to his tireless work on a wide range of committees, often as president or chairman. He was awarded an OBE in 1966. Amongst his other awards were the Mungo Park Medal of the Royal Scottish Geographical Society and Honorary Doctorates from the universities of Strathclyde and Stirling. W.H. Murray died at the age of 83 on 19th March 1996.

To reach the top and be highly respected in one's chosen field of endeavour is something achieved by only a few; to have done this in three different spheres of activity – as a mountaineer, as a writer and as a conservationist is truly remarkable. Moreover, within these different spheres he was amazingly versatile. These days, most people become experts by specialising, but Murray was an all-round mountaineer, climbing at a high standard both on summer rock and winter ice, before moving on to Himalayan mountaineering and the exploration of wild and uncharted ranges. As a writer he mastered several forms, producing both fiction and non-fiction. His conservation work encompassed a huge range of concerns and organisations to which he gave unstintingly of his time and energy, mostly for no financial reward.

The vast amount of research he did for his books, in the field and in libraries, covering history, geology, architecture, natural history and environmental topics, combined with his conservation experience, made him a leading authority on matters related to the Scottish Highlands and Islands. He was a man whose advice, opinion and support were sought by many.

A proper understanding of Murray's life and work requires that we appreciate four things about him: Firstly, his driving force was his quest to achieve inner purification that would lead him to oneness with Truth and Beauty.

Secondly, from this same quest stemmed his striving after denial of self which translated into a life of service to others. This is well illustrated by the various posts he held: Commissioner for the Countryside Commission for Scotland (1968–1980); President of The Scottish Mountaineering Club (1962–1964) and of the Ramblers Association Scotland (1966–82); Chairman of Scottish Countryside Activities Council (1967–82); Vice-president of The Alpine Club (1971–72); President of the Mountaineering Council of Scotland (1972–75).

Thirdly, was his lifelong love of mountains and of exploration. He never spoke about 'conquering' a mountain. For him, it was not about ego, but more about mountains helping him to conquer self. The fourth point we need to appreciate is that he was a quiet, modest and extremely private man who sought neither fame nor fortune, and abhorred boasting and any form of self-promotion or publicity-seeking. The consequence of this has been that he has not received the recognition he deserves. Amongst mountaineers, connoisseurs of mountain literature and professional Scottish conservationists, he is remembered and honoured, but to the general public and outside Scotland he is largely unknown. Redressing this situation has been one strand in my desire to write a biography of W.H. Murray.

Although several excellent articles and obituaries about Murray have drawn together his diverse achievements, only a full length account of his life can fully do him justice. This will be the first time that all of his 20-plus books[1] have been discussed under one cover. With the perspective of time passed and in the context of the present day, there are new things to say; and the time is right for another look at many of his misgivings about the destruction of the natural environment and the loss of wilderness areas

In the mid 1960s, I read *Mountaineering in Scotland* for the first time and was entranced by it. Although I have written other books, this will be my first biography because no other person has filled me with such a strong desire to write about them. I feel that I have at least a few things in common with Bill Murray – as a lover of mountains and of the wild places, as a fellow writer, both of wilderness topics and of fiction, and as someone who, as did he, daily meditates. I am of an age to know what climbing was like in the 1950s. I started climbing in nailed boots (who these days knows what tricounis are?) and with hemp ropes and appreciate Murray's achievement in pioneering the routes he did with such equipment.

Murray's quasi-autobiography, *The Evidence of Things Not Seen* was published posthumously in 2002. Eleven years might not seem a long enough gap for another book about him, but it was the last chance to talk to people who remembered him. Even so, with regard to a number of key people, I left it too late. However 2013, the hundredth anniversary of Murray's birth, seems a fitting time to bring out a book that celebrates the life of this remarkable man.

In writing *The Sunlit Summit* I have been aware that there is probably not enough mountaineering detail in it for the mountaineers, nor a deep enough literary discussion for the admirers of his books, and those who move in conservation circles might find it falls short of giving a blow-by-blow account of the many campaigns in which Murray was involved. At the same time, to go into too much detail on any of these aspects would not best serve the majority of readers. I have tried to overcome this by putting additional detail in the appendices and in footnotes. This approach has resulted in a large number of appendices. We decided to put the bulk of these online. Appendix 5, at the end of this book, gives further details about this. The two chapters about his winter ascents of Observatory Ridge and Tower Ridge on Ben Nevis will, I hope, give a flavour of the kind of Scottish routes Murray and his friends were tackling in the 1930s. Likewise I have given two whole chapters to his Scottish Himalayan Expedition in order to convey something of the feel of a lengthy expedition of that kind and its aftermath.

Earlier in this Introduction I indicated that the guiding light in Murray's life was his mystical philosophy. Some people are uncomfortable with this aspect of his life and they skip the passages in his books that deal with these matters. I would urge any such readers of this biography not to by-pass the two chapters which discuss Murray's philosophy, for without an understanding of it there can be no real understanding of the man.

This biography does not follow Murray's life year by year, rather it focuses on those periods when life was lived at great intensity, on key moments and turning points, and on the ruling preoccupations in his life. The last six chapters then attempt an overview and evaluation of Murray as a mountaineer, writer and conservationist, and of his life as a whole.

We learn a great deal about Murray from his own books and articles. In reading them closely and as a complete body of work, certain anomalies and contradictions are noticeable. To my mind, these are not of any great significance. Our lives are seldom conducted on logical and rational lines and memory is less like a filing clerk and much more like an editor trying to make sense of things, to fill in gaps, act as censor and to arrange and re-arrange the material into stories.

About one third of *The Sunlit Summit* is spent discussing Murray's books and Murray as a writer. To devote a substantial proportion of the book to this seems appropriate since it was as a writer that Murray elected to make a living; it is through his own writing that we learn most of what we know about him; it was his ability to harness the power of the written word that made him such a persuasive and effective advocate of his chosen causes; and it is his books which are the most tangible reminders of him today. In giving less space to his conservation work I do not mean to underrate the impact he has made in this field, nor the importance of the issues involved. Indeed, with the passage of time, and with environmental problems becoming more and more pressing, this aspect of his work becomes increasingly significant. It may well be that, in years to come, this is what he will be remembered for above all else.

I think it only right that I should say that Murray's widow, Anne, did not want a biography written about her husband. He was such a private man, she said, and he would have hated the idea. The consequence of this has been that I have not had access to material which undoubtedly would have made this a better informed account than it is. On the other hand, I may have been too late anyway. Several reports reached me of Murray, not long before his death, being spotted burning letters and diaries on a bonfire in his garden – most probably the act of a man protecting his privacy.

I admire Mrs Murray's loyalty in sticking to what she regards as her husband's wishes, but once a person enters the public domain they have forfeited their right to at least some of their privacy. Murray himself must have realised that one cannot expect to write over 20 books, some of them influential books, without his readers wanting to know more about the man who wrote them and to discuss what he said. My intention is not to intrude on his privacy except in so far as it illuminates and adds to our understanding of those areas in which he himself chose to enter the public domain.

Although Murray was married for 36 years, he wrote a total of two and a half pages about his wife and his marriage. In doing this, he was following Anne's wishes. Undoubtedly, his marriage was important to him, but I have not wanted to trespass on private territory and have written only the same amount as Murray did himself on this aspect of his life.

It has been my privilege and pleasure to get to know Bill Murray better than I did before I started writing this book; and my privilege and pleasure, too, to meet so many interesting people along the way. I repeat my thanks here to all those named in the Acknowledgements.

NOTES

1. The exact total of Murray's books depends on whether, as well as his main works, one is counting (i) books of photographs by others, which have a text by Murray which is only a small proportion of the whole book; (ii) short works written, not for mainstream publishers, but for organisations such as the Junior Mountaineering Club of Scotland, or the National Trust for Scotland; (iii) his quasi-autobiography which was unfinished at the time of his death and was then completed by his wife and published posthumously.

   Counting all categories, Murray had 25 books published. Appendix 2 shows a complete list of all Murray's published work, including his many articles, book reviews, and Forewords and chapters in other people's books.

CHAPTER ONE

THE LONGEST AND HARDEST CLIMB[1]

In February 1938, the same month that Hitler took direct control of the German military, and Walt Disney's ground-breaking *Snow White and the Seven Dwarfs* was first screened, three young men from Glasgow were mere dots on the vastness of Ben Nevis. Bill Murray, Archie MacAlpine and Bill Mackenzie, were attempting what would be only the second winter ascent of Observatory Ridge. Beset by unexpectedly poor conditions, they had been ascending and traversing unstable snow for more than nine hours. Night had fallen and they were only just beyond the half-way point. A single mistake by any one of them might mean disaster for all. They were tiring and the unremitting danger was 'not easy to bear with indifference'. Mackenzie was in the lead, cutting steps in the ice:

> 'Until my days are ended I shall never forget that situation,' Murray recalled. 'Crouching below the pitch amidst showers of ice-chips, I fed out the frozen rope while Mackenzie hewed mightily at the ice above, his torch weirdly bobbing up and down in the dark and the ice brilliantly sparkling under its beam. Looking down, I could see just a short curve of grey snow plunging into the darkness, then nothing until the twinkling lights of the Spean valley, four thousand feet below.'

The plan to make a winter ascent of this classic ridge had been hatched about a month before. As was their habit, Murray, MacAlpine and Mackenzie gathered on Thursday evening in MacAlpine's Glasgow home to plan their weekend climbing. At one such meeting in January 1938, amongst tankards of beer and maps spread out on the sitting-room floor, they discussed the ridges on Ben Nevis which, they reckoned, should be in perfect condition. Despite heavy falls of powder-snow, the strong and continuous winds would have swept them clean, exposing the older, harder, more secure snow and ice beneath. Then Mackenzie remembered that Observatory Ridge had not been climbed in genuine winter conditions since Raeburn's first winter ascent eighteen years earlier. It was a long climb – all of two thousand feet and not one, as Murray puts it, 'on which one could wander with an old umbrella.'

Soon after resolving to attempt the ridge in winter conditions, Murray sprained an ankle – not, he admits, as the result of some mountain escapade, but from slipping on the floor of a friend's house.[2] With growing impatience he rested his ankle while the days of perfect conditions slipped by and his friends regaled him with accounts of the wonderful climbing he was missing. Finally, 'sprain or no sprain, my stick went out of the window and I to Nevis with MacAlpine and Mackenzie.' And so, on Saturday 19th February, after finishing at work, they drove to Fort William. Their objective was The Scottish Mountaineering Club's Charles Inglis Clark Memorial Hut, high in the Allt a' Mhuillin glen on the fringe of Coire Leis, at the foot of the Nevis cliffs. As Mackenzie admitted, 'They lingered at the fleshpots',[3] not setting out for the hut until 8.30 pm. They lost the rough track and stumbled about in the freezing dark with loaded rucksacks. Not until midnight did they gain its warm, welcoming fug and the chance to brew up steaming mugs of rum punch.

Although referring to another occasion, Murray's report for *The Scottish Mountaineering Club Journal* of a meet held at the hut gives something of the flavour of those late night arrivals:

> 'Under the most adverse conditions of rain, mist and utter darkness, Murray succeeded in forcing a new route from the Distillery [the whisky distillery outside Fort William] to the hut. Although no beckoning light shone from its windows the snores of its occupant provided a sure and sufficient guide for the last few feet.'[4]

The hut's eight bunks, Murray says, were the best sprung and most comfortable on which he had ever slept. No doubt the long walk up to the hut or a hard day on Nevis had something to do with their perceived excellence. Murray described the hut as a school of further education. He didn't elaborate on this, but it is clear that this was a place to meet not only the top Scottish and English climbers of the day, but also a variety of interesting and eccentric characters and to learn from them. Murray captures the cosiness and warmth of that hut when he writes: 'I scrambled into my bunk. I lay back gratefully, watched the stove glow red through the darkness and listened to the wind thunder on the walls and roof.'[5] Of the joys of the glowing stove, he adds: 'Especially was this true if Archie MacAlpine was present. As fire stoker, he had the genius of Satan himself. Perhaps inspired by the latter after a heady brew, he once stoked the stove to an unprecedented redness, forgetting that he had put his blankets into the oven to warm.'[6]

Murray, Mackenzie and MacAlpine awoke that February morning to a clear, crisp, cloudless day. 'Straight from the doorway stretched the two miles of precipice, crowned with flowing snow-cornices, which blazed in the slanting sun-rays. From our feet the snowfields swept in a frozen sea to the cliffs, beating like surf against the base of ridge and buttress, leaping in spouts up the gullies.' From the hut it looked as if their predictions had been correct and that the ridges had been cleared by the wind. In front of them Observatory Ridge gradually tapered until its final thousand feet formed a delicate edge. They set out, their eyes feasting on the glinting mountainscape, the feathery powder 'squealing beneath our boots like harvest mice'.

As they approached Observatory Ridge via the base of Zero Gully, the latter seemed to them to be impregnable, so full was it with green overhanging ice. The lower flanks of Observatory Ridge immediately posed problems with loose, sugary snow, piled on ledges and slabs, threatening to slide off into space. They roped up and Mackenzie took the lead. Half an hour of searching this way and that finally yielded a possible way up. Even so, the holds on this almost vertical rib were 'distressingly far apart'. They overcame this first challenge only to find that, above it, there was more of the same. They had expected things to improve higher up where the wind should have scoured the ridge of powder-snow. Instead, they became worse. At one point, Murray was crossing a steep slab when the snow gave way beneath his feet. He slithered towards the edge and the huge drop below, just managing to stop his slide by latching onto two small finger-holds – an incident which played upon their minds, adding to the strain. In one 'loathsome and slabby gutter' the snow, which was providing the only available footing, flaked away before MacAlpine, who was last on the rope, had a chance to tackle it. Murray, directly above him, prepared to bring him up on the rope while standing on a single small foothold and with his only belay a tiny knob. It seemed inevitable that MacAlpine and the rock would part company at some point on his way up the treacherous gutter and far from certain whether Murray would be able to take the strain of it without being pulled off himself.

'When assured that all was ready and that my belay "would hold the *Queen Mary*," he calmly stubbed out his cigarette, carefully smoothed the corners of his moustache, tilted his balaclava, then with stylish glide came up that gutter like a Persian cat to a milk saucer.'

Once past the gutter they made better progress, steadily surmounting a succession of slabs, ledges, ribs and faces. When the angle of the ridge temporarily eased off they stopped for lunch on a wide stance. Below their feet the roof of the Nevis hut was a tiny red speck. They were now about mid-way through the climb. The ridge steepened again into a broad tower 70 feet high. Mackenzie disappeared round an awkward corner. The rope inched out painfully slowly. Apart from the occasional soft scuffling, 'all was silent save for the whisper of falling snow.' It took the three of them over an hour to get past those 70 feet. Now the ridge narrowed with huge cliffs on either side. Here, on the upper part of the mountain, they had expected it to be clearer, easier going. To their consternation it was smothered in huge volumes of unstable powder-snow. The sun was sinking low in the sky. They knew they were in trouble and that they had a long hard fight ahead of them. Mackenzie made the decision to leave the ridge and traverse along its western face.

Two hours later, the shelf along which they were slowly edging took them to a knife-sharp saddle and a subsidiary ridge which would lead them back to the main ridge. 'Mackenzie literally swam up these hundred feet, using the dog-stroke to cleave a passage up the massed powder.' As the sun was setting, after seven hours of climbing they found themselves once more on Observatory Ridge, but still with a long way to go. Despite their predicament, they could not but be impressed by the glorious sunset with the peaks aflame.

To give Mackenzie a rest, Murray took over the lead. Immediately he found the narrow upper section of the ridge swamped with powder held together only by 'an egg-shell crust'. It was unclimbable. The

SMC's Ben Nevis guidebook clearly stated that it was not possible to escape from the ridge into either of its flanking gullies. 'Unless we could reconcile ourselves to remaining where we were permanently the guide-book had to be proved wrong.'

In the gathering gloom they forced their way into Zero Gully. The same gully which lower down they had deemed impregnable now looked the better choice.[7] At this point in his narrative Murray pays tribute to Mackenzie and MacAlpine. With darkness falling, temperatures plummeting, fatigue setting in and their chances of survival rapidly diminishing, their cheerfulness and optimism boosted his own morale. In such circumstances, he says, 'it is the strength of the team, not of the individual, that carries the day'.

At last, in Zero Gully, with stars burning bright in the clear night sky, they found hard ice – the kind of ice in which they could cut firm, safe steps. Their hopes rose only to be dashed when they encountered yet more soft, unstable snow which continued all the way to the summit. They were tired and it was numbingly cold. The temptation was to risk it and hope that this loose layer would stay in place when they stepped on it and not avalanche into space. Experience told them, though, that they must excavate down to the hard ice beneath and then cut steps in that. Painstakingly, laboriously, they worked their way upwards, taking turns to lead. After two hours they reached the first ice-wall. Mackenzie dislodged a huge plate of snow-crust which fell onto MacAlpine's head, shattering into a thousand pieces.[8]

Another two hours went by. Two hours of hard labour or of waiting in the cold and dark, standing on small holds. With both their strength and their torch batteries fading, they overcame a second and then a third ice-wall. 'Up and up we went, digging, hitting, carving, scraping.' Suddenly, close to midnight, Zero Gully opened out and they were on the summit plateau. Mackenzie's lead that day was, says Murray, the greatest he would ever see on any mountain.

They had been in unrelenting conditions of danger for 14 hours.[9] In Murray's opinion it was the longest and hardest climb in relation to sheer strain that he was ever likely to do. 'We had learnt that when one stands on the summit after such a climb it is not the mountain that is conquered – we have conquered self and the mountain has helped us.' This second winter ascent of Observatory Ridge provided what Murray regarded as mountaineering at its best – there had been both adventure and beauty, 'the criterion of the one being uncertainty of result, and of the other, always inner purification'.

NOTES

1. The account in this chapter is based on Chapter XI, 'Observatory Ridge in Winter' in *Mountaineering in Scotland* and all quotes come from here unless otherwise stated.
2. Michael Cocker in his Chronology of Murray's pre-war climbs has this to say about Murray's mention of an injured ankle:
   'This is a curious statement because both Murray's and MacAlpine's applications [to join the SMC] show that they attempted Crowberry Gully together one of the two previous weekends' And Cocker goes on to point out that when writing about January 1939 *(Undiscovered Scotland*, page 112) Murray says, 'It even began to seem likely that we would miss a weekends climbing for the first time in eighteen months,' which suggests he didn't miss one in February 1938. Cocker concludes that Murray either made a mistake with the timing of these events or moved his injury on a couple of weeks for literary effect.
3. Mackenzie wrote his own account of the climb (SMCJ, 1938). It is interesting to compare it with Murray's account. There is no disagreement regarding the facts, but the styles are very different. Mackenzie's is a functional report, brief and to the point, understating the difficulties. Murray's is a literary essay which is expansive, reflective and dramatised, with a wider readership in mind than Mackenzie had.
4. Later, another of Murray's climbing companions, Dr J.H.B. Bell, who was then editor of *The Scottish Mountaineering Club Journal*, parodied this passage, in a footnote to an article by Murray, who had recently joined the army and was in the Middle East. The footnote gave a mock serious account of Murray forcing a route up the Sphinx outside Cairo.
5. *Undiscovered Scotland*, page 166.
6. *The Evidence of Things Not Seen*, page 37.
7. Zero Gully was not climbed in its entirety until 1957 – 19 years later – when Tom Patey, Hamish MacInnes and Graeme Nicol made the first ascent.
8. There is further mention of this incident in Chapter Seven.
9. The extent to which a winter route can vary in difficulty according to the conditions is demonstrated by the fact that, one year later, Murray repeated the same climb in six hours.

CHAPTER TWO

THE COMPANION GUIDE TO BILL MURRAY

Testing climbs like Observatory Ridge under severe winter conditions strip away the veneer and reveal a personality's true core. We learn a great deal about Murray from his reactions and behaviour on this climb and from the way he wrote about it and other climbs. For a more rounded picture of him, though, we need to see him in other situations and through other eyes.

Bill Murray was tall and lean, with a sharp beaky nose, thick dark hair and grey-blue eyes – eyes which a friend described as 'mountaineer's eyes that seemed to see to the far horizon'. Hamish MacInnes likened him to 'a frugal, contemplative eagle'.[1] Obviously he changed in appearance over the course of his 83 years – his hair thinned, he took to wearing spectacles and needed dentures. One person who knew him in later life said: 'He struck me as an old-fashioned gentleman. He was a tall, lean, spare, rather ascetic-looking man who seemed to me quiet, refined and civilised. He was reserved but certainly didn't have any of the airs and graces that one might expect given his fame and wasn't at all intimidating.'[2] Murray spoke in a polite, slightly refined way, which must have owed something at least to his mother, whose genteel accent made 'Bill' sound like 'Beel'. To say that he was slow of speech would be an understatement. It was as if he was weighing and measuring in his mind every word and sentence for content, accuracy and style as judiciously as he would were he writing rather than speaking. There were long pauses while he searched for exactly the right word. 'Sometimes it took a long time,' said a friend, 'but it was always worth the wait.' Others found it a bit disconcerting.

When Murray was 37, Tom Weir wrote an unpublished profile of him. He opens with this description of Murray:

'Study the portrait of Bill Murray. There is an air of preoccupation in the eyes. It is the face of a scholar rather than a man of action. But note the determined cast of the brows, and the leanness which betrays physical fitness. Yet if you were in his company for the first time you would remark nothing save that this tall, rather spare man, is quite self-contained, without being self-effacing. If you talk to him he will let you do most of the talking. You may think he is not listening, but the chances are you would be wrong. Behind that impassive front is the most alert brain it has been my good fortune to meet.'[3]

We are all the product of our times, influenced to varying extents by the attitudes and values that prevailed in our formative years. Sometimes we become who we are because we rebelled against what we saw as 'the old order'; and sometimes we absorb these ways of thinking and of seeing the world without even being aware of it. In most cases, we do both and Murray was no exception. When he was growing up between the two world wars the class system was in full swing; the middle classes, for the most part, had servants; and respect for authority was well embedded in most of the British population. In sport there was a clear distinction between amateurs and professionals. In cricket, for instance, there used to be an annual match in England between the Gentleman (the amateurs) and the Players (the working-class professionals). It went without saying that the captain of any county or national team had to be an amateur, that is, an educated, upper and officer class person of suitable social status.[4] Although these social distinctions were not quite so pronounced in Scotland as in England they were there nonetheless.

Shows of emotion were regarded as embarrassing and 'un-British' and were discouraged. Modesty, self-deprecation and even, to a certain degree, a lack of self-belief were regarded as attractive traits, whereas in today's 'because I'm worth it' and 'be all you can be' culture they are regarded as handicaps. People were generally much more 'buttoned up' than now. Sexual morality was a great deal sterner and more restrictive. Sex before marriage was a matter of much agonising and disapproval; people talked about 'living in sin' and to have a child outside wedlock was a social disaster both for mother and child – and these were the days before the contraceptive pill. Ignorance of matters related to sex was more prevalent than now

– many men, for example, did not know that women had periods, or only the vaguest notion about it. Homosexuality was illegal, even between consenting adults, and was punishable with a prison sentence. Anti-semitism still lingered. The term 'to jew someone,' meant to cheat them. Teenagers had only just been invented and were found mainly in America; the British Empire was still something people were proud to be part of; and, in cinemas, when the national anthem was played at the end, people stood to attention. Nobody made a connection between smoking and cancer, indeed a lot of people thought the former was good for you; no threat of nuclear war hung over the world; the idea of somebody landing on the moon was just ridiculous fantasy; there was no National Health Service or welfare state and few safety nets of any kind that individuals did not have to pay for themselves. Central heating in houses was only for the rich; people seemed hardened to cold to a much greater extent than now – nearly all public swimming pools were open-air and unheated. Murray and his friends would frequently swim in lakes and rivers, even in autumn, and think nothing of it. Men still adopted a patronising attitude to women, often regarding them as decorative appendages. It was not until 1928, when Murray was 15, that all women over 21 were given the vote. In 1918 the school leaving age was raised from 12 to 14 and in 1930 to 15. In fee paying schools, the classics still dominated the curriculum. Unemployment was at a high level throughout most of the 1920s and 30s. Murray was ten when the General Strike brought Britain to a halt and he was 19 when the hunger marches took place.

Murray had a well-developed sense of service to others and of concern for his fellow beings. 'Of all the questions ever asked by man,' he wrote, 'the most ignorant has been Cain's: "Am I my brother's keeper?" That acme of self-love is evil's real root.'[5] This belief showed itself in action in his selfless public life (documented elsewhere in this biography) and in his many acts of personal kindness to individuals. Bob Aitken, while still at school, wrote to Murray asking for his advice about how to become a mountaineer. Murray, at the time, was up to his eyebrows in work, trying to organise a Himalayan expedition. A lesser man would have ignored this letter from an unknown schoolboy. But not Murray. He replied at length, giving a great deal of practical advice, and offered, once he had returned from the Himalayas, to take Bob and a friend for a day on the hills –

which he duly did. Thereafter, Murray maintained an interest in the young Aitken, corresponding with him and encouraging him in his mountaineering endeavours.[6] Another of the many young climbers that Murray encouraged was Roger Robb.: ' Bill sent me a fine letter indicating that he had signed my JMCS [Junior Mountaineering Club of Scotland] proposal form and how best to derive experience for the membership of this club and freely noting the navigation problems around Glencoe. Bill kindly sent me a signed copy of the Glencoe rock climbing guide and instructions on what maps to purchase. All actions of a man wishing and I suppose hoping for a novice to take steps into the mountain world safely but more importantly to enjoy it and be adventurous.'[7] Murray was generous with his time, giving it unstintingly if he thought he could help. For instance he was very kind to and interested in his friend Donald McIntyre's handicapped son and made a lot of time for him. Murray spent hours at his desk writing letters to anyone he thought might be cheered by a few words from him. Not only was he generous with his time, he was generous in spirit, generous with his praise.

One of the keys to understanding Murray's life and character is to appreciate the extent to which he studied philosophy and was influenced by the teachings of the Eastern religions and by the early Christian mystics. More is said about this in Chapters Twelve and Thirteen. A strand common to all the religions he studied was denial of self – a strand in tune with the way he constantly thought of others before himself and put large amounts of time, which could have been spent in the mountains or gone into advancing his career as a writer and into earning a living, into championing conservation causes and serving on a whole range of committees related to the preservation of the countryside.

Another strand of his philosophy was his belief in Providence. His fearlessness and boldness of action was remarked upon by many who knew him and this, in some measure, stemmed from his belief that his life, his fate and the outcomes of his actions were in the hands of Providence. It was his search for truth and beauty, his belief in the unity and oneness of all things, and his practice of meditation which brought a touch of mysticism to his writing and also sometimes gave him an air of living in a world of his own, or existing on some higher plane.

A love of exploration was another characteristic which made Murray the person he was. He loved exploring mountains and wild country; his enquiring mind was forever exploring new ideas and beliefs and probing deeper into the great religions of the world; and, as a writer he explored different forms of both fiction and non-fiction, showing a remarkable versatility. 'It is indeed for striving and exploring and discovering that we are all made,' he wrote.[8]

Nearly everyone who met Murray remarked upon his modest manner. Some found it frustrating that he wouldn't expand on his exploits on Everest and other adventures. Any kind of boasting or self-aggrandisement was anathema to him and 'bad form'. On one occasion, in the Lake District, Murray and a friend were taking what they regarded as a day off from serious climbing and were indulging in an 'easy' walk when they were stopped and given a dressing down by a relative novice for not being properly equipped. Murray, one of the best known and most competent mountaineers in Britain at the time, stood there quietly and accepted the lecture without protest. The same modesty is evident in his writing. He is quick to praise his companions and give them credit and, although careful not to spoil a tale of adventure, reluctant to claim too much for himself. The prestigious Mungo Park Medal awarded to him by the Royal Scottish Geographical Society[9] he kept in the bottom of a drawer, rather than framed on the wall, as many would have done. Similarly, he preferred to be addressed as 'Mr' rather than 'Dr', despite his honorary doctorate from the University of Stirling; and he never put 'OBE' after his name on letters and never spoke about it. While in Skye (possibly in 1968), he rescued a fallen climber and helped him off the mountain and down to Glenbrittle.[10] It was typical of Murray that he does not mention this good deed, which must have interrupted his plans, in any of his books or articles; and also typical of him that he sent the rescued man a Christmas card.

Scores of people who knew Murray through mountaineering, conservation committees, through his writing, his sailing, or as friends, neighbours or partners of friends volunteered their impressions of him for this biography.[11] Obviously, these impressions were gathered only from those of his acquaintances who were still living and, therefore, come mostly from people who remembered him from the post-war years onwards.[12] Many said the same thing: that although they had known him for years, they never really knew him, for he was a reticent and private man. Even his wife, Anne, said that most of the time she had no idea what was going on inside his head. The following is a cross-section of these comments:

'Bill was awkward and shy with women which sometimes made him seem cold.'

'Bill Murray requested that I should join him on a rope up one of the easier gullies on the Buachaille Etive Mor. ... On later reflection and after several more years of climbing experience I came to realise that Bill was a sincere man in his judgment of what people are capable of doing, whatever background they came from. ... All this practical information imparted with fluency that only Bill could produce and was precise and infinitely patient when he asked you to apply what he had demonstrated. After several rope lengths of climbing he asked me to take the lead up the next few pitches. At the time and being a novice the significance of this gesture wasn't apparent, but now and from my own experience, it was a bold and carefully calculated move under all the circumstances he had to control, signifying how he could evaluate risk without endangering the party but allow adventure to be enjoyed.'[13]

'Bill tended to be modest, self-deprecating and quiet, almost too solemn in his manner and he was not as well known to the wider Scottish public as he should have been. He was a gentleman with a core of steel and the term "knightly" comes to mind.'[14]

'He could be brusque but also kind.'

'He respected other people's views and was never dogmatic.'

'An intellectual mountaineer, a man with a great breadth of knowledge.'

'On casual acquaintance he could appear distant, but to those to whom he extended his friendship, he showed absolute loyalty, infinite kindness, and touches of wicked humour.'[15]

'He used to make us his special "hoosh" as a treat and could never understand that what was appetising on the mountainside was pretty disgusting back in civilisation.'

'He always wanted and did his best for you.'

'He was a man who knew who he was and was comfortable with it. He had an enormous inner strength and stature.'

'If I had to sum him up in one word, I'd say "priest-like".'

'Bags of determination and a great companion.'[16]

'A gentle, introspective man whose writing transcended a natural diffidence to help shape the popular contemporary conception of Scotland's mountains. "Dreams are for action," he once said. And he had plenty of both.'[17]

One of the strands which runs through these comments is Murray's detachment, and the impression he gave that he lived on another level of consciousness. Murray himself recognised this when, in a letter to his sister, he described himself as 'a self-contained unit'.[18] Murray probably always was a fairly introverted character, but he became even more so after three years as a prisoner-of-war, where he endured and survived by retreating into his own thoughts: 'I learned how to concentrate by the very necessity of detachment. Having no other choice, I learned so well that it became ingrained, a permanent trait, causing in later years some social embarrassment to my friends, who would sometimes speak and not be heard.'[19]

For some people his reticence and formality made Murray appear cold, aloof, dour, self-absorbed and unfriendly, even dull. Such comments, however, seldom came from those who knew him well and, as one person said, 'He had to respect you before he opened up to you.' Some may have found him solemn, but it was certainly not his circle of friends. In a pub, he mellowed after a dram or two and his aloofness evaporated and his wit emerged. Over the years, readers of *Mountaineering in Scotland* have enjoyed his dry humour, his sense of irony and the way he gently and lovingly laughs at and with his friends, and at himself too.

Murray may have been shy with women, but those who knew him make it clear that 'he had an eye for the ladies' and 'a soft spot for pretty women'. Things he wrote in private letters show that female company was important to him. Nonetheless, there was an element of the confirmed bachelor about him. His pre-war years, his army and prison camp life were largely spent in male company. After the war, his Himalayan expeditions were all-male, The Scottish Mountaineering Club was for men only, and most of the committees he worked with were predominantly male. In a letter to Bob Aitken, then still at school, Murray invites him as his guest to an SMC reception and lecture and adds: 'the reception is rather a stuffy affair, with women guests present in large numbers, but the talk by Bonington you'd enjoy.' One suspects that his caveat about women being present is not just for a shy schoolboy, but something he felt in sympathy with himself. Four years later, he writes to Aitken: 'Congrats on acquiring the girlfriend, but give no ear to her ideas of wooing you away from climbing. Apart from which, women are one of the chief delights in life, when they're not being the reverse.' To what extent Murray's mother influenced his attitude to women is hard to say. She was a strict and upright person and, no doubt, warned him against 'fast' women. It is noticeable that, in his novels, only the women on the side of the baddies have any sensuality about them. In the late 1950s Murray had a girlfriend, Fiona Graham, to whom he proposed marriage, but was turned down. Very soon after this he met and married Anne Clarke. Chapter Thirty-Two has more to say on this.

Murray was a voracious reader from his schooldays onwards and his reading went deep. While a prisoner-of-war, from a wide range of subjects he could have studied, he chose English literature, poetry, psychology and philosophy. The kind of men Murray liked and admired were nearly all, like himself, intelligent, widely read people, with a broad range of interests and a sense of humour. Of Herbert Buck, his guru who introduced him to the Perennial Philosophy in prison camp, he wrote: 'Real moral strength is known to few ... I turned a critical eye on Buck, alert for imposture. At the end, I could find no fault. He was all that his words and acts claimed. This man was whole.'[20] Murray was clearly praising one of his younger climbing companions, R.G. Donaldson, when he said of him: 'He was very quiet and reserved. My first impression was that I had met a man in whose company no unwholesome thought could exist.'[21]

Straight dealing, integrity and wholeness were qualities for which Murray strove, and, according to many who knew him, achieved to a degree that singled him out. Here is Murray setting out the kind of person he aspired to be:

'It is a matter of experience that all feelings of disparagement, under-estimation, contempt and carping criticism are poisons that starve, stunt and wither the spiritual faculty; and that feelings of compassion, reverence and devotion are foods that nourish it and bestow energy.'[22]

What he disliked were 'humbug,' pretentiousness, boasting, and people who 'sat on the fence' or lacked the courage of their convictions. Complaining in a letter about someone, he said, 'He will trim his sails to whatever winds will give an easy passage rather than hold a true course for the ideal.' The moral strength to hold a true course for the ideal – that sums up the kind of man Murray tried to be and largely succeeded in being.

NOTES

1. In his Foreword to *The Evidence of Things Not Seen*.
2. Penny Aitken in an email to me, 22nd January 2010.
3. Tom Weir Collection in National Library of Scotland, Edinburgh.
4. When Len Hutton became the first professional to captain an England cricket team in 1952 it caused a huge controversy and many outraged letters in the press.
5. *The Evidence of Things Not Seen*, page 108.
6. In later years, Aitken was able to repay this kindness with much invaluable support and advice in matters to do with conservation. The correspondence continued throughout the rest of Murray's life.
7. In a letter to me from Roger Robb, dated 5th November, 2010.
8. These are the last lines in *The Story of Everest* (1953).
9. See online Appendix G for further details of the Mungo Park Medal.
10. This was Colin Robertson, who told me he was a bit vague on the details because of the bang to his head.
11. All those who provided this information are mentioned in the Acknowledge-ments, but only the sources of comments in print are given in the footnotes.
12. I gathered these impressions of Murray in the period 2008–2010.
13. See footnote 5.

14. From 'A True Man of The Mountains' by Rennie McOwan, in *The Scots Magazine*, December 2001.
15. From Murray's obituary by Bob Aitken, SMCJ, 1996.
16. From Murray's obituary by Bill Mackenzie, SMCJ, 1996.
17. Colin Wells, writing on ScotlandOnline, 8/8/2002.
18. *The Evidence of Things Not Seen*, page 328.
19. *Ibid*, page 302.
20. *Ibid*, page 111.
21. *Mountaineering in Scotland*, page 150.
22. 'The Approach Route to Beauty' in SMCJ, 1948.

CHAPTER THREE

THE CHILD IS FATHER OF THE MAN

Murray was only two years old when his father was killed at Gallipoli in the Dardanelles Campaign of 1915. Before the Great War his father was HM Inspector of Mines for Lancashire and North Wales. He had been based in Liverpool, where Murray was born, and it was from there that Murray's mother, Helen, took him and his sister, Margaret, five years his senior, back to Glasgow where his paternal grandparents lived. Of growing up without a father Murray says, 'the realisation of loss came later, but never did I feel wronged.'[1] Very little is known about his relatives. It is a measure of how self-contained he was that he chose not to write about them in his autobiography and never seems to have talked about them to his friends.

In general, what boys without fathers tend to lack in their upbringing is the male element of rough play and being introduced to physically challenging, risk-taking activities – all elements which mountaineering provided. Possibly this played some part in the way Murray, when aged 22, was instantly enchanted by mountains from the moment he went amongst them, instinctively knowing they would provide for his unfulfilled needs. The lack of a father in a family, particularly if there are no brothers, can also lead to a child not learning how to relate to male figures. This might, in part, explain Murray's in-built aloofness and tendency to be a loner. The 'realisation of loss' came when Murray was in his teens. He had to find his way through these difficult years without an immediate male role model or mentor. Murray was later to claim that he benefited enormously from spending his first year in the mountains on his own, profiting from his mistakes, finding out things for himself, learning to be self-reliant. He said it happened this way because he didn't know any climbers, or what clubs there were to join, but it might, at some subconscious level, have been a shadowing of how he coped with his teens.

It is possible, too, that Murray's strong belief in Providence, although triggered by an event that occurred in World War II, had a deeper origin in an unconscious yearning in his childhood for some powerful presence to watch over him and protect him. His mother fulfilled that role as best she could, but the absence of his father might have shaped Murray more than he realised or was willing to acknowledge.

Boys or young adults in families in which there is no adult male head of the household tend to take on roles of authority earlier than others of the same age. More often than not, Murray was the driving force amongst his regular climbing companions, although he was not the oldest; and it is a feature of his life that he never dodged responsibility, never found an excuse or looked the other way when someone was needed to take the lead, chair a committee or head a campaign.

Murray did not have children of his own. However, well before marriage, Murray was assuming a father-figure role in nurturing younger climbers. He enjoyed the stimulus of young minds and he believed it was the duty of the more experienced climbers to help bring on the next generation. There might also have been an element in it of wanting to act out being the kind of father he wished he'd had himself, but never did.

Some Freudian psychologists have equated feelings of, or longings for, 'oneness' with nature – something akin to Murray's lifelong quest – with regressive fantasies of being with one's mother. We were one with her in the womb and, as infants, we experienced oneness at her breast. Be that as it may, there is no doubting that Murray's mother provided her two children with a loving, caring environment and a stable home. By all accounts, though, she was over-protective of her fatherless only son. 'He was over-mothered and dominated by her,' was how one acquaintance put it. When Margaret married and moved away, Murray continued to live with his mother in Glasgow. After the war he joined her where she was temporarily living in North Wales, and later, when he bought his house on the shores of Loch Goil, she came with him. She even continued to live with Murray after his marriage and until he was in his 50s. In a letter to the young Robert Aitken (another of the young climbers he encouraged), he commented: 'It is often very hard to deal with parents ... they have difficulty in recognising that a man has grown up.'[2] The next chapter, in discussing why Murray loved mountains and mountaineering, examines the idea that mountains represent freedom and escape. More than likely, Mrs Murray senior contributed to her son's longings in this direction.

After a prolonged battle with three different government departments and a host of civil servants, Murray's mother extracted a grant from them for the education of her two children. For one woman on her own, at that time, to bend regulation-bound bureaucracy to her will showed that she was a woman of great determination with a core of steel – a trait inherited by Murray. His climbing companion, Bill Mackenzie, referred to him as having 'bags of determination,' a conclusion all readers of his books will surely arrive at for themselves, considering the difficulties he often overcame and the set-backs which he refused to allow to divert him from his goals.

From 1918 to 1928, Murray was a pupil at The Glasgow Academy,[3] a fee-paying school with a good reputation. It followed much the same lines as the English public schools of that period, except that it was not a boarding school. There was an emphasis on team games, particularly rugby and cricket, on the Officer Training Corps, on hierarchies, colours, badges of office and tradition, and a general bias towards the classics. Maurice Lindsay[4] who was at the Academy from 1926–36, wrote in his autobiography:[5]

'The weakness of the school was that if you were as disinclined to work at uncongenial subjects as I was, nobody made sure you did. Its strength, apart from the breadth of the opportunity it offered, was the unobtrusive and, on the whole, humane manner in which it inculcated self-reliance and self-discipline; indispensible qualities often glibly denigrated today.'

The first half of these school years for Murray was in the Academy's Preparatory School before he moved up to the senior school. In the latter, one of the teachers most likely to have influenced him was the Head of the English Department, Walter Barradell-Smith. A fellow member of staff described him in his pre-war years as 'a jolly man of early middle-age, solid, four-square, inclining perhaps to the portliness that rugger forwards later allow themselves; rubicund of face;

his eyes twinkling behind his glasses, as likely as not at a joke against himself.'[6] He was an omnivorous reader and a lover of literature who, under the name of Richard Bird, wrote stories for boys. Even while still at school, Murray wanted to be a writer. It must have encouraged him to know that one of his teachers was a published author.

Murray tells us that by the time he was 13 he had read 25 of Scott's *Waverley* novels and most of Robert Louis Stevenson and Alexandre Dumas. His boyhood heroes were mostly fictional, especially D'Artagnan of *The Three Musketeers*, Buchan's Richard Hannay and Ewan Cameron in *The Flight of the Heron*. Murray tells us that, whereas his school friends read as little as they could, he read as much as possible.[7] One hero, at least, was only partially fictional – his father, whom he greatly admired.[8] This was the father who was a talented musician and artist and who once, in the 1890s, skated ten miles up the frozen Loch Lomond, climbed Ben Lomond and then skated back again.

During the school summer holidays Murray's mother organised long stays in fairly remote areas of Scotland and Northern Ireland, such as Donegal, Lismore, Arran, Kintyre and the mile-wide sandy beaches of the Solway Firth where he and his sister raced against the incoming tide. These summer months, Murray says, 'bred in me a love of wild land, if not yet high land.'[9]

When Murray's sister, Margaret, started reading English Literature and Philosophy at Glasgow University, he learned a lot from her boyfriends, students, older than he, who opened his mind to new ideas and introduced him to a deeper kind of literature than he had hitherto encountered. The book which influenced his thinking most, and which he discovered for himself in his late teens, was Plato's *Republic and Dialogues*. His early encounter with the ideas of Plato and his sister's general interest in his studies in this field laid a foundation on which he was to build the philosophy that gave direction to the rest of his life.

Murray left school in 1928, aged 15. Leaving school at 15 or 16 was still quite common then. Only about two and a half per cent of the Scottish population went on to higher education in the pre-war years, compared to about 70 per cent or more these days. Murray says that, had his father been alive, he would have wanted him to go to university. Instead he became a trainee banker at the Union Bank of Scotland, studying accountancy, law, economics, stocks and shares and foreign exchange. He split his time between working at the bank and attending courses at a further education college, qualifying after four years as a member of the Institute of Bankers. Murray admitted that he had no vocation for this work. He wanted to write – which is what he did, quite often in bank hours as well as at home. He wrote short stories, which he says, produced a steady flow of rejection slips.

We know very little about these early stories. Tom Weir says they were mainly about 'people in ordinary human situations'.[10] None of the manuscripts have survived. One suspects that they were deliberately destroyed. Murray was a perfectionist in his writing and did not like draft versions or early unpublished work to be seen. When I asked Mrs Murray if I could see the draft version *of Mountaineering in Scotland* she replied, 'That really would be ratting on him.' It seems likely that it was his mother's idea that her son should leave school and go into banking. Whether this was because the grant money was running out and the family needed his income, however small, is uncertain. Lack of money does not seem to have deterred Margaret from pursuing her university studies. Murray, a serious-minded young man who enjoyed reading and studying, never at any time hints at feelings of jealousy or envy because his sister went to university and he didn't – and in the 1930s it was still unusual for women to attend. They were very definitely in the minority. The fact that she did, combined with his being in close company, as a POW, with fellow officers, many of whom would have had degrees, might have spurred on Murray in his studies and in his meticulous research for his books in some conscious or unconscious desire to show that he could be as learned as they were without needing a degree to prove it.

It was during these years with the bank that Murray found the mountains and began climbing. He joined the Junior Mountaineering Club of Scotland (JMCS). His two classics, *Mountaineering in Scotland* and *Undiscovered Scotland* do not really show the extent to which he became involved with the JMCS. He served as a committee member, then as Hon. Secretary. The indoor meetings of the club played a big part in his social life, and nearly all his climbing companions were JMCS members. In the 1930s and perhaps in the immediate post-war years he devoted to it much of the voluntary time and administrative effort that later he directed to conservation bodies. In his opinion the indoor meetings of the JMCS were as valuable as the outdoor ones, for this was where he got to know other climbers, to exchange ideas and to arrange climbs for the next weekend. Initially, while the club was still small, they met in Fred MacLeod's[11] house near Charing Cross – he who once turned up at a climbing meet direct from an all-night party, still wearing his dinner jacket in which he climbed. Later they moved to Archie MacAlpine's house in Ibrox.[12]

Murray was also of the opinion that the annual JMCS dinners were the best he ever attended.[13] The JMCS was for men only and perhaps this suited Murray who was outnumbered at home by females.

It is significant that Murray joined the JMCS, not the Ptarmigan or the Lomond or one of the other Glasgow clubs whose membership was drawn mainly from working-class or lower-middle-class climbers – folk such as Jock Nimlin, Bob Grieve and Hamish Hamilton. The JMCS became the club for aspiring professionals, bankers, account-ants, doctors and so forth. They were either students, or training for a profession, or with a foot on the first rung of their chosen career ladder. They tended to have access to cars, a key social distinction in the 1930s. Bill was of professional stock, he went to The Academy, his sister went to university, he lived in the professional West End of Glasgow. The JMCS was where he belonged. Its members were the people who, when he was a young man, helped shape his attitudes, values and views on the world around him.

Most autobiographers have quite a lot to say about their child-hood, acknowledging the truth of Wordsworth's line that the child is father of the man; and most writers will say that a major source of material for them is their own childhood, the impressionable years when everything was new and fresh and keenly felt. Yet, in his semi-autobiography, *The Evidence of Things Not Seen*, Murray gives only three and a half pages to his childhood. A strong theme running through his two mountain classics and *The Evidence of Things Not Seen* is how finding the mountains was a turning point in his life, as was his POW experience and his meeting with Herbert Buck who taught him about meditation and the Perennial Philosophy. For the rest of his life Murray strove hard to be the sort of person that these teachings held up as the ideal. It is likely, then, that he wanted to believe that he was more the product of his beloved mountains, his philosophical beliefs, his self-discipline and rigorous mental regime than he was of his childhood. Those formative early years, though, cannot be left out of the equation that was Bill Murray.

NOTES

1. *The Evidence of Things Not Seen*, page 17.
2. Letter dated 26th November, 1964, when Robert Aitken was 16 and Murray 51.
3. The Rector of The Glasgow Academy throughout Murray's years there was Dr Edwin Temple.
4. Maurice Lindsay (1918–2009) was a prolific writer and cultural proponent, producing novels, poetry, biography and literary criticism, drama and music criticism. He was also a freelance broadcaster, who later became a BBC Programme Controller, Production Controller, Features Executive and Senior Interviewer.
5. *Thank You for Having Me* (1983).
6. As recorded in *The Glasgow Academy* by Ian MacLeod, page 109.
7. *The Evidence of Things Not Seen*, page 19.
8. *Ibid*, page 17.
9. *Ibid*, page 18.
10. *Weir's Way*, page 172.
11. In 1937, when the club grew bigger, the indoor meets were held in a hotel in Bath Street.
12. Archie MacAlpine was, by then, married to Murray's sister, Margaret.
13. At the 1950 Annual Dinner of the JMCS Murray proposed the toast to 'the club'. The card for the evening shows the following text beneath Murray's name: 'Nearly all our best men are dead – Tennyson, Carlyle, Browning, George Eliot – I'm not feeling very well myself.' It is a quote from *Punch*, and typical of the kind of humorous digs members made about each other.

CHAPTER FOUR

THE SPELLBOUND SLAVE

Murray's passion for the mountain environment in all its aspects and moods radiates from every page of his two mountain classics, *Mountaineering in Scotland* and *Undiscovered Scotland* and from his accounts of his Himalayan expeditions. He did, though, explain it more succinctly in several places. Describing his feelings on arriving at the top of his very first Scottish peak – the Cobbler, near Arrochar – he wrote: 'I had never dreamt that my own country held wild land so vast. I recognised on the instant that every peak had to be known',[1] thus neatly summarising three of his strongest motives: a love of wild, remote places, the sense of freedom they gave and the thrill of exploration.

Of a solo trek across the Cairngorms he said there was both delight and danger – delight in being free of all cares, and danger because, alone, there is no room for mistakes. This paradox, he claimed, holds the secret of the mountains.[2]

Raising a bottle of beer and making a toast in the Western Desert to 'mountains' with his German captor, a fellow mountaineer, he said: 'Mountains give us some good things such as friends worth having, battles worth fighting, beauty worth seeing.'[3]

The very title of Murray's second mountain classic, *Undiscovered Scotland*, shows where his priorities lay. In this book (page 183) he refers to 'the enthralling pleasures of discovering the undiscovered country'. In an introduction to a new edition of Sir John Hunt's official account of the first ascent of Everest, Murray states: 'Exploratory quest on whatever plane is integral to living. Man cannot opt out and remain man.'[4] He greatly admired both Bill Tilman and Eric Shipton – men who preferred the exploration of unknown territory to the conquest of peaks. It was their example which led him to explore vast and little-known areas of the Himalayas.

Closely linked to a yearning for the undiscovered places is a desire for freedom. The words 'free' and 'freedom' crop up regularly in Murray's books and articles. Again writing of his reaction to standing on his first mountain summit, he said: 'Here is a field of free action in which nothing is organised, or made safe or easy or uniform by regulation; a kingdom where no laws run and no useful ends fetter the heart.' (*Undiscovered Scotland*, page 2)

Freedom implies escape, or liberation, or at least an absence of confinement, so that Thompson's contention that 'climbing is first and foremost escape'[5] seems relevant, in part at least, to why Murray was drawn to the mountains. Possibly his three years in prison camp, his years in Glasgow in what must have been a fairly suffocating job as a trainee banker, and the fact that he and his dominating mother lived in the same household on and off until he was in his fifties had something to do with it. What comes over strongly in his two classics, though, is not that he is trying to get away from something negative, but is going towards something positive.

Murray also attached a deeper meaning to freedom. Life, he says, is seen in a more detached way and in its proper perspective when contemplated from a mountain-top. Sometimes Murray used the word 'free' to mean free of noise, urban clutter and crowds. He valued remoteness and wildness for its own sake and as somewhere that wildlife and natural flora could still be found, and where there was solitude and silence which calmed the mind, let thoughts and ideas bubble up of their own volition and allowed meditation free of distractions.

Another aspect of freedom is the freedom to put your life at risk voluntarily. You choose a harder way to the top rather than an easier one because of the risk involved. Risk is what raises climbing above being just a game; it gives it a special edge and meaning, and life is never so sweet as when there is a possibility of losing it. As Michael Roberts said, 'Man can preserve his dignity only by showing he is not afraid of anything, not even death.'[6] Risk implies an element of uncertainty as to the outcome of the struggle. This is what gets the adrenalin flowing, the nerves tingling, the feeling of being really alive.

What drew Murray to winter climbing on the big routes was the nervous tension and suspense which builds up until the top is reached, giving a special quality to the final exhilaration and relaxation. For these reasons Murray was firmly of the opinion that risk should be an accepted part of mountaineering. Some climbers become addicted to risk and danger. Climbing can be a drug and such people are adrenalin junkies, for whom enough is never enough and withdrawal symptoms kick in if they are away from the cliff face for any length of time. Murray might have been edging towards this state at the height of his youthful risk-taking in the 1930s, but it was never something that took control. Then the war interrupted his climbing. After the war, he was able to state categorically that the mountains were not essential to his happiness. His comparative lack of mountaineering activity from his forties onwards bears this out.

In toasting 'mountains' with the German tank commander, part of Murray's proposal was 'battles worth fighting, beauty worth seeing'. In using the word 'battles' he did not mean that he regarded mountains as the enemy. He probably said 'battles' because he was literally in the midst of a battle at the time and it seemed appropriate in that context. Maybe, when he came to record this episode on paper, he thought it gave a stronger ring and rhetoric to his toast to have the 'b's of 'battle' and 'beauty' bouncing off each other. When Murray writes 'battle', he means something akin to a tournament, a sporting contest, a challenge to be accepted. The challenge is both mental and physical.

The mental battle is not with the mountains, but with self – against one's own weaknesses, fears, doubts, lack of resolution and narrow perspectives. In Murray's view, it was self that was conquered with the help of the mountain.

Then there is the animal physicality of the contest, 'the joy of swarming over this brow of space was out of all proportion to the technical difficultly. One's blood spins and the spirit sings. No melancholy in a man can survive such rock.'[7] At other times there was elation in facing high winds and immense satisfaction in hard physical exercise. An aspect of the physicality of mountaineering, which Murray enjoyed, is what Phil Bartlett calls 'primitivism' – getting back to the basics of survival and safety, simple food, warmth and shelter and thereby refreshing one's appetite for life.

'Most serious mountaineering takes place against a background of danger and discomfort, but only so as to provide something against which one can then play the game of trying to get as comfortable and as safe as possible. There has to be something to kick against.'[8]

Recalling his winter ascent of Tower Ridge on Nevis, fighting a gale at dusk to cross the icy gash of Tower Gap, Murray writes: 'There lies the true joy of battle, in exhilarating contest with the elements, upon mountains that may be won, yet never conquered: shared by companions who may be defeated, yet whose spirit I have never seen shaken.'[9]

Murray's mention in this extract of the joy of battle shared with companions takes us to the first of the three things he celebrated in his toast to Mountains – 'friends worth having'. When climbing companions share danger, hardship and beauty, when they put their lives in each other's hands, it creates strong bonds, a team spirit and a sense of camaraderie. The rope that links climbers on the mountain can also link them in lasting friendship. Perhaps Murray's best testimony to the friendships he formed on the mountain is his pen portraits of his climbing companions – generous, humorous, affectionately caustic, redolent with memories of good times spent together.

The challenge is both mental and physical. That the problem-solving aspect of mountaineering appealed to Murray is obvious from his descriptions of trying to work out how to surmount the seemingly insurmountable, of rising to the challenge of finding the way through thick mist, of calculating the risk, or finding solutions to the problems of winter camping. There is the joy, too, of mind and body working in harmony, of skill and craftsmanship applied through co-ordinated limbs, trained reflexes and bodily fitness. Murray had all of this and revelled in it. When good form is struck 'you rise from the dead. The world is yours.'[10] and you 'drift up the cliffs like smoke'.[11]

What Murray called being in 'good form', when rhythm, co-ordination and confidence are at their peak, is the same as being 'in the flow' (others have called it being 'in the zone' or 'in the groove'). Mihaly Csikszentmihalyi[12] specialised in flow theory and its connection to happiness and creativity. He describes being in the flow as a state of complete concentration and absorption in which your ego falls away as your whole being becomes involved in the task.[13]

In a chapter in *Mountain Experience*, Csikszentmihalyi specifically applied his flow theory to climbing: 'Flow refers to the holistic sensation present when we act with total involvement ... It is the state in which action follows upon action according to an internal logic which seems to need no conscious intervention on our part. We experience it as a unified flowing from one moment to the next in which we are in control of our actions, and in which there is little distinction between self and environment; between stimulus and response; or between past, present and future.'[14]

Murray was entranced by the sheer beauty of the mountains. His many wonderful descriptions of the mountain scene, by day and by night, in summer and in winter, make this abundantly clear – as when, for example, he describes how 'the black bristle of the Cuillin leap to the eye of the mountaineer as lightning to steel'.[15] In the last resort, he says, 'it is the beauty of the mountain world in the inmost recesses that holds us spellbound, slaves till the end.'[16] He appreciated their beauty on all scales, from the tiniest alpine flower to a vast panorama; and he responded to this beauty both with his senses and with his soul.

After Murray's prisoner-of-war experience and his discovery of the Perennial Philosophy, mysticism and meditation, the biggest single reason for mountaineering was that mountains provided not only physical exploration, but also an inner journey of self-discovery, personal development, and growth towards a oneness with the Divine, or the ultimate reality of Truth and Absolute Beauty. As Arnold Lunn put it: 'The undiscovered country of the mountains gives access to the undiscovered country of the mind.'[17]

The lack of distinction between self and the mountains, identified by Csikszentmihalyi, is very close to achieving the 'oneness' with the Divine that Murray saw as the ultimate goal both of his life and of his mountaineering.

For Murray, the way to find this unity was through an awareness and appreciation of mountain beauty, heightened and sharpened by the physical struggle and by being in the flow: 'In the quiet I felt something of the limitation of personality fall away as desires were stilled; and as I died to self and became more absorbed in the hills and sky, the more their beauty entered into me, until they seemed one with me and I with them.'[18]

Most climbers will have trembled on the brink of this kind of awareness without it necessarily holding huge personal significance.

Murray leaves us in no doubt that, for him, it was of central importance.

'In mountain days, one may win fleeting glimpses which all men who have known it have been compelled to call truth. Such, for me, has become the end of mountaineering to which the sport is a means.'[19]

Absent from Murray's motives for climbing is the collecting instinct – the instinct which leads people into Munro-bagging[20] and into ticking Corbetts[21] off the list. Nor was Murray competitive in the sense that modern professional climbers have to be, for whom fame also means better prospects, more clients to guide, revenue from endorsing equipment, higher book sales, expedition sponsorship and an increase in the amount of publicity and media coverage they will get. Perhaps, in his late teens and early twenties, there was a degree of competitiveness, but it was more like friendly rivalry than what we mean by that term today. In the hot flush of his youth there might have been an understandable desire to be the first to achieve some 'impossible' feat, but after the war – after he had embraced the Perennial Philosophy and taken up meditation – a more mature Murray regarded personal ambition and a desire for status and fame as irrelevant to what life was about.

As with all enjoyable activities, part of the pleasure lies in reliving them. Like most mountaineers, Murray had a treasure trove of memories, so that the brilliant climbs, the wonderful views, the epic adventures, the tranquil moments, the good company could be taken out and enjoyed over and over again.

After relating the arduous journey to reach Nevis, the heavy loads carried to the summit and the cold, uncomfortable night spent there, he declares: 'For all this work and unpleasantness we have, say the Philistines, nothing to show except one gully climb. Nothing to clink in our pockets, so to speak. Nothing but a memory. A memory of the wide silent snow-fields crimsoned by the rioting sky, and of the frozen hills under the slow moon. These have remained with us.'[22]

Murray's reasons for climbing were much the same as those of the majority of mountaineers, although he expressed them so much more eloquently than most. However, he recognised that the enjoyment of adventure has many different aspects to it and that it means something different to each of us, according to our temperament, skills and sensitivities. Nobody, he said, can answer for others the question, 'Why climb?'

The full answer to why people climb has physical, mental, social and spiritual components. It must also take into account the spectrum of reasons from the close-to-your-nose technical aspects of an adventure sport, to the lure of the wilderness and the urge to explore, to the aesthetics of landscape beauty and one's emotional response to this. From day to day, climb to climb, which of these receive emphasis will vary. These components can vary, too, with the phases of one's life, the physical and competitive aspects usually being stronger in youth. As we now know, mind and body cannot be separated, each strongly affecting the other. Although it is convenient to separate reasons for climbing into constituent parts for the sake of analysis, in reality they all interact and work together to produce elation, ecstasy, exhilaration, joy and happiness – words which Murray uses on numerous occasions. As he liked to point out, the original meaning of the Scots word 'daft' was 'crazy with happiness', or something that put you in this state. Therefore, he maintained, mountaineers and mountaineering were daft.

Summing up a day spent pioneering a new route on the Bristling Buttress on Sgurr na h-Uamha in the Cuillin of Skye Murray also summed up what it was that made him daft. It was the fulfilment of a creative impulse. One third of his joy in the climb was the accomplishment of it, he said, one third was the anticipation; and the remaining third a mixture of 'the multiple joys of the route: exploration, adventure, the exercise of skill and craft, the self-discipline that gave freedom, the joy of battle and the victory, the challenge and its mastery, the beauty of scene. But not all these joys together, plus the many more not mentioned, supply the reason why men climb. They are merely the by-products, gratefully accepted, often unexpected. Men climb because they love mountains; and since that love is the fundamental fact, one may safely ask the climber "Why?" – and not stay for an answer.'[23]

NOTES

1. *The Evidence of Things Not Seen*, page 22.
2. *Ibid.*
3. *Ibid*, page 80.

4. *The Ascent of Everest* by Sir John Hunt (Heron Books, 1970, by arrangement with Hodder & Stoughton).

5. *Unjustifiable Risk? The Story of British Climbing* (2010). The paragraph referred to is as follows: 'Insofar as it is possible to draw any general conclusions about a sport that prides itself on being individualistic, it is that climbing is first and foremost an escape: from the familiar to the unknown; from noise and crowds to peace and beauty; from comfort and convenience to discretionary danger; from compliance and conformity to freedom and self-reliance; from complexity to simplicity. Climbing is an escape from an existence that is useful but purposeless to one that is useless but purposeful.'

6. 'The Poetry and Humour of Mountaineering' in *The Alpine Journal*, 1941.

7. *Mountaineering in Scotland*, page 144.

8. *The Undiscovered Country: The Reason we Climb* (1993), page 60.

9. *Mountaineering in Scotland*, page 244.

10. *The Evidence of Things Not Seen*, page 307.

11. *Mountaineering in Scotland*, page 142.

12. Pronounced Mee-hye Cheek-sent-ma-hye-ee.

13. *Flow: The Psychology of Optimal Expression*, New York, 1990.

14. ed. Richard Mitchell, University of Chicago Press, 1983.

15. *Mountaineering in Scotland*, page 55.

16. *Ibid*, page 242.

17. *Mountain Jubilee* 1943.

18. *Mountaineering in Scotland*, page 138.

19. *Ibid*, page 242.

20. Munros are the 283 mountain tops in Scotland over 3,000 feet, first catalogued by Sir Hugh Munro.

21. Corbetts are the 221 Scottish peaks between 2,500 and 3,000 feet as listed by J. Rooke Corbett.

22. *Mountaineering in Scotland*, page 175.

23. 'The Bristling Buttress' in *Open Air in Scotland* magazine, summer 1948.

CHAPTER FIVE

NAILED BOOTS AND HEMP ROPES

In April 1935, having recently turned 22, Murray stood atop his first Scottish mountain, the Cobbler, near Arrochar.[1] Murray, 'a confirmed pavement dweller' up to that point, overheard a mountaineer describing a traverse of the An Teallach ridge in Wester Ross and was inspired to experience this strange new world for himself. Alone and without nailed boots, mountain clothing, ice-axe or compass, he set out to climb the mountain, kicking steps with his shoes up the hard snow and ice to reach the top. As he looked at the mountain ranges all around him, he knew he had to explore them. 'From that day I became a mountaineer,' he says.[2]

In order to fully appreciate and evaluate Murray's place in mountaineering history, we need some understanding of the context in which his climbs took place and of the pioneers who had gone before him and whose legacy and standards he was inheriting. Before World War I, Norman Collie,[3] William Naismith,[4] Harold Raeburn[5] and others had begun to open up new routes on the Scottish cliffs. Raeburn, focusing mainly on Ben Nevis, led the way in pioneering mixed rock and ice climbing in Scotland. Some of his climbs were so far ahead of their time that they went unrepeated for a quarter of a century. The climbs of these individuals were the exception rather the norm for those times. Raeburn's climbs in particular were virtually one-off. Due to lax recording, World War 1 and mild winters in the 1920s, these achievements were not fully appreciated by Murray's generation.[6]

Although many of the routes put up in this period would not compare in severity with the hardest climbs of today, the standard these early climbers achieved in relation to the equipment they had was remarkably high. Their protective clothing consisted of tweeds and they were shod with nailed boots. They had progressed beyond

simple hobnails to edge-nails along the welts, but the more effective
tricounis were yet to come. Their hemp ropes became heavy when wet
and as stiff as steel hawsers when frozen; and their ice axes were too
long, heavy and unwieldy for steep angled ice or for sustained cutting
above shoulder level.

Traditionally, Scotland had supplied the British regiments with
soldiers out of all proportion to its population, with the result
that Scotland suffered higher casualties per capita than any other
country in World War I. After the war there was almost no young
leadership left, and little taste for danger. Raeburn, now 55, was
one of the few[7] who had survived and still had the energy to take
up the challenge anew. In 1920 he made the first winter ascent of
Observatory Ridge on Nevis and published his *Mountaineering Art*.
It was heavily orientated towards Alpine climbing and outdated by
the time it was published, having been written before the outbreak of
World War I, but it did contain one short chapter which recognised,
for the first time, that climbing in Scotland could be an end in itself
and not purely as training for the Alps. There were no details of
specific climbs and Raeburn was too modest a man to proclaim his
achievements.

The generation gap created by the war, and a lack of knowledge
about Raeburn's climbs, meant that they were not followed up. His
pioneering winter climbs, in particular, were neglected because of the
very mild winters during the 1920s in which few routes came into
good condition. Another point to bear in mind is that, due to the comparative vastness of the Highlands, mountaineering in Scotland was
still in an exploratory stage. The cliffs had not become 'exhausted' to
the degree that they had in England and Wales, especially in the Lake
District, then the centre of English climbing, where all the obvious
lines were already done. Therefore, there was not the same pressure
to find harder variations and take on the 'impossible' routes.

Clark and Pyatt in their classic history of British mountaineering
say: 'Between 1919 and 1922 the majority of new climbs carried out in
Scotland were made by English parties ... The English predominance
of the immediate post-war years had one important effect: it brought
to Scotland the techniques of the increasingly difficult rock-climbing
then being attempted in the Lakes.'[8]

At this point the Scottish Mountaineering Club (SMC) published

guides to Ben Nevis and Skye, which kept the records alive and stimulated interest. A growing number of young people were finding their
way into the hills. They didn't have the required experience to join the
SMC and some, perhaps, felt they didn't quite belong there anyway,
amongst its august and predominately wealthy membership. For this
reason, in 1925, the Junior Mountaineering Club of Scotland (JMCS)
was founded by four members of the SMC. It swiftly attracted the
new generation of climbers and within a few years it was playing an
increasing part in the advance of Scottish mountaineering. The feats
and influence of its members made it in some ways as important as
its parent body.[9]

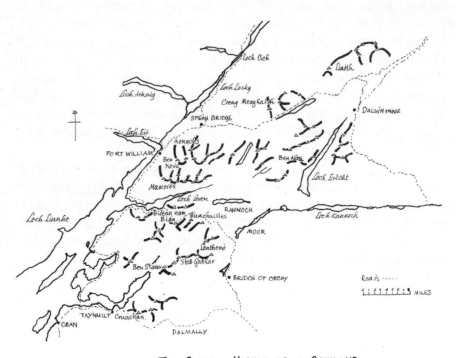

THE CENTRAL HIGHLANDS OF SCOTLAND

Then, in 1929 the SMC opened the Charles Inglis Clark Memorial
Hut (known as the CIC hut) in memory of a popular young member
who had been killed during the Great War. It was situated at the foot
of the Nevis cliffs at the head of the Alt a Mhuillin burn (on the rim
of the bowl that is Coire Leis). The presence of the hut meant that

climbers arrived at the cliffs fresh, and it lengthened the climbing day, allowing longer, harder routes to be tackled. At that time, it was the only club hut in Scotland, and yet it was hardly used at first, such was the diminished state of Scottish climbing at that time. Two climbers who did make good use of it were Bell and Macphee.

The link between Raeburn's generation and the generation of the newly formed JMCS – Murray's generation – was made by the two outstanding mountaineers of the inter-war years, Dr J.H.B. Bell[10] and Dr Graham Macphee.[11] Bell put up 70 new routes of varied character all over Scotland; Macphee focused on Nevis. These climbs, up until the mid 1920s or later, were not generally known about. Only then did people begin to learn about new routes and developments through the publication of guidebooks, through newly formed clubs which invited speakers to address their members, and through their journals and newsletters. Murray summed up the situation for himself and his fellow climbers when he wrote: 'There was a lack of inherited climbing standards ... There was no springboard. For winter work we started from scratch ... in the 1920s climbing in Scotland had to all appearances died.'[12] Then Macphee produced his Nevis guidebook in 1936. Until then the Nevis cliffs were mostly unexplored. There was a rivalry between Bell and Macphee and the latter was hard pressed to complete his guidebook because Bell kept putting up new routes on Nevis in an attempt to make Macphee's guidebook out-of-date by the time it appeared.

'The two were extreme opposites, like cat and dog: Bell small and sturdy with a strong Fife accent, one of the toughest men I have ever met, never mincing his words; Macphee big and broad with a gentlemanly drawl and quizzical tone – yet able to pull up on one arm to chin the curtain pole in the CIC Hut. He drove Bentleys ...'[13]

The exploits of these two men, in both summer and winter, stimulated and inspired the next generation of Scottish climbers. Amongst this new generation was Bill Murray. By this time, equipment had improved, although it was still a long way from modern standards. Boots now had narrow welts, sewn-in tongues, and were nailed with tricounis and clinkers.[14] Close-woven cotton garments, developed for Everest and Arctic expeditions, replaced tweeds, greatly contributing to climbers' ability to continue to operate in wet and windy conditions.

Two other by-products of Everest expeditions were cheap light-weight tents and down sleeping-bags which allowed camping at the base of the cliffs. Whereas, before, the rope used to be simply passed round a projection, slings and snap-links were introduced to increase the safety of belays.

In addition to these technical advances were better roads and cheap second-hand cars which made the mountains more accessible. The old road to Glencoe across Rannoch Moor was much rougher and narrower and took a higher route than the present road, so that it was frequently blocked by snow in winter. It was fortuitous, then, that the new road to Glencoe across Rannoch Moor had been opened the year that Murray started climbing.

Murray didn't know anyone interested in mountaineering and wandered the hills alone for several months before teaming up with his brother-in-law, Archie MacAlpine,[15] who was six years older. In addition to being an oarsman, strong and fit, he had the great merit of being the owner of a car. Rough scrambling quickly whetted their appetites for steeper rock, an appetite sharpened all the more by Murray's reading of *The British Highlands with Rope and Rucksack* by Ernest A. Baker, and Mummery's *My Climbs in the Alps and Caucasus*.[16] Murray was under the impression that climbers were 'close to gorillas, and with bulging biceps'. After reading these books, he says, 'I felt weak not only at arms and shoulders, but now at the knees too.'

Before long he joined the JMCS, MacAlpine following his example shortly afterwards. Murray did his first rock climb in November 1935 on Ben Narnain near Arrochar, at a JMCS meet; and his first winter climb – Bidean nam Bian Central Gully (Glencoe) – in March 1936. The JMCS in the 1930s contained stronger and more innovative climbers than did the SMC. It was through the JMCS that Murray met Kenneth Dunn and Bill Mackenzie, who like himself and MacAlpine were from Glasgow. The coming together of Murray, MacAlpine, Dunn and Mackenzie produced one of the strongest climbing teams in Scottish mountaineering of the 1930s.

Dunn was a young solicitor and one of the leading climbers of the Glasgow branch of the JMCS. Mackenzie, who worked at the Union Bank of Scotland, as did Murray (but at a different branch), was amongst the half dozen best Scottish rock climbers of that period, and on mixed winter rock and ice he was considered the best in Britain. Chapter Seven has more to say about these three and gives us a glimpse of how Murray saw them.

Murray did also climb with other people such as Ben Humble, Ross Higgins, Douglas Scott, W.G. Marskell, Tom MacKinnon and Douglas Laidlaw, but not with quite the same regularity. J.H.B. Bell he also climbed with fairly regularly – of whom, more later. Murray, Mackenzie, MacAlpine and Dunn stayed together for the next four years until the outbreak of war sent them their different ways. During that period they climbed in various combinations with each other, as duo, trio or quartet. They were perhaps the only team at that time which consistently climbed together, a factor which gave them an advantage over their contempories.

This was the quartet that won a place in the history of Scottish mountaineering.

NOTES

1. At various times, Murray claims that this happened in 1934, a year earlier. This discrepancy is discussed more fully in Chapter Thirty.
2. *Undiscovered Scotland*, page 3. The year after Murray left The Glasgow Academy, the school started a Hill Climbing Club and its first outing was to the Cobbler. Probably Murray wouldn't have joined, having no interest in mountains at that time.
3. Norman Collie (1859–1942), English scientist, mountaineer and explorer. He was the inventor of the neon light and the first person to use x-ray photographs for medical purposes. Most of his climbs in Scotland were in Skye, particularly in the Cuillins. By 1888 he had climbed all the main peaks on Skye. He also climbed in the Alps, the Caucasus, the Himalayas and the Canadian Rockies.
4. William Naismith (1856–1935), who owned an accountancy firm, was a founding member of the SMC, often referred to as 'the father of the club'. He made the first winter ascent of the North-East Buttress of Ben Nevis in 1896 (still a grade IV climb today). He also pioneered skiing in Scotland.
5. Harold Raeburn (1865–1926), inherited his father's brewery business in Edinburgh. He climbed extensively in Scotland. Some of his best climbs were on Ben Nevis, including the first winter ascent of Green Gully (1906), the first winter ascent of Crowberry Gully (1909) and the first winter ascent of Observatory Ridge in 1920. He also made the first Scottish ascent of Crowberry Ridge direct on the Buachaille, Glencoe, then the hardest rock-climb in Scotland (1902). He climbed in the Alps, Caucasus and Norway and was part of the 1921 Everest reconnaissance expedition, but missed most of the action through illness.
6. See Robin Campbell's Article 'The First Scottish Ice Climbers', SMCJ, 1972, page 48 for more on this.

7. Perhaps Garrick should also be mentioned here.
8. *Mountaineering in Britain*, Ronald W. Clark & Edward C. Pyatt, 1957, page 186.
9. The JMCS is now an independent body and has a larger membership than the SMC, with Glasgow and Edinburgh branches in Scotland and one in London. Even in 1939 the Glasgow branch on its own was larger than the SMC, with over 400 members.
10. James Horst Brunnerman Bell (1896–1975) was an industrial chemist who specialised in paper-making processes. He was based in Auchtermuchty and latterly in Clackmannan. He had close connections with the Grampian Club of Dundee. His climbs were more varied and covered a wider area of Scotland than those of any other Scottish climber of that period. There is more about Bell in Chapter Ten.
11. George Graham Macphee (1898–1963) was a Liverpool dentist and lecturer at Liverpool University, but was a member of the SMC and drove up to Scotland regularly. His first winter ascents on Ben Nevis include Glover's Chimney (1935) and South Gully (1936). Because he was based in Liverpool he was well placed for climbing in North Wales and in the Lake District and consequently he knew people like Menlove Edwards and Colin Kirkus.
12. *The Evidence of Things Not Seen*, page 24.
13. *Ibid.*
14. Tricounis were of hard metal which bit into the rock. They were usually saw-toothed and arranged round the welt and heel of the boot. Clinkers were of soft metal so that the rock bit into them. They might alternate with tricounis around the welt and heel and also be arranged in patterns on the sole. They could be of various shapes such as wedges or stars.
15. Archie MacAlpine (1906–1994) was married to Murray's elder sister, Margaret. MacAlpine was a dentist and, at that time, had a practice in Ibrox, Glasgow. Further details about him can be found in Chapter Seven.
16. Murray told this to Tom Weir. The notes on this interview are in the Weir Collection at the National Library of Scotland, Edinburgh. Baker's book was published in 1923. Mummery's *My Climbs in the Alps and Caucasus* was published in 1895. Murray was referring here only to how he was thrilled by Mummery's adventures. Mummery also influenced Murray's literary style. This is discussed in Chapter Eighteen.

CHAPTER SIX

MURRAY AND THE RENAISSANCE OF SCOTTISH CLIMBING

Nineteen thirty-five, the year Murray did his first climb, saw Macphee at his most active on Ben Nevis, making 11 first ascents. Ken Crocket in his history of Ben Nevis suggests that the greatest impact of Macphee's routes 'lay in their acting as an example; encouraging young climbers to follow his lead and find their own way on the under-utilised rocks and icy gullies of Ben Nevis'.[1] That year, an article by George Williams appeared in the SMC Journal describing the first ascent of Glover's Chimney on Nevis – a pure ice climb lead by Macphee. It captured the imaginations of Murray and his companions, opened their eyes to new possibilities and inspired them to search out similar ice routes in Glencoe. Murray, typically giving credit where credit is due, offered the opinion that, 'The new era opened in February 1936 when Mackenzie and Dunn were joined by J.F. 'Hamish' Hamilton for the winter ascent of Crowberry Gully – a climb of 1,000 feet, twice as long as Glover's Chimney and harder ... Having much to learn, they used full size axes and took twelve hours.'[2] This was, in fact, not a first ascent as Mackenzie thought, Raeburn having climbed the chimney at Easter 1909, but they knew nothing of this. Murray did not take part in this ascent because he didn't start climbing with Mackenzie until May of that year. Murray refers to full-size ice-axes because he and his friends were experimenting with shorter axes and found them much better on steep ice or in confined spaces. Murray credits Douglas Scott with being the first to use a shortened axe and says that this is what gave him the idea of adapting a slater's hammer for climbing purposes. Scott, however, told Michael Cocker that he copied it from a fellow climber, Bill Bennett. The shortness of the winter days in Scotland had always limited the length of climb which could be attempted. Head torches, introduced by the Mackenzie-

Murray team enabled climbs to be completed in the dark. Legend has it that MacAlpine used a head torch in his dental practice to keep both hands free and, in one of those eureka moments, realised that it could do the same for climbers.

Anyone reading Murray's *Mountaineering in Scotland* can be left in no doubt that it is his winter ascents which meant the most to him. He confirms this in *The Evidence of Things Not Seen*: 'Ice work ... was physically more exacting than summer rock and mentally more stimulating ... I have rarely enjoyed anything in life more than cutting up a long, high-angle ice pitch where balance was delicate.'[3]

The winter climbs of the Glasgow four and others at that time were done without crampons. Although, by now, crampons were available and were used in the Alps, they were not used on the Scottish mountains. Mackenzie, in an article for the SMCJ, 1947, said, 'it is not suggested here that the use of crampons is necessary for Scottish winter climbs, nor yet their habitual use is at all desirable here. To rely on crampons before one has mastered the technique of using the ice-axe on steep snow-ice is a great mistake.' Murray very much agreed that nailed boots were a better option. They gave just as good a grip on the ice; when planted carefully they did not shatter brittle or thin ice in the way that the clumsier crampon might; and they were superior on mixed rock and ice, where crampons not only blunted on the rock but were no good for delicate work and sometimes insecure; furthermore, because they had to be strapped tightly to the boots, they restricted circulation and caused cold feet. Ten-point crampons had been commercially available from about 1910. Twelve-pointers, which had two front claws, were developed in 1929 by Grivel, but these were expensive, hard to obtain and only used by the top Alpine climbers of the day. As late as 1971, when Vibram soles dominated the scene and nails were history, Murray confided to a friend that he still longed for his old boots.

In April 1937 occurred Murray's first encounter with Dr J.H.B. Bell. They were in the CIC hut below Ben Nevis with different groups and with different plans, but the connection was made and from 1938 onwards, Murray and Bell climbed together on a number of occasions. Just as Mackenzie introduced Murray to iced rocks, so Bell converted him to the strange pleasures of climbing on unclean, loose rock. Murray records Bell's dictum that 'any fool can climb on good rock, but it takes craft and cunning to get up vegetatious schist and granite'.[4]

For five years Murray climbed intensively, going from complete beginner to a high standard in both winter and summer. He completed a number of significant first and second ascents, principally in Glencoe and on Ben Nevis and established himself, along with Mackenzie, as one of the leaders of the renaissance of winter climbing on pure ice or on mixed rock and ice. He was also at the forefront of moving Scottish climbing out of the gullies and chimneys and onto the open walls where balance, flow and nerve were often more important than strength. Ullman gives a good summary of the new style at the cutting edge of which was the Glasgow group:

'One of the most remarkable developments in cragmanship has been the perfection of a technique known as balance, or rhythm climbing. It is based on the fact that equilibrium is much more easily maintained by a body in motion than a body at rest ... a tiny fingerhold or quarter-inch ledge, which would afford no support at all to a stationary climber, can yet be made to serve his ends if he uses them but momentarily, for friction on his way to another hold or ledge.'[5]

Raeburn had recommended 80 feet of rope for a party of three, which, after tying on, allowed only about 35 feet between each person. The big routes Murray and his companions were now doing, with long leads, demanded a much greater run-out of rope, so that they doubled, then tripled the recommended length and often used thinner rope than was the accepted norm. There would sometimes be 150 feet of rope between the leader and the second man and not a single protective runner[6] between them, for they rejected the use of slings and snap-links in this way. This new style of climbing dismayed the older members of the SMC. As Murray explains:

'The new generation of Scots now fell out with the old. A pillar of the pre-war school came to berate us, urging with passion in his voice that we abandon slab and-wall climbs. They were "unjustifiable" (a much used term of abuse in the 1930s), implying an irresponsible disregard for human life-values.'[7]

The renaissance in Scottish climbing in the last five years before World War II is encapsulated by E.A.M. Wedderburn:[8]

'1935 saw the rising of a new movement in Scottish climbing, in which are prominent what I can only call the "Glasgow ginger group." Most of the members of this group are members of the JMCS ... This group brings into Scottish climbing an element, hitherto not prominent, of youth and relative poverty. Scottish climbing has survived in the atmosphere in which it was started longer than has climbing in the Lakes or in Wales. It was regarded until about ten years after the war of 1914–18 mainly as a training for larger mountains and as a practice ground in off seasons for members of The Alpine Club. Such an atmosphere naturally tended to make climbing a sport for the wealthier classes ... Before the war ... the typical Scottish mountaineering party would start from some convenient hotel which they had reached the previous evening in comfortable time for dinner. ... More typical of today [1939] is the youthful pair starting out late, after making breakfast in their tent or Youth Hostel which they had reached late the previous night ... Some of them climb every week-end of the year. They appear to me to have the future of Scottish climbing in their hands.'[9]

Much of this description fits Murray. Although he was clearly a fully signed-up member of the Middle Class, he did not belong to the wealthier, leisured classes. He had only the salary of a lowly bank trainee and a limited amount of holiday. More often than not he camped in summer. His favourite camping place was Coupal Bridge at the entrance to Glen Etive, near the foot of the Buachaille Etive Mor, the mountain he climbed on more than any other. In winter he used the CIC Hut or stayed at the Inverarnan Inn (Glen Falloch), the Kingshouse Hotel (Rannoch Moor) or the Clachaig Inn (Glencoe). Initially, Murray transported himself to the mountains on a 500cc Norton motorbike. The bitterly cold journeys in mid-winter, sometimes late at night, convinced him that a second-hand car would be a better option. For eight pounds he bought an old Austin Seven, which had threadbare tyres and frequently broke down or had punctures. Those who drove with Murray reported that, such was the state of his car and his eagerness to reach the mountains, more adrenalin flowed during the journey than on the climb.

Opinions vary as to which were Murray's finest Scottish climbs, but probably everyone would agree on his breakthrough winter climbs of *Garrick's Shelf* (1937) on Buachaille Etive Mor; *Deep Cut Chimney* (1939) on Stob Coire nan Beith, Glencoe; and *Twisting Gully* (1946) on the neighbouring Stob Coire nan Lochan. And amongst his summer climbs would be his first ascent of *Clachaig Gully* (1938) in Glencoe, and repeats of some of the hardest rock routes of the day on Ben Nevis. Others might make a case for his second winter ascent of *Observatory Ridge* on Ben Nevis (1938) – the first ascent in 18 years[10] – described by Murray as 'one of the hardest battles we have had the good fortune to wage.'[11] Some might argue for the first ascent of *Parallel Buttress* on Lochnagar, done with Bell in May 1939, or the traverse of all the main summits of the Cuillin Ridge in Skye (June 1937), completed in 12 hours 20 minutes without the benefit of pre-positioned caches of food and water.

Murray himself may well have had a rather different list which would not have been compiled with the history books and his place in the development of Scottish climbing in mind, but with thought for the quality of the experience, the beauty encountered, the invigorating battle with the elements, and the enjoyment had. Amongst his most memorable days may well have been the one in August 1937, on the Cobbler, when he did 16 different climbs in one day, none of them above Diff or V. Diff in standard. Some of his climbs are described in his *Mountaineering in Scotland,* many others in the *Scottish Mountaineering Club Journal*, and all of them are catalogued in the magnificent Chronology of Murray's climbs between 1935 and 1945 so meticulously compiled by Michael Cocker.[12] A shortened version of this appears in online Appendix K.

Murray made only one visit to the Alps before the war – to Arolla in Switzerland in July 1938, when it was so wet that he fled to Skye and climbed there instead. After the war he made three visits to the Alps in three successive summers – to the Duaphine′ Alps in France (1947); the Bernese Oberland, Switzerland (1948); and the area around Chamonix, France (1949). His comparative lack of Alpine experience was due to the fact that he had neither the time nor the money for this kind of holiday. There were no cheap charter flights in those days. Travel was by train and channel ferry, and Glasgow was a long way from France or Switzerland. Allowing for a period of acclimatisation to the altitude, it was not worth going for less than a month.

In his Introduction to his Chronology of Murray's climbs Cocker has an excellent summary and overview of Murray's mountaineering in the pre-war period:

'In the 1930s most people, including Murray, who was a trainee with the Union Bank of Scotland, worked a five and half or six day week and were not free to head to the hills until Saturday afternoon or early Sunday morning. Consequently the bulk of Murray's climbing occurred on a Sunday, sometimes with a late return to Glasgow in the early hours of Monday morning. His SMC application reflects this pattern of regular weekend climbing with the addition of statutory holidays and three weeks annual leave. His activities were mainly concentrated in the Southern and Central Highlands with occasional forays to the Cairngorms and longer holidays in Skye. He only made one visit to the Northern Highlands (Torridon) before the war, one to the English Lake District and one to the Swiss Alps. In his application Murray recorded 63 climbs on Buachaille Etive Mor, 29 on Ben Nevis, 25 on the Cobbler, 9 traverses of the Aonach Eagach Ridge and the ascent of 84 Munros. Between 1937 and 1940, the period when he climbed most intensely and least distractedly, he averaged 70 days climbing and hill walking each year... When looking at Murray's record, two differences from today's activity are worth remarking on. Firstly, how often they were prepared to climb in wet weather or marginal conditions. With only one day a week available for climbing and limited annual leave they could not afford to be too particular about the conditions, and a factor in their favour was that nailed boots, routinely worn on climbs up to Very Difficult or even Severe, were almost as effective on wet and icy rock as on dry. "Rubbers" or gym shoes were only used on more difficult routes. And secondly, their use of graded climbs like Tower Ridge on Ben Nevis, or North Buttress on Buachaille Etive Mor, as a means of descent. In the era of no running belays and the maxim that "the leader never falls", the ability to down climb and retreat from a route was as important a skill as safety in ascent. This type of climbing would also have been considered good training for the Alps.'

As Cocker shows, Murray visited the Buachaille in Glencoe more often than any other mountain. From the moment he first set eyes on it, rounding a bend in the road, he was captivated by this, 'the most splendid of earthly mountains.' On the Buachaille he had some of his greatest adventures and deepest experiences. It was the mountain he instinctively chose to climb when he received the news of the outbreak of war. It was the Buachaille he selected as his last climb in Scotland before being posted abroad, and his first on his return after the war.

In these, his most active years of climbing in Scotland and in the Alps, there is no record of Murray ever having fallen (I mean here, a clear fall while leading). If he did, he doesn't tell us. However, he certainly had some narrow escapes. There was the 14-hour descent from Crowberry Ridge in appalling snow conditions, much of it in darkness and with their torch batteries exhausted, when imminent disaster was their constant companion. In his account of this retreat he does have a near fall:

'Having seen Dunn safely down and well established [on a ledge below], I followed a thought too gaily. For the fixed rope somehow rolled off its hitch above. Down I went with a rush, conscious only of one fat blue spark where a boot-nail struck bare rock. A split second later I landed astride Dunn's shoulders.'[13] Or there was the occasion on the Cuillin ridge when, in dense mist, he made a hand traverse across an overhang, swinging along with gay abandon, thinking that the main ridge was only a few feet below him. The mist cleared to reveal that he was dangling by his arms over a huge drop. One of his closest brushes with death was not on a precipice but from a near drowning at the Falls of Falloch. He, Mackenzie and Tom MacKinnon jumped across a narrow part just for the fun of it. On the return jump, Murray slipped, fell into the gorge and was swept into the cauldron. Despite the heroic efforts of his companions to save him and before the current carried him to the river bank, he entered the final stages of drowning:

'I think it is one of the most shocking moments in a man's life, when he knows that his life is lost but is not yet resigned to death. He has a feeling of despair not pleasant to look back upon. A man in that state is capable of superhuman exertions, and although "exhausted" I tapped hitherto unsuspected reserves of energy. But the forces against me were too great; for the last time my struggle weakened; then I surrendered, and sank. My past life did not flash before my eyes. Save for one thing of which I cannot write, I thought only that I had chosen a foolish way of ending my life, which might have been expended to a worthier end on mountains, where one seeks beauty, than in horseplay at a waterfall.'[14]

That one thing of which he could not write is a subject for endless but fruitless speculation. A cynic might say that it was simply a well-advised escape clause to appease all those who hoped, even expected, that they would be in his last thoughts.

Then there was the time, in 1947, when he, John Barford and Michael Ward were in the Dauphiné Alps. Barford slipped on a steep snow slope. Ward rammed his ice-axe into the snow and looped the connecting rope round it. When the strain of the rope came on the axe, its wooden shaft broke and all three went tumbling downwards. They managed to brake and came to a stop. In the process, Ward's thick woollen balaclava was knocked off his head. Murray retrieved it and put it on his own head. Shortly afterwards, they were caught in a fall of stones from the cliffs above. All of them were hit, but only Murray, thanks to the thick balaclava, remained conscious. They tumbled down the slope into a deep crevasse. Murray, who was carrying a big rucksack, was wedged near the top. Below him Barford was dead. Further down the crevasse was Ward, conscious but badly concussed and very confused. Although they didn't know it at the time, both Murray and Ward had fractured skulls. By superhuman effort Murray extracted Ward from the crevasse. Halfway down to the valley, moving at a painfully slow pace and not sure that they could keep going, they met a fellow mountaineer who refused to help them because it would have taken him out of his way.

There would also have been thousands of times when disaster was only a hair's breadth away, when he was only just on the right side of that knife-edge between glorious success and annihilation. At such times the tiniest lessening in the amount of adhesion holding man to mountain would have meant a parting of the ways. More than once, only sheer luck appeared to save him. 'I seem to have a most efficient guardian angel, and I never withhold a word of congratulation at the scenes of his master-strokes,' Murray wrote,[15] but he also said, 'Certainly "luck" is useful, but good or ill, it is often self-earned … On the mountains, nothing better discourages luck from running out than alertness. Narrow escapes come to us all in a lifetime. A good mountaineer will endeavour to control their number and balance risk with survival.'[16] Murray had more to say on the subject of alertness in a small pamphlet written for the JMCS, entitled 'Winter Climbing in Scotland' (1967), his last paragraph under the heading of 'Self-Possession' runs as follows:

'Physical fitness, the best of gear, good technique – all are totally insufficient means of survival unless a man has commonsense and stays alert. On the mountain, be aware of everything you do, every move you make, in relation to everything around you. Be aware of your companions and their movements, of the ground and its condition, of the weather and its changes. This alertness has to be maintained day-long. ... If you examine the careers of renowned climbers of the past, you will find that their best climbing was not done when they were old and wise, but when young and relatively inexperienced. They lived because a man with an alert mind and commonsense can safely go anywhere.'

Chapter Twenty-Two discusses Murray's merits as a climber and whether he can be compared to climbers of today. It is not a topic which can be addressed without first placing Murray's climbs in their context – which this and the previous chapter have tried to do. Inevitably, the major routes and first ascents are the ones which attract attention, but getting himself into the record books was never a priority for Murray. Exploration, excitement, adventure, experiencing beauty, enjoyment – these counted for more with him and could be had on lesser routes given the right conditions, the right companions, and the right attitude. Jimmy Marshall, the ace Scottish climber of the 1960s, who was decades ahead of his time, has expressed the opinion[17] that Murray was a better mountaineer than he was a climber. This was not meant in any way to denigrate his climbing ability but rather to emphasise his all-round love of mountains, not just of their most vertical parts, and his wider contribution to mountaineering through his Himalayan explorations. These aspects of Murray the mountaineer are the subject of later chapters as are his other services to mountaineering and to the conservation of the mountain environment.

According to Tom Weir: 'Bill has no doubt at all in his mind that these pre-war years on the Scottish hills were his best, and that nothing that has come to him since in the Alps or on Everest has brought the ecstasy of climbing hard routes with well-tried companions when he was physically fittest and enthusiasm was highest.'[18] The bold, determined, seemingly fearless young man of the 1930s was certainly among the best of his day on Scottish winter climbs, but that is only one part of a much bigger story.

NOTES

1. *Ben Nevis: Britain's Highest Mountain* (2009), page 123.
2. *The Evidence of Things Not Seen*, page 41.
3. *Ibid*, page 44.
4. *Ibid*, page 38.
5. *The Age of Mountaineering* by James Ramsay Ullman, 1964, page 303.
6. The leader passes the active rope through a snap-link attached to the rock by means of a sling fixed over a projection or a piton driven into a crack. Should he then fall, he is stopped by his second man below him taking the upward strain when the weight of the rope comes on the snap-link.
7. *The Evidence of Things Not Seen*, page 33.
8. 'Sandy' Wedderburn, at the outset of the war, became CO of the Scottish commandos. He requested that Murray be transferred to their Mountain Warfare Unit, but the request was denied. Later, Murray was in the same POW camp as Sandy's brother, Tommy Wedderburn, who made a daring but unsuccessful escape attempt with Alastair Cram.
9. From 'A Short History of Scottish Climbing from 1918 to the Present Day' in the *Scottish Mountaineering Club Journal*, November 1939.
10. The present-day grades of these climbs are: *Garrick's Shelf* – IV,4; *Deep Cut Chimney* – IV,4; *Twisting Gully* – III,4; *Clachaig Gully* – Severe; *Observatory Ridge* – III. The grading system for UK climbs is explained in online Appendix A.
11. From 'Present Moments' in *The Alpine Journal*, 1981.
12. Michael Cocker was born in 1955 and has climbed extensively in Britain and the European Alps as well as Arctic Norway, East Africa, the Andes, Himalayas, North America and the Canadian Rockies. He has recently retired from the NHS where he worked as a physiotherapist, a clinical specialist in orthopaedics. He is a member of the Scottish Mountaineering Club, The Alpine Club and The Climbers Club and has been a vice-president of The Fell and Rock Climbing Club. He is interested in mountaineering history and wrote and edited the *Wasdale Climbing Book* (Ernest Press 2006). He is also co-author of the book on the history of climbing on Scafell Crag, in the Lake District, due to be published in 2014.
13. *Mountaineering in Scotland*, page 59.
14. *Ibid*, page 197.
15. *Ibid*, page 158.
16. *The Evidence of Things Not Seen*, page 146.
17. In a conversation with the author, 2010.
18. *Weir's Way*, page 173.

CHAPTER SEVEN

MORE PRICELESS THAN GOLD

The four young climbers from Glasgow, Bill Mackenzie, Bill Murray, Archie MacAlpine and Kenneth Dunn, all members of the JMCS, began climbing together in 1936 and quickly gained a reputation as one of the strongest and most daring climbing teams in Scotland at that time. MacAlpine was the eldest, being 29, followed by Mackenzie, then Dunn, with Murray the youngest at 23. It was Mackenzie and Murray, though, who provided the thrust and did most of the leading. Almost every Thursday evening they gathered for supper in MacAlpine's house to plan their weekends. 'Many a new route was first made in MacAlpine's sitting-room, where we never failed to find the cheerful stimuli of blazing fire, deep arm-chairs, and tankards of beer.'[1] Probably, there was much puffing on pipes, too, for Murray, Dunn and MacAlpine were all pipe-smokers. They had all entered middle-class professions – banking, law and dentistry, but were still on the lower rungs of their respective ladders and by no means wealthy. To the four of them, with sedentary indoor jobs in urban Glasgow, the mountains called strongly come the weekend.

They were more than climbing partners, they were good friends with a shared love of the mountains. They were like-minded young men who enjoyed each other's company, had the same sense of humour and trusted their lives to each other. Together they found fun as well as adventure in the mountains. Time and again in Murray's writings he stresses that the companionship, the bond that grows between men on the same rope, and time spent in camps and huts in good company, were as important to him as the climbing itself. By your friends shall you be known, so the saying goes. By looking at MacAlpine, Mackenzie and Dunn we might hope to learn something of Murray himself – of the qualities he admired in others and of the kind of men who, in turn, appreciated him.

Archie MacAlpine (1907–1995)

Murray was 14 and Archie MacAlpine 20 when they first met. The latter, with a thatch of fair hair and 'eyes of Viking blue,' was courting Murray's sister, Margaret, and made regular visits to the Murray household in Glasgow. MacAlpine was then a student at the Glasgow Dental College. A fellow student at the time was Ben Humble, but Archie had no interest in mountaineering and couldn't see the point of it. He was, however, a university oarsman with many a trophy on his shelves. He once rowed 60 miles up the Clyde estuary to Skipness at the mouth of Loch Fyne where the Murrays were on holiday. After qualifying, he set up a dental practice in Ibrox, Glasgow and married Margaret. She it was who persuaded him to try mountaineering. The fact that he owned a car – which meant you could climb in Glencoe and be back in Glasgow that evening – was a huge bonus in the eyes of the young Murray who had himself just discovered mountaineering.

MacAlpine had a keen sense of humour and a good mimic's ear, enabling him to catch to perfection Macphee's drawl or Bell's Fife accent. He also possessed the ability to recall an almost inexhaustible fund of good stories. Murray said that only once in his lifetime had he seen an audience literally rolling in aisles. It happened when MacAlpine spoke at a JMCS dinner in the old Constitutional Club of Glasgow and recited Longfellow's *Wreck of the Hesperus,* delivered as if by a slightly sozzled upper-crust English gentleman.

> 'On mountains, the worse conditions became, whether on hard climbs, or in wet tents or bleak bothies, he never failed to lighten the fix we were in, and to lift drooping spirits. This rare talent being his to a high degree, it made him a most valued member of any rope.'[2]

Something of their shared sense of fun as a team is captured by Murray:

> 'There is a solemn canon published from time to time by the Scottish climbing clubs, in which (among other listed sins) the innocent walker is advised to avoid alcohol, but this wise declaration is immediately followed by the cheering counsel that "a flask may be carried for emergencies." Every April, after repeating the solemn canon, MacAlpine

proclaims that a state of emergency exists: his birthday. This event is of variable date, always coinciding with a good weekend on a mountain.'[3]

MacAlpine's usual role was as last man on the rope – a position which required special qualities. The last man was there to provide extra safety and, in the event of a fall, might have to hold not just the leader but the second man too. The last man had to wait longer on cold and cramped belays than the others. On snow and ice the delicate footholds had often been destroyed before it was his turn to climb and yet, to save time, he was expected to follow as quickly as possible. All these duties MacAlpine admirably fulfilled.

When war was declared in 1939 MacAlpine joined the Army Dental Corps. He was posted to the south of England where he trained in dental surgery at East Grinstead Hospital. Under the guidance of the great plastic surgeon, Sir Archibald McIndoe, he was part of the team that repaired the terrible facial injuries to British airmen. The war over, he returned to Scotland to find that his Ibrox practice no longer existed. With a wife, two young sons and a daughter to support he returned to England, opened a practice in Tunbridge Wells and accepted a post as consultant in dental surgery at East Grinstead.

Murray gives an example of his friend and brother-in-law's parenting style: for a prank Archie's two boys, Roderick and Euan, locked their father in the garage and threw away the key. Instead of hammering on the door and shouting, MacAlpine kept quiet. The boys grew uneasy as their shouts to see if he was all right remained unanswered. After a frantic search for the key which had been thrown into long grass, they opened the door. Out walked Archie without a word or a glance at his sons. 'Non action can be far more effective than violent reaction, if well chosen,' Murray concluded.[4] Later, this same Roderick was to die in a mountain accident in Norway where he was living at the time. He was only 30.

Archie died in a nursing home in 1995, aged 88

Kenneth Dunn (1911–2002)

After his schooling at Fettes, where he won prizes in classics, Kenneth Dunn studied law and was training to join his family's law firm. This is what he was doing in the 1930s, when he climbed with Murray, Mackenzie and MacAlpine. He was a gentle giant, fair-haired, broad shouldered, 14 stone and immensely strong. Donald McIntyre, in his obituary of Dunn, says: 'He was a man of many talents, who enjoyed spirited, informed discussions on topics ranging from Ancient Greek history to mechanics; geology to poetry. Each time you spoke with him, you learned something, which was delivered in a considered and erudite fashion.' McIntyre goes on to comment: 'I have often thought that Kenneth Dunn played the part of Dr Watson to Bill Murray's Holmes.'[5]

Apparently, such was Dunn's strength that he was able to hold up one side of Murray's Austin Seven while the wheel was changed – a frequent occurrence since the car's tyres were old and threadbare. He was also an excellent car mechanic, managing to repair Murray's broken down vehicle on several occasions. Murray tells us that Dunn's resourcefulness on the road was matched by the same on rock. 'With Dunn one could feel safe and relax. None of us, not even the blunt-spoken Mackenzie, were able to ruffle his built-in geniality.'[6]

In typically casual fashion Dunn once sent Murray a telegram from the remoteness of Kintyre, 'commanding' him to be prepared to climb on Nevis the next day – but omitting to state the time or place of meeting. More by luck than anything else they encountered each other at the Inverarnan Inn. Murray was all set to give him a tongue lashing, but 'You cannot damn and blast a man whose eyes sparkle with delight at meeting you. I tried; but it was no good.'[7]

A facet of Dunn's relaxed attitude to life was that he was prone to leaving his mountain boots behind; and that he was invariably still in bed when the car stopped at his house to pick him up. The others decided to tell him the starting time was an hour earlier than it really was. It so happened this was the one occasion when Dunn rose early and was ready to go. 'There was something truly great in the audacity with which he at once accused us of lateness.'[8]

Dunn's unbounded optimism was valued by his team-mates. It boosted them up many an ice-clad pitch in winter. Moreover, 'No matter how grim the prospect or precarious his own situation, he has the remarkable capacity of appearing unshakably safe and solid.'[9]

Before the war Dunn was a member of the Glasgow Highlanders in the Territorial Army, and during World War II he rose to the rank of Major. After the war he married twice and became the father of four daughters. Bill Murray was best man at his first wedding. He did voluntary work with Glasgow youth clubs and it was Dunn whom Murray assisted in taking some 'youthful Glasgow gangsters' on to the Arrochar hills. Eventually, he became Solicitor for Scotland for the Inland Revenue. As a solicitor he freely gave invaluable advice to the SMC. Probably the last time Murray and Dunn climbed together was in the famous winter of 1947. After that, professional and family life increasingly claimed his time.

Bill Mackenzie (1908–2003)

Murray was 23 when he first met Bill Mackenzie and Mackenzie was 28. Murray describes how, in May 1936, the JMCS held a meet in Glencoe. Murray wasn't there, but MacAlpine and his wife, Margaret (Murray's sister) were. It rained heavily during the day and people crammed into MacAlpine's big tent. Their camp bed wasn't equal to the challenge and collapsed. Two of the culprits were Mackenzie and Dunn. By way of apology, Mackenzie invited MacAlpine to climb with him a fortnight hence. MacAlpine said he wouldn't be able to because he always climbed with Bill Murray. 'Bring him along,' Mackenzie said. Two weeks later, when they camped in Glen Etive, Mackenzie took them on a short climb that evening. Murray recalls that moment:

'His frame was wiry, hair black, manner incisive, and speech brusque, yet he was a great bringer-on of the young and inexperienced, scorning their natural fears. He picked out a hard, near-vertical rib and went up unroped, not without trouble. I managed to follow. At the top he looked me in the eye and barked, "What else have you done?"

I hesitated. "Well Curved Ridge and the Cobbler by ..."

"Done Crowberry Direct?"

"No, maybe in twenty years if I keep at it ..."

He withered me with a glance. "We'll do it tomorrow," he snapped.

With those four words he snatched us out of the last century. As in summer, so in winter, he had me in no time leading hard rock fouled up with snow and ice, confidence boosted high by finding I could stay on the stuff.'[10]

Another wonderful little pen portrait of Mackenzie provided by Murray is when they were in the CIC hut, seated round the breakfast table one wet and windy October morning:

'"When the weather is foul," said Mackenzie – and here he paused so that his audience could hear the wind soughing round the corners of the hut – "and the rain is coming down in sheets" – at which he looked pointedly out of the small window – 'there is only one thing to do ..."

"Get back to bed," I murmured.

Mackenzie's blue eyes flashed with indignation and the nostrils of his hawk-nose distended. He looked a perfect specimen of the intolerant man of action. "The only thing to do," he sternly continued, "is to climb the hardest route on the mountain."

"Why?" asked MacAlpine briskly.

"Why!" exploded Mackenzie. "In rain you get miserable on an easy climb. But go to a hard climb and you forget the weather – all your interest goes to the rock."'[11]

It was a sore point with Bill Mackenzie that, because of the success of *Mountaineering in Scotland*, he was known in some circles as the man who climbed with W.H. Murray, whereas it would be more accurate to say that Murray climbed with Mackenzie. It was Mackenzie who took Murray under his wing and brought him on as a climber and who, on the majority of their climbs together led most of the hardest pitches. Murray gives his friend full credit for this, stating that he was one of Scotland's most able performers on summer rock and that for Scottish winter climbing, with its mixture of rock, snow and ice, he had no rival in Britain. Murray praises his blend of daring and a prudence born of experience, a combination which made him a first-class mountaineer. He sums up Mackenzie's elegant, rhythmic climbing style by quoting Hazlitt: 'Skill surmounting difficulty and beauty triumphing over skill.'[12] It is generally held that Mackenzie's finest winter climb was the first winter ascent of Shelf Route on the Buachaille Etive Mor, done in March 1937 – a frighteningly exposed 165-metre route which was years ahead of its time. When asked what made her husband tick, Mary Mackenzie (his second wife) replied, 'True grit!'[13] He certainly displayed it that day.

Mackenzie was naturally athletic, being 'wiry and lean as a courtyard cat' excelling at skiing (in Scotland, Switzerland and Norway), golf – he was a scratch player, and football – he played for Elgin City in his youth. He made several attempts to teach Murray to ski. The latter was not an apt pupil, regarding skiers as 'effete'; added to which, according to Mackenzie, he possessed two left feet.

He was educated at Elgin Academy and Robert Gordon's College, Aberdeen, then worked for the Union Bank of Scotland in Elgin before transferring to Glasgow. In 1936 he joined the Territorial Army and spent several weeks training with French Alpine troops in Chamonix. When war broke out he was commissioned in the Border Regiment and sent to France. He was evacuated from Cherbourg two weeks after the main part of the British Army had been lifted from the beaches of Dunkirk. Thereafter he was attached to Special Forces, working with mountain training units in Scotland and the Canadian Rockies. One of his duties as a commando officer was to produce the basic field manual for mountain warfare. By the end of the war he had achieved the rank of Major.

With peace restored, Mackenzie and his wife set up their own accountancy firm and business consultancy, with a range of international clients. Despite the demands which this made on his time, he still managed to climb (although never to quite the same standard as before the war), golf, fish for salmon and sea trout in his beloved Skye and ski in Scotland and on the continent. He produced a guide book to the Cuillins of Skye in 1958 and was president of the SMC 1966–68. He was still climbing in his seventies, skiing in his eighties and golfing and fishing in his nineties. He died aged 94, the last of that famous pre-war foursome to depart this world.

There was a striking contrast in the personalities of Murray and Mackenzie. The latter climbed purely for enjoyment, whereas Murray's motives were deeper and more complex. It was typical of Murray that he gloried in winter moonlight traverses, and of Mackenzie that he preferred to be in bed or at least in a warm sleeping bag. For Mackenzie climbing was just one of his several sporting activities; for Murray it was much more than this. He had a lifelong commitment to mountains in a way that Mackenzie didn't. This included the conservation of the Scottish Highland areas, whereas Mackenzie had little interest in these matters. They wrote about their mountain experiences in very different ways, Mackenzie's accounts being fairly bald, understated chronicles of fact and Murray's being crafted descriptive essays, with elements of story, character, humour and philosophy. Aitken commented in an email to me, 'We can probably say with conviction that if we'd had to depend on Mackenzie's writing-up of the great Murray-Mackenzie routes they would have enjoyed far less glamour and cachet than they did and still do.' Mackenzie was what would have been called in those days a 'hearty'. Murray, on the other hand, was an aesthete. Despite the fact that they were so unalike in many ways, there can be no doubting the strength of the bond between them.

These four never climbed together again as a team after the war. MacAlpine was in the south of England with his new dental practice and his post at East Grinstead Hospital; Dunn and Mackenzie were both married and had pressing family commitments and professional responsibilities. The experience of war would have changed all of them and Murray, after his time in POW camps, more than most. They were not quite the same people that they had been in those carefree pre-war years. In one of his SMC presidential speeches Mackenzie remarked that 'Bill saw an angel on every pitch'. This has been interpreted by some as a deliberate put down, but it seems more likely that, given the way the group teased each other and made jokes at each other's expense – all taken in the affectionate spirit in which it was meant – that there was no malice in it and that no offence was taken.

Of the four of them, only Murray remained unmarried after the war and, because of his decision to quit banking and become a writer, he was the only one without a regular job with set hours. Murray now tended to go out more frequently with other climbing friends such as Tom MacKinnon, Gordon Donaldson, Donald McIntyre and Douglas Scott. The original foursome kept in touch over the telephone, and through letters and Christmas cards. Murray was fond of his sister and his two nephews and niece and spent several holidays with the MacAlpines. The fact that the four JMCS tigers were now all members of the Scottish Mountaineering Club also helped keep them in touch with each other and they would meet on occasions like the AGM or the annual dinner. When Bill Murray and Anne married in 1960, the MacAlpines, Mackenzie and his wife and the Dunns all attended. Murray records that he sometimes went hill walking with Dunn and his son, and Mrs Mackenzie recalls that she, her husband and Murray spent a holiday in the Swiss Alps together in the late 1950s. By then, middle-age was beckoning and it seems that no serious climbing was involved. The Murrays, as a couple, regularly visited the Mackenzies in their Glasgow house. As a foursome they occasionally went hill walking but, as Murray began to do more and more sailing and became involved with his conservation work and Mackenzie's business became more time-consuming, these outings were less frequent.

Ben Humble (1903–1977)[14]

Ben Humble was born in Dumbarton in 1903, the seventh of eight brothers, the sons of the manager of Dennystown Forge. Despite rapidly advancing deafness Humble qualified in dentistry at the Glasgow Dental College. He was, in fact, a student there at the same time as Archie MacAlpine. His deafness made private practice difficult, so he turned to research in dental radiology and forensic odontology, making significant contributions in both fields.

His real calling, though, was not dentistry, but the hills, especially the Cuillins of Skye, which cast a spell over him ever since a friend took him on a walking holiday there in 1929, when he was 26. Soon he was spending more and more time amongst the Scottish hills, climbing, walking and 'howfing'.[15] The Arrochar hills, near where he lived in his early adulthood, and their many howfs, was another area that was special to him. Humble began writing about his wayfaring adventures and his first book, *Tramping in Skye*, was published in 1933. Over the years, this was followed by many others,[16] including his classic, *The Cuillin of Skye* (1952). 'There is a voice the deaf can hear as clearly as any other person – the voice of the hills,' he wrote.

Ben Humble's whole life was a response to the challenge of deafness. Despite the fact that he refused to learn to lip read, he was an excellent communicator, with an intuitive, almost uncanny, ability to follow what people were saying. He was always keen to get his point over and often took part in public debates. He carried a notebook with him and sometimes asked people to write down what they had said. Many who did not know him well, however, were unaware that he was profoundly deaf. Partly this was due to his clever use of his

vocal trademark which Murray described so well in his Introduction
to *The Cuillin of Skye*:

> 'Ben's long-drawn aaaaaah was an habitual expression. By subtle
> inflection of voice he could use it to signify equally well approval or
> censure, or to convey from the gamut of emotion any note he chose
> … His eloquent aaaaaahs could communicate more than other men's
> innumerable words.'

Humble was a man of many enthusiasms. Amongst these were
public speaking, photography and mountain rescue. He played a
central role in the creation of Scottish Mountain Rescue teams as we
know them today. For many years after their inception he was their
official recorder, keeping a record of all the incidents and call-outs
that occurred. In 1968 he was responsible for the first major mountain
safety exhibition in Scotland. In 1971 he was awarded an MBE for his
work in mountain rescue and mountain safety. He was also a keen
photographer and film maker. During World War II he produced
several educational films in order to support the war effort.[17]

Humble was one of the first voluntary instructors at the Central
Council of Physical Recreation's[18] outdoor centre, Glenmore Lodge
in the Cairngorms. In his later years he was given free board and
lodging there in exchange for his services.

Murray first met Ben Humble at a JMCS meet in 1935. They climbed
often together in 1936 and 1937, but seldom above the standard of V.
Diff. because Humble's deafness affected his balance and also made
communication difficult on a long climb. It was with Ben Humble
that Murray did 16 different climbs in one day on the Cobbler. In
June 1936 Murray went to Skye for his three-week summer holidays
(Scott and MacAlpine were there too) and teamed up with Humble
to do the traverse of the main Cuillin ridge as described in 'Twenty-
four Hours on the Cuillin,' the opening chapter of *Mountaineering
in Scotland*. It was during this holiday that Humble took his most
famous photograph, the one of Murray standing atop the Cioch with
a sea of cloud below him.

A photograph which became famous for a different reason was
one taken by Murray's sister, Margaret, on a camping weekend. It
caught Ben Humble in an unflattering moment, sitting outside his

tent eating a kipper. Murray, who was organising an exhibition of mountain photography in Glasgow, entered it under the title of 'The Humble Kipper'. Humble, a lover of practical jokes, could be touchy and over-sensitive at times if he was on the receiving end. He refused to speak to Murray for nearly two years, and then came the war years. Murray describes their reconciliation when they met by chance in Glasgow after the war:

> 'He came up to me grinning. "Three years in prison camps aaaaaah! – maybe you've been punished enough," and he held out his hand which I thankfully took.'

Although Humble and Murray were different in many ways, they also had much in common. First and foremost was their shared love of mountains. In addition to this, both were writers; and both had the same ethic of service to others, giving huge amounts of their time, unpaid, to causes they believed in. One cause which they had in common was Mountain Rescue, both having worked hard to ensure that Scotland had an efficient and properly organised system. Also, in the immediate post-war years, Murray was a regular contributor to the magazine, *Outdoors in Scotland,*[19] of which Humble was the editor. Coincidentally, both Murray and Humble had Hutchison as their middle name.

We should note that Murray's mountaineering books and articles by no means convey the full extent of his involvement with mountains or with his fellow mountaineers. As Cocker's Chronology shows, the climbs and walks Murray described in his published work were only a very small proportion of his total Scottish mountaineering. His friendships extended well beyond his regular climbing companions and he went on the hills with a wide range of JMCS and SMC members and other companions. His socialising wasn't necessarily with people in his party for that weekend. For example, in Ted Zenthon's diaries[20] there is an account of how Zenthon and a friend were camping in Glencoe at the same time as Murray and Laidlaw were camped at Coupal Bridge and how Murray dropped by their tent just for a chat; and how when Murray was giving them a lift back to Glasgow in his car, they stopped near a bridge so that Murray could scale one of its vertical piers.

Although, inevitably, the four Glasgow climbers drifted apart, it is clear from what Murray wrote in *The Evidence of Things Not Seen*, his last book, that his respect and affection for Mackenzie, MacAlpine and Dunn was undimmed and that the intense experiences shared with them had forged bonds which time could not erode. In his pre-war years he spent more hours in their company than he did with anyone else and he must surely have had companions like them and like Ben Humble especially in mind when he commented in *Mountaineering in Scotland* that through mountains he had been given friendships 'more priceless than accumulations of gold'.[21]

NOTES

1. *Mountaineering in Scotland*, page 36.
2. W.H. Murray, 'In Memoriam: Archie MacAlpine,' SMCJ, 1995.
3. *Undiscovered Scotland*, page 108.
4. *The Evidence of Things Not Seen*, page 118.
5. *Ibid*, pages 31–32.
6. Donald McIntyre, SMCJ, 2002.
7. *The Evidence of Things Not Seen*, page 32.
8. *Undiscovered Scotland,* page 111.
9. *Mountaineering in Scotland*, page 16.
10. *Ibid*, page 10.
11. *Ibid*, page 21.
12. *Ibid*, page 40..
13. In a letter to Michael Cocker, dated September, 2000.
14. Much of the information about Ben Humble I have taken from the biography written by his nephew, Roy Humble, *The Voice of the Hills* (1995).
15. Ben Humble described the art of howfing as the ability to make oneself comfortable overnight, outdoors, at any time of year. It was Jock Nimlin who first applied the word howf to any sort of rude shelter used by climbers.
16. *Tramping In Skye* (1933); *The Songs Of Skye* (1934); *Wayfaring Around Scotland* (1936); *Songs For Climbers* (1938); *On Scottish Hills* (1946); *The Cuillin Of Skye* (1952). He also produced several publications related to the area around Arrochar which he knew and loved so well: *Arrochar and District: A Complete Guide* (1930); *Rock Climbs On The Cobbler* (1940), written with the assistance of J.B. Nimlin and G.C. Williams; *Rock Climbs At Arrochar* (1954), written with the assistance of J.B. Nimlin.
17. Humble also made 'A Cragsman's Day,' 1946 and 'Holidays in Arrochar,' 1949.
18. Soon to become the Scottish Council of Physical Recreation. Later, Murray was offered the post of warden of Glenmore Lodge, but declined.
19. *Open Air in Scotland* ran from 1945–1948 and carried articles about a range of outdoor activities in Scotland such as tramping, camping, cycling, sailing, canoeing, youth hostelling, skiing. Amongst its contributors were well-known

names like, Bill Murray, Frank Smythe, Dr Fraser Darling, Ben Humble, Noel Odell, Freddy Spencer Chapman, Alastair Borthwick. It folded because of lack of advertising revenue.

20. Zenthon was kind enough to let me see his climbing diaries which he started keeping from the age of 13 and consist of four thick volumes. His daughter, Ann Gempel, used these to produce *E.R. Zenthon, His Life and Work (2011)*, a privately published account of her father's life.

21. *Mountaineering in Scotland*, page 242.

CHAPTER EIGHT

THE RELUCTANT CONSCRIPT

On 28th June, 1942, within the space of a few hours, Murray was promoted to Captain, miraculously escaped death, and was taken prisoner. This momentous day for Murray was also the lowest point for the British Eighth Army in North Africa. Tobruk had fallen to Rommel's Afrika Korps, which then swept into Egypt and captured another strategic base, Mersa Matruh. It was on this day, during the chaotic retreat which followed, that Murray was captured. Although neither Murray, nor anyone else could know it at the time, this was Rommel's last victory in the Western Desert and a change of fortunes lay over the horizon.[1]

Murray arrived in North Africa in June 1941 and commenced training in desert navigation. However, after a few weeks the 2nd Battalion of the Highland Light Infantry was rushed to Iraq to defend the Kirkuk oilfields from a German parachute drop. From there they were sent to Cyprus to guard against an expected airborne invasion. It was not until April 1942 that Murray rejoined the 10th Indian Brigade[2] in Cyrenaica (the eastern division of the Italian colony of Libya), just before Rommel's second offensive in May.

Lieutenant-Colonel L.B. Oatts, in his history of the Highland Light Infantry, describes the desert terrain in which the HLI found itself:

'The Western Desert, brown, yellow and grey, [was] a dismal prospect of shifting sand, clumps of scrub, low ridges and steep escarpments. No greenery, and no water, but a hot sun and a hot wind which would whip the sand up in an instant and blot out the sky. Of vast extent and without water or any discernible landmarks, it was certainly no country for fighting battles in. The conduct of operations was, in fact, only made possible by means of mechanical transport, without which the lines of advance of the opposing armies would have been confined to narrow and well-defined strips. With mechanical transport there were no such limitations and wide sweeps were possible, reaching far out into the desert, so that the inland flank of an army was always in the air.'[3]

The main tactic of Major General Neil Ritchie, who was then Commander of the Eighth Army, was to establish a series of defendable 'boxes' across the desert. These were encampments, surrounded by barbed wire and mine-fields. In a featureless landscape it required both exact navigation and nerve to drive through the invisible lanes in the minefields. Warfare in the desert was confusing and scattered. The military situation was constantly changing and both sides operated behind each other's fluid lines. You could never be sure who was friend and who was foe.

On one occasion Murray was sent out on night patrol to investigate an unidentified tank squadron. Under a crescent moon he, his sergeant and a full platoon covered the ground by truck before stopping and cautiously moving forward. Close to midnight they saw the tanks silhouetted against the night sky. They crawled closer. Murray whispered to his sergeant to stay with the section while he went in alone, but to clear out fast if he heard a shot or a shout. He wriggled nearer and nearer, finding no sentries, but seeing the glow of a cigarette and hearing the low rumble of voices. No enemy, he concluded, would act as casually as this when so close to the British divisions. He took a chance and stood up, walking towards them, grenade in hand. 'Someone got to his feet. "Hello," I said, "are you British or Jerry?"'[4]

Soon after this incident, Murray had a narrow escape. Ritchie's skirmishing tactics included scattering artillery batteries across the desert. Murray had sent a section of his platoon out to one of these batteries to provide protection. A couple of days later Murray and a senior subaltern went out to them by truck with rations. They were almost at the circle of guns when another British truck approached and drove into the ring's open centre. The truck was packed with German soldiers who jumped out and opened fire. Murray's driver managed to wrench their truck around and accelerate out of the circle. The battery crew and Murray's platoon section were all killed.

On another occasion, during the battle around the Cauldron, the

HLI were ordered to get in close to one of the Panzer divisions and disable the tanks by damaging their tracks with grenades. Murray regarded this mission as being every bit as suicidal as the Charge of the Light Brigade. He was outraged that General Ritchie could even think of sending infantry to attack massed tanks over open ground without armoured support. Nor did they have the benefit of surprise since a rather ineffective preliminary artillery barrage had given warning of Ritchie's intentions. As they careered towards the enemy many of the trucks carrying the HLI were blown to pieces. At last they halted. Out jumped the troops, desperately seeking cover as they advanced on foot.

'The air became loudly alive with the rush of solid shot, the whine of shrapnel and zip of bullets. I felt no fear – the nervous system had either been screwed up not to register or else shocked out of action. I half turned to see how my platoon was faring and to speak to my runner, who came hard on my heels. His body stood on its legs a yard away – but only the legs, still joined at the smoking waist. The trunk and head had vanished.'[5]

Despite heavy losses, the advance continued. The German mortars then laid a bomb-barrage backed by intense machine-gunning, pinning the HLI to the ground. A bomb landed only a yard from where Murray was lying. It blew out a crater but left him unharmed. He knew that the safest place in a bombardment is in a crater because the chances of exactly the same spot receiving a second hit were reckoned to be minimal. He was preparing to jump into the newly made crater when he felt a strong inner prompting to stay where he was. It was so authoritative, Murray said, that he obeyed and did not move. Seconds later, another bomb exploded in that first crater.[6]

The HLI were ordered to withdraw – 'We simply rose and ran,' Murray recalls. At this stage of the battle only 200 out of the 800 in the battalion were still alive. There followed a series of chaotic rear-guard skirmishes. Murray writes of unidentified vehicles racing in all directions, shells landing from invisible sources, the ground strewn with bloody and burnt-out relics. In this confusion his company was twice bombed and strafed by the RAF. The HLI were ordered to bestride the road 40 miles east of Mersa Matruh and to delay Rommel's advance as long as possible. On learning that a Panzer division had passed through Mersa Matruh and would be upon them in half an hour, Murray was told by his brigadier that, by the end of the day, he'd either be dead or a prisoner.

As dusk fell Murray, who was at brigade HQ, awaited the coming of the German tanks: 'Suddenly the tanks were there, dark bulks on top of the escarpment, twenty Mark IVs abreast. At such short range our 2-pounder guns could not miss. The shells struck them on the nose. The armour glowed red in the dusk while the shells glanced off in a shower of sparks. The tanks staggered – but came on.'[7] The Mark IVs rumbled forward, machine-gunning the ground in front of them, passing right over the HLI trenches. The tanks stopped and their crew emerged to finish off any survivors.

Lieutenant-Colonel Oatts, in *Proud Heritage*, sums up what happened (page 269): 'At one time or another every position held, including battalion HQ, had been overrun by tanks, often under the noses of the British armour. It was a poor kind of battle for infantrymen of the calibre of the HLI. There was no flesh and blood for them to fight, only armoured monstrosities spouting shells and bullets, as they converged upon the hastily-prepared positions through clouds of smoke and sand. Nevertheless, the HLI stood and fought it out as best they could.'

Somehow Murray survived. He crawled out of his slit-trench. A young tank commander was walking unsteadily towards him, brandishing an automatic pistol. The man was dazed and shaken from the pounding his tank had taken. Murray thought it quite likely that he would press the trigger. Instead, he lowered his gun.

Murray had good reason to think that these might be his last moments alive. Whatever the Geneva Convention might say, front-line soldiers on both sides accepted that if you surrendered 'too late' you had to take the consequences. It was generally recognised, too, that, in the heat of battle, the bloodlust could not easily be switched off. Murray may not have known at the time that Rommel had specifically ordered that prisoners were not to be shot.[8]

Murray was still in shirt and shorts, and starving. The chill of the desert night was seeping into his bones. The tank commander asked if he was feeling the cold.

'I blurted out, "It's cold as a mountain top."[9]

He looked me straight in the eye. "Good God, do you climb mountains?"

We were both mountaineers and still in our twenties. We relaxed. He stuffed away the pistol and could not do enough for me.'[10]

The tank commander produced food for Murray, who had not eaten in nearly two days, and gave him a British Army greatcoat (loot from Tobruk), and they toasted 'mountains' with a bottle of beer. Then Murray was handed over to the Italian infantry who had arrived with trucks to take away prisoners. The stock phrase used when Allied personnel were captured was, 'For you the war is over.' Nobody actually said this to Murray. Nonetheless, his days of active service were over.

War and conscription had meant the ruin of everything Murray and his friends valued. He said the obvious choice of armed service for him would have been the RAF. Presumably he meant that the open spaces, the wide views, the altitude and feeling of space below were things he enjoyed. Previously, however, an old school-friend had taken him up in an open biplane and shown off by doing stunts which had terrified him and put him off flying.

Undoubtedly, for someone who was not a professional soldier and who described himself as a 'reluctant conscript' Murray conducted himself with courage and coolness under fire and was a responsible officer who cared for his men. One night, with his platoon camping out in the desert scrub, Murray overhead some of his men discussing him. 'He's the kind who gets killed first,' someone said.

Murray wondered if perhaps they thought he was a bit rash on occasions and defends himself by saying in *The Evidence of Things Not Seen*, 'I felt without ambition to win a Victoria Cross.' It seems more likely that the comment was about an officer who saw it as his duty to put his own life at risk rather than expose his men – as when, for instance, he was the one who went forward to investigate the unidentified tank squadron, and when he went in person to deliver rations to a section of his platoon out in the desert.

The 2nd Battalion of the HLI was put in an extremely stressful situation and many of the men would have suffered from combat stress reaction.[11] There is no evidence that Murray was one of those who did. His conversation with the German tank commander is lucid (although this may have been mentally edited and tidied up before it was committed to paper). As a mountaineer, Murray was accustomed to coping with danger and fear.

In *Mountaineering in Scotland* (page 241), he states: 'As an infantry officer in the shambles of defeat and the prolonged rearguard actions of June 1942, I found no call upon stamina equal to that demanded by Garrick's Shelf in the winter of 1936, nor strain of suspense to match that of Observatory Ridge in 1937.'[12]

The British propaganda of the time would have everyone believe that it was a war of Good v Evil and that the British had Right on their side. Murray soon realised that, at an individual level at least, there were good people and bad people on both sides. He mentions with disgust the British airman he rescued after his plane had come down in the desert. It had run out of fuel because the pilot had used it up flying up and down strafing a German ambulance column. Murray makes a point of how his own brigade commander issued orders that no German prisoners were to be taken, and had declared that the only good Germans were dead Germans, whereas Rommel had given orders to his troops to spare prisoners. His encounter with the German tank commander, a fellow mountaineer, showed him that there was a common humanity that crossed the lines drawn by war.

He regarded some of Ritchie's decisions and the resulting carnage as madness. By the time he arrived in Italy he was close to becoming a conscientious objector.

The way Murray writes about the Desert War in *The Evidence of Things Not Seen* equals, for vividness, intensity and its ability to grip its readers, anything he wrote in his mountain classic, *Mountaineering in Scotland*. Clearly these experiences were deeply felt and lived inside him all his life. It is perhaps significant that, while in prison camp, when his experiences of being near to death in war were still only months behind him, he wrote in detail about what went through his mind when he thought he was about to die. It was not of wartime that he wrote. Instead he described in *Mountaineering in Scotland* (page 196) how he came close to drowning in the 1930s. It is as if he wanted to release these thoughts and feelings but had to shift it to a different context, less immediate and surrounded by happier memories.

On the other hand, in a letter to Gordon Smith, written in 1988, congratulating Smith on his winning entry – a satirical piece – for a mountain essay competition, Murray refers to Smith's pen as having made 'riddled corpses' of himself and fellow SMC worthies. Smith comments that he finds it astonishing that such a phrase could be 'so (apparently) casually used by someone who was so nearly that very thing.'[13] Maybe it shows that Murray had comes to terms with his harrowing war experience.

One of the things which strongly affected him and was a major influence on his whole attitude to life was his seemingly miraculous escapes from death. There was the occasion when he and his driver only just evaded the Germans who attacked the artillery post. His runner was blown in half only a few feet behind him. He had been one of only 200 survivors out of 800 advancing infantrymen. A mortar bomb exploded a yard away, leaving him unharmed; and when he had decided to jump into the crater it made, an inner voice told him not to. Murray was convinced, and remained convinced all his life, that this was not a matter of luck, but the workings of some higher power that was protecting him. He called it Providence – God's extraordinary intervention in people's lives. Over the years, Murray's writings make numerous references to Providence, of which the following extract is just one sample:

> 'It is one of the disadvantages of great experience that a man is apt to discover too many excellent reasons why an adventurous proposition should be impossible; and one of the advantages of inexperience (when high spirits go along with it) that he has an urge to attempt the impossible, which he will then achieve if Providence so disposes.'[15]
> He did, however, qualify this, in 'Present Moments' (*Alpine Journal*, 1981): 'I have not found it helpful to read into the term Providence a meaning of deity's caring provision. A man who tries to get that for himself will get nothing. It is too gross a presumption.'

His belief in Providence and his Desert War experience in general contributed to the whole-hearted manner in which he embraced the Perennial Philosophy while in prison camp – a philosophy which influenced the way he conducted the rest of his life. Murray questioned the idea of war and much about the way it was conducted, but the war also asked questions of him and he was not found wanting.

NOTES

1. Online Appendix B outlines the first two years of the Western Desert Campaign, 1940–42.

2. After the Indian Mutiny (1857–59) the Indian Army always contained British troops on a ratio of one to three to ensure that such a thing never happened again. This was unlikely in World War II, but the British regiments were usually better equipped which helped strengthen the division.

3. *Proud Heritage*, 1961, page 263.

4. *The Evidence of Things Not Seen*, page 75 (Many of the same events covering the desert war and his capture are also described by Murray in the first chapter of *Undiscovered Scotland* (1951) and in two identical articles he submitted to the *Weekend Scotsman* and *Mountain Magazine* in June 1979.

5. *Ibid.*

6. *Ibid,* page 76.

7. *Ibid,* page 80.

8. Not only was this because Rommel was a professional soldier who honoured the code but, also, as Adrian Gilbert explains in his book: 'Despite their administrative and logistic nuisance, prisoners remained a desirable commodity. They were a valuable propaganda tool: newsreels of enemy soldiers marching into captivity were a visual proof of military success. Prisoners could be used as hostages at some point in the future, and crucially, they acted as a bargaining counter to ensure reciprocal good behaviour for one's own troops captured by the enemy. They were also a source of intelligence and, subsequently, a form of cheap labour.' (*POW: Allied Prisoners in Europe 1939–1945*, 2006).

9. Midge Gillies, in her book *Barbed-Wire University* (2012), suggests that possibly mountains were in Murray's mind at that moment because, anticipating capture, he had been going through his notebooks to see if anything needed to be disposed of and, amongst his things, had been his address book with the names of all his climbing friends in it.

10. *The Evidence of Things Not Seen*, page 80. Elsewhere Murray gives a slightly different version of this event. This will be discussed in Chapter Thirty.

11. The current term 'combat stress reaction' (CSR) was not used in World War II. Known as 'shell shock' in WWI, it was usually called 'battle fatigue' in WWII. It was treated with more sympathy than in WWI, although many army doctors still knew very little about the condition. The most common symptoms are fatigue, slower reaction times, indecision, disconnection from one's surroundings, and inability to prioritise. Combat stress reaction is generally short-term and should not be confused with post-traumatic stress disorder (PTSD), although this might start as a combat stress reaction. (PTSD was not officially recognised until 1980.)

12. Murray is in error here. The winter ascent of Observatory Ridge to which he refers was made in February 1938 (as described in the opening chapter of this biography).

13. In a letter to me, October 2010.

14. *Undiscovered Scotland*, page 198.

15. *The Story of Everest*, page 14.

CHAPTER NINE

IN THE BAG

After a night spent in the open, wrapped in his newly acquired great-coat, Murray and his fellow captives were trucked to Benghazi where tens of thousands of prisoners-of-war were assembled for transportation to Italy. Within a week he was flown to a transit camp in Bari on the heel of the Italian boot. Other POWs were shipped across. Either way, it was a hazardous business with Allied aircraft and submarines on the prowl.[1]

A slow train took Murray, along with 1,500 other prisoners, to Campo 21 on a high ridge in the province of Chieti in central Italy. Here they were within view of the Abruzzi Mountains to the west, but not quite within sight of the Adriatic Sea, which lay ten miles to the east. Murray says next to nothing of these early days of captivity. Perhaps he was still too numb to register much.

Others, though, have documented the filth, the thirst, the hunger and the crowded conditions. Much of this was due to the fact that the Axis powers were unprepared for such a sudden and huge intake of prisoners. It was, they say, the worst phase of their POW years.[2] Not only was there the trauma of battle and the shock of capture to deal with, there was also some of the worst treatment and neglect they would encounter during captivity.

Added to this was the humiliation of defeat and surrender. Nearly everyone avoided the word 'surrender', using terms like 'picked up' or 'in the bag'. Those who had been ordered to surrender by their superior officers could feel slightly better about it, perhaps, but for those who had received no such order there was the nagging doubt about whether they should have fought on. Being alive when so many comrades had died could be a cause for guilt or shame as well as for thanksgiving.

In Murray's case there had been no order to surrender, but he had

no reason to reproach himself. He had resisted up to the point where
to continue would have been suicidal folly. Rather than feeling that
he had let anyone down, he felt he and his battalion were the ones
who had been let down. They had been given equipment, vehicles and
weaponry inferior to those of the enemy, and poor decisions had been
made higher up the chain of command.

Many officers felt a sense of helplessness. Accustomed to being
in control and giving orders, they were suddenly the ones who were
marched about and shouted at and surrounded by rules and restrictions. For those who were captured while the tide of war was still
flowing in favour of the Axis forces – as Murray was – the captivity
that lay ahead must have seemed like a dark, endless tunnel.

It was usual (although less so in Italy than in German-occupied
territory) to separate officers and other ranks into different camps.
Officers were generally treated better and were not required to do
any physical labour. Murray makes no comment about this. That
the officers should be with their men, looking after their welfare and
sharing the same hardships with them did not seem to have been
an issue. He and his fellow officers probably took the division for
granted. It was, after all, how the British Army conducted itself, with
the deliberate separation of officers and men – separate (and naturally
better) mess facilities and quarters, and first-class travel for officers
but not for other ranks (who travelled third class).

Furthermore, officers were drawn from the educated classes. Most,
like Murray, had attended fee-paying schools. In the early 1940s
the class system and class consciousness operated at a level hard to
imagine these days. The division between an officer and his men was
not only one of rank, but also one of class. It was said of World War I
that the officer classes of the British and German armies had more
in common with each other than with their own soldiers. While this
would not have been true two decades later, something remained of
these attitudes and values.

Captured officers were allowed to have 'batmen' or orderlies. In
most officer camps, a batman was shared by all the officers in one
room or hut, although this varied and amongst the more senior
officers the ratio was smaller. Murray makes no mention of the
presence of batmen in any of the camps in which he was incarcerated, although Campo 21 had room orderlies, mess orderlies and

British army cooks. For some officers their presence would be taken for granted or they would simply be socially invisible. For Murray, however, his lack of detail on this and other points of camp life is more to do with the fact that his account is hardly more than a back-drop to two major turning-points in his life – which we shall come to in due course.

Lieutenant John Pelly of the Coldstream Guards, who was captured at Tobruk and who was at Chieti at the same time as Murray, kept a diary and has a rather fuller description of Campo 21 than Murray gives: 'This camp is new and has only been going three weeks. It consists of six large bungalows[3] with two wings each, one bungalow (wired off) being used by the Italian guards, another for the hospital and the Commandant's Offices etc. while the remaining four are for Officer POW's. There is a central road running through the camp, there are three bungalows on either side, while the cook-house is at the end of the road. Surrounding the whole camp is a 20-foot wall, with sentry posts, searchlights etc, along the top, and with *Carabinieri*[4] patrolling continuously inside the walls. Outside the walls is a mass of wire and there are supposed to be more sentries. So it looks a tough proposition for an illegal exit. ... The whole place looks far more attractive than the transit camp at Bari, although there is still no room for recreation.'[5]

Inside the POW bungalows were rooms jammed tight with double-tiered bunks, each with a straw-filled mattress.

All descriptions of POW life put food high on the list, for there was never enough. In the first instance, it was because the Italian authorities had not been given sufficient time to organise rations for the huge influx of prisoners. Later it was because in war-torn Europe, with agriculture, imports and internal communications all disrupted, everyone was starving, civilians and prisoners alike. The camp authorities found a temporary solution by feeding their prisoners on the readily available fruit in the area – tomatoes, figs, peaches, grapes. Murray comments that, after months of eating bully beef and ships' biscuits, this sudden change in diet had catastrophic effects on their guts. All day there were endless queues outside the latrines.

A whole month of protesting finally brought a change and bread and pasta were added to the diet. When things settled down, the basic ration per day was: 1 small roll of rye bread, wholemeal macaroni, green vegetables, a small piece of hard cheese, fruit.

In his book, *POW: Allied Prisoners in Europe 1939–45*, Adrian Gilbert writes (page 99): 'The more POWs were without food the more they thought, dreamed and talked about it. There was a belief that any conversation, no matter how lofty, would turn in a matter of minutes to the topic of food . . . The culmination of all food conversations was the mythic feast that would be eaten on return to the civilian world: vast multi-course banquets with no expense spared.'

After several months the Red Cross became aware of the existence of Campo 21 and arranged for parcels to be sent and for letters to be delivered. A typical British Red Cross parcel might consist of tins containing jam, margarine or butter, cheese, meat loaf, bacon or salmon, dried milk and dried egg. There would also be packets of tea, sugar, coffee, salt, biscuits, dried fruit, cocoa and a bar of chocolate. Once its operation was in full swing, the British Red Cross aimed to send one parcel to each prisoner per week, but this seldom proved possible because of disruptions to transport. Red Cross parcels were the difference between hunger and starvation. Almost unanimously, POW accounts pay tribute to the work of the Red Cross.

Murray remembers the arrival of the first Red Cross parcels: 'The sight of those great vans in the compound, each packed to the roof with individual food boxes, seemed at first like a desert mirage.'[6]

Some of the contents of the parcels were handed in to be added to the daily meal and cooked in the kitchens. Other items were kept for consumption by individuals or by the small groups which formed to pool their resources and share a home-made stove. These stoves, made from empty tins,[7] ran on wood shavings and bits of cardboard, or any other non-edible, combustible scraps. If assisted by fans (a hand-operated system of gears) a 'blower' could boil a mug of water in under two minutes.

Next to food, cigarettes and tobacco were always in huge demand and mostly in short supply. They were paid for by the British Government and shipments went direct from tobacco companies to Geneva where they were packaged by the Red Cross and sent to the POW camps. In times of shortage, substitutes would be used such as dried mint leaves, shredded and wrapped in strips of newspaper or toilet paper, or various mixtures of dried tea leaves or coffee grounds, dried bread crumbs and manure.

Private parcels were allowed and usually contained items of clothing, books and cigarettes. These also arrived via the Red Cross. In nearly all the camps, and Chieti was no exception, the common currency for buying goods and for gambling was cigarettes.[8]

Murray guessed correctly that he would have been posted 'missing, presumed killed in action', and it was thanks to the Red Cross that he was finally able to write to his mother and tell her he was safe. She had been forced to wait six months to learn whether or not her son was alive. POWs were normally allowed to write three or four letters or postcards a month. During his captivity, Murray wrote regularly to his mother, his sister and to friends. Letters were confined to one page and were censored. Anything considered critical of camp conditions or of military value was blacked out. Letters had to be written in unjoined print rather than in normal handwriting to make it easier for the censors to read. The tone of these messages was always cheerful, making light of the hardships. Mostly this was so as not to worry his family and friends and reassure them that he was alright, but there might have been a small element of reassuring himself as well. Murray does fret, though, that some of his letters are obviously not reaching their destination.

Nearly all the prisoners at Chieti had been wearing their desert kit when captured in North Africa. Several months later they were still in short-sleeved shirts and shorts. As winter approached they took to walking about the compound draped in blankets. At last, with temperatures dropping, a consignment of serge battle dress arrived. However, their boots had been taken away 'for repair'. Murray told his mother about this in a coded letter and, thanks to her action, the War Office released 2,000 pairs of boots which were delivered via the Red Cross to Chieti.

If hunger was the pre-eminent physical hardship, its mental equivalent was boredom. Since officers were not put to work, they had time on their hands. Reading was a popular way of filling the long hours. Books were supplied through the Young Men's Christian Association, from house-to-house collections – mainly the classics of English literature, which had been gathering dust on shelves.

Organised classes were popular and were held outside when the weather was dry. Nearly all prisoners were able to lecture on something. Murray doesn't say whether he gave any lectures himself.

Since these were educational rather than for entertainment, if he did lecture, it is more likely that he lectured on subjects related to banking rather than on mountaineering.

Here is Lieutenant John Pelly again, whose diary tells us: 'Got myself into French and Italian classes in the educational programme, and also Agriculture. There is an unlimited talent in the camp, and one can take nearly any language from Russian to Zulu to Sesuto. Also engineering of all types, all sides of business management, history, literature, shorthand and Bible study, etc, etc.'

Concentration was a problem, however, when would-be-students were weak from hunger. Drop-out rates were high, particularly if there was no incentive of a certificated exam at the end.

Campo 21 also had a small theatre and John Pelly records that he was asked to write some sketches and short plays for it. Murray, who after the war turned his hand briefly to drama and who clearly had more writing talent than most of his fellow prisoners, did not contribute because he had become totally absorbed in writing *Mountaineering in Scotland*. He escaped from the everyday awfulness of life as a POW by living inside his mind amongst the mountains he loved.

In a perceptive article about Murray, Gordon Smith points out: 'It is commonplace for writers to employ the imagery of battle in describing the hazards of mountaineering, but when Murray does so, he refers to *grape-shot*, to *campaigning seasons* and to *Nelson at Copenhagen* – all images from another era, safely at arm's length from his own war.'[9]

The writing *of Mountaineering in Scotland* is the subject of Chapter Fifteen. Suffice it to note here that the decision to do so was not only a major turning-point in Murray's life, but also played a large part in helping him through his ordeal. While Murray was absorbed in his book in Italy, a fellow climber was writing about him in Scotland. The following poem appeared in the 1943 SMCJ:

'*For a Scottish Mountaineer Who Is Now a Prisoner of War*

> We are the hills of Scotland, proud and free –
> Proud to have known you, free to your behest.
> You asked for joy of life, we gladly gave;
> You longed for quietude, we gave you rest.

You sought us while the jealous heavens hurled
Their stormy wrath around your patient head.
You laughed and strove against the snowy gale,
And at our feet in peace you made your bed.

We welcomed you when sullen gloomy mist
Shrouded us round and mocked, 'He will not come';
We knew your step when ice bound us about,
And struck our tremulous singing rivers dumb.

The happiness you asked we freely gave –
The treasure that you won was but your due.
You will return to us; and in our age,
'Tis but a minute that we wait for you.

                    J.C. (with thoughts on W.H.M.)'

A second important turning-point also took place while Murray was a prisoner. This was his commitment to the Perennial Philosophy and to mystical theology. He was already interested in these topics and in philosophy in general, but in the POW camps he had time to think and to read. It was, while at Chieti, that the real foundations were laid which were to grow and develop in the next two years.

While Murray escaped into writing his book, others attempted to escape from the camp itself by going over, under or through. They went over the wall and wire by means of secretly constructed folding ladders. They tunnelled their way out; or they passed through the gates in a variety of disguises, or by hiding in vehicles.

A hard climb and an escape share certain aspects – the planning and anticipation, the adrenalin rush, the personal challenge. This was not enough to tempt Murray into trying to escape. He had no sweetheart at the time (as far as is known) or wife or children waiting for him, he thought war was lunacy and, as a mountaineer, he was practised in considering risky undertakings objectively and weighing up the odds. He rightly judged that the odds were heavily stacked against a successful escape. Escaping from the camp was considered to be only about 20 per cent of the problem. The other 80 per cent was the hard bit – travelling across a foreign and occupied country undetected and getting over the border. Only a tiny proportion of escapers ever made 'a home run' and it could take 18 months to a year to reach England. Although, officially, it was the duty of every officer to try to escape, only a very small proportion attempted it.

Since nearly all the published books, both fiction and non-fiction, films and TV programmes about POWs have focused on escaping it would be easy to believe that this was commonplace. In fact, the majority of POWs saw it as both dangerous and futile and chose to sit out the war where they were. Nor were escapers popular since everyone was made to suffer as a result of their actions – extra and unduly prolonged roll calls, standing for hours in freezing conditions or baking sun, and at much greater risk of violence than normal. Rules would be tightened, privileges withdrawn and Red Cross parcels withheld. In Campo 21, as in other camps, the authorities took to puncturing tins so that the contents had to be eaten within a few days and could not be hoarded for escape attempts.

Keen to distract their captives from thoughts of escape, the Italians decided to encourage educational and leisure activities. They provided musical instruments so that the camp developed an orchestra good enough to give concerts.

The engineers amongst the officers had built a radio. The valves and other essential parts were obtained by bribing the guards to smuggle them in. Its whereabouts in the camp was a closely guarded secret. A select few listened to the news on the radio, then posted the main items on a notice-board. The guards were thus aware of the radio's existence, but never found it. It was thought that maybe they didn't look too hard since they, too, read the notice-board, the BBC news telling them much more about what was really going on than they would otherwise have known. Murray and his fellow-officers were therefore aware of the progress of the war and knew that the Eighth Army had been victorious in North Africa, that Sicily had fallen to the Allies and mainland Italy invaded. With each success for the Allies, the camp guards grew friendlier.

When Italy surrendered in September 1943, Murray thought his release was imminent. However, German paratroopers dropped on Chieti and took the camp. Murray does not elaborate on this missed opportunity for freedom. Either he did not know what was going on at higher levels of command, or he could not bring himself to write about what he would have considered a huge let-down, amounting almost to a betrayal.

Charles Rollings sets out the facts: 'A War Office directive reached the camps telling prisoners: "In the event of an Allied Invasion of Italy, officers commanding prison camps will ensure that prisoners-of-war remain within camp. Authority is granted to all officers commanding to take necessary disciplinary action to prevent individual prisoners of war attempting to rejoin their units."

The order had originated with General Montgomery, commander of the British forces, who did not want the campaign in Italy jeopardised by thousands of POWs roaming the countryside bent on sabotage; in any case, he expected the campaign to be over in a matter of weeks ... The Wehrmacht stepped in, resulting in more than 53,000 officers and men who ought to have been freed being transferred to Germany to remain as prisoners for another two years.'[10]

The transfer was swift. In October 1943 they were ordered to pack up at short notice. By giving each man a few books to carry in addition to his own basic belongings, they managed to take with them their most treasured possession, their library. Murray stuffed down the front of his battledress tunic his own most treasured possession, the thick wad of paper that was his manuscript.

NOTES

1. A month later, an Italian troop ship, *Nino Bixio*, carrying POWs from North Africa to Italy was torpedoed with the loss of 300 POWs and with many more injured. During the next 12 months several more ships carrying POWs were attacked by the Allies. The total number of POWs who died in this way was over a thousand.
2. There are several collections of POW memories such as: *POW: Allied Prisoners in Europe 1939–1945* by Adrian Gilbert London (London, 2006); *Prisoner of War: Voices from Behind the Wire in the Second World War* by Charles Rollings (London, 2008); also websites such as the BBC 'People's War' and that of the National Ex-Prisoner of War Association.
3. Murray, however, says that there were a dozen (rather than six) stone-built, whitewashed barrack blocks. Since Pelly's diary was written at the time and Murray's description was drawn from memory more than half a century later, the former's facts are more likely to be accurate. On the other hand, Pelly says each bungalow had two wings, which might explain the difference.
4. The *Carabinieri* are a national armed force for policing both the civilian and military population. They shared jurisdiction over POW camps with the Italian Army.

5. Private collection of war memoirs at the Imperial War Museum, Lambeth; also quoted in Rollings' book (see Note 2) Lieutenant John Pelly was a POW from June 1942 to April 1945.
6. *The Evidence of Things Not Seen*, page 86.
7. The favourite tin for this was the Klim tin which was a lower, wider tin than most. Klim ('milk' spelt backwards) was a brand of powdered milk.
8. In 1943 the approximate going rate was:

    I bar of chocolate..............20 cigarettes
    I tin of biscuits..................20 cigarettes
    I tin of boot polish............25 cigarettes
    I tin of meat roll ....30 cigarettes

    The comparatively high price of boot polish might be explained by the fact that boot polish, when heated, yielded alcohol.
9. 'Sron na Ciche without cliché' in *The Angry Corrie* website, January-March 1998.
10. *Prisoner of War: Voices from Behind the Wire in the Second World* War by Charles Rolling (London 2008), page 309.

CHAPTER TEN

A RED-LETTER DAY

Amongst the wad of paper that was Murray's manuscript lay his account of a winter ascent of Tower Ridge on Ben Nevis.[1] Sitting on his bunk in the crowded room at Chieti, knees drawn up, with the box of his Red Cross parcel serving as a desk, the hunger, the discomforts and the worries would have faded away as he transported himself back to his beloved Scottish mountains and become lost in the events of that December weekend of 1939.

Britain had already been at war with Germany for three and a half months. On that particular weekend of the 16-17th, the naval Battle of the River Plate was taking place, ending with the scuttling of the *Admiral Graf Spee* off Montevideo. Although Murray had not yet received his official call-up papers he knew the army would soon claim him and his freedom would be limited. Just how restricted his life would become, he could not foresee. He and his companions were keenly aware that they should make the most of whatever time was left to them before the war took over their lives. That war and death was on Murray's mind is shown by the memo which, as secretary of the JMCS, he had already sent out to all its members. In this memo he cancelled all club meets, put the club's administration on an emergency footing and gave instructions what to do 'During my absence or in the event of death'.

Murray's companions on that December weekend in 1939 were Dr J.H.B. (Jimmy) Bell and Douglas Laidlaw. Bell was 43, Murray 26 and Laidlaw only 18. The trio met up at Crianlarich where they had a drink before proceeding in Bell's car to Fort William. On the way they stopped for fish and chips at Kinlochleven and had another drink in Fort William before setting out from Achintee, in Glen Nevis. In the dark they lost the path up to the CIC Hut at the foot of the Nevis cliffs, but were treated to a display of the Northern Lights. Bell's Log Book[2] records:

'It must have been close on midnight when we reached the hut. Therein were settled 6 St. Andrews University men who had the stove going. We lit a primus and boiled a half pint of water and dissolved 3 Oxo cubes therein, then adding two gill bottles of rum. This was brought to the boil. ... A magnificent and happy glow ensued as we drank in remembrance of the past mountaineer, A.F. Mummery.'[3]

It was in this hut that Murray first met Bell nearly three years previously. Bell was an industrial chemist, 'a short, stocky man with a bald head and wicked grin', who moved on rock as if made of india-rubber. He dressed shabbily – 'He looked like a ghillie,' commented a fellow mountaineer. He had an irrepressible twinkle and an outrageous sense of humour. Someone once said of Jimmy Bell that whatever you invented about him was almost sure to be true. Murray describes the first breakfast he had with him in that hut, which consisted of porridge, sausages, kippers, tomato soup, peas and beans all stirred up in the same pot. To Bell, as a chemist, it was just a matter of fuel intake. In the incident described in Chapter One when MacAlpine incinerated some of the hut's blankets in the stove, Murray says, with great relish, that MacAlpine considered telling the hut warden that Bell had eaten them for breakfast.

Like Bell, Murray invested time in encouraging and bringing on the next generation of Scottish mountaineers. Two young men, both in their late teens, whom Murray considered the most promising prospects for the future were Gordon Donaldson and Douglas Laidlaw. With Laidlaw, though, the relationship went deeper than simply being his mentor.

Douglas Bartholomew Laidlaw enrolled in the RAF Volunteer Reserves[4] just before the start of the war. He trained as a pilot and became a flight sergeant, flying Lancaster bombers with 626 Squadron, based at Wickenby Airfield in Lincolnshire. He was killed on 26th March 1944, aged 22, when his plane crashed near the borders of France and Belgium.[5] The details are not provided in the public records, but it is likely that he was flying either to or from a night raid on Stuttgart or Berlin (his squadron having focused on these two cities all that month). His grave is in Maubeuge Cemetery in Northern France. 'There was no man alive whom I held in higher regard,' Murray wrote.[6] Despite losing many comrades in the war and a host of relatives and friends since then, only of Laidlaw did he express such a sentiment. Perhaps he sensed in him the same mystical nature, the same response to mountain beauty and felt him to be a kindred spirit.

On the morning of Sunday 17th December, 'the sky was full of wind and sun' as Murray, Bell and Laidlaw discussed over breakfast what route they should do. They opted for 'the stirring challenge' of Tower Ridge. It is the longest and most classic mountain ridge in the British Isles, being almost a kilometre in length from start to finish.[7] The distinctive feature of Tower Ridge is its triple towers which stand out from the main cliffs and are joined by a ridge that, in places, is steep and narrow. The first tower, known as the Douglas Boulder (700 feet), is followed by the Little Tower (actually not a tower, but it looks like one from the ridge), and then the Great Tower. On the ridge on the far side of Great Tower is a sudden nick, at a point where the ridge is very narrow. This is Tower Gap. Once past this difficulty, a final slope leads to the summit plateau.[8] Like all winter routes in Scotland, the conditions vary enormously from week to week, day to day. Murray recalled that, to his knowledge, Tower Ridge had taken 16 to complete and it had also been done in four and a half hours. All of them had been on Tower Ridge several times before in summer and winter and in varying conditions. Murray, for example, records in the CIC hut log book[9] that he was there in June 1936 with MacAlpine when there was thick mist and heavy rain, 'the high water mark of discomfort and misery.' Quite often they used it as a means of descent after an ascent by some other route.

This time they began the climb with a failed attempt to find a direct line up the Douglas Boulder – something which had never been done in winter. They ran into verglas on steeply-angled slabs and retreated. This cost them a precious hour or more and the whole climb was then a race against time to reach the notorious Tower Gap before nightfall. A few years before, Bell and Frank Smythe had been forced to turn back at this point at sunset. Bell was determined that the same should not happen again. Skirting the Douglas Boulder by a traverse of the eastern side, they met powder-snow which had to be swept away before hewing steps in the very hard ice beneath. It was slow going.

Not until three o'clock did they reach the steep and looming mass

of Great Tower. 'It rose almost sheer for a hundred feet above our
heads. Its armour of snow and ice plate was complete.' They decided
to work their way round by a ledge which traversed its eastern wall.
The angle steepened and the drops below became increasingly sen-
sational. Bell, who had gone ahead unroped for most of the route in
order to save time, now tied onto the rope which joined the other two
and handed over the lead to Murray.

Murray continued cutting his way sideways and upwards until they
came to where the summer route went straight upwards to the top of
the tower. But what is relatively easy in summer can be a very different proposition in winter. The whole wall bulged with pale blue ice.
Their dilemma was whether to attempt what looked like the shortest
route but which might, in fact, take a long time to surmount, or to
continue on the long way round via the eastern traverse. Murray
could not resist the challenge, but after half an hour of very little
progress, withdrew. Further along, he found a crack just wide enough
to insert a leg and managed to wriggle up it. Beyond this he turned
a corner and was out of sight of his companions on a large snow
encrusted cliff, seamed by thin and icy ledges. 'Being not insensi-
tive to exposure, I remained constantly aware of Observatory Gully
yawning hungrily at my heels.' Scraping the snow from the rock, he
found 'slabs wrinkled like the hide of an elephant', which provided
footholds. Murray comments here that his woollen gloves helped
because the wool froze to the wrinkles, making the handholds safer.

As Murray popped his head over the top of the ridge, a strong
westerly wind smote him in the face. The sun was setting. The corrie
on the other side of the ridge was blanketed by a fleece of cloud, fired
by the low sun. The sky was red-gold, rose pink, bright green and all
hues between. Laidlaw arrived just as the sun, which was low over the
Atlantic, projected the shadow of Nevis across the face of Scotland.
The effect was 'of an anti-sun,[10] radiating not light but darkness'. One
wonders if, at some subconscious level in his mind – either when the
climb took place or at the time of writing – this impression of dark
beams reaching out towards him was due to his forebodings about
the war and the seemingly inexorable advance of the Nazi forces
across Europe.

The sun went down and the wind grew in strength. They hurried
towards Tower Gap, hoping to cross it before darkness engulfed

them. Between the Great Tower and the final upper cliffs 'the ridge hung like a tight-stretched curtain'. At the brink of the gap they looked down into deep, sheer, ice-filled gullies. A freezing wind was tearing through the gap as Murray climbed down into it. Now he had to climb up a projecting tooth on the far side, but it was glazed with the thinnest of ice upon which had grown a forest of fog crystals. At any time this would have been an extremely challenging problem, but in a half-gale, it was well-nigh impossible. They were in serious trouble. Then Laidlaw suggested trying to lasso the tooth with their rope. It seemed a desperate last hope, unlikely to succeed, but Murray thought it worth a try. He cast his loop into the wind. At the very first attempt it whipped round the projection. With the rope draped over the top, Bell tied onto one end of it, while Murray hauled on the other, sending Bell upwards. Murray and Laidlaw were dragged up in their turn.

Frozen, and buffeted by the gale, they made their way up the final easier slopes. To their surprise it was calm on the summit plateau, for the wind, on striking the cliffs at this point rose vertically upwards.

'Before us stretched vast snow-fields, shining frostily under the stars; beyond, rank upon rank of sparkling peaks. A great stillness had come upon the world. We seemed to tread air rather than crusted snow; we were light of foot; we walked like demigods in joyous serenity.'

Two weeks after this ascent Murray attended the JMCS Hogmanay Dinner at Bridge of Orchy. Years later, recalling that event, he wrote:

'I recall one member, President of the SMC twenty years on, making a girdle traverse of the dining room walls, while another, fated to be caught by the Gestapo in Prague, flicked pats of butter on to the ceiling, and a third, soon to be one of the RAF's most decorated pilots, rendering the Eskimo Nell epic. The hotel sent a big bill for material damages, but cancelled it later on counting their bar profits. It was no fitting end to an era, but it hid from us our desperation.'[11]

Tower Ridge briefly kept that desperation at bay in those early months of the war. 'Days such as these are rare indeed,' Bell wrote, 'but through them one lives life to the full.'[12] As Murray scribbled in pencil on his toilet paper, Tower Ridge again held back a dark tide of despair. In 1942 Murray was not to know that two years later Laidlaw would be killed; his book would become famous; or that this particular chapter would be made into a film.

In 1994, BBC Television showed a six-part programme under the overall title of *The Edge*,[13] made by the independent film company Triple Echo, produced and directed by the adventure film-maker, Richard Else. It was a celebration of one hundred years of Scottish mountaineering and, in particular, of the first winter ascent of Tower Ridge in 1894 (see footnote 7). One of these six programmes was a recreation of Bell's, Murray's and Laidlaw's 1939 winter ascent of Tower Ridge.

With a nod towards matching physical characteristics and age, the part of Bell was taken by Alasdair Cain, Murray by Graham Moss and Laidlaw by Mark Diggins, all first-class winter climbers based in Scotland. All three were admirers of Murray's books, having been inspired by them in their younger days. Cain was an SMC member, and the other two both professional mountain guides.[14] The BBC costumes and props departments, after some research, fitted them out with the clothing and equipment which was thought to be as near as possible to what Bell, Murray and Laidlaw would have used. Tricounis were not obtainable, so their boots were hobnailed. They carried long, wooden-shafted ice-axes; and wore knee-length breeches with woollen stockings (no gaiters), woollen gloves, waist-length tweed or woollen jackets with buttons,[15] and woollen balaclavas (no helmets). Their rucksacks were army surplus, made of khaki webbing material. They had a hemp rope and carried no pitons or other protection or aids. Mark Diggins commented that two things which struck him about the climb were the wonderful silence of it – no rustling of modern fabrics, or clank of ironmongery; and how much less weight they were carrying.

Richard Else says that he insisted that some modern protective devices were used because Cain, Moss and Diggins were climbing in unusual circumstances and it was his responsibility to ensure their safety. The unusual circumstances were that the three of them were climbing with unfamiliar old-fashioned equipment; that there were a number of places where, for filming purposes, he was asking them to repeat certain moves several times over, which increased the risk; and that, to avoid filming when other climbers were on the route, they filmed the upper half of the climb first (in the morning, when others would not yet have reached it), and the lower half second (in the afternoon, when others would have got past this bit). To enable this, the climbers were lifted onto the upper section by helicopter. This meant that they did not have the benefit of warming up on the lower slopes and gradually adjusting to the growing drop below them, but suddenly found themselves on an exposed ridge, and this presented psychological difficulties, adding to the risk. Therefore, Else felt that the wearing of a harness[16] beneath their 1930s exterior and the occasional use of modern protection equipment was justified, whilst essentially retaining the authenticity of the re-creation. Moss, Diggins and Cain had been keen to do it as near to the original conditions as possible.

The Edge was made a year before it was shown, when Murray was 80 and only three years away from dying. On the film he looks slightly frail, but otherwise in good health, alert in mind and speaking clearly and strongly. To camera he says, 'One of the principal differences from now is that we did have the mountains to ourselves. Nobody else was to be seen at all. A party of three could expect to have Tower Ridge entirely to themselves and perhaps there would be no more than six on the whole of the Nevis cliffs.' Richard Else was clearly impressed by him and told me[17] he found him to be a charming, modest, erudite gentleman, extremely generous with his time, who told his story with a wonderful freshness that was miles away from being a tired and well rehearsed performance.

Even though Moss and Diggins were both professional guides and were trained in the lost art of step-cutting (some clients like big, safe steps cut for them), they had found the prolonged step-cutting hard work. The lassoing of the rock tooth was frustratingly difficult, involving many attempts and a slight reshaping of its snow covering before they managed it. Using ice-axes without slings and trying to grip them in woollen gloves had been another problem, as had cold feet caused by the nailed boots. The nails or hobs, embedded in the welts and soles, conducted the heat away from the boots and feet. In the film you can see the rope billowing out in the wind. If not the 'half-gale' of the 1939 ascent, it was close to it. No wonder, then, that Richard Else, who had hoped to include some of the conversation of the three climbers as they went about their task, found he had to cut most of it out because their language had been so ripe!

Alasdair Cain summed up the experience: 'Having climbed the route a few times in modern gear, it made a considerable difference climbing it in the gear of W.H. Murray's day. In terms of safety, speed and standard – not as safe, not as fast and feeling a bit harder and definitely more committing.'[18] Richard Else spoke for everyone involved in the filming when he said, 'We all completed the film with a renewed appreciation of Murray.'

There can be little doubt that Murray's winter ascent of Tower Ridge in 1939 with Bell and Laidlaw was special to him. A 'red-letter' day he called it. When, in 1946, *Open Air Magazine* asked him for an article, he could have selected any of the 23 chapters of *Mountaineering in Scotland* which were close to being ready for publication, but it was 'Tower Ridge in Winter' which he chose to give them.[19] In 'Rocks and Realities,' the last chapter in *Mountaineering in Scotland*, which sums up the essence of his mountaineering experiences and draws things together, he closed the chapter and the book by recalling his fight in a gale at dusk to cross the icy gash of Tower gap.

NOTES

1. This became Chapter XIV, 'Tower Ridge in Winter' of *Mountaineering in Scotland.*
2. Bell's Log Book is now part of the Bell Archive in the National Library of Scotland, Edinburgh.
3. This brew was always known as 'Mummery's Blood'. Sometimes Bovril was used instead of Oxo cubes.
4. The Royal Air Force Voluntary Reserve was formed in 1936. When war broke out in 1939 the Air Ministry employed the RAFVR as the principal means for aircrew entry to serve with the RAF. A civilian volunteer on being accepted for aircrew training took an oath of allegiance ('attestation') and was then inducted into the RAFVR. Normally he returned to his civilian job for several months until he was called up for aircrew training.
5. In *The Evidence of Things Not Seen* there is a photograph of Laidlaw in uniform (photos following page 64). The caption to this reads, ' ...he died in 1942, piloting a bomber over Germany, the rest of the crew having bailed out.' This is incorrect on three counts: (i) he died in 1944; (ii) he did not die while over Germany; (iii) the official records of 626 Squadron show that, out of the crew of seven, five died in the crash. Only two managed to bail out. One was captured and became a POW; the other, with the help of the French Resistance, finally made it back to Britain.
6. *The Evidence of Things Not Seen*, page 108.
7. The first winter ascent of Tower Ridge on Ben Nevis was made in March 1894 by Norman Collie and party. This was the year the Highland Railway opened,

enabling travel by rail to Fort William. According to the Nevis Observatory records, the snow was lying more heavily than it had done for ten years. Collie likened it to the Italian Ridge of the Matterhorn.

8. The old Ben Nevis guide book describes Tower Ridge in the following terms: 'A long (600 metre) but pleasant V. Diff. in summer, this is one of the most famous and finest winter days out in the UK and good preparation for Alpine ridges further afield. Make no mistake – a serious outing for a grade III route.' Since then, Tower Ridge has been upgraded to IV,3. Ken Crocket in his book, *Ben Nevis*, explains: 'the revised rating was the result of a request by the Lochabar Mountain Rescue Team who were becoming over stretched by repeated rescues of parties who had underestimated the climb. The technical standard of Tower Ridge is reasonable, but it is a long expedition by Scottish standards and the major difficulties are high on the route.'

9. Past CIC Hut Log Books are now part of the SMC archive held at the National Library of Scotland, Edinburgh.

10. Bell, in his account, uses the same word 'anti-sun' to describe this phenomenon. They must have discussed it at the time or soon after, when this word was used by either him or Murray, and it stuck in the minds of both of them.

11. SMCJ, 1975. Archie Hendry, who was at this dinner, thought that Murray had slightly embellished this account.

12. *A Progress in Mountaineering*, page 165.

13. It won a Scottish BAFTA Award that year.

14. Later, both became involved with the Scottish Avalanche Information Service, with Diggins as its co-ordinator.

15. Possibly they might not have worn these jackets, which belonged more to pre-World War I days than post-war. Murray says in *The Evidence of Things Not Seen* (page 27) that a spin off from Everest expeditions had been windproof anoraks and that 'no one wore tweed jackets'. Photographs of Murray and his climbing companions confirm this. Also, by then, Murray was using a shorter ice-axe.

16. In Murray's climbing days the rope was simply tied round the waist, which, in the event of a fall could cause broken ribs or internal injuries. A harness distributes the impact over a wider area of the body and is made of flat, wide webbing which does not cut into the body.

17. Telephone conversation, 24th August, 2011. In this same conversation Else told me that Alfred Wainwright held Murray in the highest esteem. (Wainwright, 1907–1991, is best known for his *Pictorial Guides to the Lakeland Fells*.)

18. Letter to me, 19th April 2010.

19. There are some variations in text between the *Open Air in Scotland* version and the *Mountaineering in Scotland* version which came out a year later. These are discussed in Chapter Twenty-Nine.

CHAPTER ELEVEN

SOMEHOW I WAS HAPPY

After four days in crowded railway cattle trucks, the prisoners being transferred from Chieti tumbled out to find themselves in Bavaria, at Moosburg. For the British and Commonwealth officers this was a transit camp, but for the Russians and Poles who were there, it was a concentration camp, a death camp. The Nazi theory of the Aryan master race was being applied here. While the British, regarded as being closest to Aryan stock, had a roof over their heads, the Poles and Russians spent all day and all night in their open compounds whatever the weather.[1]

The batch of prisoners from Chieti stayed at Moosburg for over two months in filthy, cramped conditions, beset by fleas, lice and bed bugs. Breakfast was black bread and mint tea; and for dinner it was potatoes and turnips. 'We lived like rats in a slum,' was how Murray described it. It was winter and bitterly cold. In an effort to keep warm at night Murray practised regulated shivering, letting the body shiver for five seconds in every half minute. Then, in early December 1943, they were again herded into cattle trucks and clanked eastwards for three days through a winter landscape, ending up at Oflag VIII F,[2] Mahrisch Trubau in Bohemia, the western province of Czechoslovakia. Murray does not mention it, but they were handcuffed during the journey.

Captain Ted Johnson of the London Irish Rifles tells us: 'The handcuffs were hopeless and archaic, so were easy to remove. At the end of the journey we handed them to our escort – he was not amused.'[3]

Almost the first thing that happened on arrival was that they were ushered into a large, bare hall where they had their names and numbers taken, were searched, photographed and finger-printed. Murray's thick wad of paper, covered in writing, was discovered on him. He was bundled into a side-room which was empty except for a table and chair. A Gestapo agent began interrogating him while another stood behind him. Their suspicions were aroused because, they insisted, he had tried to hide the paper and not carried it openly. The Gestapo were convinced it was some kind of coded report containing military intelligence gathered while in the various camps or while journeying between them, which he was going to pass to Czech patriots or escape with it to England.

This experience and his time at the Moosberg camp altered Murray's attitude to war. Up to that point he had encountered only Rommel's Afrika Korps – professional soldiers he respected, in particular the tank commander who had helped him. The Gestapo, though, changed his mind. He understood now that some wars had to be fought.

In the end, they had to let him go, but they kept his manuscript and he never saw it again. Murray had been working on it for nearly a year and a half and the book was almost finished. Anyone who has spent just one day working on a report only to have it disappear off their computer will appreciate the depth of his despair and agony of mind. The fact that he decided to write it all over again displayed as much courage, determination and strength of mind as overcoming the crux of any of his most difficult climbs ever did. Even if *Mountaineering in Scotland* had been a lesser book than it turned out to be, its completion under these circumstances would still have been an achievement worthy of the highest admiration.

Mahrisch Trubau was generally reckoned to be the best camp they had been in – at least, at first. There was plenty of space, the dormitories had double glazed windows and the Red Cross and YMCA parcels arrived with a pleasing regularity. The library grew to over 8,000 books, and plays, concerts and Sunday services were organised. There was even a Masonic Lodge. An extensive choice of course was laid on, at a more advanced level than at Chieti. Textbooks were sent by the Educational Books Section of the Red Cross, as were exam papers. The Germans allowed the completed papers (written under strict exam conditions) to be sent back to Britain for marking.[4]

Despite the Red Cross parcels they were permanently hungry and resorted to scrounging from the bins outside the kitchen of the German garrison, searching for prized titbits such as potato peelings and cheese rinds. Washing up was easy because the plates had always been licked clean.

Realising that their numbers included mountaineers from Britain, Canada, South Africa and New Zealand, Murray started up a mountaineering club, which met regularly to hear talks and share experiences and compare notes on routes done. Amongst those who joined was Tommy Wedderburn, a younger brother of Murray's friend, Sandy Wedderburn – he who was in charge of the Mountain Commandos.

Also in Oflag VIII F was Alastair Cram,[5] a fellow member of the Junior Mountaineering Club of Scotland. Cram had been in the other group that was trying to make a first ascent of Clachaig Gully when Murray and his group were there on a similar mission.[6] Murray said of Cram that he was 'quite the most remarkable man I have met in this war'.[7] Unlike Murray, Cram was an escaper. He made more escapes than anyone else in World War II. At one time, Cram asked Murray to join him in an escape which involved some climbing ability. Murray refused. Relations between them were fairly cool after that.[8]

Cram was not the only escaper in the camp. Numerous attempts were made, each attempt bringing forth long hours of punitive standing in the compound and disruption to studies. Murray comments that none had final success. 'All escapers were in due course returned to their camp of origin, alive if caught by the army; dead if caught by Gestapo, who sent ashes back in a box.'[9] Other accounts claim that there were a few 'home runs' from Oflag VIII F at that time.[10] More than likely, people drew different conclusions from the uncertain information, speculation and rumours that were floating round the camp. Murray would probably have felt more comfortable with an interpretation which made escape seem futile.

It was here, at Oflag VIII F, that Murray received an invitation from Herbert Buck to attend his class on the Perennial Philosophy. This was the second great turning point in Murray's life. Buck's immense influence on Murray is explored in a later chapter.

As at Chieti, a radio was built and kept hidden in the camp. News of German defeats on the Russian front, of bombing raids on Germany, the fall of Rome, and then the Normandy landings on 6th June 1944 kept hope alive. It was generally thought, though, that deliverance was more likely to come from the Russian armies which were making rapid advances through Poland and Romania. For Murray, as for everyone else in the camp, the wait seemed interminable as they grasped at every scrap of news, trying to guess what it might mean in terms of their chances of survival.

With the advancing Russian Army drawing ever nearer, the Senior British Officer banned all further escape attempts. Czech patriots had warned that the SS[11] were murdering POWs in camps further east rather than see them released by the Russians. The tunnels dug under the electric fence at Mahrisch Trubau had to be reserved for a mass break-out to forestall any similar atrocity. Weeks of tension and speculation went by, the Russians drew closer, and then the order came to pack up and be ready to move to another camp.

Yet another long journey by cattle truck brought them to Oflag 79, a former parachute regiment barracks in Saxony, outside Brunswick (Braunnschweig) in northern Germany. Conifer woodland screened the camp from the open plain beyond. The library of books had travelled with them from Mahrisch Trubau.[12] Lectures and studies resumed and Murray continued working on his manuscript and studying the Perennial Philosophy under Herbert Buck. It was largely due to these two forms of escape that, despite the grimness, starvation and stress, Murray says, 'Somehow I was happy.'[13]

Brunswick was within reach of Allied air forces. Thousand-bomber raids were now regularly taking place across Saxony. The camp was surrounded by legitimate industrial targets, including an aircraft engine factory, so that the prisoners were constantly at risk. The RAF did the night-time raids. The leading aircraft ringed the camp with flares so that that those following knew not to bomb inside that area. But, according to Murray, the daylight raids by the US Air Force were a different matter: They kept above 30,000 feet and off-loaded at random, the result being several hits on the camp causing death and injuries to POWs as well as guards. So dense was the smoke and the dust from the ruined cities around them that, for the next nine months, both sun and moon were obliterated.

One daylight raid by American Flying Fortresses wiped out the German garrison at the camp. Unfortunately, crouching in the cellars and deafened by the exploding bombs, the prisoners were unaware of this. When they emerged all they saw were burning trees around the camp. They could have walked out, but were too dazed and bewildered to realise it. By the time the smoke had cleared and the dust settled, an emergency guard had been moved in.

Transport was so disrupted that Red Cross parcels dwindled to one a week, then one a month and finally stopped completely. 'We were truly starving. The guards no longer dared send their Alsatians into the compound at night. We had commandos in plenty trained to kill. Any dog, and cats too if they strayed into camp, went straight into the pot.'[14] Murray's hair started falling out, he had to cut down his walks in the compound and climbing stairs brought on palpitations. TB was rife throughout the camp. Morale amongst the weakened and starving officers declined sharply. People became more ruthless and selfish.

In the midst of this misery and suffering there occurred a wonderful moment. It was Christmas Eve and for once there was no air raid. In the compound someone began to sing 'Silent Night'. Others gathered round and added their voices to the carol. Soon the entire complement of prisoners was standing in the open, singing. Then the Germans joined in, even the sentries, war and its horrors briefly forgotten, enemies united by the beauty of the music.

A fellow officer at Brunswick called a meeting and proposed that they should pledge time and money, if they survived, to founding boys' clubs in Britain's cities. It was an act of faith, both in the future of Britain and in their own future. Murray attended this meeting, but does not say whether he pledged himself to the cause. A Brunswick Boys' Club does exist in Glasgow, but Murray makes no mention of having any hand in setting it up.

Through the three illicit radios secreted in the camp they learned that the Allied armies were advancing swiftly on all fronts. Berlin fell to Russian forces on the last day of April 1945. The American Ninth Army swept through Saxony so fast that the SS had no time to evacuate the camp. With shells whistling over the camp, the Germans fled. Some of the guards stayed, no longer guarding the gates. They had nowhere to go. The first American trucks arrived at the camp. Chocolate bars were distributed, one to each prisoner.

'I remember still that swift run of heat through the body, as if from neat whisky. More solid food was dispensed gradually not because in short supply, but by good reason of our incapacity to digest richer diet. Our first white bread tasted like cake.'[15]

Murray's story of their release differs in several respects from the one given by others.[16] He says that the Americans arrived on May Day of 1945, but other accounts put this event at April 11th or 12th. Murray says they were flown home after four days, not, as others would have it, after waiting impatiently for several weeks because the POWs in nearby camps, which were for other ranks (i.e. those who were not officers and therefore had been forced to do hard labour) were in a much worse state and had to be given priority.[17] A detail, not mentioned by Murray, perhaps because he was not an actual eyewitness to the event, was that the American trucks were headed by a jeep in which stood a huge red-headed sergeant, smoking a large cigar. Maybe, put in the context of his whole life and viewed from the perspective that another 50 or so years gives to an event, these details were not important to Murray. What was important was that he was free, he was back in Britain and a whole new set of challenges lay ahead.

NOTES

1. What Murray witnessed was happening in camps all over occupied Europe. The Germans captured approximately 5.7 million Russians. Through harsh treatment, shooting, starvation and overwork, well over half of them died. In some camps the death toll amongst Russian prisoners was 90 per cent. Not only did the Nazis regard Russians as subhuman, but the Soviet Union was not a signatory to the Geneva Convention, so that Russian prisoners were not protected by these rules, nor eligible for Red Cross parcels and other aid.
2. In the German system (but not in Italy) POW camps for officers were called Oflags (short for *Offizierslager*) and camps for other ranks were known as Stalags (*Stammerlager*). Airmen were prisoners of the German airforce who ran Stalag Lufts which included both officers and NCOs (non-commissioned officers such as corporals and sergeants).
3. From the BBC Archive, 'The People's War' – an archive of World War II memories submitted by the public to the BBC. www.bbc.co.uk/ww2peopleswar/
4. The pass rate was about 78 per cent of those who sat the exams.
5. Alastair Cram (1909–1993) was educated at Perth Academy and the University of Edinburgh. He started his working life as a solicitor in private practice at the Scottish Bar. In World War II he served initially with the Royal Regiment of Artillery then was transferred to the SAS. While with the latter he was taken prisoner. Cram was involved in more escapes than anyone else in World War II. He was awarded the Military Cross in 1945. He played an important role as a prosecutor of Nazi war criminals in the Nuremberg trials. Later, he served as a Judge in Kenya at the time of the Mau Mau uprising. In 1965 he became Governor-General of Malawi. See *Almost Home: the life of Alastair Cram* by David Guss (as at May 2013 date of publication yet to be announced).

6. As described in Chapter X of *Mountaineering in Scotland*.
7. In a letter to his sister, Margaret, dated 5th December 1943.
8. This is according to Cram's wife, Isobel, in a letter to me dated 10th June 2009. Murray's admiration seemed to remain undimmed despite any coolness on Cram's part and he wrote a very positive obituary of Cram for the 1995 SMCJ.
9. *The Evidence of Things Not Seen*, page 100.
10. *Prisoner of War: Voices from Behind the Wire in the Second World War.* Charles Rollings, 2008.
11. SS is an abbreviation of *Schutzstaffel* (Protection Squad). The SS was originally formed as Hitler's bodyguard, but soon grew into a large and complex organisation, ranging from elite military corps to national security services. The Gestapo – the Secret State Police – was under the administration of the SS.
12. When the war ended the prison camp libraries were sold off to book dealers. Books with an Oflag stamp in them still crop up in second-hand bookshops.
13. *The Evidence of Things Not Seen*, page 102.
14. *The Evidence of Things Not Seen*, page 109.
15. *Ibid*, page 110.
16. An article, 'Lion-hearted POW's Vision still Lives on', by David Charles, *Liverpool Daily Herald*, 2nd January, 2008, based on the POW diary of Captain Tim Marshall. This is corroborated by the account given by Lieutenant William Bompass in his diary (Imperial War Museum Collection). Murray, in *Undiscovered Scotland* (page 8), does give April as the month of his release, but this is only a passing reference.
17. The British and Commonwealth POWs might have been impatient, but the last German POWs in Britain were not repatriated until November 1948 because they were needed as farm labour.

CHAPTER TWELVE

WIDE OPEN TO THE MESSAGE

While a prisoner-of-war in Oflag VIII F at Mahrisch Trubau in Czechoslovakia, a meeting occurred which changed Murray's life. He was strolling in the compound when a young English officer he'd not met before came up to him and introduced himself as Herbert Buck, Indian Army.[1] 'It seems to me,' Buck said, 'you're ready to start on the Mystic Way. Would you let me give you instruction?'

Murray was startled and on the point of giving a curt refusal when he looked into Buck's eyes and found himself saying, 'Yes'. As he climbed the stairs to his dormitory, he was filled with an inexplicable sense of joy.[2]

Herbert Buck and his teachings made an impression on Murray that was profound and lifelong. Further information about this charismatic young man is provided in online Appendix C.

In June 1945, soon after his release, Murray wrote to his friend and fellow climber, Douglas Scott.[3] Telling Scott about his three years of imprisonment, he says, despite the hardships and starvation: 'Of all the years of my life, it is these last three that I would on no account forego. When I went into the bag in 1942 I could see no purpose in life and was filled with a sense of frustration and depression. But for the first time in my life I then had the leisure to think, to be still.' Towards the end of his life, looking back on his POW experience, Murray is quite clear that, 'those prison years were the most profitable of my life … Years had been wasted, but I had started – albeit a little late – and despite the outward circumstances of my prison life, a facet of the present experience was a sense of wellbeing and peace.'[4]

Murray was not referring to his writing. Both in his letter to Scott and in his autobiography the context makes it clear that he is discussing his spiritual development.

Writing about his quest to find glimpses of that 'beauty which all men who have known it have been compelled to call truth' Murray says, 'it has become the end of mountaineering to which the sport is a means.' Of this spiritual adventure on which he had embarked, he says it is 'a joy surpassing all that mountains offer.'[5]

The significance of these words needs to be realised if Murray, the man, is to be fully understood. Murray, one of Scotland's top climbers at that time, who had missed only two weekends of climbing in three years; Murray who had spent glorious days and nights on the Scottish mountains and described them so vividly, is saying here that mountaineering is only a means to a greater end and that, in relation to what really matters, the joys of the spiritual life are more rewarding than anything else.

In *Undiscovered Scotland*, written soon after the war, he asks (page 14) whether mountains are necessary for happiness or the true completion of a man, and gives his answer: 'Quite to the contrary. So little are they necessary that one of the happiest years of my own life was one of the three spent in a prison camp.' That year was the year he met Herbert Buck.

From the point of meeting Herbert Buck onwards, the quest to find self-fulfilment through union with the Divine Essence, with Absolute Beauty and Truth, was the most central and important thing in his life. To try to understand him on any other terms than this is to misunderstand him.

Murray says that he was alert to the possibility of Buck being an imposter, but that he could find no fault. 'He was all that his acts and words claimed. The man was whole – an occurrence so rare it arrests.'[6]

'It seems to me you're ready,' were Buck's words to Murray and he was right. Although Buck was three years younger, the impact he made upon Murray was huge. Murray was in a state of readiness, receptive and open wide to Buck's message. It was as if everything that had happened to Murray so far had prepared him for this moment.

Writing of a pre-war 24-hour adventure in the Cuillin of Skye, Murray says: 'Here, for the first time, broke upon me the unmistakable intimation of a last reality underlying mountain beauty; and here, for the first time, it awakened within me a faculty of comprehension that had never before been exercised.'[7]

Describing his feelings when sitting on the summit of Sgurr nan

Bannachdich in Skye in 1936, after making a solo ascent, Murray wrote: 'Let the mind soar like the highest-mounting bird, self-surrendered to the infinite, and an infinite spirit seems to flow into one. This is the law of grace. Thus seeds are sown from which a rich harvest of philosophy may be reaped in its season. But I was too inexperienced to reap then.'[8]

Now the season for reaping had arrived. The mountains had given Murray a feeling that he was on the brink of some important revelation. After completing a winter ascent of Crowberry Gully in Glencoe, Murray says, 'The mountain and the world and I were one. But that was not all: a strange and powerful feeling that something as yet unknown was almost within my grasp, was trembling into vision, stayed with me until we reached the cairn, where it passed away.'[9] Now the opportunity had come to make himself worthy and to receive the withheld revelation.

A prime factor leading to this readiness was Murray's love of exploration and adventure which went beyond physical adventure and included a willingness to depart from the orthodox, to explore his inner self and undertake a difficult spiritual journey. This same sense of adventure, of course, led him to the mountains, to the wild places. It has been well documented[10] that mountains and closeness to nature in general can trigger mystical feelings, a sense of something greater than the individual, an expansion of the inner self, and a feeling of the oneness of all things. Such feelings would have been reinforced in Murray by having read about them in books by mountaineers he respected.[11]

Research has also shown that there is a carry-over from one intense experience of this kind to the next. Each time one of these episodes occurs the threshold is lowered and the visionary experience is won more easily the next time. Such experiences will therefore happen with greater frequency. When Murray met Herbert Buck he had been engaged in nearly five years of regular climbing. His threshold had been lowered.

Parallels have been drawn between deserts and mountains as places for contemplation, meditation and mysticism and Murray had clearly found the Western Desert, with its vast spaces, open skies and its solitude, a mind-expanding place. The ordeal of battle and the prospect of imminent death, too, can be a mind-bending, perspective-changing experience.

As previously noted, the German offensive in the Western Desert led to an experience which gave Murray a lifelong belief in Providence. Undoubtedly, the incident in the crater awakened Murray, in a direct and personal way, to the existence of a Higher Power.

Similarities can be found between the deprivations of a POW camp and the vision-inducing régimes undertaken by religious mystics and shamans. By the time Murray met Buck he had been a prisoner for over two years. As Adrian Gilbert shows in his book, *POW: Allied Prisoners in Europe 1939–1945*, quite a number of POWs were helped towards a greater spiritual awareness by their POW ordeal. He includes an account (page 159) by Terry Frost who later became a well-known painter: 'In prisoner-of-war camp I got a tremendous spiritual experience, a more heightened perception, and I honestly do not think that awakening ever left me.'

The mountains, the desert, battle, the POW camps had all been deeply felt experiences for Murray which had put him in a state of readiness to receive the teachings of Herbert Buck. So, too, had his interest in philosophy which existed before he met Buck. In a letter to his sister, dated July 1940, before his captivity, Murray tells her of this interest and lists some of the books he is reading.[12] Then, while Murray was still at Chieti POW camp in Italy – again, before he met Buck – he was sent[13] a copy of Aldous Huxley's *Grey Eminence* which had been published two years previously. It is a biography of Father Joseph (1577–1638), a French Capuchin monk and confidant of Richelieu, being mainly about the inner struggles between Joseph's faith and mysticism and the world of politics which he had entered. As a background to this, Huxley included a chapter discussing the religious ideas current at the time and their origins.

Of this chapter (Chapter 3) Murray said that it was the first time he had encountered a good summary of European and Asian mystical tradition. 'The plain common sense of it all appealed to me . . . my exploratory instinct sharpened . . . my finding of mystical theology was like stumbling into an oasis. Its water was pure. I drank.'[14]

When Huxley, Murray and Buck used the word 'mysticism', each probably understood slightly different things by it. In general, mysticism is the search for direct union with Reality, that is to say with the underlying, unifying force that pervades everything and which is sometimes also called the Divine Essence, Ultimate Reality, Truth, or God. The word 'direct' here is important because it implies a personal, first-hand connection with this force rather than receiving second-hand knowledge of it through rituals, and God's appointed representatives on Earth.

According to Huxley, Father Joseph, the subject of *Grey Eminence*, was strongly influenced by *The Cloud of Unknowing,* a book by an anonymous 14th century English author, a book which Huxley describes as 'one of the finest flowers of medieval mystical literature.'[15]

The author of *The Cloud of Unknowing* counsels his readers not to seek God through knowledge but by spiritual union with Him through the heart. He also says that if they 'die to self' they can become aware of the divine element within them. Murray makes several references to *The Cloud of Unknowing* in his writings[16] and had clearly studied it during his incarceration. It was one more factor in making him wide open to the teachings of Herbert Buck.

NOTES

1. Before Independence in 1947, the majority of officers in the Indian Army were British. Indians now refer to this as the British Indian Army to distinguish it from their own post-independence army. In the pre-war years advancement for an officer was difficult in Britain without a private income and many less privileged young men chose the Indian Army for their career.
2. *Evidence of Things Not Seen*, page 9.
3. Not to be confused with the English mountaineer, Doug Scott, born 1941, who made the first ascent of the south-west face of Everest with Dougal Haston in 1975.
4. *Evidence of Things Not Seen*, page 102.
5. *Mountaineering in Scotland*, page 234. Murray says much the same thing again in *Undiscovered Scotland*, page 14.
6. *The Evidence of Things Not Seen*, page 111.
7. *Ibid*, page 4.
8. 'The Cuillin Ridge and Blaven' which first appeared as an article in SMCJ, 23, 1942.
9. *Mountaineering in Scotland*, page 207. Murray also expresses a similar thought on page 226: 'Something underlying the world as we saw it had been withheld.'
10. See online Appendix D.
11. For example, Alfred Mummery, Edward Whymper, Leslie Stephen, Geoffrey Winthrop Young, Tom Longstaff.
12. This letter is shown in the Appendices of *The Evidence of Things Not Seen*. In this letter he says he is reading Leslie Stephen's *An Agnostic's Apology* (1893) and another book comparing yoga and psychoanalysis (both books, he says, were lent to him by Donaldson); also C.E.M. Joad's *Philosophy For Our Times,*

which had come out only a few months earlier – one of Joad's central thoughts was that truth and beauty are absolute, not relative and subjective – a belief strongly held by Murray.

13. In *The Evidence of Things Not Seen* Murray says that this book was sent by his mother, but in a letter from POW camp to Archie MacAlpine, dated 17th April 1943, he suggests it was sent by Gordon Donaldson, whom, he says, 'has displayed a genius for selecting the books I most appreciate.'

14. *The Evidence of Things Not Seen*, page 90.

15. Within the compass of that small book, Huxley explains, lay the essence of Dyonesian mysticism and a neat summary of the doctrines of St John of the Cross. Dionysius the Aeropagite (a member of the Athenian Council of Elders) was St Paul's first Athenian convert, whose books used material derived from Plato and from the Hindu Vedantic tradition. St John of the Cross (1542–1591) was a Roman Catholic mystic, a Carmelite friar and one of Spain's greatest lyric poets who wrote *Dark Night of the Soul*, a narrative poem about the soul's difficult journey from its bodily home to its union with God – a journey which has similarities with the Buddhist stages of truth awakening. This book and his *The Ascent of Mount Carmel* are considered by many to be the high point of the western tradition of mysticism.

16. Murray uses the phrase 'cloud of unknowing' in 'Rocks and Realities' in *Mountaineering in Scotland*, page 243: 'Wisdom standeth at the top of high places. From our promontory we look up to the cloud of unknowing that wraps the last height, and from its radiance we know the summit is in sunlight.' On page 226, he writes, 'not half the wonder had pierced the cloud of our blindness.' In an article 'The Approach Route to Beauty' (SMCJ, 1948) he tells his readers, 'we must die to self,' exactly echoing the author of *The Cloud*. In *The Scottish Himalayan Expedition* (page 2) he also quotes a passage from it.

CHAPTER THIRTEEN

APPROACHING THE SUNLIT SUMMIT

Although Buck, in his initial encounter with Murray, used the term 'Mystic Way', Murray subsequently refers to Buck's instruction as being concerned with the Perennial Philosophy.[1] This is the notion that there are universal truths – The Highest Common Factor of all religions – about the nature of humanity and reality, recognised across the centuries by all cultures.[2] It is the eternal philosophy which underpins all religions and, in particular, the mystical streams within them where the self becomes one with the 'Absolute Principle of All Existence'. The Perennial (or Eternal) Philosophy emphasises experiences which are illuminating for the individual such as meditation, contemplation, and prayer; and it pays less attention to religious organisations, rituals and the outer trappings of worship.

There are four points that all the major religions and philosophies stress and which, therefore, are given pride of place by the Perennial Philosophy. Firstly is the laying aside of self as a way to enlightenment. Secondly, the great mystic traditions of both East and West proclaim the unity and harmony of all things.[3] Thirdly, they teach that this ultimate harmony (or Reality, or Absolute Truth and Beauty, or God) is beyond the intellect alone – the word is not the thing it describes, the menu is not the food. Following on from this is the fourth common factor: the belief that Reality can be realised through transcendental meditation.

Transcendental meditation is meditation which transcends or goes beyond the physical, observable world to a spiritual state where glimpses of the Truth are possible.[4] Scholars of mysticism strongly emphasise that, although it gives a direct connection to the Divine Essence, it is definitely not a short-cut. Great effort, hardship and discipline are required. Only then, says the author of *The Cloud* 'will He sometimes peradventure send out a beam of ghostly light,

1 Murray on the Cioch in Skye. Ben Humble's best known photograph, taken in June 1936, when there was still full daylight at 9 pm.

2 This photo was taken on the same evening as Plate 1. Murray commented that Humble would spend hours trying to get the right shot.

3 Murray climbing in Skye with the Cioch below.

4 Murray (standing) with Rob Anderson on the Cuillin ridge, Skye. It was Anderson who drew the maps and diagrams for several of Murray's books.

5 Murray, Douglas Laidlaw (sitting) and Dr. J H B Bell outside the CIC Hut during the exceptionally hot summer of 1940 that was overshadowed by war.

Scottish Mountaineering Club.

STATEMENT OF THE QUALIFICATIONS FOR MEMBERSHIP OF

(Candidate's Full Name), _WILLIAM HUTCHISON MURRAY_ (Age), _32_

(Occupation),

(Other Mountaineering Clubs to which the Candidate belongs) _J.A.C., J.M.C.S._

(Residence), _NEUADD PARK, CAPEL BANGOR, ABERYSTWYTH, WALES_

Extract from Rule 38—

"Every Candidate for election as an Ordinary Member of the Club shall be proposed by a Member, and seconded by another Member, both having personal knowledge of the candidate and general knowledge of his qualifications. The candidate shall supply, on a special form to be obtained from the Honorary Secretary, a list of his Scottish and other Ascents, stating the month and the year in which each ascent was made, or a statement of his contributions to Science, Art or Literature in connection with Scottish Mountains. Such list must be signed by the candidate, and by the two Members acting as proposer and seconder. It may also be signed by any other Members desiring to support his candidature."

To ensure the candidate's application being considered at the Annual Meeting of the Committee in October, applications must reach the Hon. Secretary not later than 30th September. It is desirable that every candidate should have attended a Meet before applying for membership.

DATE OF ASCENT (ONLY THE YEAR AND MONTH NEED BE STATED).	ASCENTS.	SNOW OR ROCK CLIMBS AND NAMES OF COMPANIONS. CLIMB LED AND ANY SPECIAL REMARKS.
April 1935	The Cobbler and Narnain Ben Lede and Ben Vane	led by self marked ✗
May "	Ben Laoigh The Cobbler, Ben Ime, Ben Vane	

6 Part of the first page of Murray's application to join the SMC. 'Occupation' has been left blank because, in 1945, Murray was still in the army and uncertain of his future.

Dunn
Murray
Humble
Mackenzie
Scott
Geo. Roger

7 A pre-war group outside Lagangarbh, Glencoe.

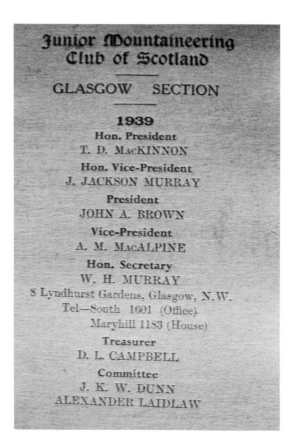

Junior Mountaineering Club of Scotland

GLASGOW SECTION

1939

Hon. President
T. D. MacKINNON

Hon. Vice-President
J. JACKSON MURRAY

President
JOHN A. BROWN

Vice-President
A. M. MacALPINE

Hon. Secretary
W. H. MURRAY
8 Lyndhurst Gardens, Glasgow, N.W.
Tel—South 1601 (Office)
Maryhill 1183 (House)

Treasurer
D. L. CAMPBELL

Committee
J. K. W. DUNN
ALEXANDER LAIDLAW

8 JMCS membership card, 1939. Murray's address on the card is his mother's house.

1937		
Feb, 7—Informal Meet	Inverarnan (for Killin)	
24—Lantern Lecture.	B. H. HUMBLE	
Mar. 7—Informal Meet.	Inverarnan (for Crianlarich)	
21—Lantern Lecture.	W. M. MACKENZIE	
26/29—EASTER MEET.	Aviemore or Loch Laggan	
Apr. 25—Informal Meet.	Arrochar	
May 15/17 Informal Meet.	Coupal Bridge	
June 13—Informal Meet.	Kingshouse	
19—Afternoon expedition to Loudoun Hill		
July 17/19 FAIR MEET	C.I.C. Hut, Ben Nevis	

1937		
Sep. 25/27 AUTUMN MEET.		Corrie
Oct. 10—Informal Meet.		Inverarnan
20—Lantern Lecture.		To be announced
Nov. 7—Informal Meet.		Bridge of Orchy
17—Annual Dinner		
29—Lantern Lecture.		To be announced
Dec. 5—Informal Meet.		Arrochar
13—ANNUAL SECTION MEETING and Photographic Competition Judging		
31 to 1938 Jan. 3	NEW YEAR MEET, Annual General Meeting and Dinner of the Club	Dalmally

Informal Meets. Members will be postcarded.

Nevis Hut. Use of the C.I.C. Hut is available (to members only) on application for the keys through the Secretary, and by kind permission of the Scottish Mountaineering Club.

9 JMCS programme for 1937. The JMCS was at the centre of Murray's climbing activities and of his social life.

10 Percy Unna in 1932. Unna, a former president of the SMC, was one of the NTS' greatest benefactors and was passionate about keeping the mountains unspoiled.

11 Dr 'Jimmy' Bell who climbed frequently with Murray and whose exploits spanned the pre and post First World War years, linking with the newly formed JMCS and helping to keep Scottish climbing alive.

12 Tom Longstaff in the Alps, 1904. Murray greatly admired Longstaff and his uncompetitive attitude to mountaineering.

13 POWs at Chieti, Italy. Taken in 1942 at the time when Murray was imprisoned there.

14 The first moment of freedom. A jeep of the American Ninth Army arriving at the gates of the Brunswick prison camp in Germany in the Spring of 1945.

15 1950 Scottish Himalayan Expedition. Dotial porters carrying heavy loads at 18,000 ft to camp 3 on Bethartoli Himal.

16 Gorges and rushing torrents sometimes gave way to calmer waters and time for contemplation.

17 Tea break during one of the many long treks through the Eastern Garhwal region of the Himalayas. Tom Weir holding up his mug.

18 The Sona glacier beneath one of the peaks of the Panch Chuli.

19 Dotial porter with the head of a goat which had been executed for a feast. Goats in this part of the Himalayas were also used as pack animals by the local people.

20 Loading a jhopa, a kind of yak, for the trek from Dunagiri to Malari. The agreed load for each jhopa was 160 pounds.

21 Camp 2 on the unsuccessful attempt to climb South Lampak Peak. Behind the tent is the 7,000-foot wall of Tirsuli. Note the evidence of a recent avalanche.

22 The Central Pinnacle at 18,000 feet on Uja Tirche. Murray, Scott, Weir and MacKinnon went on from there to make a first ascent of Uja Tirche's North Ridge (20,350 feet).

23 'Number your red-letter days by camps, not by summits, ' Tom Longstaff wrote in a letter to Murray. In camp was where expeditions could relax, enjoy their surroundings and the company.

24 Payday for the porters. Murray at the table with Weir behind.

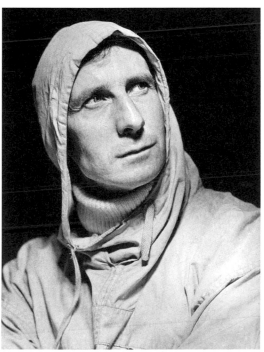

25 Murray wearing a monk-like cape at Darmaganga. Next to him is Douglas Scott.

26 This portrait of Murray, taken in a professional studio, was used on the cover of his autobiography.

27 1951 Everest Reconnaissance Expedition.
From left to right: Eric Shipton, Michael Ward, Bill Murray, Tom Bourdillon.

28 Ang Tharkay,
the head Sherpa who
bartered with the
Tibetan border guards
west of Everest and
saved Murray, Shipton
and Ward from arrest
and imprisonment.

29 Thyangboche Monastery where the 1951 Everest Reconnaissance Expedition stopped on their way to Mount Everest. Murray declared this to be the most beautiful place he had ever seen.

30 Hillary sees the Khombu glacier and the Western Basin from the flanks of Pumori, confirming that this might be a possible route up Everest.

31 Yeti footprints
west of Everest , seen
by Shipton's group
and then by Murray's
group two days later.

32 Sir John Hunt in
conversation with
Geoffrey Winthrop
Young in 1953, soon
after the former's
return from leading
the expedition that
made the first ascent
of Everest.

piercing the cloud of unknowing that is betwixt thee and Him.'

In a letter to his sister, dated July 1944, four months after meeting Buck and taking instruction in meditation, Murray tells her: 'Philosophy ends in theory, science in speculation, Art in intuition, institutional religion in faith: Nowhere direct knowledge. They stop one with an overhang. But there is a route winding through the overhangs to the summit. The peak has been often climbed. The route is old but the start is hard to find. I have been shown the start and I find that it goes. The purpose of life and the goal and the way have become for me clear as crystal. I have learned more in 4 months than during the last 30 years. The point is that the summit may be reached in this life. To refuse the ascent is to deny the lessons of life, and to deny the development of the only part of you that is enduring.'[5]

Murray's concept of Beauty is drawn from Platonism.[6] Plato's Theory of Forms stated that abstract forms or ideas are the highest and most fundamental kind of reality, and that there are transcendent perfect archetypes, of which objects in the everyday world are imperfect copies. *In Mountaineering in Scotland* (page 6), Murray echoes this theory when he says, 'The one Beauty pervades all things according to their nature, they have beauty by virtue of participating in it.' *In Highland Landscape* (page 9) he explains his criteria for judging the beauty of a landscape: 'Beauty stands here for the perfect expression of that ideal form to which everything that is perfect of its kind approaches.'

Plato's influence can also be seen in Murray's choice of title for the penultimate chapter of *Mountaineering in Scotland* and for the first article he wrote for the SMCJ after his release – 'The Evidence of Things Not Seen'.[7] In both of them he laid out more explicitly than anywhere else, what his philosophy and beliefs were. The title is a quote from *The Epistle of Paul the Apostle to the Hebrews*, Chapter 11, verse 1:[8] 'Now faith is the substance of things hoped for, the evidence of things not seen.'

Parallels have been drawn between this verse and Plato's Allegory of the Cave which appears in his work *Republic*. The allegory is presented in the form of a fictional dialogue between Socrates and Plato's brother, Glaucon. Plato imagines a group of people who have lived chained in a cave all of their lives, facing a blank wall. The people watch shadows projected on the wall by things passing in front of a fire behind them, and begin to ascribe forms to these shadows. According to Plato, the shadows are as close as the prisoners come to seeing reality. He then explains how the philosopher is like a prisoner who is freed from the cave and comes to understand that the shadows on the wall (the evidence of things not seen) are not reality at all. This is the substance of what Murray hoped for – that he might see reality, truth and beauty in their purest forms. 'The fulfilment of life's purpose will be found in oneness with reality,' Murray wrote to his sister.

Both through reading *The Cloud of Unknowing* and the works of Evelyn Underhill,[9] Murray would have been exposed to the teachings of St John of the Cross. Some of these teachings, which Murray is likely to have noted, were that God dwells in every soul; that the practice of self-knowledge is the first requirement for advancing towards the knowledge of God; and that absolute self-giving is the only path from the human to the Divine.

Murray's philosophy is often equated to Zen Buddhism. Murray certainly studied Buddhist texts, and Zen Buddhism,[10] with its greater emphasis on meditation and on closeness to nature, is what would have interested him most. Clearly there were other influences on him besides Zen. However, to equate his philosophy to Zen is a short and convenient way to summarise much of his thinking, since Zen shares with the world's major religions many of the mystical elements which lie at their heart – as does the Perennial Philosophy.

Zen, the Perennial Philosophy and Murray all place great importance on meditation. It is probably the most important thing that Herbert Buck taught him. Murray continued to meditate regularly all his life. He saw it as the way to open the spiritual eye and expand the soul. In *The Evidence of Things Not Seen* (page 98) Murray explains that meditation, with full use of the reasoning process has to give way at long last to: 'an alert stillness of mind that allows its conclusive leap into the spiritual realm beyond time and space. There were no short cuts, no easy ways, no let-offs, but many falls and defeats, therefore a need of over-riding commitment.'

He explains it in a different way in *Mountaineering in Scotland* (page 4): 'Mercifully, it is by this very process of not understanding that one is allowed to understand much: for each one has within him "the divine reason that sits at the helm of the soul", of which the head knows nothing.' Murray is quoting Plato here. Online Appendix E has more about the meditation techniques used by Murray.

Closeness to the mountain landscape was, for Murray, a means of glimpsing Absolute Beauty or Truth or God. Because of this, some people have assumed that he was a pantheist, that it was Nature and the mountains themselves which he worshipped. This wrong assumption has been further encouraged by the fact that Murray greatly admired the Lake Poets such as Coleridge and Wordsworth who dabbled with pantheism. This was a hugely important point for Murray, striking at the very heart of his belief. In his view, such pantheism would have been mistaking the altar for the deity.

When Wilfred Noyce, in a favourable review (*Alpine Journal* 58, 1952) of Murray's book *The Scottish Himalayan Expedition*, implied that Murray was a pantheist, Murray was outraged. He wrote a stiff letter to *The Alpine Journal* (AJ 59, 1953), complaining that Noyce 'ascribes to me "a sense of oneness with the mountain universe around whose name men call God". Let me say at once that I wrote no such nonsense. The reviewer would foist onto me a pantheism that I detest, and which I hold in less honour than a relatively healthy agnosticism … It is not the mountain universe, but the integrating principle of the universe whose name men call God.' Murray makes his point again in *Mountaineering in Scotland* (page 243): 'Mountains here discharge their highest service. A man of balanced intelligence will not make a religion of mountaineering; neither will he fail, by mountains, to be brought face to face with it.'

Mihaly Csikszentmihalya, in his work *Flow: The Psychology of Optimal Expression* (New York, 1990), says there is a strong connection between being in the flow while engaged in creative activity and meditation. (Reference has already been made to Csikszentmihalyi's work in Chapter Four.) His research has found that people who experience flow while being creative find it enhances their ability to achieve deep meditative states; and people who have found a path to deep meditation also find that they experience flow more regularly than otherwise.

There can be no doubt from the intensity of Murray's writing in *Mountaineering in Scotland* that, for long periods at a time, Murray was in the flow while he worked on the book in captivity. Nor is there any doubt that his finding of mysticism and the meditation which accompanied it was an equally intense experience for him. These two factors, working together, intensifying and enhancing each other, go a long way to accounting both for the brilliance of Murray's classic of mountain literature and for the strength and depth of his mysticism.

The fulfilment of life's purpose, Murray wrote to his sister, is to be found in oneness with reality. In the letter to Douglas Scott (previously mentioned), Murray explains how deeply the discovery of mysticism had affected him and changed his life. He refers to a complete reorientation of his outlook on life. It was like being born again, with fresh eyes a new mind and a heightened sense of beauty. His bodily health improved too, he says, until starvation took its toll. He tells Scott, 'I realise that the Beautiful, the Good, the One, Brahman, or God or ultimate reality – give it whatever name you please – could in fact be known and realised within oneself in this life. The way to do it I found in mystical training.'

He likens the mystic way to climbing a mountain, saying that, although he was a long way from the top, he knew it was climbable. 'Therefore, when I came out of these prison camps life for the future did have a meaning. I could see and understand much of the purpose of it and had a single-minded intention of trying to get to the goal. If ever a summit was in sunlight this one is.'[11]

The American Ninth Army liberated them and arranged for Dakota troop carriers, assembled at a nearby airfield, to fly them home. The Dakotas had seen a lot of service and were way past their best. Murray describes[12] how his unease was justified when, on landing in England, the plane directly behind him crashed. According to Murray, among those killed, only a few miles from his home, was Herbert Buck.

However, it seems that Murray was mistaken. Herbert Buck did not die then. He returned home and married his pre-war sweetheart. While still in military service he was killed when his RAF plane crashed en route for Malaya where his SAS unit had been posted. He died on 22nd November 1945,[13] more than six months later than Murray records in *The Evidence of Things Not Seen*. It may well be that, such was the confusion when scrambling into the Dakotas, Murray only assumed that Buck was aboard the one behind him. Then, on hearing vague reports of his death in a plane crash, mistakenly supposed it was the same crash. Although Murray's version turns out to have been based on the evidence of things not seen, as it were, his final words about Herbert Buck came from the heart: 'My meeting him in Mahrisch Trubau had been the most important personal experience of the war. And the most far-reaching.'[14]

Murray's study of the Perennial Philosophy convinced him that denial of self was an essential condition for reaching the spiritual 'sunlit summit'. It led him into a life of service to others. To mountaineering and conservation causes he gave unstintingly of his time and energy; and stories abound of acts of kindness to individuals, in which he put others first and himself second. Murray was not one to simply pay lip service to his beliefs. He lived by them.

NOTES

1. Huxley's book *The Perennial Philosophy* was not published until 1946, so the term was not borrowed from there. It was already in current use, although popularised by Huxley. Murray also used the term 'Mentalism'. Today, this is associated with stage performances involving feats of memory or mind control, but in the 1940s it meant deep mental focus and meditation.

2. One wonders why Murray made no reference to the World Congress of Faiths, founded in 1933 by the Himalayan explorer, Francis Younghusband. Its aims were to bring together all religions and to recognise a common spiritual dimension in all humans; and for people of all faiths to share their spiritual quest.

3. That Murray was studying the philosophies of both East and West is clear from the books he was reading while a POW. More information about this is provided in Section 2 of online Appendix E.

4. There are, of course, many other definitions of, and debates about, what is meant by Truth – conformity with the divine intellect (St Augustine); pure love and pure truth are identical (Joseph Ratzinger); beauty is truth, truth beauty (Keats); Truth is the answer to the ultimate questions (such as what is the meaning of life? What is the nature of Beauty? What is Reality?).

5. This letter is in the possession of Ken Wilson who published *The Evidence of Things Not Seen*. I am indebted to Mike Cocker for drawing my attention to his own copy of it.

6. Plato was a Greek philosopher, one of Socrates' students, who lived in the third century BC. His ideas influenced much of Christian thought, particularly its mysticism.

7. This was also the title of his autobiography. However, the title for this was chosen by Ken Wilson after Murray's death.

8. It is now generally believed that Paul was not the author of this epistle.

9. Evelyn Underhill (1875–1941) was the author of 39 books, more than 20 of which were about mysticism. She immersed herself in the writings of St John of the Cross. Her monumental volume, *Mysticism* (1911), reveals her knowledge and appreciation of his teachings concerning the mystic life. He was, she claims, 'at once the sanest of saints and the most penetrating of psychologists.' After the

war, Murray is known to have had books by Evelyn Underhill on his shelves. Since most of her books were published before the war, it is likely that he was reading them while a POW – sent to him in parcels, or borrowed from the extensive camp library.

10. Zen Buddhism emerged in the seventh century AD in China – over a thousand years after the original Buddha lived on earth – and spread throughout South East Asia.

11. In *Mountaineering in Scotland* (page 243), published three years after this letter, Murray again uses the same imagery. Writing metaphorically he says, 'and from its radiance we know the summit is in sunlight.'

12. Murray's account of this event is in *The Evidence of Things Not Seen*, page 111.

13. There is a grave at Reading Crematorium where a Commonwealth War Graves Commission plaque bears his details, including the date of his death. This is also confirmed by the Indian Army Records and by his niece, Sheila Jepps.

14. *The Evidence of Things Not Seen*, page 111.

CHAPTER FOURTEEN

RECOVERY AND REDIRECTION

On arriving in England after being debriefed, given a medical examination, issued with a ration book, a new uniform, a travel warrant and five pounds, Murray spent the night in London and then travelled by train to a farmhouse near Aberystwyth in Wales where his mother and sister were living. He had been given two months leave and he planned to spend it there recuperating.

Murray was naturally lean. At the peak of fitness, despite being tall, he weighed only ten stone four pounds, yet in the prison camps he lost two stone. No wonder he describes himself as looking like a skeleton. For the first month after release he could not walk on the flat for more than ten or fifteen minutes without feeling faint, having palpitations and feeling as though his chest was being crushed. Initially, he thought he must have TB. The physical effects of starvation were plain to see, but slowly disappeared as he recuperated in North Wales, cared for by his mother and sister who plied him with fresh farm produce.

The physical effects of incarceration could be cured by a healthy diet, but the mental effects could not always be treated quite so easily. Nearly all POWs experienced short-term problems after release – feeling disconnected, anxious, having nightmares, or being overwhelmed by the proximity of women after several years deprived of their company. It was difficult to get out of the habit of scavenging, like slipping bits of broken biscuit or bacon rind into one's pocket or hoarding useless bits of wood or scrap metal. Those responsible for the debriefing process reported that, instead of filling in the forms, the recently released POWs stole the pencils. After years of living with the same people, going into a room full of strangers could be quite an ordeal; and many found themselves too frightened to cross a busy road. Others felt they were strangers in their own homes. The divorce rate was higher amongst ex-POWs than in any other group of ex-servicemen.

Added to this were financial problems. Instead of returning to find a sizeable nest-egg of accumulated pay, officers discovered that one third of it had been deducted during their period of captivity because their board and lodgings had been provided by the Germans.[1] Murray gives us a glimpse of this state of mind when, on arriving in London, he says he felt 'inept at foraging for myself amid the bustle of a big city';[2] or when, living with his mother and sister on the Welsh farm, he says: 'I had well nigh forgotten what female kindness was like, its depth of personal warmth, and civilising influence. They in turn were learning how uncivilised men could become without them.'[3] His difficulties in coming to terms with civilian life with all its worries, responsibilities and demands upon his time are clear when he says, 'I exchanged the freedom of the prison camps for the chains of civilisation',[4] and that he felt less free than he had in prison.[5]

All this is considered normal and to be expected under the circumstances. It is when these symptoms persist or develop into depression, alcohol and drug abuse, and a range of associated health and social problems that it becomes known as Post Traumatic Stress Disorder (PTSD). These symptoms can suddenly occur later, sometimes years later. The main body of research into PTSD has been done in America, funded by the military. One 40-year study of 62 former World War II POWs[6] revealed that half of them suffered from PTSD in the year following their release and that, of these, one third still exhibited symptoms 40 years later. Other studies of former POWs have found an even higher proportion with persistent symptoms, but significantly lower PTSD figures for combat troops who avoided capture. Murray did not consider himself to be harbouring any invisible wounds of this kind.

In a postcard from Brunswick POW camp to a friend, E.R. Zenthon, dated 26th Feb, 1945, he writes: 'After this experience I have little hope of climbing severes again. I am literally a skeleton; but very well in mind and spirit.' Four months later, in his letter to Douglas Scott, he says, 'At all events I can now say that three years imprisonment has done me no physical injury, although at the time I thought it had wrecked me. Mentally, or if you like spiritually, it has done me nothing but good.'

Yet there is a possibility that the war affected him more than he realised or cared to admit. One of the symptoms of PTSD is avoidance – avoiding activities, places, thoughts or feelings that remind you of the trauma. Murray consistently refused to speak about his wartime experiences, particularly his POW years. He did, though, write briefly about it in the first chapter of *Undiscovered Scotland* (1951) and again in 1979 in a couple of articles when explaining the background to the writing of *Mountaineering in Scotland,* and then he used the same text in his early eighties for *The Evidence of Things Not Seen*. In all these accounts he misses out quite a lot of the nastiness, the beatings and the humiliations.

Combat and captivity are shared challenges and dangers which must surely have created bonds of comradeship every bit as strong as did climbing or going on expedition together. Yet Murray says nothing of close relationships formed, mentions nobody by name – except Herbert Buck with whom he had a teacher-student relationship, and Alastair Cram with whom he had a distinctly cool relationship – and after the war appears not to have kept in touch with anyone he knew in the HLI or in the POW camps. Nor did he join any ex-POW or regimental associations. One might have expected that, after looking at the Abruzzi Mountains day after day from behind barbed wire at Chieti and longing to be amongst them, he would have returned after the war and climbed there, but he did not. It's as if he deliberately severed all contact with a part of his life he wanted to forget.

Nearly all therapists would now agree that talking about and writing about bad experiences is healing and that bottling up one's feelings, suppressing or denying them has the opposite effect. It has been said, jokingly but with a deal of truth in it, that nothing could have prepared British officers for POW life better than their public school upbringing[7] with its dormitories, close living, harsh discipline, all-male atmosphere, sparse food and separation from family. Unlike most of his fellow officers, Murray did not have this kind of background. After the war he appeared to have a permanent cough and by the time he was 70 he was not going up the hills at all because of problems with his lungs. Respiratory problems are one of the symptoms of PTSD.

The counter-argument is that to make a connection between Murray's respiratory problems and PTSD is mere conjecture, backed by no real evidence. His smoking habit, breathing extremely cold air in the mountains in winter and the effects of high altitude are more obvious causes. It is true he had changed, but almost nobody was quite the same after the war as they had been before it, and Murray was less likely than most ex-POWs to be amongst those who suffered from PTSD. His mountaineering had given him a physical and mental toughness and fortitude which exceeded that possessed by all but a few of his fellow captives.

By writing about his memories as he worked on his draft of *Mountaineering in Scotland,* Murray escaped into his mind and into the mountains he loved. Of the last grim year at the Brunswick camp, starving and unsure of their fate, he wrote: 'During this last year I had not once thought of myself as imprisoned. I lived on mountains and had the freedom of them. I felt able to wait on the SS machine-gunners, or whatever else fate held in store, without undue apprehension ... One has always to make the best efforts one can, but having made them, they have still to be seconded by Providence. Since that was now seen by me as a law of life, I reckoned efforts should be made hopefully, and the outcome resigned without any more self-concern to God's will.'[8]

In addition to his mountain memories there was his meeting with Herbert Buck and his embracing of the Perennial Philosophy which gave him an immense spiritual lift. Furthermore, Murray attended a variety of other classes. Later research discovered that POWs who studied were less likely to suffer PTSD. As one camp education officer put it at the time: 'We try to communicate the faith that there are things of the mind unbounded by time and place and that captives may escape beyond the barbed wire into fields of knowledge and delight. Those who know this freedom of the intellect are the happiest people in this camp.'[9]

In a letter dated 21st October 1946, to Geoffrey Winthrop Young, a mountaineer who had lost a leg in World War I and whom he greatly admired, Murray wrote: 'I think that I might now tell you that during the worst days of imprisonment, when I thought for a while that I would never be able to climb again, I was saved again and again from the worst excess of self-pity by the recollection of what happened to you in the last war and how you have faced up to it. Your own misfortune helped me to see my lesser one in proper perspective and helped me maintain a mental stability during those three years.'[10]

On this evidence it appears that Murray suffered no long-term trauma and, as he claimed, even benefited from the experience, finding time to think, read, be still, meditate, learn and write. If he never spoke of his war experience, as much as anything, it might have been out of his natural reticence and modesty, his horror of self-pity or of seeming to boast about hardships endured, particularly when others had suffered more than he had. He would have seen it as another instance of bad form to elaborate on such things.

It is interesting, though, that in 1965, twenty years after his release, Murray makes reference to his POW experience in his novel, *Dark Rose the Phoenix*. One wonders why he never fully used this rich material, or used it earlier – he wrote novels to make money and POW stories and escapes were highly popular.

In this novel, Schlinkel, a former Nazi, was heavily involved in the extermination of the Jews before disappearing at the end of the war and covering his tracks. On page 209, speaking of Schlinkel (who is under the alias of Seidl), Ross (one of the three main good guys), says: 'He deeply impressed me; in fact he gave me a shiver up the spine. Until one meets a man of this stamp, one doesn't realize how much good there is in the run-of-the-mill criminal, our common jail-stock. Seidl had the mark of the long-trained Gestapo agent – an animated corpse quality, which marks the man from whom practically all good has been wrung out.'

This scene has a close similarity to the passage in *The Evidence of Things Not Seen* recounting Murray's interrogation by the Gestapo: 'These were the first men I'd met able to put a shiver up my spine. Their facial expression was not mean or nasty, which might have implied some element of humanity. Gestapo agents seemed to be men from whom all good had been wrung out, leaving an animated corpse. My flesh crept. I had never appreciated before how much good there is in the common criminal.' (page 93)

Murray's mention of this incident in fiction precedes his mention of it as fact by nearly 15 years (his first factual account of this appeared in *Mountain Magazine* in June 1979). It is as if he found it easier to relive it through fiction and fictional characters before taking full ownership of it. And it also shows that, although Murray did not speak of these things, they were still in his mind. Although *Dark Rose the Phoenix* is one of Murray's least known novels and not considered his best, it probably had great significance for him in that Schlinkel, the former Gestapo agent, is later shown to have some good in him, to have reformed and is ultimately forgiven by Ross and allowed to live. Maybe it took that long for Murray to find forgiveness in his heart for those Gestapo men.

Just over a month after arriving at the farmhouse in Wales, Murray began to feel his energy returning. Early in June 1945, on hearing from Bill Mackenzie that he was in Glasgow, Murray decided to join him for a couple of days. Five years previously Murray had laid up his pre-war Morris Eight in a Glasgow garage. He found it in perfect condition, having been looked after all this time by the garage owner at no extra cost. It even fired up at the first swing of the starting-handle. In one of his most moving chapters Murray recounts in *Undiscovered Scotland* his first real climb after the war. His last climb in 1941 had been the Buachaille Etive Mor, and his first now could be none other. He tells Mackenzie they will have to go very slowly, take the easiest possible route and not expect to reach the top. Then, as the Buachaille comes into sight, he decides they should at least try for the top. As they walk towards it, he thinks that maybe he could manage a rock-climb as long as it's an easy one. And, of course, they end up doing quite a hard climb.

'We went over the Crowberry Tower to the summit. When I clapped my hand on the cairn I suddenly remembered my blank despair when I last stood here and made the same movement and found I could laugh at my folly. For this day had been for me another rebirth.'[11]

Murray spent the remainder of his leave assisting a Mountain Commando Unit stationed near the farm in North Wales to improve their climbing standards. Murray's application to join the SMC lists a number of climbs he did there in June and July. One of the people he climbed with was Chris Preston who later that summer made the first ascent of Suicide Wall (on the Idwal crags, near Ogwen, North Wales) which, at the time, was the hardest route ever climbed in Britain and a major advance in standard.

When his leave ended Murray was posted as adjutant[12] to a Royal Engineer's unit in the Vale of Leven near Dumbarton – a posting which did not make many demands on his time (his office staff did most of the paperwork) and enabled him both to continue work on the final stages of his book and, since he was not more than two hours' drive away from Glencoe, to accept J.H.B. Bell's invitation to write the first rock climbing guide to Glencoe.

Murray's ability to cope with his freedom was helped by the fact that it came in stages. Release from POW camp was followed by release from the Army which was eased by the relaxed discipline at the Vale of Leven, like a kind of half-way-house to civilian life. On being demobbed in April 1946, Murray reported to his pre-war employers, the Union Bank of Scotland, who had paid his salary throughout the war. He was given a post at their Charing Cross (Glasgow) office. While he searched for a house in Glasgow, suitable for himself and his mother, both of them stayed with Douglas Scott.

Scott's diary records that Murray arrived there on 17th May 1946, and that the following month he, Murray, Dunn and 'Hamish' Hamilton took a group of youths from a Glasgow boys' club up the Cobbler. After the war a Brunswick Boys' Club was set up in Glasgow. Whether Murray had anything to do with this, or whether these boys were from that club is not known. Dunn organised the outing. Maybe it was a 'taster' for Murray to let him see whether he wanted to get more involved in that kind of youth work with lads who belonged to gangs which fought each other with razors, bicycle chains and even firearms. Although Scott says the boys did well and were very keen, from Murray's point of view it wasn't a success. He must have hoped for something like his own rapturous reaction on reaching the Cobbler's summit for the first time and was disgusted when one of the young men sat down at the top and read a newspaper without ever looking around him. Possibly this experience was instrumental in shaping a rather less than enthusiastic attitude towards organised outdoor education for young people.

Murray wrote that, as a youth, he was 'adrift, as if rudderless on wide and windy seas.'[13] As he explained to Douglas Scott, 'When I went into the bag in 1942 I could see no purpose in life and was filled with a sense of frustration and depression.' In prison camp he found a spiritual goal to aim for. He had also put in many hours of solid work towards becoming a writer and a published author – something he had wanted to be since his schooldays. And yet, when he was demobbed, he was uncertain as to the final direction he should take.

'I came out of prison camps with one clear idea in mind: I wished to enter monastic life. I did not want that for refuge but to find spiritual fulfilment. A monastery would allow single-mindedness. I came out of the Army with two other clear ideas: to earn my living as an author and to make a return to the mountains. Mountains enthralled me still. None of the ideas was wholly incompatible with the others.'[14]

Murray decided to enter a monastery for a trial period of one week. It has been suggested that part of the reason Bell recruited Murray to do the Glencoe guidebook was that he could see the direction in which Murray's thoughts were heading and tried to give him something that would keep him in Scotland and keep his mind off such ideas. Anyway, if this was the plan, it didn't work. Murray chose Buckfast Abbey[15] on the banks of the River Dart in Devon because he knew several RAF pilots who had gone there. The Abbey was a Roman Catholic community of Benedictine monks, but this did not bar Murray, a non-Catholic, from coming for a trial period. The Abbot and leader of the community at the time of Murray's visit was Abbot Bruno.[16]

Something of the nature of the monastic life Murray was considering is conveyed in *The Rule of Saint Benedict*, a book of precepts about how Benedictine monks are expected to conduct themselves. It provides teaching about the basic monastic virtues of humility, silence, obedience and service. It requires monks to give away their property, either to the poor or to the monastery, and live in poverty. There is no stated requirement to remain celibate, but this was a separate provision for monks of all orders. The Benedictine motto is *'ora et labora'* – prayer and work, and the Rule contains a great deal about what prayers should be said and when.

The Rule gives no provision for leisure as such, but does state that physical work should be balanced with periods of study. It also states that, every year each monk should receive a reading list or 'codex' and is expected to read every book on the list over the course of the year. New monks had a probationary period of one year. If, at the end of that time, they still wanted to join and had proved satisfactory, they were made full members. Once they had joined, they were expected to remain in the monastery in which they had made their vows until their deaths. In general, the Rule aims at productive community living, seeking a middle and moderate way between individual zeal and strict institutionalism.

At Buckfast Abbey the monks ran a profitable farm, kept bees, taught in school and made medicinal wine. Later in life, Murray must have been rather dismayed to find that Buckfast wine had become the drink of choice of Glasgow's drunks. During the war the monks also ran the local fire brigade. On top of this, they attended Divine Office, the seven rites of day and night – Matins at 5.15 am, Lauds 6.30 am, Prime 7.30 am, Terce and Conventual Mass 9.00 am, Sext and None 12.45 pm, Vespers 6.30 pm, Compline 9.00 pm. The doors were locked just before Compline and everyone had to be in by then.

Murray had a small room to himself. He was expected to attend Divine Office, being woken at 4.55 am by a monk who went around swinging a bell. Murray ate in the refectory with the whole community, where meals were eaten in silence. He was forbidden to speak except to the Guest Master in his own room. Murray says he made good use of the library while there. According to the Abbey's archivist, the library at that time was well stocked with books on theology, scripture, spirituality, monasticism, and general religious matters.

There are similarities between this monastic regime and the POW way of life – an enclosed, all-male, celibate, institutional life where the inmates were locked in at night. It is possible that, at some sub-conscious level, Murray was drawn to it because it was like the place where he had found happiness. However, the week-long stay was enough for Murray to decide against the monastic life. He states that he might have sought conversion to the Roman Church, but for two things: he must accept the Church's way to fulfilment as the only way, and believe in the infallibility of the Pope. Murray believed neither to be true. 'Somewhat reluctantly' he decided to reject monastic life, 'which in some ways would have suited me well.'[17]

Maybe he had not studied the Rule until he was at the Abbey and had not realised until then the degree of commitment involved or that the likelihood of getting away to his beloved Scottish mountains, a long way from Devon, was slim. 'I could not gainsay my joy in the natural world,' he writes.[18] 'I saw no sure benefit in shutting myself away from it when already it had given me so much good.' At no point does Murray mention the required celibacy as a factor in his deliberations, a point which would have caused much agonising amongst most healthy young men. Stress and starvation are both well-known libido inhibitors and it could be that their effects had not yet worn off and that sex was not as prominent in his thoughts as it might have been.

A rumour persists, unsubstantiated by solid evidence, that Bill Mackenzie and other friends 'rescued' him from the monastery, in much the same way as parents now extricate their children from the clutches of modern cults – that he was intending to stay much longer than a week and they went down to Devon and persuaded him to change his mind with some forceful talking. We will probably never know if there is any truth in this.

What we do know is that, although he rejected the monastic life, his commitment to the Perennial Philosophy, to mysticism and meditation remained undiminished. Murray tells us that, for the rest of his life he continued to take instruction. He does not say where he did this or with whom. It seems likely that his reticence about this was deliberate, probably because, from the start, he had been eclectic in his search for the path to fulfilment and he did not want a label put on him or to be associated with one particular religious organisation. Various guesses have been that it was a lay order of the Franciscans,[19] or one of the Buddhist centres in the west of Scotland. A transcendental meditation centre now exists in Glasgow, but that did not open until the 1970s.

When Murray emerged from POW camp, he was bubbling over with his new-found philosophy and spiritual rebirth. His article in the 1946 SMC Journal, 'The Evidence of Things Not Seen', his letter to Scott, and numerous passages in *Mountaineering in Scotland* all attest to this. It's as if he couldn't wait to tell the whole world about it. At the same time, he must have known that some of his fellow members of the SMC would regard him as a crank and an 'oddball' for his views. Dent, his publishers, requested that he removed his more spiritual passages from the book, fearing they would put off readers and impede sales. Murray insisted that they stay in. To bear witness to your beliefs when they are unfashionable, and when you know they will mark you out as different from your colleagues and make you an outsider, takes courage and conviction. Murray had both. In the end, his 'joy in the natural world' took priority over monasticism. It was a decision which led directly to the rest of his life being spent in mountaineering and exploration, in working to preserve the Highland landscape and in using his undoubted writing skills to convey to others this joy and an understanding of what was worth preserving.

NOTES

1. The Treasury kept the money for its own purposes.
2. *The Evidence of Things Not Seen*, page 112.
3. *Ibid*, page 117.
4. *Ibid*, page 111.
5. *Ibid*, page 127.
6. American Journal of Psychology, 1986, Speed N., Engdahl B., Schwartz J., and Eberly R.
7. By public school, I mean here a fee-paying boarding school.
8. *The Evidence of Things Not Seen,* page 109.
9. Quoted in Adrian Gilbert's *POW: Allied Prisoners in Europe 1939–1945*, page 199.
10. Letter in the archives of The Alpine Club Library, London.
11. *The Evidence of Things Not Seen*, page 122.
12. In the British Army an adjutant is responsible for, or assists with, the administrative side of a regiment.
13. *The Evidence of Things Not Seen,* page 17.
14. *Ibid, page 126.*
15. The Abbey was founded in 1018, but ceased functioning as a monastery with the dissolution of the monasteries under Henry VIII. It went into private ownership until 1882 when the monks bought it back and began restoring it. Buckfast is the only mediaeval monastery to have been restored and used again for its original purpose. The rebuilding and restoration would still have been in progress at the time Murray was there.
16. Father Bruno Fehrenbacher, Abbot from 1939–1956.
17. *The Evidence of Things Not Seen*, page 130.
18. *Ibid*.
19. Murray clearly had a strong interest in St Francis of Assisi and, in the early 1950s, he wrote two plays about him. St Francis (or Francesco Bernadone as he was then known) was captured when on a military expedition against Perugia and spent a year as a prisoner-of-war. Murray would have identified with that, and also with St Francis' attraction to the hills around Assisi and his love of nature and the environment. Franciscans prayed with their eyes open, praising the beauty they saw around them, as typified in the prayer 'A Song of Brother Sun' (also known as 'The Canticle of the Creatures') – another thing which would have struck a chord with Murray.

CHAPTER FIFTEEN

GENESIS OF A MOUNTAIN CLASSIC

Murray's first published book, *Mountaineering in Scotland*, appeared in 1947 and has never been out of print since. Sixty-six years later it is still selling in bookshops and on the internet. This chapter is the story of that book, of how and why it came to be written. Chapter Sixteen looks at the reviews and at changing reactions to it over the years. Chapter Seventeen analyses what made it such a great book and why it made the impact it did. Chapter Eighteen considers the literary influences on Murray; and Chapter Twenty-Nine examines Murray's craftsmanship as a writer, including sample passages from *Mountaineering in Scotland*.

More than 30 years after the publication of *Mountaineering in Scotland*, Murray wrote an article in the *Weekend Scotsman*, entitled 'Genesis of a Mountain Classic'[1] in which he described how his first book was the product of three years in prison camps. In this article he wrote of how he had been captured in the Western Desert in 1942 and had wasted nearly a year at Chieti prison camp before, 'My imagination took fire at last from two slow-burning matches.'

These two things, these two slow-burning matches, which had kept mountains in his mind despite the trials and traumas he had endured, were the snow-capped Gran Sasso Mountain, the highest peak of the Abruzzi Mountains, which he saw daily from behind barbed wire; and his captor in the desert, the German tank commander, a fellow mountaineer with whom Murray had raised a bottle of beer and toasted 'Mountains'.

Murray had wanted to be a writer since his schooldays. While training to be a banker before the war he had written short stories (rejected) and several published articles for the *Scottish Mountaineering Club Journal*. Now the old urge to write returned and became compulsive. In a letter to Robert Aitken, dated 5th July 1967, Murray refers to *Mountaineering in Scotland* as simmering in his mind 27 years ago, which means that he began thinking about it, at some mental level, in 1940, two years before he became a POW. In the article 'Genesis of a Mountain Classic', Murray mentions his pioneering winter climbs and says:

> 'Hardly more than a dozen climbers in Scotland were involved in such work. The rest had little notion, and most none at all, of what Scottish rock could offer in winter. Many had the idea that our climbs were "unjustifiable" (then a fashionable word for damning hard moves and routes) I ... wanted to dispel ignorance of the rich harvest available on winter rock, and to propagate the fierce joys of fetching it in.'

So he knew, in general terms, what he wanted to write about. Once he had recovered from the trauma of battle, of capture and the initial shortage of food at Chieti, he was ready to start writing. Immediately a problem arose – there was no paper on which to set down his words. A diet heavily subsidised by local fruit meant that toilet paper, the only paper available, was urgently needed for its intended purpose. As Murray recounts it, the solution to his problem arrived in the form of *William Shakespeare's Complete Works* sent to him via the Red Cross by his mother. He realised immediately that the fine India paper of this volume would make excellent toilet paper, thus freeing his ration of Italian toilet roll for writing on.

'I felt sure Shakespeare would approve,' Murray commented.[2] However, in a letter to his sister, dated 5th December 1943,[3] after he had been moved on from Chieti, he asks her to tell his mother to send writing paper and also toilet paper. Failing the latter, his mother should send old Penguin books. Then he says: 'I have preserved Shakespeare and Byron so far.' It seems that this colourful story, often repeated in articles about Murray, may have been the result of a little 'improvement' and authorial licence.

Murray set up a makeshift desk using the top of his Red Cross parcel and sat on his top bunk, pencil poised. He knew he wanted to write about mountains and to share with others his love of them and his varied experiences amongst them, but beyond that, he did not know how or where to begin and he was without diaries, maps or reference books. His first page stayed blank for two days. At last into his mind surged the memory of a glorious 24 hours in Skye. He started writing. To his astonishment the pencil kept moving. 'As if with a will of its own it kept filling the pages.'[4]

Murray found that his ability to recall details improved with practice. As a prisoner, he had time to give it his almost undivided attention. Over a period of months the trickle of memories became a full flood.

Some commentators on Murray's work have expressed doubt as to whether he could really recall as much as he says he did. They cite the huge number of word-perfect quotes in *Mountaineering in Scotland* and the wealth of small details about the routes taken, the rock formations and the climbing moves that were made. Some of the quotes could have come from the books on hand in the extensive prison camp libraries – more than 8,000 books, mainly the classics of English literature. However, Murray later told a friend that the quotations were from memory and that, with practice, he had managed to recover them, but that, once back in civilisation, the 'power' vanished. As for recalling minute detail – other authors have experienced the same phenomenon, including the author of this biography.[5]

Murray would have been helped in this by his meditation. Self-hypnosis techniques which people use to recall their past are very similar to the kind of meditation which Murray learned while a POW. This is not to say that he deliberately practised self-hypnosis in order to bring back the details of his pre-war mountaineering, but, meditation does calm the mind, eliminates distractions and increases ability to concentrate. Through meditation he would have improved his capacity for letting go of the conscious mind in the here and now and travelling elsewhere.

His memory, remarkable though it was, did sometimes require assistance. In the same letter of 5th December 1943, quoted above, Murray desperately wants to be sent the pre-war articles he had written and says, 'Please tell me the names of the following peaks which I fail to remember and require – North West of Bidean, second of Buachaille and corrie between, peak of South of A'chir ridge.' A memory for names, of course, is not the same thing as an ability to recall vivid personal experiences.

Murray had several months after the war to polish and redraft his book and had access to the notes and references he had been denied while a POW. On many of the adventures he describes, he was accompanied by friends against whom he could later check the facts. While still doing the final corrections on his book, Murray was filling in his application form for membership of the SMC. For this, he entered details of every climb he had done up to that point. Clearly, he needed to check his facts for this. It seems highly likely, therefore, that most of the details in *Mountaineering in Scotland* were checked after the war and were accurate.[6]

Where Murray may have departed from exactly recapturing the moment as it really was is in describing his emotional, spiritual and mystical responses to the mountains. Although his mysticism was there in embryo from before the war, it did not burst into full life until 1943 and 1944 – at the same time as he was in full flow with *Mountaineering in Scotland*. It seems likely that the older, more mature and mystically aware Murray reinterpreted his feelings about those youthful 1930s climbs and responded to them as the person he was at the time of writing, rather than the person he was when he actually made the climbs. Murray himself records a comment made by his friend and brother-in-law, MacAlpine, along rather similar lines: 'Does beauty move climbers as much as their later writings suggest?'[7]

Worried by the number of escape attempts, the Italian authorities at Chieti tried to divert the prisoners' attention to other things by providing recreational facilities, including writing paper. Work on the book progressed, but then had to be put on hold for two months when Murray and his fellow-prisoners were moved to Moosburg where the terrible conditions and overcrowding made writing impossible. Then he and his fellow prisoners were sent to Mahrisch Trubau (Oflag VIII F) and Murray suffered what at the time seemed like a huge setback. His manuscript, which he considered to be almost finished, was confiscated by the Gestapo.

As has been mentioned, many of the POW camps had well-organised education programmes. The German authorities allowed exam papers to be sent back to Britain for marking and certification. Included in this agreement were the manuscripts of prisoners who had written books of various kinds while in captivity, which could be sent back to publishers and literary agents in Britain.[8] Whether or not this opportunity was available to Murray, or whether he was unaware of it, we do not know. It is possible that he couldn't bring himself to send off something that wasn't quite ready. Had he done so, the story of *Mountaineering in Scotland* would have been a different one and the book itself would not have been the same.

Showing enormous fortitude and determination, Murray started all over again. Now, though, his approach to his book had changed.

'Our hunger intensified. I no longer believed that I would climb mountains again, but felt impelled to get the truth of them on paper. Nor did I want, as before, to write specifically about hard climbs, or to enlighten anybody about techniques and winter severities. I wrote because I must, shedding the twin humbugs of understatement of difficulty and exaggeration of danger and likewise of reticence about feeling for beauty ... I had a mind to say what I'd found of beauty and delight, effort and fun. I would try for truth only, and while knowing that it could never be said, still I would try.'[9]

The second draft, which he believed at the time to be the final one, was finished on his thirtieth birthday in March 1944. Murray says that on re-reading his manuscript he found many flaws. Between March 1944 and April 1945 – first at Mahrisch Trubau and then at his final camp, in Brunswick (Oflag 79) from where he was freed – Murray set about improving *Mountaineering in Scotland*, polishing, deleting, extending.

On the day of his liberation from POW camp, his manuscript was nearly lost for a second time. He had transferred it from its usual place under his tunic to a suitcase. He heard, just in the nick of time, that the suitcases would be travelling separately, so he took it out and kept it on him. He never saw his suitcase again.

Back in Britain, posted to a fairly undemanding job, he was able to continue his redrafting. In March 1945, a year after completing the book in longhand, he finished typing his manuscript. Despite all his hard work, he did not feel confident of success. In June 1945 he wrote to Douglas Scott, saying, 'I haven't even tried to find a publisher; for I have still some work to do on the book ... Goodness knows if I will ever get it published anyhow. It may not be good enough, and I've no graft with any publisher!'[10] However, soon after this, he sent it to J.M. Dent & Sons of London.[11] He chose Dent because he had heard that their literary director was a member of The Alpine Club and might be disposed to at least read a book on mountains.

Two months later Murray heard from Dent that they wanted to publish *Mountaineering in Scotland,* but wished to make some editorial cuts. Their professional reader[12] was of the opinion that Murray had expressed his thoughts too freely and that some of the mystical and philosophical passages should be removed. Murray refused, arguing that, 'the book had to be as it was – written from the heart of a holocaust and not written as if on home ground.'[13] In his opinion writers who were too cautious produced dead books.[14] Dent accepted his position and sent him a contract.

Dr J.H.B. Bell, Murray's early climbing mentor and editor of the SMCJ, tried to persuade him to delay publication for several years, but Murray was keen to go ahead with it. Murray told Tom Weir later that he was glad he had done so.[15] In a letter to Peter Hodgkiss,[16] dated 30th March, 1987, Murray has more to say about this:

'When I told JHB in 1945 that I was going to look for a publisher for a book I'd done in the prisons, he tried his best to dissuade me. I was too young, he said, and should wait until I had more years of experience behind me, and could speak with authority, and with proper balance and perspective. I'd then be heard with far more respect etc. I listened and had to agree that he was possibly right. On the other hand, I knew that a climber's hard work is done when he's young and relatively inexperienced, not when he is old and wise – and it might be the same with writing too. Of course, the book, my book, had now been written, and I was not going to sit on it any longer, so Bell's words fell on deaf ears.'

Perhaps, too, Bell could see that Murray was bubbling over with his new-found Perennial Philosophy and mysticism and thought that, given time, he might simmer down and modify some of his more high-flown passages.

The editorial director of J.M. Dent & Sons who worked with Murray on preparing *Mountaineering in Scotland* for publication was Ernest F. Bozman, a fellow mountaineer.[17] So began the task of going through the text with a fine-tooth comb, indexing, selecting photographs and discussing the maps and drawings. The latter were done by Edward R. Zenthon, an artist and fellow member of The Scottish Mountaineering Club, with whom Murray had kept up a correspondence while a POW. This 1947 first edition contained 32 full plate black and white photographs. In the Acknowledgements page Murray thanks 'all the photographers, whose names are given elsewhere'. Unfortunately there must have been a slip-up or an editorial oversight, because the names are not given elsewhere. However, we know that the bulk of the photographs were supplied by Murray himself, by his friend, Douglas Scott, who after the war set up as a professional photographer, and by W.S. Thomson, at that time one of the leading landscape photographers in Scotland.[18]

Mountaineering in Scotland was published in August 1947, priced 18 shillings.[19]

The final version consisted of 23 chapters or essays, covering some of the highlights of Murray's pre-war adventures in the Scottish mountains and embracing 'hard routes on rock, snow and ice, as well as on high plateaux and long ridges and wide moors'. The final chapter, 'Rocks and Realities', is a more generalised essay about mountaineering and the deeper meaning that mountains had for him. In this chapter (page 239), in defining a mountaineer, he also defines the range of experiences which his book covers: 'Indeed I can hardly pretend to myself that a man is a true mountaineer unless he knows his mountains winter and summer, on cliff and summit ridge, by day and night, in fair weather and foul.'

He then goes on (page 243) to elaborate on this: 'I thought not only of the ends but of the ways of striving, for the one adds lustre to the other; not only of the solemn hours but of the familiar joys of mountaineering, for in these too there is beauty: dawdling under a blue sky up the crest of a sun-warmed ridge; the irrepressible gaiety of rope-mates, forcing wet slabs in mist and windy rain; stimulating doubts upon the ice-bulge in an unclimbed gully; the plunge into a shining tarn; the crackling fire in an inn after blizzard – the beauty of living and of life itself. Of all such days I thought, and before I knew what I was about, of these I found myself writing. In truth, I wrote with no dark design of enlightening others, but because I could not help myself.'

Out of a total of 23 chapters, five had been written and published before the war, while three more were published in other forms post-war in the period before the book came out. Most of these pre-war articles, written for the *Scottish Mountaineering Club Journal*, were altered slightly and expanded for their inclusion in *Mountaineering in Scotland,* often adding a slightly more mystical note. (Note 20 at the end of this chapter gives an example of the sort of changes Murray made.)[20]

In nine of the accounts a significant proportion of the action involves walking or climbing at night, experiencing scenes such as when 'The moonlight cast our shadows long and thin upon the snows, and before us the buttress swelled in a silver wave to the summit, bearing us up firmly to the starred sky;' or the time when, 'A mysterious twilight, like that of an old chapel at vespers, pervaded these highest slopes.' Often, part of the total experience of night climbing or camping out is witnessing sunset and sunrise and *Mountaineering in Scotland* contains marvellous descriptions of both.

These night scenes mostly occur because long hard winter routes, attempted when daylight hours are limited, can lead to reaching the top after dark. Sometimes they happened because of a late start due to various delays, but whereas others might have then made alternative plans, Murray and his companions invariably went ahead, despite knowing that darkness would overtake them. They had discovered that, with head torches (of which Murray and his group were the early pioneers) and given the reflection of light off the snow, climbing at night in winter did not present difficulties. Murray loved the magic of night and, unlike most mountaineers of his era, he actively planned to be up there as the sun set, the moon rose and the stars emerged.

'It is in winter and by night that the mountains are most studiously avoided, despite that when the peaks are snow-capped and the moon full, visibility of twenty to twenty-five miles is by no means exceptional … if you are alone, as you should be sometimes, go up to the main ridge of the Mamores and walk the shining snow waves that link Stob Ban to the spire of Binnein Mor; only your boot nails sound on the frozen snow-crust, so that when you stop to listen – and listen – you can hear an utter silence that no one has ever heard in company … You will know more of the world's song than can be set forth in books.'[21]

A bare summary of the factual content and provenance falls a long way short of capturing the spirit of the book or explaining why it came to be regarded as a classic of mountain literature. These things are the subject of other chapters. In the penultimate chapter Murray wrote, 'From the deeps of the earth to the uttermost star above the whole creation had throbbed with a full and new life; its music one song of honour to the beautiful.' That is what *Mountaineering in Scotland* is – a song of honour to the beautiful and to beauty. 'Therefore let us speak of the unspeakable, for there is no speech so profitable,' he wrote (page 222). This is what Murray had the courage to attempt in *Mountaineering in Scotland*. In doing so, to many readers he brought inspiration and vision and found for them the words they could not find themselves; he articulated thoughts which had lain beneath the surface of their minds; he said things which, for the first time in their lives, they recognised once he had said them.

NOTES

1. 2nd June 1979. The same article appeared in the same month in *Mountain Magazine* under the title of 'To Write a Book'. It was later the basis for several pages of text in Chapters 9,10 and 11 in *The Evidence of Things Not Seen*.
2. *The Evidence of Things Not Seen*, page 87.
3. This letter is in the archives of Ken Wilson. A copy of it was shown to me by another researcher.
4. This became the opening chapter, 'Twenty-Four Hours on the Cuillin'.
5. In writing my memoirs of growing up in India, more than half a century after leaving that country, by intense focus, self-hypnosis, finding books, films, photographs and other materials that would jog the memory, I was able to recall things which I had thought were lost forever – such as the names of all 50 boys I had been at school with, and the titles of all the books on the shelf in my father's study. At the same time there are memories which I cannot say for sure are real rather than being imagined.
6. The matter of accuracy is further explored in Chapter Thirty.
7. *Undiscovered Scotland*, page 108.
8. The German Army officials who ran the prison camps were not the same as the Gestapo, who might well have suspected that coded messages were being sent back to Britain this way.
9. *The Evidence of Things Not Seen*, page 100.
10. This letter is clearly dated 26th June, 1945, and yet in *The Evidence of Things Not Seen* (page 128) Murray says that J.M. Dent and Sons expressed a desire to publish his book a month earlier than this, in May of 1945. Murray's memory appears to be at fault here.
11. Dent and Company was founded in 1888, becoming J.M. Dent & Sons in 1909. It was best known for its Everyman series which made over 1,000 volumes of the classics available to the public. It was purchased by Weidenfeld and Nicolson in 1988. It now forms an imprint of the Orion Publishing Group.

12. Dent's reader was R.L.G. Irving, then a housemaster at Winchester, and was known to Murray. George Mallory, who died on Everest in 1924, was a pupil at Winchester. It was Graham Irving who introduced him to mountaineering. The latter is not to be confused with Sandy Irvine who died with Mallory on Everest.

13. *The Evidence of Things Not Seen*, page 129.

14. Jane Austen would have agreed with this. She once summed up a novel of a lesser writer by saying, 'The risk was not taken.'

15. This information comes from the notes Weir made when interviewing Murray to gather material for his chapter, 'Murray's Way' in his own book, *Weir's Way* (1981). These notes are in the Weir Collection in the archives of the National Library of Scotland. This part of the interview was not used in the published chapter.

16. Peter Hodgkiss was the owner of the Glasgow-based Ernest Press. The letter was a response to Hodgkiss asking Murray for his opinion on Bell's book, *A Progress in Mountaineering*, which he was considering republishing. In the letter, Bell's advice is being used to illustrate why Bell's book did not take off – it lacked the fire and spark of youth. Bell had waited too long before writing it. I am indebted to Joy Hodgkiss for showing me this letter.

17. Bozman was also a French scholar. Another of the books he edited was *Mountain Essays by Famous Climbers*, published by Dent in 1933. He was a regular contributor to *The Climbers' Club Journal*. Bozman would have known about Murray already because he co-authored *British Hills and Mountains* (Batsford, 1943) with J.H.B. Bell. In this latter book, writing of mountaineers, Bozman says, 'I am a convert to their faith, a member of the rank and file. I know enough to be able to imagine the great deeds of courage and patience and of self-sacrifice that have been offered on the mountains, and I can see the thousand desperate battles that have been fought and won on lonely precipices by the leaders and pioneers.'

18. In 1954 Murray and Thomson jointly produced a book, *The Highlands in Colour*, with an Introduction by Murray and colour photographs by Thomson.

19. In the old currency, before decimalisation, there were 20 shillings to the pound. In 1947 a new Ford Popular car cost £80, the national average for a three-bedroom, semi-detached house was £750, and a bag of chips cost 1d.

20. For example, Chapter XVII 'New Year on Ben Nevis' appeared in the SMCJ of November 1940 under the title of 'Night Up There: Hogmanay on Ben Nevis'. One can imagine the London publisher, Dent, worrying that readers south of the border might not be familiar with the word 'Hogmanay'. In describing the sunset from the Nevis plateau, Murray has added the sentence: 'We felt dazed, as though the eyes of the soul had been blinded by too much wonder.' The section about Gardyloo Gully has been expanded from half a page in the SMCJ to four pages in the book. The difference is probably accounted for by the constraints imposed by SMCJ editorial policy concerning length. On the final page in the chapter the load they carried has crept up from the original 110 lbs to 115. And the ending is different, introducing a slightly more mystical note.

21. *Mountaineering in Scotland*, page 239.

CHAPTER SIXTEEN

LIKE A METEOR TRAILING LIGHT

Reviews of *Mountaineering in Scotland,* all favourable, began appearing in newspapers, magazines and journals in the autumn of 1947 and, for the next 66 years up to the present day, like a meteor trailing light, it has been accompanied by praise and admiration. The following extracts give a flavour of the reviews and comments at the time of, or soon after, publication.

'Climbing in the British Isles has so far failed to inspire a book which the mountain fraternity can accept as a classic, but *Mountaineering in Scotland* may one day be acclaimed as such. (Arnold Lunn in the *New Statesman*)

'A notable contribution to the mountain literature of the world.' (*Glasgow Daily Record*)

'Seldom, in a book dealing with mountains, has an author so success-fully grappled with the philosophical implications of his sport, and many will feel grateful to him for expressing in words what they have so often but dimly felt.' (*Open Air in Scotland*)

'The charm of the book is in its author's power to convey both his zest in physical triumph and the spiritual refreshment he gets from high places.' (*Observer*)

After commenting that it was odd that the literature of mountain-eering in Scotland was so small, the *Scotsman* review of November 1947 went on to say: 'This admirable book will please the general reader because of its excitement and the author's literary artistry. It will find favour with the experienced climber for the detailed descriptions of the routes followed. Everywhere Mr Murray's passionate love of the Scottish hills is evident.'

'His book, *Mountaineering in Scotland* has no equal amongst Scottish mountain literature.' (J. Courtland-Simpson in a letter of support for Murray's application to join the Alpine Club, October 1948.)

Describing his immediate reaction to *Mountaineering in Scotland*, Tom Weir later wrote: 'I was in Bournemouth, working as a surveyor, when the book came out in 1947, and I knew I was reading a classic as adventure followed adventure with a dimension of action and powerful description that made you feel that you were one of his companions on the rope, so clearly was each character brought to life.' (*Weir's Way*, 1981)

'W.H. Murray's *Mountaineering in Scotland* is in a class by itself.' (Tom Longstaff in his book, *This is my Voyage*, 1950)

Almost as soon as *Mountaineering in Scotland* was published, Geoffrey Winthrop Young wrote a letter to Murray which must have meant more to him than even the most glowing review:

'My dear Murray
    Your book has just come out. And it damnably spoilt my morning writing. I have not resisted dipping twice and deep into Cir Mhor and Sron na Ciche. Then I shall read it really. Oh, thank heaven at last – for someone who can write! ... I am going to have enormous pleasure, I see, out of it. I feel safe with you, straight off, and that means a lot, after all the sympathetic reading I do of climbers' efforts-to-record!
    I see at once that you have written a book – and the first book – worthy of the subject, that is of Scottish climbing of the high order. I am glad that it was left until you did it! I'll probably write again when I've read and digested ... but here's my first burst of delight – Glory be! – a climber's book, and yet a writer's too!'[1]

There was general agreement that the quality of the writing in *Mountaineering in Scotland* was superb and following these good reviews, the book sold well. In 1962 Dent issued a new edition. This was described as containing revisions. They must have been very minor ones because close scrutiny by Murray afficionados has failed to find any significant changes, except in a slight reorganisation of the index and a rewording of the Acknowledgements. In the original 1947 edition, Murray acknowledges, 'the members of the Junior Mountaineering Club of Scotland, who taught me to climb.' This was changed to: 'I want especially to thank W.M. Mackenzie, J.K.W. Dunn, and A.M. MacAlpine, with whom I learned the craft of climbing.' In 1966, Dent brought out the book as one of their Aldine Paperbacks (price 45p). This edition had no photographs in it and a rather lurid cover, better suited to a cheap fiction title, which Murray detested – all the more so because it showed two climbers on a crag making liberal use of pitons in a way that would have horrified him.

In the meantime, Murray was working on his next book and in 1951 Dent published *Undiscovered Scotland*. Some reviewers and, indeed its subsequent publisher, have rather loosely summarised this book as dealing with his post-war climbs. In fact, five of the chapters deal with pre-war climbs.[2] *Undiscovered Scotland*, often referred to as a companion volume to *Mountaineering in Scotland*, followed much the same format. It was a series of 22 essays, with similar maps, illustrations and black and white photographs.

Like its companion, the book covers a wide range of mountaineering experiences in Scotland, has a good ration of night scenes, maintains the spiritual and mystical themes and continues Murray's one long answer to why he loved mountains and mountaineering. This and the central theme of discovery give continuity to the individual chapters. The first chapter, 'The Undiscovered Country', contains a wonderful sweeping overview of the Scottish mountains and a magnificent summary of why people, himself in particular, are drawn to them. As in *Mountaineering in Scotland*, the book is rich with wonderful phrases and descriptions.

Murray would never speak about his desert war and POW experiences, but, here he writes about them for the first time. There is a greater emphasis in this book on the joys of exploration. Its very title proclaims this. As well as covering Glencoe, Nevis and Skye, as before, there are also visits to Rum, Arran, Glen Affric, Benalder Forest and places further north than he had previously ventured. Tom MacKinnon, Bill Mackenzie and Douglas Scott are still there. Archie MacAlpine, who had moved south of the border after the war to take up a dental practice, figures less often, as does Kenneth

Dunn, who appears mostly in the pre-war climbs which are included in the book. On the other hand there are new climbing partners in Donald McIntyre, Bill Tennent and Michael Ward, as well as other, less regular companions.

A greater proportion of easier climbs and walks are found in *Undiscovered Scotland* than in *Mountaineering in Scotland*. By the time he began work on the former Murray had produced his climbing guidebook, *Rock Climbs: Glencoe and Ardgour* (1949), which included easy and moderate climbs as well has the hard ones. This had given him an appreciation of the needs of the average club climber.

In his chapter entitled 'The Forgotten Cliffs of Aonach Dubh' he writes (page 74): 'New climbs of extreme severity are not hard to find in Glencoe, but the discovery of simple and modestly difficult routes is so hard that something like an intervention of Divine Providence is required for their revelation. It was our remarkable feat this day to have made on Aonach Dubh no route of real severity. That East Cliff was a humble and generous cliff, giving freely the sound climbs that are the daily bread of the rock-climber; therefore of more value than many airy severities that I happened on in the past. On the East Cliff all men may climb.'

Overall, there is a more mature and softer feel to *Undiscovered Scotland*. As Tom Weir says, 'The reader is made aware that the writer has discovered more than remote places where hand and footholds are scarce. There is an air of tranquillity about this work, a feeling that mountains matter more than the mere climbing of them.'[3]

Almost inevitably, *Undiscovered Scotland* was overshadowed by *Mountaineering in Scotland*. Without the same combination of special circumstances which surrounded the creation of the latter, it was expecting the impossible that Murray should write with the same intensity and brilliance. These two books are often referred to as his 'two mountain classics'. And it could be argued that *Undiscovered Scotland* does deserve to be called a classic, but it does not quite match up to *Mountaineering in Scotland* – very few books of that genre can. Reviews were fewer, favourable but not ecstatic.

The publishers, Dent, issued a one-page 'prospectus' for the book (a leaflet to advertise it, a copy of which is held in the National Library of Scotland). This could hardly be said to be an objective description, but few would disagree with what it said: 'Mr Murray writes as he climbs – with skill, balance, philosophic good humour, and a continuous regard for his fellow men – and to read these further chapters on his Scottish climbs is to rope up behind an acknowledged expert and a most fascinating companion.'

It is interesting that Murray says not a single word about *Undiscovered Scotland* in his autobiography, *The Evidence of Things Not Seen*. Whether he was disappointed with how it turned out and dismayed that the former magic had been just out of reach, it is hard to say, since he never seems to have mentioned it again.

In 1979 a compilation volume, incorporating both books, was published by Diadem Books and reprinted in 1980, 1982, 1986 and in paperback form in 1992. Bâton Wicks[4] took it over and issued the two-book volume in paperback in 1997, with several subsequent reprints. This combined volume contains 16 black and white full plate photographs, compared to 32 for *Mountaineering in Scotland* alone in 1947. Presumably, this smaller number of photographs was in the interests of keeping down the price of a book that was approaching 500 pages in length. The front page, the page with both titles on it, states: 'With twenty maps and diagrams by Robert Anderson'. However, the maps and diagrams for *Mountaineering in Scotland* are clearly the same as those done for the 1947 edition, which were attributed to E.R. Zenthon; and a different hand has drawn the maps and diagrams for *Undiscovered Scotland,* which have been signed 'RA' – obviously Robert Anderson, an artist and friend of Douglas Scott who occasionally climbed with Murray.[5]

This combined volume has been referred to as 'the great bible of Scottish climbing';[6] and the website 'Undiscovered Scotland' – one of the best internet tourist guides for Scotland, particularly in relation to the Highland regions and outdoor activities – was so named in its honour. Ken Wilson, owner and manager of Bâton Wicks, was almost certainly correct in saying, 'If I hadn't put the two together, *Undiscovered Scotland* would have withered on the vine.'[7] Lovers of mountain literature have him to thank for maintaining the availability of these two wonderful books over the years.

In the 66 years since it was first published, *Mountaineering in Scotland* has continued to attract reviews and assessments in journals, books and, in more recent years, on a variety of websites. In the 1960s and early 70s, Murray's mountain writings fell out of favour. It was a period of strong youthful rebellion against the values of the past, the older generation and the 'Establishment' in general. Murray and *Mountaineering in Scotland* were regarded by some as being in this category. There was a certain amount of mockery of Murray and his books, most of it of a gentle and affectionate kind, as epitomised in Tom Patey's song, 'The Ballad of Bill Murray', the last verse of which goes:-

> 'In that Tournament on Ice, Death or Glory was the price
> For those knights in shining armour long ago –
> You must forage for yourself on that ghastly Garricks Shelf
> With every handhold buried deep in snow.
> Murray did his Devil's dance on each microscopic stance
> Recording his impressions of the view,
> There was green ice in the chimneys and black ice at the crux
> And not a single piton or a screw.'[8]

The song is a tribute to Murray in that it is packed with references to things mentioned in *Mountaineering in Scotland* and its humour relies on Patey's audience knowing Murray's work and recognising these references – which it would have done.

It was also a time of rapid developments in climbing techniques, some of which were seen as breaking the old rules and taboos, the kind of rules which Murray was perceived to uphold. Murray, who as a young climber had upset the 'old-guard' of the SMC with his new approach, was now regarded as being behind the times. Des Rubens,[9] in 'W.H. Murray Revisited',[10] gives us a glimpse of the irreverent but affectionate way in which at least one group of climbers thought of Murray and his classic book.

Writing of how *Mountaineering in Scotland* harked back to a bygone age, Rubens says: 'Nightly readings were held at base camp at 14,000 feet [in Pakistan]. For us, Bill was a heroic figure of a more innocent age. This was not so much through the quality of his climbs, though we respected these. Rather, through the images conjured by his writing he articulated much of what we felt of our own early experiences of the hills ... We envied his personal discovery of the empty hills of the Thirties. To us, his time was a Golden Age of Scottish mountaineering ... As students at the tail end of the Sixties, our

respect for the man and his contemporaries was coloured by the anti-
authoritarianism of the time. The tales brought back by student club
representatives attending SMC dinners were eagerly awaited. These
tales of our (still living) Victorian mountaineering heritage were as
remarkable to us as to those scientists who discovered the living fossil
coelacanth brought up from far down in the Indian Ocean. ... During
those student days a Bill Murray evening was held. The parts of the
Bills, Archies, Bells *et cetera* were allocated for historic re-enactments.
Mrs Malloch was played by a bewildered girlfriend roped in for the
occasion. Quantities of Mummery's Blood were consumed and readings of the Works were held ... *The Works*, as *Mountaineering in
Scotland* and *Undiscovered Scotland* were referred to, were critically
analysed, and phrases stockpiled for use in times of drama ... Despite
this infantile taking the piss (well, it was so much youthful fun), we
were with Bill. Whilst sometimes gently derided, the spirituality of his
writings struck a vibrant chord.'

By the late 1970s and 80s people were becoming more environmentally aware, more conscious of what they might lose and of the need to
appreciate and conserve our natural flora and fauna and our unspoilt
areas of landscape. There was a cultural swing towards nature and
wilderness writing, past and present. At the same time there was a
growing awareness of the concept of emotional intelligence and of the
need to be in touch with one's feelings. These factors, the increasing
number of people taking to the mountains for recreation, and the
appearance of the 1979 double volume in paperback, helped bring
about a revival of interest in *Mountaineering in Scotland* which has
continued to the present day.

Later reprints of the combined volume carry a review by David
Rose from the *Observer*:

'The writing is sublime with descriptions of climbing that come close
to the Buddhist idea of ahisma, the shedding of self. It offers a more
complex but satisfying answer to the question, of why climb, than
Mallory's "because it's there".'

In 1982 Jim Perrin[11] wrote a perceptive article about Murray and
other post-war Scottish mountaineer-writers in which he described
his two books as having 'the best descriptions ever written of this

particular landscape ... You could say that Murray strives too hard at times to define the indefinable, you could say that he invests his set pieces too richly and too often with roseate glow; you could say that his attempts at humour can be a little solemn and ponderous. For all that, along with Tilman, whom he knew and with whom he climbed, he is my favourite mountain writer, and the best of them all on British themes.'[12]

Chris Bonington, in a 1983 review of Joe Tasker's *Savage Arena,* wrote 'There are very few mountaineering books that become both a representative expression of a certain era and, at the same time, inspirational bibles to the younger climbers of that period. Two immensely important books for me in this context were W H Murray's *Mountaineering in Scotland* and Hermann Buhl's *Nanga Parbat Pilgrimage.*'[13]

Another of Murray's admirers is Robert Macfarlane.[14] Writing of *Mountaineering in Scotland*, Macfarlane gives his opinion that it 'must stand as one of the finest expressions of the power of the wild to act, even in retrospect, even remotely, upon the mind.'[15] In an article for the *Guardian* about Nan Shepherd[16] he says: 'Like her friend and fellow modernist novelist Neil Gunn, and like the Scottish explorer-essayist, W.H. Murray, Shepherd had read deeply in Buddhism. Shards of Zen philosophy glitter in the prose of all three writers, like mica flecks in granite. Reading their work now – with the fusion of Scottish culture and Buddhist metaphysics – remains astonishing: like seeing a Noh play performed in a kailyard, or chrysanthemums flourishing in a corrie.'[17]

Macfarlane was later asked by the *Guardian Review* (16 March, 2009) to recall the book that for him best captured somewhere special in Britain. He chose two books: Edward Thomas' *The South Country*, and Murray's *Mountaineering in Scotland.* Of the latter, he wrote: 'To my mind it's one of the major works of 20th century Scottish landscape literature.'

These days, of course, many books are reviewed or discussed on the internet. Here are extracts from Colin Wells'[18] retrospective view of Murray's two classic books on the website, *Scotlandonline* (www.scotlandonline.com): 'At the same time as Murray's climbing star was on the wane, his wider influence was just beginning, thanks to the publication of *Mountaineering in Scotland* (written while incarcerated as a Prisoner-of-War), followed four years later by *Undiscovered Scotland*. These books, written from an earnestly passionate personal viewpoint, with an intensity unprecedented in climbing writing, were phenomenally successful and continue to be avidly read to this day. Murray's writing style was heavily influenced by a homespun mysticism which lends a mesmerising metaphysical other-worldliness to his accounts of the inter- and post-war climbing scene in the Highlands. ...

'In the immediate aftermath of a world war which had devastated Europe, such quasi-religious metaphors for the healing power of the Scottish mountains resonated with readers battered by half a decade of attrition and austerity. ... Murray's unabashed wallowings in the spiritual communion he feels with the Highlands may exude the charm and innocence of another era but it's a style which still has the power to move many readers.'[19]

The internet bookstore, Amazon.co.uk, encourages customer reviews. These contributors may not be professional literary critics, but they do show the views of a writer's current fans, of connoisseurs of that particular genre and of ordinary readers. Here is an extract from one which was highly rated by other users of the site: 'I applaud and respect W.H. Murray for his attempts to move on from captivating views of mountain landscapes or gripping accounts of climbing, to lead into compelling views or mesmerizing exposition on the meaning of life. *In Mountaineering in Scotland* he confirms his belief that "our understanding of mountains is broadened and deepened toward the understanding of all things created". Each [of these two books is] a magnificent mountain commentary in its own right – this superb-value omnibus edition should continue to inspire and influence generations to come.' (Contributed by D. Elliott, 25 March 2009.)

And one from another regular contributor, Robert Aitken: 'Bill Murray's *Mountaineering in Scotland* has a well-known mythology of its own, having been written on toilet paper in a POW camp. Now 55 years old, this book stands in the same relationship to Scottish climbing and to Scottish climbing literature as Leslie Stephen's 'Playground of Europe' does to alpine climbing and literature: it provides both the style and tone for the activity, and the yardstick for all subsequent books about it. The climbs Murray describes, even his fierce pioneering winter climbs of the 1930s, may now simply be test pieces for climbers at an early stage of their apprenticeship, while the expression may seem formal and a bit dated. Life moves on.

'But the quality of the writing, both in describing climbing action and in evoking landscape across the diversity of Scotland's mountains – on rock or ice, by day and by moonlight, in spring sunshine or in winter blizzard – carry the reader off into a uniquely exalted world of intense mountain experience. All Scottish climbers should own this book, even if it is the only book they own; so should anyone with an interest in the highest quality writing about mountains and mountain landscape.' (2nd February 2002)

Amazon also run 'Listmania' in which customers can create their own lists of top ten or top twenty books in any category or subject they wish. The combined volume of *Mountaineering in Scotland* and *Undiscovered Scotland* consistently figures in these lists – usually in the top half if the subject is books about climbing in Britain, or a bit lower down if the lists also include books about mountaineering in the Alps, Himalayas and other parts of the world.

Similarly, the website, *Outdoors Magic* (www.outdoorsmagic. com) features a list of Top Ten Mountain Books, in which *Mountaineering in Scotland* consistently holds a high place , with the following comment: 'Why's it great? Still perfectly encapsulates the feeling of Scottish winter climbing along with an inspirational love for the hills made all the more poignant by the knowledge that it was written in captivity. Blessed with our advanced front point crampons and reverse-pick axes, all we can do is marvel at the toughness of these men cutting steps laboriously up sheer gullies. For a perfect winter day we suggest climbing a classic Bill Murray route then reading the original ascent description and marvelling at it. For a perfect winter day's reading we just suggest this book. It makes you want to be in Scotland.'

On Murray's death in 1996, a renewed appreciation for *Mountaineering in Scotland* was expressed in the many obituaries which appeared, as exemplified in an extract from the one by Robin Campbell:[20] 'His first book and its sequel *Undiscovered Scotland* (Dent, 1951) are inspirational writings – the *Iliad* and *Odyssey* of Scottish mountain writing ... Murray's books led hundreds of climbers in the fifties on to the crags, told them how to behave when they got there and explained to them why they liked it so much.' (The full text of this obituary is shown in online Appendix I.)

Over the years certain myths have grown up around *Mountaineering in Scotland*. According to the myth the entire book was written in POW camps, from memory and on toilet paper (or scraps of paper, as one account had it); Murray never stopped writing, even in the terrible concentration-camp conditions at Moosberg; and the manuscript was then delivered straight to the publisher. None of this is accurate. Five of the chapters had already been published in the *Scottish Mountaineering Club Journal* before Murray was captured in 1942. Only a part of the first draft was written on toilet paper (the draft confiscated by the Gestapo), and it looks as though the toilet paper was not obtained, as myth would have it, by swapping it for pages from the works of Shakespeare. All of the second draft was written on proper writing-paper provided by the camp authorities. At Moosberg he stopped writing for two months. After completing the final manuscript, Murray had almost two years to rewrite, change and polish it, including a year back in Britain when he had access to his notes and to reference books and maps and was therefore able to check if his memory had been correct concerning events and his many quotes.

This myth, for the most part, is not of Murray's making – although he never went out of his way to deny it – but is the result of reviewers and journalists wanting to believe what would make their copy more compelling, and of publicists with an instinct for what makes a book more buyable. That the story behind *Mountaineering in Scotland* has acquired embellishments is some sort of compliment to the book – it shows that there is something about it that has captured our imaginations and calls to us.

A reviewer of *Undiscovered Scotland* wrote: 'Murray has hitherto confined his writings to describing his activities in Scotland. I hope that he will feel the urge to include some account of his experiences in other parts of the world in his next book.'[21] – a hope which was fulfilled, for Murray's next book was about his first experience of an even greater tract of undiscovered country, the Himalayas.

NOTES

1. Letter as reproduced in *The Evidence of Things Not Seen*, page 334.
2. Murray gave no dates for several of his chapters. Two of these, however, can be placed as pre-war or early war years because he is describing climbs done with Douglas Laidlaw who was killed during the war. They can be identified by the climbs he listed for his SMC application.
3. Unpublished notes in the Tom Weir Collection, National Library of Scotland, Edinburgh.
4. Diadem Books Limited, established in 1978 by Ken Vickers and Ken Wilson, was sold to Hodder and Stoughton in 1989 and was run from within the Hodder group with Wilson as publisher. Following the Hodder/Headline merger, Diadem publishing ended in 1993. Wilson left the company and set up Bâton Wicks to publish new titles and steadily re-acquire the Diadem list. Both Diadem and Bâton Wicks titles predominately concern hill-walking, mountaineering and rock-climbing.
5. Ted Zenthon was a member of the London JMCS. He met Murray on several occasions when he came to Scotland to climb. He was a trained draughtsman and had previously illustrated E.C. Pyatt's *Sandstone Climbs in S E England*. Robert Anderson died in 2010, aged 101. He occasionally climbed with Murray and is mentioned in *Undiscovered Scotland*, page 58. (Not to be confused with Sheridan Anderson who created the cartoons for *Mirrors in the Cliffs*.)
6. On the website 'The Glencoe Mountaineer'.
7. Telephone conversation with me, May 2010.
8. Tom Patey (1932–1970), was a doctor by profession and one of Scotland's top climbers in the 1960s, achieving outstanding successes in Scotland, the Alps and the Himalayas. He is best known to the general public for his part in the televised ascent of the Old Man of Hoy. He was much in demand as a singer at gatherings of climbers. His verses, including this ballad, can be found in his book, *One Man's Mountains* (1971).
9. Des Rubens later became President of the Scottish Mountaineering Club.
10. Winner of the W.H. Murray Literary Prize, 2000. This annual prize is run by the Scottish Mountaineering Club Journal and was started in 1998.
11. Jim Perrin was one of Britain's top climbers in the 60s and 70s and is one of Britain's most brilliant living essayists on travel and climbing topics. Twice winner of the Boardman Tasker Prize, he is the author of *Menlove*, (1985), a biography of Menlove Edwards. Amongst his other books are *On and Off the Rocks* (1986), *Yes, To Dance* (1990), *Travels with a Flea* (2003), *The Climbing Essays* (2007).
12. 'The Ice Climbers' in *Climber and Rambler* magazine, Oct. 1982.
13. *Alpine Journal*, 1983.
14. Robert Macfarlane is the author of *Mountains of the Mind* (2003; winner of the Guardian First Book Award and the Somerset Maugham Award), *The Wild Places* (2007) and *The Old Ways* (2012). Macfarlane is seen as the inheritor of a tradition of nature writing which includes John Muir, Richard Jefferies and William Cobbett, as well as contemporary figures such as John McPhee, Barry Lopez and Roger Deakin. He is generally grouped with a number of recent

British writers who have provoked a new critical and popular interest in writing about landscape.

15. *The Wild Places*, page 71.

16. Nan Shepherd (1893–1981) was a Scottish novelist and poet. Her modernist novels portray the restricted and often tragic lives of women in contemporary Scotland. She was a keen hill-walker and her poetry expresses her love for the mountainous Grampian landscape. In his article, Macfarlane was writing about her non-fiction book, *The Living Mountain* (written in the 1940s about the Grampians, but not published until 1977).

17. *The Guardian*, 30th August 2008.

18. Colin Wells is the author of *A Brief History of British Mountaineering* (2001) and *Who's Who in British Climbing* (2007).

19. These extracts are part of an online review, 2002, of Murray's last book, *The Evidence of Things Not Seen*.

20. Robin Campbell is the archivist for the SMC. The obituary he wrote for Murray appeared in The Alpine Journal, 1997.

21. R.M.P. Hartog, *Climbers' Club Journal*, 1951.

CHAPTER SEVENTEEN

ANATOMY OF THE SUBLIME

In previous chapters we have looked at Murray's passion for mountains, at his philosophical and mystical beliefs, and at the intensely creative crucible of his POW years, all of which have a bearing on the character and content of *Mountaineering in Scotland*. Because his book is written in a personal way, Murray's personality and character are relevant, too, and these include his values, beliefs, attitudes and sense of humour. Therefore, everything that shaped these, that is to say the whole of Murray's life up to that point, has relevance to the kind of book that *Mountaineering in Scotland* turned out to be. There are, however, specific reasons why it is such a special and well-loved book.

Mountaineering in Scotland was the first book ever to be written purely about Scottish mountaineering. The book was an eye-opener to many mountaineers of the day, particularly the accounts in it of winter climbing. By describing his own joy in mountaineering in a variety of situations, Murray provides one of the most comprehensive accounts ever written of why people climb. He shows us, through his own personal responses, how mountains satisfy our physical, emotional, social, psychological and spiritual needs.

Online Appendix D, 'Mountains and Mysticism', looks at how the act of climbing, the physical and mental effort and the release of tension between pitches or at the finish, induces receptive states of mind, intense feelings and heightened perceptions. In no small measure, Murray's openness to these states of mind and his ability to articulate them has warranted the use of the word 'sublime' by several reviewers and contributed to making *Mountaineering in Scotland* a classic which has stood the test of time.

Murray said that he wanted to write *Mountaineering in Scotland* free of the twin 'humbugs' of overstating the dangers and hardships, and of understating them. The latter, seen as a virtue by some, as showing a becoming modesty and a manly stiff upper lip, was the fashion for mountain writing in the 1930s. Murray thought this made for dull writing and wanted to throw off these constraints. He had to solve the problem facing all adventure writers who write in the first person – how to thrill their readers and give them the full flavour of the drama and the danger without seeming to boast or be trying to grab too much sympathy and glory.

Murray successfully walks the tightrope, using a mixture of strategies. Sometimes he employs cool but undramatised assessments of the dangers. At other times he uses understatement, not in a spirit of false modesty, but with a sense of irony, humour or parody. Here he is in typical trademark mode: 'The last few airy feet, where one trusts to edge-nails on a shelving ledge, freshened us not a little.'

Whenever possible he ensures that others, rather than himself, take the credit for the difficulties overcome. Occasionally he brings out rather quaint, old-fashioned phraseology, usually to avoid describing some dangerous situation in a way that, to him, would seem too dramatic and breathlessly excited: 'I felt a pardonable anxiety to eschew any step too palpably irreversible,' or, 'This was an error of judgment for which I met condign reward.'

In order not to make himself the centre of attention when any heroics were afoot, he might resort to 'one' instead of 'I'.

A further reason for the success of *Mountaineering in Scotland* is that Murray often gives his adventures an appealingly romantic slant as if he were a knight of old, jousting with crag and cliff, entering the lists for a tournament on ice,[1] or questing for the Holy Grail. When presenting the TV programme, *The Edge*, Cameron McNeish commented, 'Mountaineering was still a romantic tale and Bill Murray its true story-teller.'

At the front of *Mountaineering in Scotland* Murray chose to quote four stanzas of Geoffrey Winthrop Young's poem, 'Knight Errantry'.[2] The poem speaks of a 'magical land of hills', of the 'perils of knightly zest', and of 'vigil in dreamlit cave' and 'gleams of the vision that Merlin gave'. In his letter to Geoffrey Winthrop Young requesting permission to use this poem,[3] Murray tells him that these lines are 'most appropriate to the text of the book.'[4]

This kind of escape was what the public wanted in austere post-war

Britain, with its fuel and food shortages, grey utility clothes and grey faces. Murray transported them to a magical realm above the clouds where the sun shone and the stars glittered. Perhaps for different reasons, this is still a place to which many of us are happy to be carried on the wings of Murray's words. Murray's romanticism was that of a young man, as was the spirit of life and energy which imbues his accounts of his adventures.

As we saw in Chapter Fifteen, 'Genesis of a Mountain Classic', his friend J.H.B. Bell tried to persuade him to delay publication. In the same letter referred to in that chapter, written 40 years after the publication of *Mountaineering in Scotland*, Murray asks himself, 'what if I had held back?: The book would be very different, and also much better written. I am appalled now when I re-read what I wrote then – the clichés ("avoid like the plague" etc. etc.), the excessive quotes from other people's works when I should have written what I felt myself in my own words, the loose statements, set down without proper reflection, the too formal phrasing of thoughts – a host of such errors would now have been swept away. In fact, I itch to rewrite the book, except that it's not worth it. BUT, if I did this, or had waited as Bell advised until my old age, I am sure the life would have gone out of the book. Inexperience always produces errors, lots of them. Likewise, it doesn't put a stopper on open expression of real feelings and ideas.'

Admirers of this classic, I feel sure, will be glad that Murray did not delay publication and did not rewrite it. The passage quoted above does, however, demonstrate Murray's perfectionism. Despite all the polishing, editing and redrafting, he is still not satisfied. He was a true craftsman – an aspect of his writing which is discussed in Chapter Twenty-Nine.

Another appealing facet of *Mountaineering in Scotland* is that it is both serious and humorous. It is a book which treats its readers with respect, as intelligent beings. It would be hard to find many other mountaineering books of that period which contain passages about Beauty, Truth, immortality, wisdom, humility and peace, and quote from the likes of Buddha, Goethe and Plato, and even have them as items in the index. Yet, at the same time, there are veins of irony and dry, sardonic humour running through it and an entertaining turn of phrase.

Sometimes he feigns a heartless self-interest as when an enormous plate of snow-crust is dislodged and falls on top of MacAlpine's head: 'MacAlpine gave a hollow grunt, at which the hairs of our balaclava helmets rose on end, for he carried the rum (for my ankle) and seemed about to depart with it hutwards by the shortest route.' (Page 107)

Or he might indulge in a tongue-in-cheek exaggeration as when ascribing to 'Mummery's Blood' miraculous properties: 'This mountain elixir consists of equal parts of navy rum and Bovril, served boiling hot. Its effect on both mind and body is nourishing, warming, strengthening; it lowers angles, shortens distances, and improves the weather.' (Page 163)

That *Mountaineering in Scotland* can attract readers who have no prior interest or knowledge of mountaineering is due not only to his ability to evoke the power of mountain landscape but also to this humour and the entertaining little cameos and pen portraits of his friends.

Two things, above all others, make *Mountaineering in Scotland* an outstanding book. First and foremost is the quality of the writing. This aspect of the book merits a chapter to itself and is discussed in Chapter Twenty-Nine. Secondly, it was unusual for its time, and indeed, unusual for any period, although less so now, in that it contains a spiritual and mystical dimension.

Quite early on in the book he states: 'Until we are aware in the midst of our climbing that mountains are but the sign of things higher, we may be climbers, but we have not begun to understand mountains, or mountaineers.' (Page 29)

At one level, then, *Mountaineering in Scotland* may be an account of his adventures in the Scottish mountains, but at another level it is the story of his search for these 'things higher', for that 'last reality underlying mountain beauty', which he saw as the same thing as ultimate Truth, or God. It is the story of his quest to find unity and harmony with these absolutes. 'On mountains it is that spiritual part that we unconsciously develop. When we fail in that all other success is empty.' (Page 138) In several of his chapters the climax of the essay is not overcoming the crux of a hard climb, completing a route, or reaching the summit, but achieving, however fleetingly, a sense of oneness with nature, the mountains and ultimate Reality.

In addition to the fact that Murray had talent in abundance, passion for his subject and the craftsmanship and determination to go with it, there were exceptional circumstances which all came together to produce an exceptional book. The circumstances in which the book was written meant that, for the majority of the essays or chapters, there was a fairly lengthy gap between the actual event and Murray writing about it in his prison camp.

Robert Louis Stevenson, who strongly influenced Murray's writing as we shall see in a later chapter, would have approved of this:

> 'I allow a considerable lapse of time to intervene between any of my little journeyings and the attempt to chronicle them. I cannot describe a thing that is before me at the moment, or that has been before me only a little while before; I must allow my recollections to get thoroughly strained free from all the chaff till nothing be except the pure gold; allow my memory to choose out what is truly memorable by a process of natural selection; and I piously believe that in this way I ensure the Survival of the Fittest.'[5]

The war made time for Murray's pre-war mountaineering experiences to be internalised or 'cooked in the subconscious' instead of being committed to paper in a raw state. It allowed the pure gold to emerge.

Murray was forced to write his book without access to his diaries and the notes he kept about his climbs. As he says himself: 'I came in the end to realise that diaries are a trap that I'd been lucky to escape. Too many expedition books, and other exploratory tales, stay dull because their author blindly copies from diaries – a temptation all too easy to fall into when time is short and distractions many. To bring a tale alive, he has to relive it in his own mind, which means to recreate.'[6]

These same circumstances, with Murray divorced from his normal life and far from his beloved Scottish mountains, contributed to the timeless quality of a book in which the chapters are not in chronological order and the years and seasons occur in happy disorder.[7]

Then there was the loss of his original, nearly completed, manuscript to the Gestapo. It seemed like a disaster at the time, but turned out to be a blessing in disguise. Not only did it allow Murray to start again with a different aim in mind, but, in the effort to recall what he had previously written, there was a further process of distillation and purification. Other authors, who have lost all or large chunks of their work, have said they were certain their second version was better, sharper and more exactly as they wanted it to be than the original had been. Having to recreate his memories without benefit of diaries had made Murray's tales come alive, and now they were doubly subjected to this creative process.

Another factor, another special circumstance, which may well have contributed to the quality of *Mountaineering in Scotland* was the enforced abstention from writing, for over two months, while at Moosberg. Overcrowding and the appalling conditions stopped all work on his book. There can be no doubt, though, that it was going on inside his head, as if in a pressure-cooker, building up in intensity, waiting to burst afresh onto paper.

The awfulness of his surroundings which made Murray escape into his own mind and memories and the big blocks of time available to him brought an intensity and focus to his writing which allowed him to achieve a state of flow – the state achieved in sporting and creative activities when a person is totally absorbed in what they are doing and everything seems to flow naturally.

In Chapter Thirteen of this biography the relationship between meditation and being 'in the flow' was discussed. Read again the same paragraph with Murray's writing of *Mountaineering in Scotland* in mind:

'Mihaly Csikszentmihalya, in his work *Flow: The Psychology of Optimal Expression* (New York, 1990), says there is a strong connection between being in the flow while engaged in creative activity and meditation. His research has found that people who experience flow while being creative find it enhances their ability to achieve deep meditation; and people who have found a path to deep meditation also find that they experience flow more regularly than otherwise.

'There can be no doubt from the intensity of Murray's writing in *Mountaineering in Scotland* that, for long periods at a time, Murray was in the flow while he worked on the book in captivity; and there can be no doubt that his finding of mysticism and the meditation that accompanied it was an equally intense experience for him. These two factors working together, intensifying and enhancing each other, go a long way to accounting for the brilliance of Murray's classic of mountain literature and the strength and depth of his mysticism.'

The next chapter considers the literary influences upon Murray, but nobody could mistake a passage from one of Murray's books for one written by anyone else. His style is unique and distinctive and has as much to do with the expression of his own personality as it has with the influence of others. Murray's style has various 'trademarks', such as the use of the word 'high' to mean 'great', quaint phrasing and an unusual word order, the employment of double negatives; and his colourful similes: 'I went at it [cutting steps in the hard snow] like a buccaneer digging pieces of eight.' Or Donaldson, about to embark on a difficult section of the climb, who 'remained as unperturbed as an aristocrat on the scaffold'. Writing of the midges at their campsite, he says, 'Almost every night witnessed scenes of disorder and sounds of torment, dire enough to pour balm on the soul of a Torquemada.'[8]

Perhaps a chapter which examines what goes into the creation of a book as sublime, quirky and distinctive as Murray's should give more examples of it. However, almost every chapter in this biography quotes from his writing. Although this is done to illustrate points other than have been made here, nonetheless, they serve, as would almost any passage, to demonstrate the quality of his writing.

NOTES

1. 'Tournament on Ice' is the title of Chapter XII in *Undiscovered Scotland*.
2. *Collected Poems of Geoffrey Winthrop Young*, London,1936. The poem consists of 10 stanzas, of which Murray quotes stanzas 7, 8, 9 & 10.
3. This letter is in the Appendices to *The Evidence of Things Not Seen*.
4. Murray's friend, B.H. Humble, had a book, *On Scottish Hills*, published the previous year (1946) which contained a Foreword by Geoffrey Winthrop Young. Possibly this encouraged Murray to approach Young about using his poem.
5. In the travel essay, 'From Cockermouth to Keswick', 1871.
6. *The Evidence of Things Not Seen,* page 88.
7. This is a point Michael Cocker makes in his Introduction to his Chronology of Murray's Scottish climbs (see online Appendix K).
8. Torquemada was a prominent member of the Spanish Inquisition in the 15th century, notorious for his use of torture.

CHAPTER EIGHTEEN

FROM COLERIDGE TO CHANGABANG

No anatomy of a book would be complete without looking at the literary influences on its author and it is upon this aspect that this chapter focuses.

In considering these influences on *Mountaineering in Scotland* there is no attempt to deal with them in order of importance. Murray himself probably could not have said who or what influenced him most, not only because literary influence is a complex web, but also because, like all good writers, he internalised, reinterpreted and subconsciously synthesised, so that what emerged was very much his own creation. The literary influences on Murray are, therefore, treated in a roughly historical order.

Twenty per cent of all the quotes in *Mountaineering in Scotland* are drawn from writers associated with the Romantic Movement; and a similar percentage from Victorian writers. To quote somebody does not necessarily mean your main content, approach, style or techniques are influenced by them, but it does give a rough guide to what Murray had read and absorbed.

The Romantic Movement in literature was at its height in the first half of the 19th century. It was a reaction against the rationalism of science and increasing industrialisation. It therefore emphasised emotion, passion and the natural world. The two Romantics whose influence upon Murray is the most obvious are William Wordsworth and Samuel Taylor Coleridge. The essayist, William Hazlitt, although not a Romantic, was a friend of these two poets and took part in their philosophical discussions. His influence, too, can be traced in Murray's writing.

In the early years of Coleridge's friendship with Wordsworth, despite being two years younger than the latter, it was he who was the driving force. His walks in the Quantocks in the English West

Country stirred deep feelings and elicited descriptions of views over the sea and of sunsets. In a letter to his brother he declared: 'I love fields and woods and mountains with almost a visionary fondness.'[1] He explored the effect of nature on the imagination and how nature could help him transcend himself. He believed that nature represented a physical presence of God's word. In his poem 'The Lime-Tree Bower' he develops the theme of unity between the human and the divine in nature, a theme very much in tune with Murray who frequently expresses a feeling of oneness with the mountains. Coleridge spent some time in Germany and was regarded as the most influential English interpreter of German Romanticism of his generation. He was also strongly influenced by the empirical philosopher, David Hartley,[2] and even called his son Hartley. If Murray took on board some of Hartley's teachings, it is likely to have been indirectly through the English Romantics, especially Coleridge.

According to Coleridge's biographer, Richard Holmes,[3] philosophy, not poetry, was Coleridge's main concern. Holmes connects the storm-tossed journey and the trials of the Ancient Mariner with Coleridge's spiritual voyage and sees both the Mariner and Coleridge as seeking to express a mystical quality at the heart of experience.

Holmes states (page 38): 'The overall character of the *Biographia* is that of a spiritual autobiography: the voyage and trial of a writer seeking for truth, beauty and salvation.' This could also be seen as a neat summary of what *Mountaineering in Scotland*, at one level, is about. Murray must have wondered whether such a book should be attempted and would have been encouraged by Coleridge's example. Shelley described Coleridge as a hooded eagle 'who sits obscure in the exceeding lustre and the pure intense irradiation of the mind'[4] – a description which would have fitted Murray and is not unlike Hamish MacInnes' view of him as 'a frugal, contemplative eagle'.[5]

Two of Wordsworth's works, in particular, demonstrate the affinity between him and Murray – his poem 'Tintern Abbey' (1798) and his 'Preface to the Lyrical Ballads'.[6] In the opening stanza of the first of these works Wordsworth and Murray have very similar responses to a mountain scene:

'.......................... Once again
Do I behold these steep and lofty cliffs,
That on a wild secluded scene impress
Thoughts of more deep seclusion; and connect
The landscape with the quiet of the sky.

In the second stanza he exactly reflects Murray's feelings, when in captivity, about the mountains he is missing so much (or Murray reflects his):

'These beauteous forms,
Through a long absence, have not been to me
As is a landscape to a blind man's eye:
But oft, in lonely rooms, and 'mid the din
Of towns and cities, I have owed to them
In hours of weariness, sensations sweet.

Wordsworth goes on to speak in this poem of the harmony to be found in all things, and then come these lines, which Murray, on various mountain tops, overawed by the magnificence around him, echoes again and again:

'And I have felt
A presence that disturbs me with the joy
Of elevated thoughts: a sense sublime
Of something far more deeply interfuse,
Whose dwelling is the light of setting suns,
And the round ocean and the living air,
And the blue sky, and in the mind of man;
A motion and a spirit, that impels
All thinking things, all objects of all thought,
And rolls through all things ...'

Jim Perrin, in 'The Ice Climbers',[7] his masterly analysis of Scottish mountain writers, refers to 'a sense of dialogue' between Murray and Wordsworth's Preface to the *Lyrical Ballads*. There are passages in this Preface which state the need for long and deep thought, and the need for regular, disciplined habits when it comes to meditation and the cultivation of an appreciation for beauty. 'It has therefore appeared to me that to endeavour to produce or enlarge this capability [the perception of beauty] is one of the best services in which, at any period, a Writer can be engaged.'

Here is Murray: 'May it not be possible, by some practical method to help one's mind to grow in awareness of beauty, to develop that faculty of perception which we frustrate and stunt if we do not exercise? The answer is that growth may be given to the spiritual faculty as simply as growth and health are given to the body.'[8]

It was in the Preface that Wordsworth put forward the idea that poetry takes its origin from 'emotion recollected in tranquillity,' which just about describes what *Mountaineering in Scotland* is – a reliving, a recreation of intense emotions during a time of enforced leisure. Murray may have absorbed some of the vocabulary of the Romantics, but more importantly it was their philosophy, their approach route to beauty, their values and attitudes which he found attractive and which reinforced what he was already thinking and feeling.

To quote Perrin again (discussing *Mountaineering in Scotland* and *Undiscovered Scotland*): 'The philosophy which underpins the work may be borrowed, but it is nonetheless deeply felt and informed by the fine qualities of the author's mind. And he synthesizes it majestically in these two books of linked essays.'[9]

Hazlitt (1778–1830) was seventeen when he first met Coleridge, who was six years his senior. 'The light of his genius shone into my soul, like the sun's rays glittering in the puddles of the road,' Hazlitt wrote of him.[10] Wordsworth and the essayist, Charles Lamb, were on the curriculum of every respectable British school in the 1930s, and it may well be that, in his studies of these writers, Murray was led to Hazlitt. He certainly encountered him later when a book of his essays was sent to him while he was in prison camp.[11] The chapters in *Mountaineering in Scotland* and *Undiscovered Scotland* are sometimes referred to as essays. This proximity to the essay form, as employed by Murray, is due, to a large extent, to his use of Hazlitt's essays as a model.

The essay takes a huge variety of forms and any precise definition is problematic. One suggested definition is: 'Any brief composition in prose that undertakes to discuss a matter, express a point of view, or persuade us to accept a thesis on any subject whatever.' There are certain recurring features which might be regarded as helping to recognise this elusive genre. The essay often addresses personal and particular concerns; it is exploratory in nature; its persuasiveness is based on its distinctive style; at the heart of the essay is the voice of the individual.

All these criteria would apply to any of Murray's chapters, which clearly go beyond being solely an account of an adventure. They are an expression of his burning desire to share with us the beauty and excitement of the mountains and the friendships forged there; they explore the many reasons why he is drawn to the mountains and seek to understand the nature of Truth and Beauty and the path to achieving oneness with the ultimate Reality; and, yes, the style is distinctive and we would not mistake his words for anyone else's.

Most essays can be put into one of two categories – formal, or informal. Murray's essays would fall into the latter category, assuming a tone of intimacy with his readers, and writing in a self-revelatory, sometimes whimsical, way. Hazlitt was a master of both forms and Murray his willing pupil. Hazlitt's essays are light, but always floating on a platform of profound philosophical understanding. They never begin with any 'throat clearing', but pitch right into the argument or action. Hazlitt's own term, 'gusto', best captures his approach to his essays and the way he musters language and imagery to catch things difficult-to-describe with verve and energy, employing, as he does so, a remarkable range of literary allusions and quotations. His essays are the voice of a man passionately involved with his subject. Remove the name of Hazlitt from this paragraph and replace it with that of the author of *Mountaineering in Scotland*, and it would be an accurate description of Murray the essayist.

In the main, the writers of the Romantic Movement responded to what they saw from the valleys and had little direct experience of what lay above the tree line. It was not until Victorian times and the 'golden age' of mountaineering that any true mountain literature emerged. Victorian literature was mostly the product of middle and upper class authors. Words typically used to describe the writing of this period would be: energetic, erudite, expansive, descriptive. Some of this fits Murray, but only if it carries no hidden meaning such as verbose or over-long, for one of the hallmarks of Murray's writing is economy. Every word is weighed in the balance and has to justify its presence on the page. Of the Victorian mountaineer-writers, Murray specifically mentions Mummery,[12] Whymper[13] and Leslie Stephen.[14]

In a speech entitled 'Writing about Climbing and Landscape' Murray said: 'Most of us who are given to writing can sometimes come away with a sentence or two that is just right. A few can get a whole paragraph, or even a scatter of paragraphs through a book-length work. Men who can do that rank high. For me, Mummery could sometimes do it. He first brought me to see that climbers and writers (in fact most humans) have this in common, that we are not rational beings ... we are usually moved to act less by logic than feeling. This stands out clear in the best mountain writing.'[15]

One such passage, for example, might have been Mummery's appreciation of 'the great brown slabs bending over into immeasurable space, the lines and curves of the wind-moulded cornice, the delicate undulations of the fissured snow ...'[16]

There are echoes of Mummery to be found in *Mountaineering in Scotland*. This is not to suggest, in any way, that plagiarism is being employed here. It has been suggested, however, that certain echoes of other writers might be a deliberate act of homage. It seems more likely, though, to be a matter of various passages making a deep impression and becoming internalised and part of him.

For example, here is Mummery: 'No feeling can be more glorious than advancing to attack some gaunt precipitous wall with "comrades staunch as the founders of our race." Nothing is more exhilarating than to know that the fingers of one's hand can still be trusted with the life of a party ... quite impossible to look down the tremendous precipices of the Little Dru without feeling in each individual nerve the utter disintegration of everything human which a fall must involve.'[17]

And here is Murray: 'When a leader turns down from the last impossible rocks and hears the rising wind buffet on white-veiled cliffs, fast fading into night, and on looking down, watches his party again and again enveloped in clouds of drift-snow, torn from storm-swept ridges, he may feel, as I have, an instant's suspicion that the prospect is somewhat grim for hope. An instant later his rope reminds him that he is tied to men of high heart, that whatever the outcome, they, at least, will not falter.'[18]

From Whymper, in particular, Murray would have learned the value of including vivid pen portraits of his climbing companions

and of writing, not only of the triumphs, but also of the disappoint-
ments, frustrations and failures. In all three – Mummery, Whymper
and Leslie Stephen he would have noted and appreciated the wry
humour, the readiness to give praise and credit where it was due, and
the total lack of conceit or boastfulness, but rather a modesty which
under-played the danger, yet managed to convey the adventure and
the thrill of it. All three wrote with awe, respect and humility.

Robert H. Bates in his *Mystery, Beauty and Danger*[19] is of the opinion that: 'Leslie Stephen's essays still are among the finest examples
of mountain literature.' It was he, Bates says, who did more than
any other writer of that period to persuade a largely disapproving
Victorian public that mountaineering was not some unjustifiably
dangerous and useless pursuit which should only be done, if at all, for
scientific reasons, but something from which was to be gained true
joy and a renewal of the spirit. It was a message which was lost from
sight when later authors wrote earnestly only of fact and practicalities. Murray's hymn of praise, with Leslie Stephen as a guiding light,
was instrumental in raising it once more into prominence.

It is possible that the mountain writer, Conway,[20] was also an
influence on Murray. Robert Aitken noticed an unconscious parallel between Murray's description of the Lost Valley in Glencoe in
Mountaineering in Scotland (page 112) and Conway's of the Glacier
de la Plaine Morte in the Western Oberland in *The Alps from End to
End* (page 153). When Aitken asked Murray about this, he readily
agreed that the likeness was there. Although there had been no copy
of Conway's book at the Chieti or Mahrisch Trubau prison camps,
Murray knew he had read it before the war and thought the passage
must have lodged in his mind and that the general tenor of it had
subsequently popped out at the appropriate moment.

In his speech about writing, climbing and landscape, Murray was
addressing the British Mountaineering Council and spoke only about
British writers who were also mountaineers. However, at another time,
he did mention[21] that he had studied and been influenced by the essays
of Robert Louis Stevenson.[22] This being the case, he would have studied Stevenson's *Essays in the Art of Writing*. Murray employs many
of the techniques advocated by Stevenson. Chapter Twenty-Nine, 'A
Supreme Craftsman at Work', looks at some examples of this.

Stevenson, in this essay, says that each phrase of each sentence should 'gratify the sensual ear'. A good test of whether this is happening is to read aloud the piece of prose in question. Anyone who has read any part of *Mountaineering in Scotland* aloud will know that its rhythms and pleasing clusters of sounds roll off the tongue, giving to the physical act of reading it, as well as to listening to it, immense gratification. Stevenson, too, admired and emulated Hazlitt. He described Hazlitt's essay *On Going a Journey* as 'so good that there ought to be a tax levied on all who have not read it'.[23]

One more Victorian who possibly influenced Murray, and who was himself indebted to the Romantic Movement, was the famous art critic, John Ruskin (1819–1900). In an excellent article, written to mark the reissue of the combined volume of *Mountaineering in Scotland* and *Undiscovered Scotland,* Gordon Smith says: 'That he [Murray] had read Ruskin is clear, given that he quotes him briefly on page 54 of *Mountaineering in Scotland.* What is not clear, but nevertheless is an interesting subject for speculation, is whether he had read Ruskin's *Modern Painters,* and in particular the chapter *Of the Open Sky.* In this essay Ruskin argues that the sky has an immense importance in art, and that the beauties of sunrise and sunset have moral significance, offering us divine messages.'[24]

Smith goes on to say that Murray's work is notable for its brilliant descriptions of the sky and that some are suggestive of the famous painter, J.M.W. Turner, whom Ruskin regarded as the absolute master of skyscapes. To Ruskin, Truth and Beauty were inseparable, a view very much in line with Murray's own beliefs. In his three-volume *Modern Painters* (Volume 1 was published in 1843), Ruskin was one of the first to apply aesthetics to landscape. He wrote more than 50 pieces about the main features of the landscape and the sky, analysing what made them pleasing to the eye and discussing criteria by which to judge their beauty.

When Murray did the same in *Highland Landscape* (1962), he may well have referred to Ruskin. Like Wordsworth and other Romantics, Ruskin believed that God was present in nature. Perceiving beauty in nature, he held, led one closer to goodness and to the universal moral laws. This is not an exact fit with what Murray believed, but it is close. Amongst the many influences on Murray's mysticism and philosophy as expressed in his books (and as discussed in Chapter Thirteen), might possibly be added the name of John Ruskin.

Some 37 years after completing *Mountaineering in Scotland*, Murray posed the question, 'If I were once again a beginner, who would I chose today as my writing and climbing paragons?' And he answered it by saying: 'I have no hesitation. They are Peter Boardman and Joe Tasker.[25] They do really say directly and simply what mountains mean to them ... Pete and Joe re-lived their climbs in the writing. They recreated them, and the mountains too – more still, they brought each other intensely alive ... they kept balance between the two worlds, the subjective and the objective, and made each real, the one between the lines, the other in plain words.'[26]

Others have praised these two books for their gripping pace, for being self-effacing and not too technical, for their honesty, for their personal insights and for glimpses into the inner workings of ordinary human beings attempting extraordinary feats and for capturing companions with clarity and sensitivity. These are all qualities Murray would have appreciated since they are recognisable in his own writing. Murray must have been pleased that Boardman quotes or refers to him in his book on five occasions.

Surprisingly, Murray did not acclaim Bill Tilman's books in the same way.[27] Although he mentions him as amongst the best twentieth century mountain writers, Murray did not rate him as highly as Boardman or Tasker – unlike Jim Perrin who thinks Tilman's *Ascent of Nanda Devi* is probably the finest expedition book ever written; or Jan Morris who said his *Everest 1938* was the best of all the Everest books.

The literary influences on Murray were many and varied. These writings he absorbed and made his own, suffusing them with his own magic.

NOTES

1. *Collected Letters of Samuel Taylor Coleridge*, edited E.L. Griggs, 1956.
2. I am indebted to Jim Perrin for pointing this out to me. Empiricism is a theory which asserts that knowledge comes primarily from sensory experience (in contrast to rationalism, for example). Hartley (1705–57) believed in the biblical promise that we would all eventually become partakers of the Divine Nature.
3. *Coleridge*, Richard Holmes, 1982.
4. From the poem 'Letter to Maria Gisborne' (1820), published in *Posthumous Poems*, 1824.
5. In his Foreword to *The Evidence of Things Not Seen*.

6. *Lyrical Ballads*, a collection of poems by Wordsworth and Coleridge, was first published in 1798. For the second edition in 1800, Wordsworth wrote a Preface, explaining his approach to poetry.

7. 'The Ice Climbers' by Jim Perrin in *Climber and Rambler* magazine, Oct. 1982.

8. 'The Approach Route to Beauty,' SMCJ, 1948.

9. It should be borne in mind that Perrin's comment, perceptive though it is, was written twenty years before the publication of *The Evidence of Things Not Seen* in which Murray revealed, for the first time, the origin of his philosophy and his mysticism, not all of which was 'borrowed' from Wordsworth and the Romantics.

10. In his essay, 'My First Acquaintance with Poets', first published in *The Liberal*, 1823.

11. Murray told Jim Perrin this on one of the occasions when the latter visited him at his home.

12. Albert Frederick Mummery (1855–1895), political economist and mountaineer. With several first Alpine ascents to his name, he was one of the best-known mountaineers of his generation. He was killed in an avalanche on Nanga Parbat in the Himalayas. His book, *My Climbs in the Alps and Caucasus* (1895) is one of the classics of mountaineering literature.

13. Edward Whymper (1840–1911) was an illustrator, mountaineer and explorer (Greenland, South America, Canadian Rockies), best known for his first ascent of the Matterhorn in 1865 and the tragic accident which happened on the descent. Author of *Scrambles Amongst the Alps* (1865) and *Travels Amongst the Great Alps of the Equator* (1892).

14. Sir Leslie Stephen (1832–1904), Eton and Cambridge University. He was ordained but renounced his faith, probably influenced by the current debate concerning Darwin and his *Origin of Species*. He was the father of Virginia Woolf. His best known books are *The Playground of Europe* (1871) and *An Agnostic's Apology* (1893).

    As editor of *Cornhill* magazine, Stephen was influential in encouraging Robert Louis Stevenson, who, in his turn, influenced Murray.

15. A speech given in 1984 to the British Mountaineering Council. This speech is also reproduced in an Appendix to *The Evidence of Things Not Seen*. In this speech, Murray also names climber writers of a later period, but gives no indication of the extent of their influence on him – Geoffrey Winthrop Young, Frank Smythe, Eric Shipton, Bill Tilman and Tom Longstaff. From what he says elsewhere it would seem that it is their attitudes and values he has taken on board, rather than their writing style.

16. *My Climbs in the Alps and Caucasus*, page 360.

17. *Ibid*, page 333–334.

18. *Mountaineering in Scotland*, page 237–238.

19. *Mystery, Beauty and Danger: the Literature of the Mountains and Mountain Climbing Published in English before 1946*, Robert H. Bates, 2000. The period considered by this book does not cover Murray's classic, published in 1947.

20. Sir Martin Conway, later Lord Conway (1856–1937), was Professor of Art at University College, Liverpool, and later became Slade Professor of Fine Art at Cambridge University. His two best known mountaineering books are *Climbing*

and Exploration in the Karakoram Himalaya (1894) and *The Alps from End to End (1895)*.

21. In a conversation with Robert Aitken.

22. Robert Louis Stevenson (1850–1894), essayist, short story writer, travel writer, novelist. Best known, amongst his many books, are: *Travels with a Donkey in the Cevennes* (1879), *Treasure Island* (1883), *Dr Jekyll and Mr Hyde* (1886), *Kidnapped* (1886).

23. In 'Walking Tours', originally published in *Cornhill Magazine*, 1876.

24. 'Sron na Ciche without cliché', on the *The Angry Corrie* website, Jan. 1998.

25. Peter Boardman (1950–82), was a British Alpine and Himalayan climber. In 1976 he joined forces with Joe Tasker, another top climber of that period, to make the first ascent of the West Wall of Changabang, then regarded as the hardest climb in the Himalayas. His book about this ascent, *The Shining Mountain* (1978) is one of the great works of mountain literature. Joe Tasker (1948–82) wrote his own superb account of this ascent – *Savage Arena* (1981). They died together on the North-East Ridge of Everest in 1982. The Boardman Tasker Prize for Mountain Literature was founded in memory of these two climbers and writers. Murray was one of the judges for this prize in 1985, along with Sir Jack Longland and Al Alvarez. The prize that year went to Jim Perrin for *Menlove,* a biography of the climber Menlove Edwards.

26. See note 15.

27. Harold William Tilman CBE, DSO, MC and Bar (1898–1977), English climber and explorer, renowned for his Himalayan climbs, including two expeditions to Everest, and for his epic sailing trips in Patagonia and beyond. He and Shipton were once both coffee growers in East Africa and they climbed together there. During World War II he was dropped behind enemy lines to fight with Albanian and Italian partisans. Author of over 20 books.

CHAPTER NINETEEN

I NEED CURB MY DREAMS NO LONGER

In an article for *Mountain Craft*, Murray stated that all the pleasures of mountaineering could be enjoyed to the full in this country, with the exception of exploration of unknown country. 'Exploration has always been for me the foremost motive in rock snow and ice climbing. But keenest enjoyment needs an unmapped range.'[1]

That Murray's thoughts had been on the Himalayas and its vast tracts of unmapped country is shown by his letter to Douglas Scott, dated June 1945. Scott was in India at the time, still in the army, and Murray ends his letter with the words: 'I do hope you manage to get into the Himalayas. How about a small expedition there after the war?[2]

Douglas Scott did manage to get into the Himalayas briefly. On his own he reached the fringes of the Garhwal region – a region which has been described as the most beautiful mountain country in the world. What he saw filled him with a burning desire to return.

'Perhaps you are wondering,' Scott said, 'how it came about that a party of unknown climbers set off for Himalaya in 1950. It was very simple. A classic example of pure chance, or as Bill would have said, Providence. All because, being posted to India during the war, in 1945 I was able to get two weeks leave in Garhwal, in the Indian Himalaya. From my tent I gazed in awe at the shining peak of Nanda Ghunti. After demob I thought of little else but how to get back. By 1950 I had a plan and with it managed to persuade two old climbing friends, Tom Weir and Tom MacKinnon to join me. MacKinnon was a chemist and his work was invaluable, but we needed a fourth – someone who, as well as great climbing ability, had confidence in administration, dealing with bureaucrats of all kinds – Bill Murray was invited.'[3]

Bill Brooker[4] was also asked by Douglas Scott to join, but had just left school and was due to start at university that autumn; and, being a penniless student, did not have the money to pay his share of the expedition expenses.[5]

So that was the expedition team – just four – Scott, Murray, MacKinnon and Weir, all Glaswegian, all in their thirties, all at that time unmarried, all raring to go. Tom gives a quick sketch of himself and Murray's other two companions in his book, *East of Katmandu*,[6] describing them as 'men of patience and determination, who know when to stop smiling and get down to business; as for me, impetuous by nature and quick to anger.'

THE 1950 SCOTTISH HIMALAYAN EXPEDITION

Murray caught something of the flavour of each of them when he described in *The Scottish Himalayan Expedition* (page 139) what they read in the tent at night – he himself was studying some condensed notes on philosophy, Weir was reading Homer's *Odyssey*, Scott the Four Gospels and MacKinnon had forgotten to bring anything.

Although none of the four had climbed in the Himalayas, it was a strong party. Murray had climbed on various occasions both before and after the war with Scott and MacKinnon, either separately or together. Murray described Scott as 'the most beautifully stylish rock-climber who ever tied himself onto my rope.'[7] Scott, MacKinnon and Weir climbed with each other more regularly. All had climbed in the Alps, MacKinnon ascending over 70 Alpine peaks before 1940 and managing to put in seven summers in the Alps on either side of the war years. Scott was the next most experienced in this respect.

The least experienced climber in the group was Tom Weir. Nonetheless he was a tough, all-round mountain man and a good ski-mountaineer. Weir (1914–2006) was the Glasgow-born son of a locomotive fitter. Like Bill Murray, Tom lost his father in World War I. He started his working life in a grocery and became one of the band of young men from Glasgow and the West of Scotland who, in the years between the two wars, escaped urban poverty at the weekend by exploring 'the great outdoors'. During the war he served in the Royal Artillery doing a mixture of clerical work and being a battery surveyor.[8] He spent most of the war on the south coast of England with defensive batteries, but was posted to Germany in 1945 as the war in Europe was coming to an end. After the war he worked as a surveyor with the Ordnance Survey, giving up his job to seize this chance to go to the Himalayas.

Like Murray, Weir was a writer. Later he also became a popular broadcaster.[9] Throughout his adult life Weir campaigned ceaselessly to protect some of Scotland's finest landscapes. At the time of the 1950 expedition Murray's interest in conservation was largely dormant. It could well be that Weir had a hand in awakening it.

In the year following the Scottish Himalayan Expedition Weir and Scott joined forces again for exploration in northern Norway. Then in 1952 Scott, Weir and MacKinnon were back in the Himalayas in the Rolwaling region; and after that in the High Atlas range of North Africa.

Douglas Scott (1911–2008) was two years ahead of Murray at Glasgow Academy. They did not know each other at school but met later through the JMCS. Scott began his working life in the design room of Templeton's carpet factory in Glasgow. Robert Anderson also worked there. Scott took him climbing and introduced him to Murray. It was Anderson who did the illustrations for the later editions of *Mountaineering in Scotland*. Scott served in the Royal Corps of Signals during World War II, being posted first to Orkney and then to India. After the 1950 expedition National Geographic magazine used some of his photographs which encouraged him to set up as a freelance photographer. 'Anything except weddings,' he would say.

A large proportion of the photographs in Murray's books are Scott's (and quite a number were Weir's). Scott also took part in expeditions to Norway, Kurdistan, East Africa (including Mount Kilimanjaro) and Greenland. He made his final major expedition in Greenland, aged 67. After retiring to Spean Bridge, he continued to climb, trek, ski, go sea-kayaking and take photographs.

In an obituary in the SMCJ, Iain Smart wrote of Scott: 'For the first fifty years of his life Douglas was Scotland's most successful bachelor, the focus of much admiration. For the next forty-seven years he was Scotland's most successful husband. When he and Audrey got married Dougie's life expanded. Audrey was adventurous in her own right and she and Douglas led a life of physical, intellectual and cultural endeavour ... they were both bold ski mountaineers in Scotland and the Alps. They canoed extensively in the Western Isles and explored the world furth of Scotland from Poland to Africa.' Before he died, aged 97, he was the last remaining member of the 1950 expedition.

Tom MacKinnon (1914–1981) trained as a pharmacist before taking over his father's chain of chemist's shops. He was a big man, six foot and fourteen stone, with red hair. It was MacKinnon who dived into the seething waters of the Falloch when Murray was drowning. In addition to the expeditions he did with Scott and Weir, he was on Kangchenjunga in 1955, twice reaching over 25,000 feet. The New Zealand climber, Norman Hardie, who was on the same expedition, wrote in his autobiography (*On My Own Two Feet*, 2006) that MacKinnon was 'a hard worker and an excellent expedition companion'. In later years Tom MacKinnon became an enthusiastic yachtsman.

In many ways this was an impressive group of people. Weir received the first ever Lifetime Achievement Awards from the John Muir Trust in 2002. Murray received an OBE and Weir an MBE. MacKinnon, Murray and Weir all became presidents of the Scottish Mountaineering Club, and Scott a vice-president. MacKinnon (1955) and Murray (1952) were both awarded the Royal Scottish Geographical Society's Mungo Park Medal for their contributions to extending geographical knowledge of remote areas.

Murray says that when he was approached about joining Scott and the others, the decision was effortless. 'I need curb my dreams no longer.'[10] It was just the sort of expedition he wanted, with people he knew and liked, who all shared the same desire that it should be a small-scale, lightweight, low-budget venture on which they lived off local produce as much as possible. Murray admired and was influenced by Eric Shipton who, along with Tilman, much preferred to explore with a small group. Murray was definitely of one mind with the others about exploration and travel through unknown country being as important as climbing peaks. The cost of the expedition was divided equally between the four of them, with a possibility of recouping a major part of it afterwards from lectures, magazine articles, and from a book, which it was agreed Murray would write.

The first thing Murray did as the expedition administrator was to allocate tasks. Scott consulted maps and drew up an overall plan of action and a schedule; Weir took charge of the packing and transport of supplies and equipment; and MacKinnon was responsible for stocking the fairly comprehensive medicine chest.[11]

Something of Murray's brisk, thrusting style is captured in Weir's account of the expedition: 'Bill Murray certainly did not waste time. From him came a sheaf of papers marked Battalion Orders, and outlined what had to be done immediately.'[12]

Murray gave himself the job of consulting experienced Himalayan travellers such as Dr Tom Longstaff and H.W. Tilman and of making contact with members of the Himalayan Club in India to ask for their assistance in organising transport and porters at that end of the operation. Once in India, Murray also took on responsibility for negotiating with the Dotial and Bhotia porters, agreeing on loads, pay etc. With his experience as an officer in the army and having come in contact with Indian troops in the Western Desert, he judged that he was the one best suited to this task. Perhaps, too, he thought himself better suited to imposing discipline should it be needed. As a young lieutenant he was surprised to find that, when the men under him had to be reprimanded, he seemed to have a natural talent for it, provided he rehearsed inwardly beforehand. So when Perimal, a Dotial porter, received 'a whole-hearted cursing' from Murray, it was born of practice on erring soldiers of the Highland Light Infantry.

The expedition has been variously known as the Scottish Kumaon

Expedition, the Scottish Garhwal and Almora Expedition, or the 1950 Scottish Himalayan Expedition. Kumaon[13] was the large wedge of mountainous Indian territory between Nepal and Tibet which was divided into two districts: Garhwal in the north west part and Almora in the south east.

The plan was in six stages, ranging west to east across the three river gorges of the Dhauli, Gori and Darma, all flowing in an approximate north-south direction. The first phase was to attempt to follow the line of the Rishiganga (a tributary of the Dhauli River) and then the Tisul Nala (a tributary of the Rishiganga) which would then put them in a position to make an attempt on Bethartoli Himal (20,840 feet). They would then retrace their steps back to the main Dhauli River and move upstream in a north easterly direction to the village of Dunagiri. From there they would undertake a reconnaissance of the Lampak range. On its completion they hoped to be able to climb some of the peaks on the Uja Tirche glacier on their northern side, including Uja Tirche itself (20,350 feet).

The fourth phase of their plan was to move east from Lampak and find a way through the Girthi gorges which connect the Dhauli and Gori river systems, thus linking two of the great trade routes between India and Tibet – they could find no record of this having been done before. They would then move south along the Gori river before branching further east to pass through Ralam village and then on over the Ralam pass and into the valley of the Darma. Here, they planned to reconnoitre the five connected peaks of Panch Chuli. Their objective was to look for a possible route to the 22,650 foot summit.

In short, the overall plan was to travel some 450 miles in four months, clockwise in a huge semi-circle, through little-known country (to outsiders, that is), exploring the great ring of mountains of which Nanda Devi is the centre.

This was a bold and ambitious plan for a small group, none of whom had any experience of Himalayan climbing and who spoke no Hindustani. What is more, they were trying to get things together in a period of severe post-war austerity and shortages. They had only eight weeks to prepare, it being essential that they left Britain in April in order to reach Ranikhet (where the real trekking started) by May. The arrival of the monsoon in the Dhauli region was normally the end of June. Therefore stages one and two had to be completed before then. In going north after this to Lampack and focusing on the mountains on the northern side of the range, Scott cleverly planned to move out of the monsoon-affected belt into an area of low rainfall. Then, when they returned south again for the final two stages of their plan, the monsoon would be over.

This was the first post-war Himalayan expedition from Britain and the first ever all-Scottish Himalayan expedition. Murray took 274 pages in his expedition book to tell of their adventures and, even then, admitted that there was much that had been left out or only half told. This biography, therefore, cannot hope to do more than give a flavour of the expedition and a few incidents and impressions on the way.

On arrival at Ranikhet Murray had his first sight of the Himalayas: 'A great cloud-screen rose tall above the curve of the world. I was about to turn away disappointed when a wild thought made me raise my head higher. They were there, an Arctic continent of the heavens, far above earth and its girdling clouds, wholly divorced from this planet ... They seemed out of this world. The wonder of it all has never left me.'[14]

At Ranikhet they hired 18 Dotial porters. Murray writes of his admiration for them and of his tough but mutually respectful negotiations with them. He gives descriptions of various individuals such as Ram Badur who elected to inflate the lilos each night, a task he performed with such enthusiasm that they were as tight as drums and the stoppers almost impossible to remove. Almost every day there was a pass to climb or a gorge to penetrate via narrow paths; ravines to cross, crags to turn and precarious river crossings to be made. Hard days were relieved by valleys with wooded slopes and meadows filled with flowers and birdsong, and villages with colourful, friendly, curious mountain people whom MacKinnon, the red-haired giant with a magic box, treated for a wide range of ailments.

A maze of ridges made the finding of a route into the Rishi Gorge difficult. Murray, deceived by the scale of things, set off on his own to reconnoitre a way ahead. He had to ascend and then descend four long gullies before finding a pass the porters could use. Night had fallen, he was utterly exhausted and he had no food. The situation was partially saved by discovering in his pocket some sweets given to him as a parting gift by a lady from the Old Tricouni Club of Glasgow. When he finally dragged himself back to camp he was running a high temperature and too tired to eat anything but a spoonful of stew.

With great physical effort, the four Scots and their Dotial porters forced their way into the inner curtain of ridges. As they topped a rise they were suddenly confronted by Nanda Devi (25,645 feet). 'It filled the whole world, a vast projectile bursting arrow-like from the bent bow of the Rishi Gorge. Essentially it was a rock mountain and the greatest that we had ever seen or imagined ... [it] hurled itself through thin air, tapering to a flame tip, white upon blue space.'[15] They were now tantalisingly close to their objective of Bethartoli Himal, but were slowed by miles of low, tangled scrub and thorn. On one of these days, they took four hours to cover half a mile.

From a base camp near the snout of the Bethartoli Glacier they set out to climb Bethartoli Himal with four of their fittest Dotials, five days rations and a tent. At night in their first camp, 'the nearest of the great peaks, Rishi Kot, turned to us an edge like a cutlass but black as gun metal. ... Changabang in the moonlight shone tenderly as though veiled in bridal lace.' Later they had to send the porters back because it was becoming too dangerous for them, and then they themselves were defeated by an impassable gap in the ridge.

Their next attempt was on the nearby unclimbed peak of Hanuman (19,930 feet). They reached the final ridge only to be turned back once more by an unclimbable chasm.

By mid June they had moved north to the village of Dunagiri in the Lampack region – a virtually unexplored area, surrounded by unclimbed, unnamed peaks. While in the village MacKinnon treated a girl's badly infected foot, which she would surely have lost had nothing been done. Murray wrote that perhaps they had achieved something of more importance here than the main objectives of the expedition could ever hope to do.[16]

For the benefit of future expeditions they wanted to gain a clearer idea of these ranges by observing them from some of the lesser peaks. Poor weather, however, thwarted their efforts. Assisted by hired yaks they moved further north to Malari. Continuing on, this time using hired goats to carry the bulk of their new supply of ata (the local flour), they crossed a high pass and then descended to Lampak across hillsides covered in wild flowers.

The Lampack group formed a vast horseshoe of ten 20,000 foot mountains which fed the Uja Tirche Glacier. They thought they had spotted a way up the North Ridge of Uja Tirche and their hopes rose of ascending their first ever 20,000 foot peak. They established base camp at the foot of the glacier, then took all six of their porters up to Camp 2. The chief difficulties which lay ahead were a series of pinnacles which obstructed the main ridge and two ice walls, each of about 200 feet. They managed to by-pass the pinnacles round or near their bases.

The difficulty of the ice walls, Murray said, was made greater by the nervous strain induced through being on an unclimbed mountain of vast scale at an altitude of 19,000 feet. Whereas technical difficulties in the Alps were part of the fun, in the Himalaya they were not enjoyable. Above the first ice cliff, 'the edge twisted up in huge, swinging zigzags, raw edged and corniced.'[17] They reached the summit at 2 pm.

With the snow softening and deteriorating under the sun, they began their descent. They had two near disasters, once when Weir went shooting down the slope to be held on the rope, and again when MacKinnon did the same. At one point, on a long traverse on uncertain ice, Murray had a run-out of 200 feet of heavy hemp rope dragging at his waist. Scott later said of this traverse by Murray that it 'must have been one of the finest feats of icemanship up to that time in the Himalaya.'[18]

The last part of the descent was completed in darkness. They reached camp after 18 hours on the ridge. Only shortly before publication of the expedition book, when it was too late to change it, did Murray discover that this was not the first ascent, Major General R.C.A. Edge, Ang Chuck, Gyaglen and two other sherpas having reached the summit in 1937.

A few days later, Matbir, one of their Dotial porters, a young man of 18, presented Murray with a bunch of wild flowers. This charming, spontaneous and unembarrassed act made a deep impression on Murray. 'I tried to think of men whom I had met outside the Himalaya, who in unaffected grace of manhood could stand comparison with Matbir. I was unable to think of any.'

Over 40 years later, in his final book, he refers to this incident: 'In our experience of the high Himalaya there occurred nothing to make a more lasting impression on my mind than this trivial incident. Again and again it recurs, accompanied by one or other of its witnessed opposites: Italian sentries at Tobruk staving in a prisoner's face with rifle butts; one pundit of British mountaineering disparaging another; the corpse-like face of a Gestapo agent interrogating me at Mahrisch Trubau. From these I can turn to Matbir at Lampak and feel a respect for man.'[19]

The next part of their plan was the traverse of the Girthi Gorge – a stark and arid place, with bare rock walls rising to the top of Uja Tirche. Contouring 1,000 feet above the river, on frighteningly narrow tracks, they were, nonetheless, delighted by the colours in the rocks and the many scents which arose in the enclosed gorge from flowering bushes. On one occasion they discovered a fine cave with a patch of flat ground just big enough for a tent. Sometimes they made only three or four miles in seven hours.

After six days and 22 miles they were through the gorge and the village of Milam lay below them. At Milam, Len Moules, the medical missionary, and his wife treated them to a vast and very welcome meal;[20] and here 'Big Tom' MacKinnon had to depart, three months away from his business being all that he could spare.

They continued south down the Gori for two marches, passing through Milari where they engaged a fresh batch of local Bhotia porters. Beyond Milari they encountered a group of shepherds. One of their Tibetan mastiffs sprang at Murray's throat. He only just managed to fend it off with his ice-axe before a shepherd beat it back with rocks.

Their route then took them eastwards to cross the Yankchar, the first of the Ralam passes. To the north and east lay range after range of unclimbed 20,000 foot peaks. Finally, after laborious step cutting below the imposing North Face of Chaudhara, they were through the Ralam pass at 18,500 feet. The last great uncertainty now lay ahead, the five-peaked Panch Chuli.

Considering that this was basically a reconnaissance expedition, that the difficulty of the peaks around them was high, even by Himalayan standards, and that it was the monsoon season, they had thought they would be lucky if they managed to climb even one of the peaks they had targeted. Their expectations of achieving the summit of Panch Chuli, therefore, were not high. If they discovered a route that might take some future party to the top, they would be content.

During the first week of August they established three camps and then moved to the upper levels of the Sona Glacier. The upper edges of Panch Chuli were so thin that, over a stretch of a thousand feet, they could see the sun shining through the ice. Their attempt on the main peak failed when they were turned back by 800 foot cliffs peppered with stone falls.[21]

Murray was not unduly upset by this defeat, any more than he was by others during the expedition – they attempted nine peaks and were successful on five. Murray fully accepted that uncertainty is a feature of exploratory mountaineering. 'The Himalayan traveller who cannot acquire such a philosophy and apply it will find that however long his life it will not be a happy one.'[22]

They withdrew down the Darmaganga into the Almora region, covering 160 miles in 15 days, losing height all the way, enjoying the cultivated landscape, the birds and the monkeys, finally returning to the point where they had started out – Ranikhet.

Looking back on their four-month journey, Murray recalled Dr Longstaff's advice to mark their red-letter days by camps, not summits and knew it to be good advice. 'Himalayan climbing did not seem to us be better than Alpine, for altitude is against full enjoyment. But the travel *among* the mountains – surely it can have no equal in the world! Full of uncertainty and variety, daily change of scene – always some new, unexpected encounter – it taught us much of permanent value. To my own mind the most important knowledge is how to enjoy the present without worrying for the future … The art of mountain travel is the art of being bold – bold enough to enjoy life – now.'[23]

Years later, Murray summarised some of his outstanding memories from that expedition:[24] The milk white granite spire of Changabang soaring in the moonlight; the wild Himalayan rhododendrons in full bloom, pale purple, scarlet and pink against the gleam of snow-covered mountains; the peaks beyond the Rishiganga flashing like sharks' teeth; Uja Tirche thrusting its silver wedge to the moon; Matibir presenting him with a bunch of flowers.

NOTES

1. 'Somewhere in the Middle of Nowhere', *Mountain Craft*, spring 1968.
2. Although the war in Europe had ended when Murray wrote this letter, the war against Japan had not and, for Scott in India, was still very much on the agenda.
3. Slide lecture given at the first Mountain Festival in Fort William, 2003.
4. William D. Brooker, Vice-president SMC 1970–72, President 1972–74, edited *A Century of Scottish Mountaineering* (1988).

5. Margaret Brooker, Bill Brooker's wife, supplied this information in an email to me, in October 2011.
6. *East of Katmandu* is an account of the Scottish Nepal Expedition, consisting of Weir, George Roger, Scott and MacKinnon, which explored the area west of Everest in 1952.
7. *Mountaineering in Scotland*, page 47.
8. Battery surveyors determined the accurate location of artillery batteries and target elements so that units could co-ordinate their firepower more effectively.
9. Weir wrote about his teenage adventures on foot and bike and about his love of the wildlife and the mountains. By 1950 he had published his first book, *Highland Days*, and had several articles published in *The Scots Magazine*. With typical humility and generosity he later said, 'my first book, *Highland Days* was such a damp squib compared to W.H. Murray's thrillingly descriptive and philosophical book *Mountaineering in Scotland*.' However, he was soon to become a successful freelance writer and photographer, well known for his writings on wildlife and nature and for his stunning photographs. By the time their two lives ended it was Weir who was the better known to the general public. In addition to several more mountain travel books he wrote a popular monthly column in *The Scots Magazine*. This was followed by an even more popular STV series, *Weir's Way*, which won him the STV Personality of the Year Award 1978.
10. *The Evidence of Things Not Seen*, page 151.
11. The most common complaints on Himalayan expeditions were headaches, indigestion, enteritis and dysentery.
12. *Weir's World*, page 51.
13. Boundary lines have changed since 1950. The Kumaon area has been redefined and, since 2007, has been part of Uttarakhand State.
14. *The Evidence of Things Not Seen*, page 210.
15. *The Scottish Himalayan Expedition*, page 87.
16. *The Evidence of Things Not Seen*, page 1.
17. *Ibid.*
18. In an obituary of Murray, SMCJ, 1996.
19. *The Evidence of Things Not Seen*, page 192.
20. Len Moules was a member of the Himalayan Club. He and Murray must have had a lot in common because, during the war, as a Major in the Royal Engineers, he fought in the Western Desert, and like Murray, narrowly escaped death at Mersa Matruh. Moules wrote a book, *Some Want it Tough*, (1958) to which Murray wrote a Foreword.
21. While on this climb Murray spotted an alternative and better route which was successfully climbed by Chris Bonington and Graham Little in 1992.
22. 'Scottish Kumaon Expedition' in *Himalayan Journal* 1950–51.
23. *Ibid.*
24. *The Evidence of Things Not Seen*, page 211.

CHAPTER TWENTY

BOLDNESS HAS GENIUS

Just as the totality of an expedition includes the months of preparation, so also does it embrace time spent after the return writing
articles and books, giving lectures to pay off the expenses, doing the
accounts and tidying up loose ends. It is once they are back that the
rumours start. Speculation was soon rife as to whether the strain
of living so close together for four months had permanently soured
relationships between Murray and his three companions, Scott, Weir
and MacKinnon.

Any expedition, with people living at close quarters, in conditions of
physical and mental stress, puts a strain upon relationships. Shipton,
a veteran of many an expedition, describes some of the tensions than
can arise: 'All manner of things, great and small, are liable to promote
discord. Garrulity is notoriously hard to bear; silence can be no less
trying. Even an unconscious display of virtue can be as intolerable as
any vice, gentlemanly poise as hasty temper, efficiency as clumsiness,
knowledge as ignorance, energy as sloth. In conditions of boredom or
nervous strain one is quick to resent the way a man drinks his soup
or wears his hat, or the silly manner in which his beard has grown,
or a thousand other trifles that in normal circumstances would pass
unnoticed. When one is short of rations it generally seems that one's
companion has secured the larger part of a meal; and he invariably
occupies more than his share of the tent.'[1]

Minor irritations and quarrels were bound to arise. Shipton mentions silence being as annoying as garrulity and Murray was a silent
man, living inside his head a lot of the time. In the previous chapter,
Weir's comment about Murray's commanding style as an organiser
has been noted. He mentions it again in *East of Katmandu*, where,
writing of the expedition they did the following year without Murray,
he says: 'Our expedition is a democratic one, with no appointed

leader. Jobs get done by someone undertaking them rather than by anyone formulating a plan or laying down an order.'[2] This could have been a cause of tension, as could the fact that Murray was the only one of the four who had been a commissioned officer during the war. Memories of the immense gulf between officers and 'other ranks' which existed in those days might not have entirely faded, it being less than five years since they were all demobbed.

Some of the letters that passed between Murray and Weir do, at times, tend to have the tone of an officer addressing one of the ordinary ranks. Rhona Weir says that Murray often went off on his own in the evening to sit on the hillside and meditate. As Shipton points out, the fact that he absented himself could have worked either way, either lessening his aggravation quotient or increasing it.

Douglas Scott's wife, Audrey, thought that there had been a cooling of relations between Murray and her husband after the expedition, but certainly no big rift. A point of conflict might have been over the porters. Apparently Murray didn't think anyone else could handle the porters because only he understood their religion.[3] Scott, who was the only one who had lived in India and been to that area, could reasonably have pointed out a weakness in Murray's case. Scott himself remarked that he found Murray 'rather I', (as in me), meaning that he felt he was a bit too self-absorbed.[4]

The war had probably changed Murray more than it had changed the others. He was not the same person that Scott and MacKinnon had known before the war and the full realisation of this might not have come until they spent so much time with him at close quarters.

It has also been rumoured that MacKinnon left the expedition early because he'd had enough of Murray's company. Murray and Weir (both in books) and Scott (in his lecture notes) all state that the reason he left was because he couldn't leave his business unattended any longer. This seems likely to be true and not some kind of cover-up. Not many people can take more than three months off work. Scott and Weir had both given up their jobs to go on the expedition and Murray was a freelance writer, but MacKinnon was not in the same situation and did have a business to manage.

It is worth noting that in the obituary Murray wrote of MacKinnon he said: 'Outstanding in his character was an abounding good nature. It positively overflowed to benefit all in his company, this too at every level of circumstance. For example, I never knew him lose his temper (something I can say of no other sorely-tried friend), not even during the weeks and months of a Himalayan expedition, when minor causes build up, and everyone gets tired and stretched.'[5]

Nonetheless, the rumours persist that MacKinnon, in particular, found several months of Murray hard to take. Clearly the issue of conflict within the group did need addressing, for as early as page 2 of *The Scottish Himalayan Expedition*, the official expedition book written by Murray, he hastens to address the matter: 'For my own part I could not have wished for men whom I liked better. This latter point is of extreme importance; for going on expedition is like getting married – a man has to live with his companions over long periods when all are at their worst ... it is their weaknesses that stand out, as mine do, dismal and made great. Our knowing of these things in advance does little to ease the situation when we are out in the field.'

Later in the book (page 251), he goes on to say: 'Lack of privacy makes prolonged camp life a test of self-discipline. After several months of living in tents, if men commit no murder it is entirely through fear of public opinion. Throughout the expedition I should cheerfully have slain every one of my companions at quite frequent intervals but for the need of tiresome explanations to relatives.'

Murray takes a slightly tongue-in-cheek, humorous tone here, but there is no doubting that the irritation was mutual. However, the fact that he can openly express this and that the others would have seen the manuscript in advance and let it pass, would seem to indicate that no real or lasting damage had been done.

What is clear is that none of the other three saw very much of Murray after the expedition and that he was not invited to join them when they returned to the Himalayas the following year. Partly this lack of contact is accounted for by their busy lives. Communication between young friends commonly decreases as work, marriage and other commitments take over. People can still regard each other as good friends even though they do little more than exchange Christmas cards. Undoubtedly and inevitably there were quarrels, but it is clear from things said and written since then that these were generous and big-hearted men, not the kind to bear a grudge and always quick to give each other credit and praise whenever possible.

For two years after the expedition there was considerable correspondence between Murray and Weir about expedition matters.[6] These letters are amicable in tone and occasionally contain general chat about what climbs they have recently done or congratulations on something written by one or the other. They seek each other's advice – Murray about what camera to buy, Weir about how best to advance his career as a photographer. They also read and comment on each other's manuscripts. There is one sharp note sounded by Murray – when he thought that an article by Weir about the 1952 Swiss Everest Expedition did not adequately acknowledge the contribution of the 1951 Everest Reconnaissance Expedition, of which Murray was the depute-leader. Weir, although a little hurt, is contrite and the spat is soon forgotten.

Murray occasionally scolds Weir. For example: 'On no account print, publish or sell for reproduction another photo of me clad in oilskins. Apparently the Herald readers all think of me as permanently bearded and aged 60.' But the scolding is self-mocking, too, admitting to a streak of vanity. There is also disagreement about Weir's photographs, Murray suspecting that Weir had kept back the best ones for his own book and only sent the second-best to illustrate articles in magazines and journals (both Murray's and Weir's).[7]

In his book, *Weir's Way* (1983), Tom Weir devoted a whole chapter to singing Bill Murray's praises, admiring his writing and his climbing achievements. It is significant, though, that in this chapter Weir says that, when he went to Murray's house at Lochwood to interview him for the book, it was the first time he had been there. That is to say that, in more than 30 years since they were on expedition together, this was his first visit. The Murrays, as a couple, occasionally visited the Weirs as a couple; and Anne Murray stayed with Rhona Weir to be near the hospital when Bill Murray was ill. People have said that Weir did not like Murray, but that is not quite the same as saying that he disliked him. He might not have chosen him as a close friend – they were very different sort of people – but he certainly respected him.

The agreement, made before they set out for the Himalayas, was that all money earned from lectures and from articles in newspapers, magazines and journals and from accompanying photographs, would be pooled and go towards paying off expedition expenses. Murray would also write the official expedition book. Weir later wrote his own book, but this seems not to have come within their financial arrangement. Murray was the one in most demand as a supplier of articles. Clearly he was the one spending far more time on the writing than any of the others. Murray accepted this uncomplainingly, but he did complain when asked to do something similar again for the 1951 Everest Reconnaissance Expedition.

In his book, *In This Short Span*,[8] Michael Ward includes a letter to himself from Murray in which the latter rails against The Alpine Club and the Royal Geographical Society, the joint sponsors of the 1951 Everest Reconnaissance Expedition who seemed to think that all moneys raised from articles, lectures and books should go entirely to the funds of the Himalayan Committee – a situation that was unacceptable to Murray. Referring to the arrangement he had with Scott and Weir, he says that all his earnings for that year, which formed over half of their combined contribution, went towards meeting the expedition's expenses, leaving him with no personal income. 'I could not enter such an arrangement again, otherwise I should literally and truly starve, and my dog too, and my mother would have to go to some less pretentious dwelling place.'

Between them, Murray, Scott and Weir gave lectures (usually accompanied by slides) to the Royal Geographical Society and The Alpine Club (who had partly sponsored the 1950 expedition as well as the one in 1951), and repeated the same for a fee at organisations such as the Royal Central Asian Society, the University of Cambridge Mountaineering Club, Glasgow Literary Society, the Mountaineering Association, the Royal Society Dublin, the Cairngorm Club, The Scottish Mountaineering Club, and gave public lectures at Foyles in London, the Mitchell Library in Glasgow, Usher Hall in Edinburgh, Paisley, Bromley, Bexhill and Manchester. This schedule, the demand for articles and trying to write the book at the same time imposed a heavy burden on Murray. In a letter to Weir, dated 30th December 1950, he says he's had to write a further 4,000 words for an article while, at the same time, trying to produce 1,000 words a day for the expedition book. In the same letter he goes on to say: 'It has been a wonderful month at Lochwood frost, sunshine, clear blue skies have been continuous all December. I regret I can't get any climbing this winter when it's turning out such a good one.'

Aided by his sister, Margaret, to whom he sent the manuscript for typing, *The Scottish Himalayan Expedition* was published by Dent in 1951. It contained four pages of colour plates and 32 pages of black and white photographs taken by Scott and Weir. As with later editions of *Mountaineering in Scotland*, Robert Anderson drew the maps and diagrams.

The shorter, summarised versions of the expedition, written for magazines or as given in *The Evidence of Things Not Seen* tend to focus on the basic facts of the expedition and on the mountaineering. The book, however, gives a much more rounded picture of the expedition as a whole, with wonderful descriptions of the approach march, a lot to say about the culture and society of the regions they passed through and a keen interest in the people met and in the Dotial and Bhotia porters as individuals. Murray has more to say than in his previous books about the flora and fauna to be seen. Scott and Weir, whose own diaries are full of observations on the birds and mountain flowers, must surely have influenced him.

In one of his letters to Weir, Murray comments that, in his sister's opinion, it was a better book than his last two. J.H.B. Bell was of the same mind. Despite the accolades received by *Mountaineering in Scotland* and *Undiscovered Scotland*, Bell states in a review[9] that this is 'easily his best book'. Perhaps Bell, who was uncomfortable with Murray's mysticism, welcomed the fact that this element was not so prominent in Murray's third book. Bell also commented that: 'Human relations with the Dotials, Bhotias and other Himalayan peoples are described with full interest and shrewd humour. The porters are all live characters.'

In the review Bell praises the excellent quality of the photographs by Scott and Weir, saying that the mountain studies of Uja Tirche and Panch Chuli are outstanding. He thought that the chapter on the ascent of Uja Tirche was the highlight of the book. Bell sums up the expedition's achievement: 'It is true there are attempts on other big peaks which are unsuccessful but these are big unknown Himalayan peaks. They are valuable reconnaissances. The expedition completed its main programme of exploration without mishap and covered much new ground.'

The Times Literary Supplement gave it a favourable review: 'The lively narrative, eloquent photographs, maps and diagrams make it easy to follow those competent, humorous Scots round those heavenly mountains.'

The *Glasgow Herald* praised it: 'Mr Murray makes a high art of descriptive and persuasive writing ... The photographs in colour and black and white convey the most lucid impressions of the Himalayan scene.'

A rather different reaction to the book came from Audrey Scott who said: 'I was unable to finish Bill Murray's book when he became so patronising about how he was on a different plane of understanding with the Dotials than the other three, which, knowing the sympathy that Douglas and the others always established with the local people and porters, I think is very unlikely.'[10]

Surprisingly, considering this was his first visit to the Himalayas when everything would have been new and wonderful to him, Murray's account in *The Scottish Himalayan Expedition* is not overflowing with superlatives. With the onset of the monsoon many of the peaks and vistas were obscured by mist and cloud; and altitude and fatigue sometimes took the edge off their appreciation of the beauty around them. The most likely explanation, though, is that, surrounded by such magnificence and fresh, strong impressions, it was impossible to pick out any one thing for special praise. It could also be the case that Murray let Scott and Weir's excellent photographs speak for themselves.

A phenomenon arising from the publication of this book was the way one passage near the beginning caught the attention of all sorts of people, most of whom had no interest in mountaineering or exploration and probably had never read the book. It now ranks amongst the most famous quotes in the English language. Almost every website supplying quotations contains this passage in part or in its entirety. Self-improvement programmes, books and websites of the 'seven steps to being all you can be' variety have adopted it in a big way, as have keynote inspirational speakers and aspirational projects and givers of business enterprise or personal advice. In his influential book, *Earth in Balance* (1992), about the world's ecological predicament, it was used by US Vice-president, Al Gore.

Murray is describing the early days of organisation and their efforts to get the expedition off the ground. After days of dithering and indecision, they took the plunge and booked their boat passages to Bombay.

'Until one is committed, there is hesitancy, the chance to draw back, always ineffectiveness. Concerning all acts of initiative (and creation), there is one elementary truth the ignorance of which kills countless ideas and splendid plans: that the moment one definitely commits oneself, then Providence moves too. All kinds of things occur to help one which would not otherwise have occurred. A whole series of events issues from the decision, raising in one's favour all manner of unforeseen incidents, meetings and material assistance, which no man could have dreamt would have come his way. I learned a deep respect for one of Goethe's couplets:

> 'Whatever you can do, or dream you can, begin it.
> Boldness has genius, power and magic in it!'[11]

The Himalayas had worked their magic on Murray. He was to return there again and again.

NOTES

1. *Upon that Mountain*, 1943.
2. *East of Katmandu*, 1953, page 2.
3. As mentioned in a discussion with me, September 2010.
4. Said in a conversation between Mike Cocker and Douglas Scott in about 2006.
5. *Alpine Journal*, 1982.
6. Weir Collection, National Library of Scotland, Edinburgh.
7. Letter in Weir Collection, 27th November 1950.
8. *In This Short Span*, 1972, page 62.
9. SMCJ, 1952.
10. In a letter to me, 2nd October 2011.
11. No end of pundits have pointed out that the couplet at the end of this passage is not a direct quote from Goethe's *Faust*, but a rough paraphrase or a very inaccurate translation from the German. Murray's lines are an expression of the same thought, but not a quote.

CHAPTER TWENTY-ONE

EVEREST[1]

After World War I, with Nepal closed to foreigners, the British had almost exclusive access to Everest, via Tibet, for the next 30 years. Throughout the 1920s and 1930s all attempts to reach the summit of the world's highest mountain had therefore been from the north, approaching it up the Rongbuck glacier. Mountaineers had often speculated about the possibility of tackling Everest from the south and west, but there was insufficient information about whether or not this might be feasible, and permission to approach Everest from the Nepalese side had always been denied.

Interest in a southern approach to Everest through Nepal began to grow when, after World War II, the Nepalese government relaxed its rigid policy of exclusion. From 1947 onwards several expeditions were granted permission to enter the country for scientific or mountaineering purposes, including the first ascent of Annapurna (26,493 feet) by a French group – the highest mountain yet climbed by man. Then an American party, which had also invited H.W. Tilman, made the first visit by westerners to Everest's southern slopes, travelling up the Khumbu glacier and sighting the great icefall. They could add no new information about the glacier's upper reaches.

As Murray put it: 'It was not what they discovered but the fact that they were there at all that was so stimulating an event.'[2]

When, in 1950, China invaded Tibet and closed its frontiers to foreigners, the 'traditional' route to Everest from the north was no longer possible. If Everest was to be climbed at all, it would now have to be from the Nepal side.

Enter Michael Ward. Murray first met Ward in 1945 when the former was 32 and the latter was a young medical student at the University of Cambridge. Murray describes their first encounter at Harrison's Rocks in the south of England which led to their friendship. 'There I met a slim black-haired youth of twenty, who offered to show me some of the easier climbs first. I should have taken note of his bright, sardonic eye. He instead put me on the hardest, and stood back grinning when I failed to get off the ground.' Later, they camped and climbed together in Rum, climbed on Nevis with John Barford, and then the three of them were together in the Duaphiné Alps in 1947 when a serious accident occurred. Barford was killed and Murray and Ward spent ten days together in the same room in a French hospital.

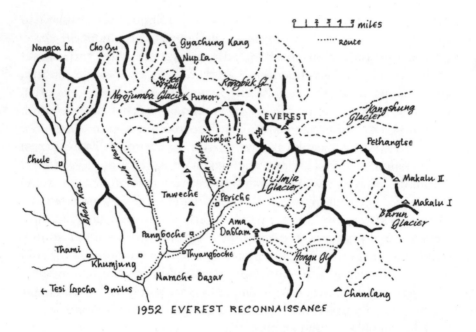

1952 EVEREST RECONNAISSANCE

Early in 1951 Ward, then a national serviceman in the Royal Army Medical Corps, made an important discovery. Sifting through the chaotic archives of the Royal Geographical Society, he found two unmarked brown envelopes. Inside were photographs taken on covert flights over Everest in 1945 and 1947, revealing features of the Nepal side of the mountain, including the South Col. Ward thought he could see a possible route to the top from the Western Cwm. He examined other photographs taken by earlier expeditions from vantage points overlooking the border with Nepal and by the Houston-Westland flight.[3] His researches in the Royal Geographical Society archives also unearthed the forgotten Milne-Hinks map.[4] All this information added up to what appeared to Ward as the key to the ascent of Everest.[5] He took his findings to his friend, Bill Murray.

It looked as though there might be a route via the Khumbu[6] icefall and the South Col which lay beyond it. As far as could be seen, the slopes below and above it appeared possible, but the photographs showed nothing of the South Col itself. Information about the western slopes of the icefall was essential before any decisions could be made about whether an attempt on Everest from this side was feasible. A reconnaissance expedition was needed.

Mallory[7] had seen Everest's Khumbu Glacier in 1921 from the North-East Col of Pumori. He wrote in his diary: 'We are not sorry we have not to go up it. It is terribly steep and broken ... It was not a very likely chance that the gap between Everest and the South peak could be reached from the west. From what we have seen now I do not much fancy it would be possible, even could one get up the glacier.'

The following year he added the comment: 'The single glimpse obtained last year of the western glacier and the slopes above it revealed one of the most awful and utterly forbidding scenes ever observed by man.'[8]

Coming from so respected a mountaineer as Mallory this estimate of the route to the summit via the Khumbu glacier and the South Col made the Himalayan Committee[9] slow to take the initiative in mounting an expedition from the Nepal side. Ward and Murray, however, looked at the evidence with different eyes. 'Where the light of hope can shine, the eye of faith may see and believe,' Murray wrote.[10]

The initiative came from Ward, with the aid of Campbell Secord,[11] a friend, a forceful personality and a member of The Alpine Club. They put a proposal to the Himalayan Committee for an Everest reconnaissance expedition to get underway in the autumn of 1951. The party would consist of Murray as leader, Michael Ward, Tom Bourdillon,[12] Alfred Tissières[13] and Campbell Secord. Both Tissières and Secord had to withdraw.

At this point, Eric Shipton[14] returned unexpectedly from China. He had been the Consul General in Kashgar, but communism and the Red Army put an end to that post. Murray, who had already done the major part of the organisation, decided to step down as leader and offer the position to Shipton. 'This was the arrival of the right man at the right moment. We asked him to lead the expedition because no man alive knew Everest better than he.'[15]

Shipton accepted, although he was sceptical about the chances of success by the route they proposed to reconnoitre. At the last moment the President of the New Zealand Alpine Club sent a telegram to the Himalayan Committee, asking if any of the New Zealanders currently climbing in Garwhal region could join the party out there. These were Edmund Hillary, Earle Riddiford, George Lowe and Edmund Cotter. At first, Shipton was going to refuse the offer but then concluded that the group needed strengthening. He sent a reply saying, 'Send any two,' leaving the Kiwis to decide amongst themselves whom these two should be. The argument was won by Hillary and Riddiford. Murray and the others were not immediately aware that Shipton had done this.

The group from Britain assembled at the railhead at Jogbani in south-east Nepal late in August 1951. Here they were met by Angtharkay and twelve Sherpas.[16] After engaging local porters they began their march to Namche Bazar. Hillary and Riddiford met up with them about half way there, at Dingla.

Hillary couldn't help wondering what the four men they were about to meet would be like: 'Of course we knew all about Shipton, his tough trips, his ability to go to great heights, and his policy of having cheap and mobile expeditions by living largely off the land. He was certainly the most famous living Himalayan mountaineer. But what did he look like? And what about his three companions? I'd never heard of them … For all I knew they might shave every day; they might be sticklers for the right thing. We'd have to smarten up a bit and watch our language.'[17]

When they did finally meet them, Hillary was relieved: 'I have rarely seen a more disreputable bunch, and my visions of changing for dinner faded away forever.'

Shipton welcomed them and introduced his three companions. What Hillary saw was: 'Bill Murray, a dour Scotsman who had led the first all-Scottish expedition to the Himalayas the previous year; Dr Michael Ward, a well-built young chap with an easy impetuous manner … and Tom Bourdillon … an enormous chap, obviously as strong as a horse. I knew he had a fine record of formidable climbs in the Swiss Alps.'[18]

Shipton had expected the march to Namche to take a fortnight, but the early onset of the monsoon, with its flooding and swollen rivers, an attack by hornets and desertion by their porters doubled the time it took. On 25th September they set out on the final stage of the trek to their base camp, now only 25 miles away to the north-east. On the first night after leaving Namche they stayed at Thyangboche Monastery, which Murray said was the most beautiful place he had ever seen. He was clearly impressed by the three huge figures of the meditating Buddha and with the monastic atmosphere of study and contemplation. Murray tells us that the Lama received them with great kindness, but if he was able to converse with the Lama on matters dear to his heart he makes no mention of it.

Three days later they established base camp at 18,000 feet under Pumori. While Riddiford, Bourdillon and Ward began the work of finding a way through the icefall, Shipton, Hillary and Murray climbed the flanks of Pumori to obtain a view of the Western Basin.

The party was reasonably confident of finding a way through the icefall. The success of the reconnaissance and of attempts on the summit from this side would depend upon what Shipton, Hillary and Murray, while on Pumori, saw of what lay above the icefall, what lay between the upper basin and the Col. 'Gradually these slopes disclosed themselves. They were straightforward, not too steep, even when seen face on, free of stonefall from Lhotse, and they were obviously climbable.'[19]

Back in camp Riddiford reported that he thought a way could be found through the icefall. It had become obvious, though, that Murray, Bourdillon and Ward were not yet acclimatised and also that the snow was too loose and powdery. In order to let the snow settle and to get fully fit before resuming the assault on the icefall, they decided to explore the mountains to the south and west and return in two or three weeks' time. Hillary and Shipton set off to find out more about the mountains south of Everest, while the others, together with six Sherpas explored the Nup La and the Hongu Basin. This was exactly the kind of exploration that both Shipton and Murray really enjoyed. Indeed, both write about this phase of the reconnaissance expedition at greater length and with much more enthusiasm than they do about finding a route up Everest.

Hillary observed: 'Even the most enthusiastic Everester tended to develop the attitude of: "Let's go and find we can't climb it! Then we can go away and get down to some really enjoyable exploration!" It was something of this attitude that influenced us to take only seven-teen days' supplies with us.'[20]

Shipton and Hillary arrived back at Everest five days before Murray and his group and re-established a base camp at the foot of the icefall. Without waiting for the others they set about completing the route through the icefall, but were held back by massive new falls of ice, and crevasses which had opened up where none had previously been. However, by 28th October all six in the party and several Sherpas were above the icefall, looking down on its broken and tortuous descent. Murray formed the impression that the glacier moved in a series of uncoordinated jerks. Each time this happened it created anew a jumbled chaos of ice blocks and chasms which sometimes favoured climbers and sometimes hindered them. 'None the less it was already clear to us that the icefall in its present state could not be used as a packing route to supply high camps.'[21]

A short distance from the top of the glacier they encountered the biggest crevasse they had ever seen, splitting the glacier from side to side – about one hundred yards at its widest and one hundred feet at its narrowest. They did not have ladders or sufficient rope to cross it. They could go no further and returned to camp. At the end of October they packed up and returned to Namche Bazar.

In Murray's opinion, the main advantage of the new route from the south was that the most serious difficulties occurred lower down before the climbers were too exhausted and their physical condition had deteriorated at extreme altitude, but the icefall would always be a hazard and the route passed through an area of avalanches that swept down the Western Cwm.

From Namche Bazar they began a second period of exploration, this time of the passes west of Everest. The 'sahibs' paired up, each taking some Sherpas with them, and moved off in different directions. Riddiford and Hillary into the Rowaling gorge, Shipton and Ward through the Menlung pass and beyond; and Murray and Bourdillon through the Nup La to inspect Cho Oyu from the north-west.

Returning from there Murray and Bourdillon found what they thought must be yeti tracks and followed them for nearly two miles. When they caught up with Shipton and Ward, they learned that they, too, had seen them a couple of days earlier when they were fresh and more sharply defined. Sen Tensing, who was with Shipton and Ward had no doubt that they had been made by a yeti. He said he had seen one two years earlier near Thyangboche Monastery. He described it as having reddish brown hair, about the same height as a Sherpa and with a slightly pointed head.

Their westward exploration had now taken them to the border between Nepal and Tibet. A return route via the Rongshar gorge, virtually unknown to Europeans, proved too big a temptation, despite the fact that part of it lay in forbidden Chinese territory. They decided to move through this part at night to avoid being spotted by any guards that might be in the area. It was a long hard march and they stopped for a rest. They were so tired that they fell asleep and didn't waken until daylight. No sooner were they on the move than they were surrounded by a band of Tibetan militia brandishing swords and pistols. Shipton suggested that Angtharkay, the head Sherpa, tried bribery. The expedition kitty was down to its last one thousand rupees (about £75) and Murray doubted if it would be enough. After much bargaining and angry shouting the Tibetans agreed on seven rupees – approximately the cost of half a sheep!

Murray summed up his expedition by saying: 'Behind us lay three months of exploratory travel through mountain ranges either little known or hitherto quite unknown. They had been packed with incident, new discoveries, varied peoples and constant surprise. We seemed for a while to have led enchanted lives.'[22]

Following the 1951 reconnaissance, the Himalayan Committee had intended to mount a full-scale attempt on Everest in 1952, only to find that the Swiss had been given priority for that year by the Nepalese authorities. A joint Swiss-British attempt was mooted but negotiations broke down, so it was agreed that the Swiss go first in 1952 and the British in 1953. To prepare for their turn in 1953 the Himalayan Committee invited Shipton to lead an expedition to Cho Oyu to the west of Everest. The aim was to test the latest high altitude equipment and clothing, try out new oxygen systems and further prepare a core group of climbers for a British attempt on Everest the following year.

To be picked for the Cho Oyu venture was virtually to book a place on the Everest team. Selected by Shipton were Hillary, Riddiford, Ward, Bourdillon, Secord, Charles Evans, Ray Colledge, George Lowe (another New Zealander), Alfred Gregory and Dr Griffith Pugh, who was attached to the party to carry out physiological research. All of the 1951 reconnaissance team had been included except Murray. Shipton's biographer states, 'Murray was not included because of his poor performance at altitude and his meagre technical skill on glacier ice'.[23]

That Murray had been slow to acclimatise is true, although Murray himself is fairly reticent about this in his various accounts. The second reason might seem surprising until we remember that Himalayan glacier ice is a great deal harder than anything Murray might have encountered in Scotland or the Alps and climbing it demanded a different technique. Shipton's explanation was simply that Murray had not been available.

In 1952, the year of the Cho Oyu expedition, Murray was busy working on *The Story of Everest*. There was huge public interest in Everest and in the forthcoming British attempt. Murray and his publisher rightly judged that this was exactly the moment to bring out a book on the subject. Also the Himalayan Committee expected Murray to recover for them some of the money they had spent on the 1951 Reconnaissance Expedition and this involved him in a heavy schedule of lectures and article-writing. He needed to earn money both for himself and for the Royal Geographical Society.

The book was an account of all the expeditions to Everest, from the first one in 1921 up to the present moment, including the 1951 Reconnaissance Expedition, and the two Swiss attempts in 1952. It was published while the 1953 British expedition was already under-way, and the outcome uncertain. The final chapter looked at the chances of success and also discussed the ethics of using oxygen.

Murray was against it. In his opinion it would be much more rewarding to attain the summit without the use of oxygen. He countered the argument that climbers already employed artificial aids in the form of boots and axes by saying that these were instruments of the craft of mountaineering, to be used with skill. Oxygen, on the other hand, enhanced the natural powers of the body – that very thing which a climber wants to test against the mountain. Its use, he thought, was akin to taking drugs.

Being absolutely up to date and catching the interest of the public, the book sold extremely well. It made more money for Murray than any of his other books, being translated into eight languages. It went into several editions, the final chapter of these later editions being amended to complete the story of reaching the summit – and one which was in print before Hunt's official expedition book came out.

There has been conjecture as to whether Murray was, or was not, selected for the Cho Oyu expedition. One line of thought is that he was not invited and so decided to write his book instead. The counter-argument is that he was selected, but because he earned his living from writing, he gave this priority. Those favouring the first proposition point out that both in *The Scottish Himalayan Expedition* and in *The Evidence of Things Not Seen* Murray strongly makes the point that boldness pays off; that if you really want something and go for it, somehow Providence will provide. Therefore (they say), Murray would be unlikely to let the matter of money hold him back from going to Cho Oyu.

However, a letter held in the archives of the Alpine Club swings the matter towards the latter proposition. It is dated 23rd November 1951, while he was on his way back from the Everest Reconnaissance (he gives his address as 'the British Embassy, Katmandu') and written before any hard thought had been given to who might go on another expedition the following year. He was writing to two friends, a married couple, Mabel and Donal Glegg. They had asked him to try to obtain for them some Tibetan mastiff pups, but he had been unable to do so.

He says: 'It seems to us there will have to be another expedition in May [of the next year] … For my part, I have been to the Himalayas two years running and I doubt if I would go a third time in succession. I have to earn my living, and my house and grounds at home are falling into wreck and ruin through 2 years' neglect. But if there is to be an Expedition it should be quite possible, and no great trouble, to get you two pups, whether I am there or not.'

Before Shipton was replaced as leader of Everest 1953, he named the men he would like as the nucleus of his team,[24] stressing that they should all be between 25 and 35. Murray in 1953 had just turned 40 and he was not among those named. Shipton also stated that he wanted Charles Evans as his deputy leader, not Murray who had held that position in the 1951 reconnaissance expedition. The possibility that Shipton would not have selected Murray for Cho Oyu, whether he had been available or not, cannot be ruled out.

Shortly before Murray set out on the 1951 Everest Reconnaissance Expedition, Tom Weir had written: 'It is an honour for Scotland that this home-trained mountaineer should be chosen for a reconnaissance on the great South West face of the greatest mountain in the world, Mount Everest, 29,014 feet.[25] For Bill Murray, this month and the next will be the culminating endeavour of a distinguished career which goes back to 1935.'[26]

From his last sentence it is clear that Weir, also, thought Murray too old to be included in any future Everest party.

It is only natural that a mountaineer should want the chance to stand on the summit of the world's highest mountain, or at least be part of the team that succeeded in meeting the challenge. In this, Murray was no exception. Despite his reservations concerning large-scale expeditions, the danger from avalanches and from the uncertainties of the icefall that the Sherpas would be exposed to, and the loss of the magic and mystique that surrounded Everest, he wanted to go.

In a newspaper interview he is reported as saying: 'Yes, I was sorry I didn't have the chance. I would have liked to have been there.'[27]

Although he was not in the 1952 Cho Oyu party, he must have hoped he would be picked for Everest 1953. After all, had political events not conspired to bring Shipton back to England, Murray would have been the leader of the 1951 Reconnaissance Expedition. Tom Longstaff, the well-respected Himalayan veteran, obviously thought Murray should have been included when he wrote saying, 'I was shattered when I learned you were not going with the Everest party.'[28]

After the Cho Oyu training expedition, Secord and Riddiford complained to the Himalayan Committee about Shipton's chaotic organisation and lack of drive to get things done. By now the British 1953 Everest Expedition had become strongly associated with national prestige and with the international competition to be the first nation to attain the summit. This being the year of the coronation of Queen Elizabeth II, it was regarded in exalted circles as being highly desirable that the New Elizabethan Age started with a triumph on Everest. Only a large-scale, military style, meticulously organised expedition was likely to succeed. Large expeditions, nationalism, competition, fanaticism, putting peak bagging above exploration – all these were anathema to Shipton.

A series of emergency meetings of the Himalayan Committee[29] and behind-the-scenes discussions took place. Shipton was offered co-leadership with Hunt up to Base Camp, with Hunt the sole leader from then onwards. Shipton was not prepared to remain in the party with Hunt. Their philosophies and temperaments were too conflicting. He offered to resign and his resignation was accepted. Larry Kirwan, a committee member gave it as his opinion that 'if ever there was a case of the right thing being done in the wrong way, this was it'.

It is just possible that the criticisms levelled at Shipton and his subsequent resignation had some bearing on Murray's non-selection by Hunt. Murray was seen as being very much of the same mind as Shipton regarding the size of expeditions, their priorities and the adoption of a non-competitive approach. Tom Bourdillon turned down his invitation to be part of the British 1953 Everest Expedition out of loyalty to Shipton, but was later persuaded to change his mind. It would have been entirely in character if Murray had done the same, but the situation never arose.

From what Sir John Hunt[30] wrote in his book, *The Ascent of Everest* (1953), it seems that he never seriously considered Murray as a candidate. He states in this book that he was looking for four qualifications based on age, temperament, experience and physique.

Age: 25 to 40 – Murray was on the outer limit of this bracket.

Temperament: 'There was the need to be sure that each one of the party really wanted to get to the top … any one of us might be called upon to make this attempt.' In Murray's view the true joys of mountaineering were spiritual and reaching the top was not the real goal.

Experience: Compared to many of those hoping for a place Murray's Alpine experience was fairly modest as was the amount of high altitude climbing he had done (as opposed to Himalayan exploration at lower altitudes). Alastair Cram had been one of those who wrote to Hunt requesting to be considered. In his reply, Hunt said: 'The standards are very high indeed, for apart from a good many Himalayan post-war parties to choose from, this season, 1952, has seen an all-time record for British guideless climbing in the Alps, especially by the under thirties.'[31]

Physique: Hunt seemed to be looking for strongly built men.

Hunt also thought it important that everyone should 'fit in'. Murray was not part of the Alpine Club clique which probably did not help, and he was known for being a bit of a loner. Hunt finally selected a party of 13, which became 14 when Tenzing was invited to join as one of the climbing team. Hunt also drew up a list of five reserves. Murray was not on this list either.

Murray was too much of a gentleman to complain or make an issue of it. He maintained a dignified silence and his final book contains no hint that he thought he had been unfairly treated. He reviewed Hunt's *The Ascent of Everest* in generous terms[32] and in an Introduction to a special edition of the book[33] he praised Hunt's qualities and commended him for firmly rejecting proposals that the book should be entitled 'The Conquest of Everest'.[34] Also, in a letter to his sister, he described Hunt in favourable terms and then says, 'The fact remains that Shipton deserves to command greater respect as a mountaineer than Hunt. But I have no doubt that Hunt is the better leader for Everest.'[35]

A newspaper article claimed that Hunt never acknowledged his debt to Murray.[36] This is not the case. Hunt stated: 'So it came about that another expedition, initiated by M.P. Ward, W.H. Murray and C. Secord, and led by that renowned veteran of pre-war Everest expeditions, Eric Shipton, was sent out with a small reconnaissance party ... This brilliant Reconnaissance of 1951 not only traced a hypothetical route to the top – it proved to be the most practical line in the light of later experience – but forced a way up one of the most formidable sections of it ... These, the Reconnaissance of 1951, the two Swiss attempts and the Cho Oyu experiments, were the immediate milestones behind the final journey to the top. The knowledge provided by all four expeditions ... governed my planning.'[37]

On 29th May 1953, after two unsuccessful expeditions by the Swiss the previous year, Hillary and Tenzing became the first climbers to stand on the summit of Everest.[38] Murray did not learn of this success until two weeks later. Having completed *The Story of Everest*, he was back in the Himalayas, doing the kind of mountain travel he liked best. In the company of John Tyson[39] and a small group of Sherpas, he was exploring the Api and Nampa regions of West Nepal,[40] penetrating the Kali and Seti gorges, and spending several days in Chinese-held Tibet. Murray describes how he sent one of his Sherpas to a nearby village to recruit more porters prior to moving camp and how the Sherpa returned with a pot of honey wrapped in a newspaper. It had been sent by a swami Murray had met earlier. When he unwrapped the pot he saw the headline and realised the swami's true intention had been to send him the news that Everest had been climbed.

When Murray told the Sherpas, one of them shook his head in wonder, and exclaimed, 'There will be no living with Tenzing now!' Murray says that when he met Tenzing later, he found his modesty unaffected by his fame. Murray's feelings on receiving this news were mixed. He was thrilled that the route he had helped to pioneer had brought success, 'but dismayed that the world's summit was no longer inviolate. Its old inspirational value had, I felt, been diminished ... That "success" was the most damaging to mountains and to real mountaineering that there has ever been.'[41]

In Murray's garden, on the shores of Loch Goil, is a piece of Everest rock.

NOTES

1. This chapter is based mainly on the accounts given by Murray in Chapter XIII of *The Story of Everest*, Chapter 32 of *The Evidence of Things Not Seen*, his article 'The Reconnaissance of Mount Everest, 1951' in *Alpine Journal* 1952, and Eric Shipton's *The Mount Everest Reconnaissance Expedition 1951*. Other sources used were Michael Ward's *In This Short Span*, Edmund Hillary's *High Adventure*, and Peter Steele's biography of Shipton *Eric Shipton: Everest and Beyond*. Details and viewpoints vary slightly, but there is agreement on the basic facts.
2. *The Story of Everest*, page 142.
3. In April 1933 two British bi-planes (Westlands) attempted to make the first successful flight over Mount Everest. The attempt was funded by Lady Houston and closely supported by the RAF. They were caught in a tremendous down-rush of air, but eventually scraped over the southern peak by a few feet. Both planes were equipped with cameras, but a heat and dust haze prevented any useful photographs being taken (also the camera operator in one of the planes became unconscious when he trod on his own oxygen line). However, later that year the four pilots made a second, unofficial, flight and managed to take perfect photographs.
4. In 1945 A.R. Hinks, mathematician, cartographer and secretary of the RGS, combined the information from the 1933 aerial photos and Spender's 1935 map and photos to create a composite map of Everest. This map, beautifully drawn by H.F. Milne, and generally referred to as the Milne-Hinks map, depicted with accuracy both the Nepalese and Tibetan side of the mountain for the first time.
5. Ward wrote in more detail about this in 'Mapping Everest' (*Cartographic*

Journal, June 1994) and with P.K. Cark in 'Everest 1951: Cartographic and Photographic Evidence of a New Route from Nepal' (*The Geographical Journal*, March 1992).

6. In some of his earlier writing, Murray prefers to spell this Khombu rather than Khumbu.

7. George Herbert Leigh Mallory (1886–1924) took part in the first three British Everest expeditions in the early 1920s. On the 1924 British Everest Expedition he and his partner, 'Sandy' Irvine, disappeared from sight high on the North-East Ridge. His body was not found until 1999. Whether they reached the summit is still a subject for speculation.

8. The Mallory diaries are in the archives of Magdalene College, the University of Cambridge.

9. The Himalayan Committee, formerly known as the Everest Committee, is a joint committee between The Alpine Club and the Royal Geographical Society. Its function is to scrutinise proposals for Everest expeditions and, if approved, help support and fund them.

10. *The Story of Everest*, page 143.

11. Campbell Secord (1913–1980) was a Canadian by birth who, from the 1930s onwards, chose to live in Britain. As a student he climbed in the Canadian Rockies and later he climbed with Frank Smythe in the Alps and became a member of The Alpine Club. During the war he flew Liberators for Coastal Command before becoming an industrial consultant to the government. In 1947 he was part of a mainly Swiss team that made an attempt on Rakaposhi.

12. Tom Bourdillon (1924–1956) was a major figure in the renaissance of British Alpine climbing. After graduating from Oxford he had a career as a physicist in rocket research. He also did important experiments into the use of oxygen at high altitude and was put in charge of the oxygen equipment on the successful 1953 Everest Expedition. On this expedition he and Charles Evans, who were chosen to make the first bid for the summit, came within 300 feet of being the first men to the top. Three days later, Hillary and Tenzing succeeded. Bourdillon died in a climbing accident in the Alps in 1956, aged 31.

13. Alfred Tissières (1917–2003) was a Swiss climber with an impressive list of Alpine ascents. He was a member of The Alpine Club who, at that time, was a research scientist at the University of Cambridge. He went on to become an internationally known molecular biologist, giving this priority over climbing.

14. Eric Shipton (1907–1977) was an indefatigable explorer of remote ranges and a man whose Everest experience was greater than anyone's in his lifetime. He favoured small-scale, low-budget expeditions. He began his adult life as a coffee grower in Kenya. Here he first met Bill Tilman with whom he climbed Mount Kenya. In 1931, with Frank Smythe, he reached the summit of Kamet, the highest peak climbed at that time. He took part in all four Everest expeditions in the 1930s, being the leader of the 1935 Everest Reconnaissance Expedition. During World War II Shipton was a British Consul in Kashgar in Central Asia. Following a series of other diplomatic posts he returned to Kashgar in 1946 as Consul General. He took this opportunity to explore the mountains of Central Asia. In his mid-fifties he traversed the Southern Patagonia Icecap. He is the author of eight books on travel, exploration and mountaineering.

15. *The Story of Everest*, page 144.
16. Sherpa is not simply another word for a porter who carries loads. The Sherpas are an ethnic group who live in the Everest region amongst Nepal's highest mountains. They are acclimatised to high altitude and are therefore often employed for the harder high altitude climbing and load carrying. For lower altitudes porters are engaged who are not necessarily Sherpas, particularly when the starting point is outside the Sherpas' home area.
17. *High Adventure*, page 37.
18. *Ibid,* page 38.
19. *The Story of Everest*, page 152.
20. *High Adventure*, page 43.
21. *The Story of Everest*, page 162.
22. *The Evidence of Things Not Seen*, page 219.
23. *Eric Shipton: Everest and Beyond* by Peter Steele (1998), page 170.
24. Those named were Hillary, Lowe, Ayres (New Zealand's top ice climber and Hillary's mentor), Gregory and Bourdillon. Out of the running were Secord and Riddiford, both having quarrelled violently with Shipton during the Cho Oyu expedition; and Shipton asked for Charles Evans as his deputy leader.
25. In 1955 the official height of Everest was adjusted to 29,029 feet; and in 1999 it was again adjusted to 29,035 feet, although there is debate about this new figure.
26. Notes for a profile on Murray, the Weir Collection, National Library of Scotland, Edinburgh.
27. Article by Jack Webster, 'The Grand Old Men of the Hills' in *The Herald*, 18th March, 1995.
28. Murray quotes from this letter in *The Evidence of Things Not Seen*, page 223.
29. The minutes of these meetings of the Himalayan Committee are in the Royal Geographical Society Archives, London.
30. John Hunt (1910–1998) trained to be an army officer at Sandhurst and was then seconded to the Indian Police. While in India he climbed in the Himalayas. During World War II he trained troops in mountain warfare and later served in the Middle East and Europe, where he commanded the 11th Indian Infantry Brigade. When the call to Everest came he was at the headquarters of the Allied Staff Central European Command. At the time John Hunt was invited to lead the Everest expedition he held the rank of Colonel. Immediately after the Everest success he was knighted and became Sir John Hunt, and later Lord Hunt. His full title, at the end of his life was Brigadier Henry Cecil John Hunt, Baron Hunt KG, PC, CBE, DSO.
31. This letter is in The Alpine Club archives, London.
32. In the *Scottish Geographical Magazine*, December 1953. Murray did slip in one little dig, though, saying, 'Parts of the book read like an Army manual on administration.'
33. A special edition brought out by Heron Books in 1970.
34. However, an American edition, published by Dutton, New York, did entitle it *The Conquest of Everest*.
35. This letter, dated 13th October, 1952, is included in *The Evidence of Things Not Seen*, page 339.

36. See note 27.
37. *The Ascent of Everest*, pages 5 & 6.
38. Although the 1953 Everest expedition was designated as a British expedition, the two climbers who reached the summit were a New Zealander and a Sherpa who was Indian by birth. It was not until 1975, 22 years later, that the first British citizens, Doug Scott (the English climber, not the Scottish one) and Dougal Haston, stood at the top of Mount Everest.
39. John Tyson was a recent graduate of Magdalen College, Oxford, who lived in Edinburgh. He had been to the Himalayas the previous year. Part of his reason for accompanying Murray was to conduct research into the nature and distribution of Asian food crops and seeds at high altitudes and to collect plants and insects for the British Museum.
40. Murray gives a full account of this in his article 'The Exploration of Api' in *Blackwood's Magazine*, April 1954; and Tyson has an account: 'Exploring the Api and Nampa group, Western Nepal' in *Alpine Journal*, 1954.
41. *The Evidence of Things Not Seen*, page 239.

CHAPTER TWENTY-TWO

WHO IS THE BEST CLIMBER IN THE LAND?

It was often said of Murray that he was utterly fearless. Although there are passages in his writing where he does admit to being frightened, what is evident in most of his accounts is an air of cool, calculating detachment from a man so completely committed to the task in hand that fear is banished. 'On mountains, fearlessness is a good companion,' he said, 'provided fear is there too as the watchdog.'[1]

Most ace climbers of today would expect to stay at the top of their sport for a decade, perhaps more if they are lucky. Murray and his friends only had four years at the top before the war interrupted them. They never regained that position in Scottish climbing. After the war Murray moved on to a different, larger scale of mountaineering – Himalayan exploration. A younger generation with a different approach and new techniques superceded those who had brought about a renaissance in Scottish climbing in the 1930s.

The Creag Dhu club (formed in 1930 and drawing mainly on young working-class Glaswegians) now came into its own, pushing up the standard. Cameron McNeish tells how: 'Murray continued to climb in his beloved highlands, but did not try to compete with the new generation of climbers like John Cunningham, Tom Patey, Jimmy Marshall and Hamish MacInnes. They were taking climbing into new realms of difficulty, and as Murray observed "had a speed and confidence we simply hadn't possessed. After we had climbed the Garrick Shelf on the Buachaille our immediate feeling was one of 'never again'. These fellows were starting with climbs like that, taking them almost for granted." Another era was about to begin.'[2]

In evaluating Murray as a climber three points should be made right away. Firstly, he was part of a team. The achievements of the Mackenzie-Murray-Dunn-MacAlpine rope were team achievements, as were his climbs with Bell, Marskell, Scott, Donaldson, Laidlaw and others. In most of the key ascents, Mackenzie and Murray alternated as the lead climber and, on several of them it was Mackenzie who led the crux. Because it was Murray who wrote so eloquently about their adventures, the spotlight has shone on him, but Murray himself was always the first to give credit to his companions. It was a sore point with Bill Mackenzie that he became known as the person who climbed with Murray, whereas in fact, he would point out in his forthright way, it was Murray who climbed with him – a view which Murray himself endorses.

Secondly, valid comparisons cannot be made between people climbing in the 1930s with hemp ropes, nailed boots, old-fashioned ice-axes and the minimum of protection, and modern climbers with the vastly superior equipment available to them. To name but a few of the aids which Murray and his contemporaries did not have: lighter, stronger, more flexible ropes, specialised adhesive footwear, resins, more effective ice-axes, single-point crampons, and an array of iron-ware that had not hitherto been employed. The latter (including wedges, nuts, chocks, bolts and ladders) both enabled 'the impossible' to be overcome and increased the safety factor on difficult moves beyond all recognition since the early days of the JMCS.

Furthermore there have been huge strides forward in training facilities, with indoor climbing walls and access to gymnasia, weight training and advances in sophisticated strength and fitness programmes for climbers. The pre-war climbers did not have the benefit of special mountain weather forecasts[3] or of an avalanche warning service. In both cases experience, an instinct honed over the years[4] and close attention to local knowledge were required to a greater degree than they are today. Mountain rescue, too, was in its infancy – no trained teams, no special equipment, no dogs, no helicopters, and no telephone at the Kinghouse Hotel in Glencoe, instead a strong emphasis on self-reliance. Nor can fair comparisons be made between strictly amateur, weekend climbers and professional or semi-professional, virtually full-time climbers.

There is also the matter of psychological barriers. Once something has been done for the first time, without anything else changing, it becomes easier for others to follow. As soon as Roger Bannister broke the four-minute mile barrier, others found that they, too, could do it. Every generation builds upon the advances made by the previous one and standards rise. Mummery famously captured this truth when he declared: 'It has frequently been noticed that all mountains appear doomed to pass through three stages: An inaccessible peak – The most difficult ascent in the Alps – An easy day for a lady.'[5]

Anyone who completes one of Murray's first ascents today and thinks it wasn't all that difficult, should remind himself of these things. They should remember, too, that when you do a climb for the first time you don't know what lies ahead, you don't know what problems might be encountered around the next corner, or whether a promising line will peter out, leaving you stranded, perhaps in an irreversible position. These routes were done without benefit of guide book, or dotted lines on a photograph or the knowledge that it was possible.

Robin Campbell, archivist for the SMC, and Jimmy Marshall have both expressed to me the opinion that Murray and his peers of the JMCS brought Scottish winter climbing back from a period of decline to where it had been in Raeburn's day, but did not advance it beyond that point (Campbell also expressed this view in his obituary of Murray in the Alpine Journal 1997). Murray would have agreed with the first half of that assessment, but not the second.

In a historical piece, looking back on the development of Scottish mountaineering in the period 1935–40, Murray stated: 'Mackenzie was the pre-eminent iceman of the time. He and J.K.W. Dunn, A. MacAlpine and Murray formed a team devoted at first to numerous reascents of the great buttresses and ridges of Ben Nevis and Glencoe as well as the ice-holding gullies like S C Gully … the standards of earlier climbers were thus re-established and then, by more frequent advantage taken of hard conditions, greatly exceeded.'[6]

As every ice climber knows, snow and ice conditions vary enormously from day to day, month to month, year to year. No ice climb is ever quite the same twice and can vary in standard quite dramatically – another reason why one should be cautious about making comparisons. Murray mentions 'hard conditions' in the passage above because the decade before the war was remarkable for its severe winters in Scotland with freak conditions in the mountains – huge ice bosses and bulges, iron hard ice, giant overhangs and other hazards seldom encountered. The winter of 1939–40 was the coldest winter in Western Europe for one hundred years and the year of 'the blizzard of the decade' in Scotland. It is difficult to say for certain, but, in repeating Raeburn's climbs, he and his friends might have been doing them in much harder conditions than the old master.

Had the war not taken Murray away from the mountains when he was in top form, he might well have had an even more impressive list of ascents than he did. Moreover, he devoted a whole year in 1946 to revising the Glencoe guidebook, which involved checking and repeating a huge number of low grade climbs. If Murray had been the sort of person who was concerned with massaging his ego, enhancing his reputation, outshining rivals, and bagging first ascents by using every artificial aid possible, his record would have reflected this, but he was not that kind of person.

One of the biggest problems in discussing Murray's achievements in relation to those of later generations of climbers is that climbing values and ethics, for the most part, were not the same. Murray's aims and motivations, attitudes and values were, in some respects, closer to those of Geoffrey Winthrop Young (1876–1958) and the Edwardian era than they were to the post-World War II era. When Murray started climbing, the general feeling in Britain was that it was an amateur sport. Murray's attitude in this respect is well illustrated by the fact that he declined to write a fifth mountaineering book (about his Himalayan expedition to Api) because he didn't want to earn his living, directly or indirectly from climbing.

In those days only the minimum of artificial aid was acceptable, and the accepted attitude was that climbing was a private affair between man and mountain and not concerned either with seeking publicity or with competition. Murray, who admired Shipton, strongly identified with the latter's statement that 'directly people allow the element of competition to *rule* their activities and care *more* for trophies or record breaking or acclamation than for a real understanding of their craft . . . they are in danger of losing the real touchstone of values which alone makes anything worthwhile.'[7]

By the time of Murray's death in 1996, the top climbers were mostly professional climbers, dependent on sponsors and publicity, in competition with each other for fame and funding, needing to supply the news-media with new and ever more eye-catching ascents. The two eras are so different in their attitudes and approach that their players cannot be directly measured against each other. It is rather like trying to compare two runners in a cross-country event. The first runner has entered because it's a scenic route and he wants to enjoy the view along the way and he likes the camaraderie of the occasion. The other is there because he wants to finish ahead of everyone else and prove he is the best. If each achieves what he hoped for, judged on their own terms, they are both winners, but their achievements cannot meaningfully be compared.

In his biography of Young, Alan Hankinson writes: 'There was much that Geoffrey disliked about recent trends in mountaineering. He noted in the diary: "My type of mountaineering, I feel, grows more and more out of date, as technique and mechanism take the place of our romantic pioneering." Shortly after, he wrote: "In fact, and philosophically, I am dropping out of the mountain social world. I don't like modern climbing ways, and technical stunting. And the old romance and distinction are no longer there. Bill Murray I except ..."'[8]

That the two amateur mountaineers were on the same wavelength is confirmed by Murray when he wrote: 'I liked Geoffrey Young's attitude to mountains and mountaineering, for these attitudes were mine too ...The principles are simple: that the true joys of mountaineering are spiritual and only to be had when the climber, however high or low his skills, goes to the mountains because he loves and respects them.'[9] Jimmy Marshall summed up much of Murray's outlook on mountaineering when he told me[10] that he thought Murray was a well-balanced person who had climbing in its proper perspective.

Collecting summits was something Murray deplored. He enjoyed hill-walking and taking in a summit or two along the way, and he understood others people's enjoyment of it. The Chronology of Murray's Climbs (online Appendix K) shows how he often chose to walk in the mountains rather than climb on some part of them. What Jim Perrin described as the ego-fuelled 'status-and-collecting-tickability view of climbing'[11] roused his ire. 'Munromania' as he called it, had, in his view, more to do with the collecting instinct, the Protestant work ethic, and the need to set oneself targets than it did with the love of mountains.

Something of the old pre-war attitudes is conveyed in Murray's position in what was then a current debating point in climbing circles – the use of crampons, pitons and other climbing aids. Murray shunned the use of crampons on Scottish mountains because he thought nailed boots were better suited to the conditions. There were ethical reasons, too, for not using them. In discussing the use of crampons, Macphee tells us (SMCJ, 1938), that 'most people consider that their use tends to lessen the sporting nature of Scottish winter climbing'.

Bill Brooker told me[12] that, in those days, the use of crampons was seen as a form of cheating. Much the same applied to the wearing of 'rubbers' (gym shoes or plimsolls), which Lord Chorley declared was cheating because 'it didn't give the rocks a chance'.[13] Even mountain huts were regarded with suspicion in some quarters. As late as 1948, J.B. Nimlin was saying in the SMCJ, 'Are huts the beginning of a movement to make the mountains fit for climbers rather than climbers fit for mountains? ... I like to think that I meet the mountains on the same terms [as Mummery and his contemporaries] and without the use of modern weapons like pitons, which, if properly used, will enable me to defy even gravity!'[14]

The common attitude in the 1930s towards the use of pitons is summed up by E.A.M. Wedderburn: 'One must distinguish between two entirely different ways of using pitons: as direct aids to climbing, as in steeple-jacking, or as safeguards where the natural rock provides no belay. Although the first method has already made its appearance in British climbing (in the Lake District), I can only say that it does not appeal to me. But I have been able to satisfy myself that the use of pitons in the second way, that is, purely to safeguard, is, on new climbs at least, unexceptionable.'[15] Murray would have agreed with Wedderburn on this[16] and he would have acknowledged that a rope is the greatest artificial aid of them all.

Murray expressed his feelings on the topic in no uncertain terms, in The Craft of Climbing.[17] While acknowledging that we need to keep danger within manageable proportions, he thought that there must be an element of danger present. Without it there is no reality in the adventure. In the same chapter he deplored the use of pitons on rocks of Severe standard or less and went on to say, 'There was a time, not long ago, when action so poor spirited was unheard of – men who could not force a new route without a piton turned back and left it to someone who could ... It is irrational vanity to nail that obstinate pitch for the sake of a claim to a first ascent. Who is the best climber in the land? The slam of hammer on piton cries "Me – me –me!"'

Clearly, Murray preferred to climb well at a slightly lower standard than to climb badly at the highest standard. A similar feeling is expressed by Jimmy Marshall. In a newspaper interview[18] he was asked whether he thought the winter climbers of today, with their fancy gear, have it easy. He replied: 'No, I don't think so because they're taking it to further extremes. Obviously these guys are very fit and very competent ... I've got a lot of respect for them. But I find it appalling when I see people who are not as good as them sort of crawling up with two axes, on their hands and knees, virtually. There's no sense of balance or anything. I find that an eyesore.'

Exploration of unknown country was more fulfilling for Murray that ascending some unclimbed peak, and being in tune with the spirit of the mountain more satisfying than reaching the top. 'Does it matter,' he asks, 'whether a man gets to the very top? If he penetrates to the heart of the Leac Mhor the mountain is his.'[19] This was not the statement of some middle-aged man, running out of steam, making a virtue of necessity, it was written when he was in his prime.

As a mountaineer Murray was playing by different rules to the majority of today's top climbers. We are not comparing like with like. This does not mean to say that we should not try to assess the man and his achievements, but it should be done within the context of his own times, in the perspective of the high standards being achieved at the same time in England and Wales, in the Alps and other parts of Europe[20] and mindful of what he himself saw as worthwhile goals.

Murray laid out what he saw as the worthwhile goals when he wrote: 'Throughout the last sixty years it has been the policy of the Scottish Mountaineering Club to honour the mountaineer rather than the specialist.'[21]

The all-round mountaineer was his ideal. He maintained that a man is not a true mountaineer unless 'he knows his mountains winter and summer, on cliff and summit ridge, by day and night, in fair weather and foul. For until then he understands them incompletely; he is still in his novitiate, however expert a specialist.'[22]

The judgement of those who climbed in the same era as Murray or were within a few years of it – those close enough to appreciate his climbs in their proper context – was that he was one of the best of his day, particularly on mixed winter climbs. Douglas-Hamilton, in his review of *Mountaineering in Scotland*, said of Murray: 'He is himself an outstandingly skilful rock-climber, his speciality is the high standard and long winter climbs. There is no finer exponent in the whole country today of this type of climb.'[23]

Tom Patey, writing of Murray's classic winter routes, said that they 'inspired everything that followed; Garrick's shelf on the Crowberry Ridge is the prototype of the modern ice climb.'[24]

Hamish MacInnes' opinion was that 'The "ice crowned castles" of Bill's career, such as the stubborn Garrick's Shelf on Buachaille Etive Mor, stand the scrutiny of time. Not many mountaineers of this new millennium would relish scaling the glassy rampart wall of Crowberry Ridge with the bare trio of necessities – an antiquated ice axe, nailed boots and a hemp rope that resembled, when frozen, a steel hawser.'[25]

Mark Diggins, who took part in the recreation of Murray's winter ascent of Tower Ridge,[26] said he thought that, in those days, with the gear they had, more planning, skill and experience was required and that some modern climbers are flattered by their equipment and are not as good as they think they are.

Ted Zenthon, who used to climb the sandstone outcrops near London without using his hands, relying on his feet and balance alone, told me[27] that Murray's balance and technique was as near to this ideal as possible and that 'he was a joy to watch'.

With the perspective of time and taking into account Murray's later explorations in the Himalayas and his role in the Everest reconnaissance expedition, he has come to be seen as a great all-round mountaineer – an assessment that would have pleased him, although he wouldn't have cared overmuch what either his contemporaries or posterity thought of him. He actively strove to overcome vanity and ego, to serve others rather than himself and to find in the mountains, not glory and fame, but truth, beauty and spiritual fulfilment.

NOTES

1. *The Evidence of Things Not Seen*, page 146.
2. *The Edge: 100 Years of Scottish Mountaineering* (1994), page 59.
3. The *Glasgow Herald* published a daily weather chart, but these originated in London and were often out of date by the time they were seen by the reader.
4. Murray, in *Mountaineering in Scotland*, page 230, writes about how the experienced mountaineer is protected by an instinctive feeling for the state of the mountain and the presence of danger. Mark Diggins, director of the Scottish

Avalanche Information Service, confirmed in a discussion with me, that, despite modern technology, this instinct is still important.

5. *My Climbs in the Alps and Caucasus*, 1895.
6. *The Scottish Highlands*, 1976, page 215/216 – a view which Murray repeated later in *The Evidence of Things Not Seen*, page 39.
7. *That Untravelled World*, (1969).
8. *Geoffrey Winthrop Young: poet, mountaineer, educator* by Alan Hankinson (1995), page 326–7.
9. *The Evidence of Things Not Seen*, page 145.
10. In a telephone conversation, 20th October 2010.
11. *Yes, to Dance* (1990), page 32.
12. A telephone conversation with Bill Brooker in October 2010. Brooker was SMC president 1972–74 and knew Murray.
13. Quoted in Douglas Milner's chapter in *Classic Rock* (ed. Ken Wilson), 1978.
14. This kind of attitude is paralleled by the Arctic explorers of an earlier era who regarded most innovations as diluting the challenge, spoiling the contest between man and the elements and therefore some kind of 'grubby subterfuge'.
15. SMCJ, 1934.
16. Murray, however, does admit to following Bell up a climb on Lochnagar when the latter used a couple of pitons as direct aids to overcome a difficult section (*Mountaineering in Scotland*, page 127).
17. *The Craft of Climbing* by W.H. Murray and J.E.B. Wright, 1964, pages 25–27.
18. *Scotsman*, 1st February, 2010.
19. *Undiscovered Scotland*, page 66.
20. In 1938, for example, while Murray, was doing some of his hardest routes in Scotland, the even harder North Wall of the Eiger was being climbed.
21. In his Introduction to *Rock Climbs in Glencoe and Ardgour* (1949), which he revised and edited for the SMC.
22. *Mountaineering in Scotland*, page 239.
23. *Alpine Journal*, November 1947. Murray most likely would have denied this and pointed out that Mackenzie was more deserving of this accolade.
24. *One Man's Mountains* (1971), page 4.
25. In MacInnes' Foreword to *The Evidence of Things Not Seen*. In this same Foreword, MacInnes does point out that, on the climb referred to, Murray carried a slater's hammer rather than an antiquated ice-axe.
26. See Chapter Ten for more details of this and more about Mark Diggins.
27. In a conversation with Ted Zenthon at his house in Loughborough, February 2012 when Ted was aged 93.

CHAPTER TWENTY-THREE

HIGHLAND LANDSCAPE

In 1961 Murray was commissioned by the National Trust for Scotland (NTS) to produce an evaluative report on the Highland landscape. The NTS was founded in 1931 to promote the preservation of historic buildings and places of natural beauty. The former had clearly been the priority. The Trust was aware that for 30 years natural scenic beauty in the Scottish countryside had not enjoyed the same level of official protection as the buildings under its care, or, for that matter as Scotland's wildlife had under the care of other organisations. The Trust urgently needed up-to-date information on which to base decisions. Murray was given the task of undertaking a survey and producing a report which would identify and describe Highland regions of supreme landscape value and outstanding beauty, to report on the distinguishing characteristics of these areas, and to assess recent changes or future threat.

As recalled[1] by Jamie Stormonth Darling,[2] then the Director of NTS, the commissioning of the report was driven by the Trust's dislike of Tom Galbraith, Lord Strathclyde, Chairman of the North of Scotland Hydro-Electric Board from 1959–1967. Galbraith's mission was to harness water power at every opportunity regardless of its damage to the landscape and despite protests by NTS. According to Stormonth Darling, his close friend, Michael Noble, who was then Secretary of State for Scotland for the Tory government, encouraged the Trust in this because he (Noble) thought the Hydro Board, under its ambitious chairman, was getting out of control.

The NTS was finally spurred into action when the North of Scotland Hydro-Electric Board announced its intention to dam the famous gorge of upper Glen Nevis. The Board had already spoiled three Scottish glens of supreme beauty – Affric,[3] Cannic and Strathfarrar. As Murray saw it, 'The dams with their new roads had dispelled the natural atmosphere of these remote mountain passes; eroded the unusual beauty of their ancient woodlands and rivers, and so, too, the spiritual quality that wildland conveys to walkers – a refreshment beyond the physical. The proposed addition of Glen Nevis to the list of depredations inflicted was one too many.'[4]

Added to the activities of the Hydro-Electric Board were those of the Forestry Commission. In an attempt to replace the massive amount of timber felled during the war years, the Commission's sitka plantations were dressing the West Highlands in a dark green uniform of close-packed trees.

Highland Landscape was the first definitive study of the landscape of the Scottish Highlands – the largest area of mountainous and semi-wild land in Britain. Murray was selected for this challenging assignment for several reasons: Foremost was his reputation as the author of two classics of mountain literature. Robin Campbell, archivist to The Scottish Mountaineering Club, says of Murray: 'While his prose style was very effective and finely wrought, what was truly remarkable about it was a rare and peculiar talent for capturing mountain landscape in a way that compellingly exposed its character and beauty. This talent was seized on by the National Trust for Scotland, who appointed Murray as their Mountain Properties Advisor and commissioned a survey of Highland landscape.'[5]

Then there was Murray's impressive experience of the Scottish Highlands – more than 30 years of climbing its mountains, walking its moors, plateaux and hills, exploring its nooks and crannies and travelling through its landscapes. There could be no doubting Murray was a huge admirer of the Scottish Highland landscape and would do his very best to make a case for preserving it.[6]

Thirdly, Murray was at that time the Vice-president of the Scottish Mountaineering Club (he took over as president the following year). His appointment by the NTS may well owe something to the influence of the SMC since the project was being funded through the Trust's Mountainous Country Fund which was the benefaction of Percy Unna, a former President of SMC. In those days, Stormonth Darling said, the SMC and other bodies of that kind worked much more closely with the NTS and were 'all part and parcel of the Trust'

A further reason may have been that Murray was known to be a determined and honourable man, a man who invariably finished what he started and delivered what he promised.

'No one before me had attempted such a survey,' Murray wrote.[7] There had, in fact, been two post-war reports commissioned by the government in 1945 and 1947 chaired by Sir J. Douglas Ramsay which identified areas that should be considered for national park status. Legislation on these two reports did not proceed mainly because of pressure from landowners and the lack of any organised and concerted counter pressure from outdoor recreational interests for greater access rights. If Murray knew of the two Ramsay reports he makes no mention of them, nor of the NTS report *Scotland in Trust,* published just before the war which listed the key buildings in the care of the Trust and the iconic landscapes which were seen to be under threat. These reports did little more than produce lists and were short on both analysis and description. A more persuasive report was clearly needed and Murray was the man equipped to do it.

The Trust wanted the survey completed by late summer or early autumn, so for practical reasons the survey was restricted to the Highlands and excluded the Borders, Lowlands, Islands and the coastal strip. But for this, Murray would have identified a greater number of landscapes worthy of protection. Indeed, some of his favourite areas were excluded by this restriction, particularly where the sea and the sea lochs come together: 'There are two hundred and seventy-six mountains in Scotland. To anyone who sees them at all seasons, their unique virtue becomes that wedding of rock and water portrayed to such perfection down the Western seaboard from Cape Wrath to Arran. ... The Atlantic and the lochs ... of all mountain settings the most brilliant.'[8]

Murray chose 52 regions to survey. Each was then traversed on foot and surveyed from the lowest ground to the mountain tops. Murray had four months to complete his task. He was very recently married and, instead of a more conventional honeymoon, he and his wife embarked on the survey. They spent that summer living in a small tent in wild and lonely places during an exceptionally wet and windy period of weather. When asked how they endured four months in a tent, Anne Murray said, 'Oh, we were used to it. It was what we did all the time, anyway.'

Twenty-one regions were finally selected for their outstanding beauty. These were:

Moidart, Glen Nevis, Loch Arkaig, Knoydart, Glenelg, Kintail, Applecross, Ben Damph & Coulin Forests, Torridon, Loch Maree, Strathnasheallag & Fisherfield Forests, Inverpolly and Glencanisp Forests, Glen Affric, the Cairngorms, Balmoral Forest, Tummel

Valley, Benalder Range, Blackmount with Rannoch & Glencoe, Glen Lyon, Loch Lomond, the Trossachs.

Murray's main conclusion in this report was that: 'The ugliness that has grown up in so many of our towns arrived there insidiously, creeping in by degrees through lack of over-all direction, foresight, or control. The same situation is arising in the Scottish Highlands. The outstanding beauty of the Highland scene, which is one of the nation's great natural assets, has been haphazardly expended and no account kept.'

The following year, in a letter to the SMCJ, Murray summed up his findings and impressions by saying that great changes had occurred in the Highlands, mostly within the last 15 years, and mostly from hydro-electric works, forestry and tourism. Of the 21 regions which he had identified as being of outstanding natural beauty, only seven remained unspoiled and free from threat. In the next decade, he warned, the rate of change was likely to accelerate. It was not change we should fear, for some changes were beneficial, 'but haphazard change, uncontrolled and undiscriminating.'[9]

Murray concluded the opening overview of his report by calling for the formation of a body with the authority and power to control the indiscriminate abuse of the Highlands. He ended with these words: 'If action to that good end be not taken now, the Scottish people will lose by neglect what remains of their natural heritage.'

Landscape evaluation was in its infancy in the 1960s and Murray had no models to follow. Since then, techniques have been developed which are now used by landscape consultants. Mostly, these methods are a mixture of quantitative assessment and of subjective approaches. In the first category, checklists might be used to quantify the amount and type of woodland in an area, settlement patterns, or the number of water features. In the second category, evaluations from a range of viewers might be gathered (either in the field or using photographs or slides) employing various categories and scoring systems and then finding the average mark. Some of these systems, Professor Linton comments (1968), 'are better suited to the vocabulary of the estate agent than to that of the scientist or responsible planning officer.'[10] Even if a landscape assessment model had been available, it is unlikely that Murray would have used it. It seems much more likely that he would have done what he did and trusted in his own judgement.

The main problem of evaluating Highland landscape lay in its diversity, from sparse bare rocks to rich woodland, from remote wilderness to cultivated valleys. In Murray's view, however, there was a simple and universal criterion which could be applied.

> 'My choice of areas of outstanding beauty was determined, of necessity, on the criterion of beauty itself. Beauty is the perfect expression of that ideal form to which everything that is perfect of its kind approaches. The idea of beauty is innate in our minds, so that outward expressions of it can be recognised. Had the mind no idea or criterion of beauty within itself, no number of outward exhibitions would suffice for its recognition. Hence, in my survey, regions were selected on the criterion of beauty as I saw it.'[11]

Murray read widely in the field of nineteenth century mountain literature. He was therefore aware that attitudes to mountains are not universal or fixed for all time. During mediaeval times mountains were frightening and mysterious places to be avoided. It was not until two hundred years later that travellers began to visit them. Wealthy young Englishmen on the grand tour in the eighteenth and early nineteenth centuries wrote about the Alps with distaste as a type of landscape which was far removed from what was then the accepted idea of beauty.[12] Our changing perception of mountain and wilderness areas has been well documented by writers such as Marjorie Hope Nicolson, Robert Macfarlane and Robert H. Bates.[13]

By the time Murray wrote his report for NTS he had completed several expeditions to the Himalayas and spent many days in the company of Dotials, Bhotias, Sherpas and other mountain people in the areas to which his explorations took him. He would have observed that their cultures embraced different ideas of beauty about the human body, buildings, ornaments and dress, music and song and about the scenery around them.

Both these difficulties – criteria for landscape beauty varying across history and across cultures – Murray answers in *Undiscovered Scotland* (page 222), written more than ten years before he undertook his survey: 'Beauty gets a very different reception from different men. Its manifestation through the mountain scene may be refused reception in one century and not another according as prejudice veils men's eyes or detachment clears them. A particular acceptance or rejection of that kind is in the long run of no great consequence; for beauty is manifest in the whole natural creation, and men will find it where they feel disposed to look.'

This 'where they feel disposed to look' is often influenced by the kind of landscape that was imprinted on a person's mind during childhood, which then sets the standard and the criteria of landscape beauty for that person, be it the stark beauty of the red Australian Outback, the rolling quilted farmlands of England, or the bright colours of Bermuda. Writing of his summer holidays as a boy, spent on remote Scottish islands and coastal areas, Murray says they 'certainly bred in me a love of wild land, if not yet of high land.'[14]

That Murray should hold the views he did about beauty is not at all surprising. The fact that he had supreme confidence in his own judgement and the boldness to act upon it, free of self-doubt, was what made him a great climber. It was how he lived his life. More than that, though – he saw universal harmony and beauty, God and the human soul as inextricably linked. His statement that 'Beauty is the perfect expression of that ideal form to which everything that is perfect of its kind approaches' is a major tenet of the Perennial Philosophy which guided his life; and it was also a belief expounded by Plato whose works Murray closely studied.

In his survey Murray analyses why the areas he chose had beauty, and he identified certain ingredients of a beautiful Highland landscape – the beauty as he saw it. Frequently mentioned in *Highland Landscape* (but in no particular order) are: variety, irregularity and surprise, contrast, pleasing combinations of loch and mountain, wide and open views, scale, majesty and grandeur, the shape and form of mountains, moving water, interesting or rare flora and fauna, mixed native woodland.

Another factor, not always specifically stated, but implied or underlying Murray's descriptions is unity. Murray believed that landscape beauty is more than a collection of disparate features, but a result of them coming together as a unified, harmonious whole. It is the way that features combine which makes a place special. The whole should be more than just a sum of its parts. The concept of universal harmony was at the heart of Murray's philosophy and mysticism.

Although Murray did not regard wildness and remoteness as essential qualities for selection for his final list – he does include inhabited and cultivated locations and areas close to urban centres – phrases like 'air of seclusion', 'mountain sanctuary', and 'utter remoteness', crop up regularly. It is worth noting that, except for the upper regions of the higher mountains and the Flow Country in Sutherland (the largest area of natural bog-land in Europe), all of Scotland's seemingly wild country is the result of human activity – a fact which led Dr Robert Lambert to comment: 'In Great Britain, and in Europe as a whole, wilderness is so far removed from our historical and cultural traditions that we have little understanding of what it should be in its purest form.'[15]

In other, later writings Murray does make a distinction between areas of outstanding natural beauty and wilderness[16] areas, valuing wildness and remoteness for their own sake. For example, in a letter to the *Scottish Mountaineering Club Journal* (May 1969), he says: 'There is a strong case for certain areas being safeguarded as "wilderness" areas. These would be remote areas where the intrusion of man and man-made things would be at an absolute minimum – above all, the vehicle would be excluded. Entry beyond a certain point should be only for those prepared to carry their requirements on their backs.'

Murray put inverted commas around the word 'wilderness' here because he was well aware that definitions of wilderness vary and generate strong feelings and that there was a move towards using the term 'wildland' as more accurately reflecting the situation in the UK.

Murray knew that the word 'wilderness' was a sensitive one in the Scottish Highlands with its associations with the Highland Clearances. To many Gaelic Scots the wild areas of the Highlands represent a wasteland that was once a thriving crofting community. These lands were systematically cleared of their tenants during the early 1800s to make way for sporting estates and the widespread grazing of sheep. Hence the widely held view that the land is not empty, but emptied.

Phil Bartlett, in his book *The Undiscovered Country* (Ernest Press, 1993) adds the concept of natural piety to the discussion of wilderness and wildland: 'There is something in the mountain environment and the way we operate there whose gift is a feeling of belonging and rightness regained, and there is a point beyond which that feeling disappears. Can you feel it in the English Lake District? Most of the time, yes. Can you feel it in Langdale on an August Bank Holiday? I say, no. … Sooner or later it will be impossible to duck the vital question: *what are the essential qualities needed to preserve natural piety? …* But really, it's absurdly simple: it's emptiness we want.'

Although Murray was nearing the end of his life when this was written, the chances are that he read it. He would have agreed with it.

One of the advantages of employing someone with Murray's depth of experience of the Highlands was that he could describe them in all seasons and at different times of day, not just as he saw them during the four months of summer and early autumn of 1961 when he carried out his survey for the NTS. We should consider, too, that Douglas Scott, with whom he had spent several months in the Himalayas, was a professional photographer and Tom Weir, another companion on that expedition, was a semi-professional photographer. They would have reinforced what Murray undoubtedly knew already: the difference that the quality of light makes to how a landscape looks – the subtleties of early morning or late evening light with their soft tints and long shadows; the dramatic effects of cloud and mist, the sky reflected in water; and the way a landscape can change in a matter of seconds as the sun breaks through or clouds boil up.

This, too, is appreciated in his report, as, for instance, in his description of Crowberry Tower: 'Early on a Winter's morning, when the mountain is snow-clad, the most tremendous view is to be had of it from Kingshouse. The sun's rays stretch level across the moor and flood the great cone with fire.'

Whether there is an absolute standard for landscape beauty or for beauty in general is a matter for endless debate. Murray chose to rely on his instincts and judgement. No landscape assessment model developed since then has been able to move very far from the subjective opinion of the observers involved. It has been more a matter of finding ways of achieving consensus and consistency. The Countryside Commission for Scotland (later to become Scottish Natural Heritage) undertook a major review in 1978 – *Scotland's Scenic Heritage* which identified 40 NSAs (National Scenic Areas) in Scotland in need of conservation.[17]

The Introduction to this review states: 'We have not found or been able to develop any completely objective system capable of satisfactorily comprehending the selection of scenery in a way which would satisfy the essential aesthetic aspects of the appreciation of natural beauty and amenity. The review has therefore been carried out on a systematic but subjective basis.'

John Foster, who was then Chief Officer for the Countryside Commission for Scotland (CCS), gave his account of this: 'From the outset I was well aware of Bill's valuable and relevant skills [Murray was on the Board of the CCS] and when it was decided to undertake a similar survey for landscape quality designation I found Bill an enthusiastic supporter. However, I considered it first necessary to try to find an objective basis for carrying out the work on the ground. From his past experience Bill did not think this possible and indeed in discussion with him I began to have reservations myself. However, a reputable firm of landscape consultants was appointed, as sought by the Commission. After some months of intensive (and expensive) study I had to admit, and the Commission accepted, that no evidence of a positive objective methodology was showing itself. ... Bill was by no means triumphant in having confirmation that his initial thinking was correct and gave useful advice during the surveying period. At the conclusion of the fieldwork Bill gave further helpful support in the ultimate choice of the 40 areas accepted, but not formally designated, as National Scenic Areas by the Scottish Office.'[18]

'Beauty in things exists merely in the mind which contemplates them.' (David Hume, *Moral and Political Essays*, 1742), or as popular wisdom would have it – beauty is in the eye of the beholder. In Murray's case, it was a very experienced and well-informed, alertly sensitive, respectful, appreciative and clear-sighted eye.

The publication in 1962 of *Highland Landscape* was a landmark both in the identification of, and in the conservation of, the natural beauty of the Scottish landscape. It gave the NTS the ammunition it needed to argue its case with local and national government; and it acted as a bench mark for just about every report on Scottish scenic beauty that followed it.

One of Scotland's leading mountain country consultants, Robert Aitken, gave his opinion that 'this reticent little book has exerted a profound and sustained influence on the conservation of landscape in Scotland ... The effect of *Highland Landscape* was not dramatic, but it has been pervasive. With Tom Weir's campaigning against the Nevis scheme, and with wider economic and political forces, it helped to dam the flood of hydro development. It became part of a swelling wave of conservation awareness that led in 1967 to the creation of the Countryside Commission for Scotland. When the Commission struggled to pioneer convincing techniques for objective landscape classification, it ultimately fell back on a subjective evaluation in which the influence of *Highland Landscape*'s descriptions shines out.'[19]

Referring to the CCS report of 1978, Aitken said, 'It's easy to see the substantial influence of *Highland Landscape* and Bill's other writings about landscape, both in the selection of National Scenic Areas and in the text that characterises the areas and justifies their inclusion.'[20] Later, he wrote: 'Its superb characterisation of our diverse topography, often close in quality to blank verse, are endlessly quoted in area studies such as that of the recent Cairngorm Working Party, proving – if proof were needed – that no-one has yet improved on them. As with the writings of Sir Walter Scott, Bill's articulation of the essential qualities of Highland landscape has permanently enhanced our perceptions.'[21]

John Mayhew, former Head of Planning for NTS and president of the Association for the Protection of Rural Scotland, told me that Murray's report had led the way in landscape preservation, that no report since then had really replaced it, only reinterpreted or updated it, and that he 'still pulled it off the shelf' whenever he wanted to think through a problem. Robert Lambert, in his book *Contested Mountains,* describes *Highland Landscape* as 'one of the most important books of the twentieth century about rural Scotland'.

Lord Wemyss (the Earl of Weymss and March), who was then Chairman of the NTS, in an enthusiastic Foreword to *Highland Landscape*, said, 'This is a book which one can read for pleasure or instruction. ... We have had for many years a ranking order for Scotland's mountains, based on the criterion of height. This is the first time anyone has tried to evaluate the Highlands in terms of natural beauty or of scenic interest. It is agreeable to believe that in the future "Murrays" will command as much attention and respect as the "Munroes" and no able-bodied person – resident or visitor – will be content until he or she has penetrated every one.'

This well-intentioned compliment and genuine appreciation of Murray's ground-breaking work must have caused Murray to shudder on two counts. Firstly, Munro-bagging was anathema to him and, in his opinion, not in the spirit of true mountaineering; and secondly, the idea of every able bodied person in the country tramping through these beautiful and largely secluded areas would have appalled him. Here, from the outset of his dealings with the NTS, lay the seeds of conflict, both with the NTS and within himself.

NOTES

1. Notes on a telephone conversation between Bob Aitken and Stormonth Darling in April 1996. Notes taken at the time by the former.
2. Sir James Stormonth Darling (1918–2000) served as an officer with The King's Own Scottish Borderers during World War II and was awarded the Military Cross. After completing a law degree at Oxford, he became the longest serving Director of NTS, occupying that position from 1949–1983. Known for his dynamic and charming personality he considerably increased the membership of the Trust and the number of properties under its care.
3. In Chapter 4 of *Undiscovered Scotland* Murray lovingly describes a camping trip to Glen Affric, made in 1945. He wrote in *The Evidence of Things Not Seen* (page 128) that it was 'the finest of all Scottish glens or indeed of any I have seen in the Alps or Himalaya'.
4. *The Evidence of Things Not Seen*, page 309.
5. In Memoriam: obituary of Murray in *The Alpine Journal*, 1997.
6. Seven years previously he had written: 'I have availed myself of this privilege [the freedom to travel] and travelled in twenty countries between the United Kingdom and High Asia. The most spectacular highland scene is the Himalayan. Along the Tibetan frontier of Nepal its dramatic form sweeps to climax around Everest. It is magnificent, but not to be lived with: its too theatrical design could become a monstrous monotony. I have been forced by experience to a conclusion that I never anticipated when I first set out – that the most brilliant colour, the finest subtleties of light and shade, the most varied and contrasting beauties of natural scene, are to be found not at the ends of the earth but on our own doorstep.' (Introduction to *The Highlands in Colour* by W.S. Thomson (1954), which was a book of photographs.)
7. *The Evidence of Things Not Seen*, page 309.
8. *Mountaineering in Scotland*, page 228.
9. SMCJ, May 1962.
10. *The Assessment of Scenery as a Natural Resource* in *Scottish Geographical Magazine*, December 1968. Professor David Linton (1906–1971) was Professor of Geography at Sheffield and Birmingham.
11. The idea that the criteria for landscape beauty might be innate receives support from Stephen Kaplan with a theory somewhat removed from Murray's philosophical or spiritual starting point. Kaplan, Professor of Environmental Psychology at University of Michigan, has demonstrated that, when groups are given a range of landscapes to choose from, it is possible to predict which one they will prefer. This, he argues, is because our primitive ancestors were hunter gatherers and we still have an instinctive preference for the type of landscape which once gave the best chance of survival under those circumstances – that is, a savannah type of landscape with both trees and grassland. Savannahs had a higher density of large meat-bearing animals than elsewhere; they had distant views for spotting the prey and trees which provided fruit, shade and refuge. (*Environmental Preferences in a Knowledge-Seeking, Knowledge-Using Organism* by Stephen Kaplan *in The Adapted Mind* ed. Jerome Barkow *et al* OUP, 1992).

12. The shifting standard by which landscapes are judged is illustrated by the following two descriptions of Rannoch Moor:

    The first comes from the pen of the Rev.John Lettice in 1792: 'An immense vacuity, with nothing in it to contemplate, unless numberless misshapen blocks of stone rising hideously above the surface of the earth, would be said to contradict the inanity of our prospects.' *(John Lettice Letters on a tour through various parts of Scotland, in the year 1792 London: 1794. Available in Glasgow University Special Collections Department.)*

    The second is Murray himself. He starts in the following vein and continues to extol the moor for another six and a half pages: 'It was that eastern view from the Glencoe summits that won me – the sparkle of the numberless tarns at noon – the phosphorescent gleam of their night-eyes – the spike of Schiehallion pushing up beyond blue haze at the far rim, thirty miles away. I had been fascinated, too, by the distant flight of wild swans and great flights of smaller birds coming on to Loch Ba and Loch Laidon, which stretch in a linked waterway ten miles across the moor.' (*Undiscovered Scotland*, page 155)

13. *Mountain Gloom and Mountain Glory: the Development of the Aesthetics of the Infinite* by Marjorie Hope Nicolson (1959); *Mountains of the Mind: A History of a Fascination* by Robert Macfarlane (Granta, 2003); *Mystery, Beauty and Danger: The Literature of the Mountains and Mountain Climbing Published in English before 1946* by Robert H. Bates (Peter E. Randall, 2000).

14. *Evidence of Things Not Seen*, page 18.

15. *Contested Mountains: Nature, Development and Environment in the Cairngorm Region of Scotland 1880–1989* (Whitehorse Press, 2001), page 269).

16. Broadly speaking there are three main categories of wilderness definition: (i) anthropocentric definitions – areas which give the appearance or feel of wilderness to those who visit them. The concept of relative wilderness falls within this definition; (ii) biocentric definitions which define wilderness by the extent to which its flora and fauna are natural or original. This definition encompasses the concept of 'second-hand' wilderness – areas which have returned to the wild, but do not necessarily support the same flora and fauna as before; (iii) geographical definitions – distance from roads, habitation and other man-made intrusions.

17. There are 40 identified areas compared to the 21 selected by Murray in his report because the 1978 report was not confined to the Highlands and included coastal areas, Lowlands, the Western Isles, Orkney and Shetland. All the areas listed in *Highland Landscape* are represented in the CCS report, but are divided up and named differently in some cases.

18. Letter to me, October 2010.

19. Extract from 'His Single Measure was Beauty' in the John Muir Trust Newsletter, 2007.

20. In an email to me.

21. Extract from Aitken's obituary of Murray, SMCJ, 1996.

CHAPTER TWENTY-FOUR

SAVING THE WILDLANDS

The research for and the writing of *Highland Landscape* brought to Murray an awareness he had not previously possessed of the need to protect the Highland landscape. For example, whereas he now objected to new roads which brought tourists to beautiful places in numbers that caused erosion, in his youth he had been full of enthusiasm for the new road which enabled him to reach Glencoe so much faster than before; or when he compiled his Glencoe climbing guide, he did not foresee that, 20 years later, he would be protesting that too much information was being made available about the glen, enticing people into its remote sanctuaries.[1]

Perhaps, influenced by his conservation-minded friend, Tom Weir, and by Anne, whom he had recently married, Murray was already becoming more aware of the need to save his beloved mountain landscapes, but 1961, the year he started working on *Highland Landscape,* was a definite turning point in his life. From then onwards, protecting Scotland's wild and beautiful places, particularly the mountain areas, became one of his chief priorities, consuming an immense amount of his time and energy.

By then, the problem had been compounded by a huge increase in car ownership, by new and better roads, paid holidays, the rise of a host of new clubs promoting outdoor activities of all sorts and which organised slide lectures and group outings; more outdoor journals with enticing photographs; and the increased popularity and activities of the Scottish Youth Hostel Association. Murray described the social revolution that followed World War II as 'an earthquake effect that sent tidal waves of humanity rolling into the Scottish countryside at weekends and holidays.'[2]

In the 1960s people did not have a 'green' mindset as many do these days. It was a rare thing for landscape protection or environmental issues of any kind to be in the minds of planners and politicians, let alone on their agendas. A great deal of work, lobbying, campaigning, fact-finding, education and quiet persuasion needed to be done. For Murray, the means of doing this was through the positions he held in four organisations: the National Trust for Scotland (NTS), the Countryside Commission for Scotland (CCS), the Scottish Country-side Activities Council (SCAC) and the Mountaineering Council of Scotland (MCof S).

Shortly after the NTS published *Highland Landscape*, Murray was appointed as their Mountain Adviser (for a modest honorarium) and remained in that post for the next 20 years. A major area of contention between Murray and the officers of the NTS was over the application and interpretation of the Unna Rules. In 1935, the Glencoe estate of Lord Strathcona had come up for sale. Percy Unna,[3] who was then president of the SMC, sent out an appeal to mem-bers and to all other mountaineering clubs in Great Britain to raise funds for its purchase. Then, two years later, he also purchased the Dalness Forest which included Buachaille Etive Mor and Buachaille Etive Beag. The bulk of the money, in both cases, came from his own personal contribution. He presented these two purchases to the recently formed NTS.

In 1937 Unna wrote (see Appendix 3 for the full text of this letter) to the Chairman and Council of the NTS expressing his wish that this land be held on behalf of the public and preserved for their use in a primitive condition without development or active management. Unna foresaw the huge pressure these wild places would come under from increased numbers of visitors. He stated in his letter that there should be unrestricted access but that it should not be made easier to get into these mountains – for example, no improvements to the existing paths and no new paths, no bridges over the River Coe, no way-markers or shelters, no fixed ropes or other aids on difficult bits. These wishes, agreed to in writing by the NTS, became known as the Unna Rules.

After World War II the number of climbers, walkers and sightseers visiting the Glencoe area increased hugely, bringing problems to the NTS in how they managed this property. Throughout the 1960s and 70s, under the leadership of Jamie Stormonth Darling,[4] the Unna Rules were seen as impractical and not applicable to a situation which had changed enormously from the pre-war years. Besides which, the NTS needed to raise revenue and wanted to attract the public to its properties. It felt it had an obligation to the public to make them more accessible and to publicise them more. In doing this, in Glencoe (and elsewhere), it acted against most of Unna's expressed wishes.

An obtrusive and unsightly visitors' centre (or so Murray thought) was erected near the foot of Clachaig Gully. The Centre stocked pamphlets directing walkers to the beauty spots and extolling the charms of 'the Lost Valley'. Signposts were put up, old paths improved and new ones made[5] and a bridge built across the River Coe – justified by the NTS in that it gave quick and easy access to the mountains for rescue teams. It did, but it also gave quick and easy access to a multitude of walkers. Up till then, some fairly difficult boulder hopping across churning waters had been required, which weeded out the faint-hearted and those not suited to the rougher ground ahead. The attitude of the NTS was that Unna's letter contained guidelines rather than hard and fast rules, and that guidelines had to be interpreted, and decisions made, in the light of changed circumstances.

Murray, on the other hand, was in no doubt that Unna wanted the points which he had laid out in his letter implemented for all time. He was entirely of one mind with Unna and strongly opposed to the breaking of the Unna Rules. Whereas NTS officials claimed they were merely responding to demand and encouraging responsible use, Murray thought they were deliberately creating demand to an extent that was causing erosion and other damage to the natural beauty of Glencoe. Rennie McOwan told me[6] that 'some people ducked the row who should not have done so, but not Bill'.

McOwan wrote in an article: 'An unpleasant element entered the debate. Members who protested about anti-Unna decisions tended for a time to be ostracised by some senior members of Trust staff. The Trust's newsletter refused to carry letters on the subject ... A confidential staff memo in connection with the Trust's later acquisition of Ben Lomond said that Unna's name was not to be mentioned.'[7]

Within the NTS Murray did not find sufficient support for upholding the Unna Rules. However, as president of the Scottish Mountaineering Club (from 1962–64) he was able to lobby for this and other aspects of mountain conservation. Then, in 1970, he, Sandy Cousins, Donald Bennet and others reconstituted the ailing Association of Scottish

Climbing Clubs into the Mountaineering Council of Scotland. Its purpose was to represent the interests of mountaineers in Scotland, including matters relating to access and preservation. Bill Mackenzie became its first president and Murray took over from him. (Murray's presidential address to the MCofS, delivered at the end of his term of office, is given in full in online Appendix F and includes his views on mountain rescue, outdoor education and other matters).

Murray recognised that Stormonth Darling had the forceful personality and dedication needed to get things done. However, he did not appreciate having his advice ignored, or sometimes being deliberately left off the invitation list for meetings and functions. Frustrated and in order to gain a free voice, he resigned from the NTS in 1982.[8]

In 1967 the Countryside Commission for Scotland was established by Act of Parliament.[9] Murray was appointed as one of the founding Commissioners (member of its board) and served three consecutive terms of four years. This made him one of the longest-serving Commissioners in the history of the CCS (Brian Parnell also served three terms and Duncan Ross served four). The remit of the CCS was 'to develop facilities for the enjoyment of the Scottish countryside and to conserve its natural beauty'.

As with the NTS Murray felt that its priorities were in the wrong order. The CCS was handicapped by lack of any real powers and by its power of grant to local authorities being set too low. Again, as with the NTS, Murray had years of frustration and disappointment ahead of him. He had to work with and through what was there and to use the systems that were in place, imperfect though they might be. In his opinion many of the appointed commissioners knew very little about the Scottish countryside. 'I noticed at meetings that those who knew least were the most fluently vociferous, feeling able to speak with most confident assurance.'[10]

Murray recounts[11] how he opposed a proposal to build a caravan site on the Isle of Staffa.[12] The Commissioner who proposed it upbraided Murray and declared that a chance to offer employment to the inhabitants of Staffa was worth more than preserving its wild scenery. Murray had to tell him that Staffa was uninhabited and never had been inhabited.

Robert Aitken commented: 'Bill's own standards of judgement and integrity were of the very highest, while pretension was entirely absent from his character. Usually humorously tolerant of human foibles, he was scathing of what he saw as arrogance, wilful ignorance, underhand dealing, or naked selfishness.

'What Bill did bring to the Commission was his total commitment to mountain recreation and mountain landscape, a field knowledge of Scotland virtually unmatched (especially in the early days) by staff or other members, and quiet authority. The commission was to draw heavily on these assets when it formulated its system of scenery protection in *Scotland's Scenic Heritage* in 1978.'[13]

In the same obituary Aitken said that Murray probably found it difficult to make common cause with fellow Commissioners of very disparate interests to form or join any kind of power bloc with them. Findlay McQuarrie, who worked with Murray at NTS, saw him as someone who usually took a balanced view, always listened to what others had to say, had a pragmatic streak and a fund of common sense. 'He was a person who preferred to be behind the scenes, although others pushed him to the fore.'[14]

John Foster,[15] a former Director of CCS, had this to say: 'In his 12 years as a Commissioner Bill Murray brought an unrivalled knowledge of mountain country and its recreational use to his colleagues ... All his extensive involvement with responsible voluntary organisations helped to make Bill an important contributor to the development and progress of the Commission as a national agency ... He did not speak at length or all that often, but ... when he did members listened to what he had to say ... Bill was a valuable member of the Commission and in his three terms of office did a power of useful work, most of it quietly and without fuss.'[16]

On one occasion, Murray was so incensed by the Forestry Commission waymarking a route to the top of a mountain that he pulled out all the posts and dumped them at the roadside. He then phoned the Commission and told them what he had done.

One of the voluntary organisations Murray was involved with was the Scottish Countryside Activities Council. In 1967, the same year that the CCS came into being, the Ramblers Association (Scottish Area), of which Murray was president at the time, held a conference in Glasgow, attended by a range of outdoor organisations. The title of the conference was 'The Scottish Countryside – The Future'.

Murray opened the conference with a speech on 'The Scottish

Countryside Today'. He pointed out that the newly formed CCS had put preservation as its second priority, not its first. Preservation, he said, was a positive attitude, a determination to hold what was excellent and improve what was not. Murray listed a number of subjects of mutual concern to outdoor organisations: preservation; access to open country; freedom to camp in mountain and coastal areas; rights of way; a need to retain the old roads and tracks (new motor roads were often built over famous old tracks); the retention of deciduous woodlands. Murray then stated that when people acquired a more intimate knowledge of the countryside, they cared for it and behaved well in it. Information officers and wardens had a vital role to play in this.

He then went on to say that: 'The amenity societies had a mutual concern to retain remote wilderness. This could not exist together with development of it. The whole interior of areas such as the Cairngorms ought to be held untouched, with development checked at the circumference. Wild country was a thing of very high value. It was a value that had been greatly underestimated by all but a very few planners. ... It could only be kept wild by leaving the interior unimpaired for the enjoyment of future generations. Development was not reversible.'

Murray said that the outdoor/amenity societies should speak with one voice to the CCS and should get together to ensure this happened.

Out of this suggestion emerged, the following year, the Scottish Countryside Activities Council, with Murray as its first Chairman. It represented a wide range of interests – rambling, mountaineering, camping, caravanning, cycling, skiing, youth hostelling and a variety of clubs and organisations which supported or promoted these activities. Sometimes it was difficult to obtain consensus and it took a man like Murray to handle potentially divisive situations.

'Bill fostered and directed SCAC from 1968 to 1982 with understated authority and sagacity. He commanded immense respect and affection from the members. SCAC was never intended as a radical lobbying force – the varied interests of its member organisations have always acted as a constraint on the more exuberant factions – but it became, and has survived as, a useful consultative and representative forum, a respected moderate voice.'[17]

The years when Murray was serving on the NTS, the CCS, the

MCofS and SCAC were the years when debate about national parks in Scotland was in full swing. Between the report, *A Park System for Scotland*, produced by CCS in 1974 and the first national parks in Scotland lay a 28-year gap of debate, in-fighting, compromise, political manoeuvring (especially by the powerful landowners) and procrastination.

Murray was heavily involved in this debate. He had already made a significant contribution to it through his survey, *Highland Landscape*, which identified areas of outstanding beauty in the Scottish Highlands. Now he was involved in advising the NTS and the CCS, helping frame proposals, responding to draft papers, and co-ordinating the responses of SCAC members to these various reports, papers and proposals. As always, his personal response was that preservation of wild land should have priority over easy access; and that there should be some areas where access was limited. Murray himself did not favour the use of the term 'national parks'. He thought it would give the public the wrong impression of their purpose and attract people to them in numbers that would harm the natural environment.

It was not until six years after his death that the first national park in Scotland was created (Loch Lomond and Trossachs National Park, 2002. The Cairngorm National Park followed in 2003). Murray would not have been entirely happy with the fact that when they finally came into being, these two parks, unlike those in most other countries, had a duty to promote economic development as well as to protect the natural environment.

A sample of the cases Murray undertook and the tasks he was required to perform will give a flavour of the variety of conservation work in which he was involved. In 1968, almost at the outset of its existence, the CCS had to deal with a proposal to renovate the Coruisk coastal path in Skye[18] and build a bridge over the River Scavaig. This, it was claimed, would greatly facilitate mountain rescue. The CCS approved the plans despite opposition from Murray, one of their own Commissioners. His despair and disappointment almost caused him to resign.[19] A year later the path and the bridge were badly damaged, returning the difficulty of access to its previous level. The official cause of this damage was 'a winter storm', but it seems to be an open secret that its demolition was a planned act of protest.

Another case into which Murray put a great deal of work was the proposal to extend skiing facilities in the Cairngorms by developing Coire an t-Sneachda, Coire an Lochan and Lurchers Gully. Murray rallied opposition to it through SCAC[20] and the MCof S. He declared that mechanical ski-lifts, car parks, toilets and cafés in this remote and beautiful part of the Cairngorms would be 'the selling of a people's birthright'.[21] He gave evidence to this effect at the public inquiry in Kingussie.

'Diffident as he was, he manifestly did not relish any part of that experience, but the sincerity and passion of his evidence clearly carried much weight with the Reporter.'[22]

Other tasks Murray undertook were, for example, Heritage Assessment for CCS (tax exemption for owners of estates deemed to be of national heritage significance); or looking at issues arising from the development of North Sea oil and its impact on the environment – for instance, going on a fact-finding mission for the NTS to Wales to observe the damage done by an oil-spill.

Aitken summed up much of Murray's work with SCAC: 'Under Bill's chairmanship SCAC actively promoted the conservation of wild land in Scotland, drew on Adam Watson's survey work on bulldozed tracks in the Cairngorms to badger CCS and the Scottish Office into limiting further damage, led the campaign against the Grampian Way long distance footpath proposal, and carried out useful surveys on topics ranging from rights of way in Central Scotland to camping and caravanning problems in the Highlands.'[23]

Because Murray had strong views and was well known for his ability to express them powerfully, one might suspect that a streak of intolerance, even fanaticism went with it. Those who knew him and worked with him, however, said that in committee meetings, hearings, inquiries and the many memos that flowed from his pen, he was even-handed and fair-minded. In an article for *The Scots Magazine*, for example, he wrote: 'We need a balanced development of farmland, forestry, and recreation.'[24] He was not against developments if they were in the appropriate places and did not go too far, or reach a point when 'the process no longer gives, it robs'.[25]

In all his conservation work the Unna Rules were his ideal and never far from his mind, but he was there at a time when the general opinion of his colleagues was against them; and he was working with officials who, for the most part, had a knowledge of and a feeling for the Highland landscape that did not match his own. He became a founding Trustee of the John Muir Trust (JMT)[26] in 1984, believing that here was an organisation that would put preservation first and recreational access second. As with the NTS and the CCS he found that their point of compromise with developers, politicians, the reality of crofters and landowners and the pressures of modern society was not his.[27]

His frustration is shown in a letter to Aitken (31st August, 1985):

'I will be astounded if they [the Trustees of the John Muir Trust] consent to strict rules and if they do not I will be getting out. I wasted years of time on the NTS and on CCS playing games with men who never were in earnest about conservation of wild land and who did not in reality give a damn about what happened to it. I was so slow in leaving that I now feel guilty (of my own stupidity) ... Perhaps compromise cannot be avoided. I remember Morton Boyd[28] saying to me (after a CCS meeting) "On conservation, never compromise." I learned he was right.'

Murray and other supporters of the Unna philosophy have been accused of being selfish, élitist and even ageist (in that not many people over seventy can get into the hills without a bridge or two and paths to help them). His stance, some said, was denying important local and national needs. This is not a fair or an accurate assessment. Murray's aim was not to fix things so that only he and his fit friends could enjoy the mountains free of the riff-raff masses, but to ensure that, for future generations, there was still something left to enjoy. He, like Percy Unna, was taking a long-term view, foreseeing the huge pressures that social changes and an increasing population would bring.

Half a century later, an article in the JMT Journal supported Murray's judgement: 'Time and again we discover that the important national need that demanded somewhere beautiful be destroyed turns out to have been the important need of a few individuals who make a lot of money for themselves, but impoverish the potential of an area forever.'[29]

Nor was he trying to restrict access to all the wild or mountainous areas in Scotland – only to the heartlands of the most scenically beautiful, the most environmentally sensitive, and those places most in danger of being spoiled. Murray emphasised that wilderness should not be confused with areas of outstanding natural beauty (although the two might overlap). It might seem obvious to us now, but it needed pointing out then, that wild and remote areas cannot remain wild and remote if they are tamed. Furthermore, rather than being some old-world reactionary from the days of class privilege, when mountaineering was a sport for 'gentlemen' who instinctively understood 'the code', he was ahead of his time in valuing wild land for its own sake and not as something that was there purely for the convenience and enjoyment of mankind.

'Wildland is not there simply to minister to our need of recreation … Land and wildlife have their own being in their own right. Our recreation is an incidental gain, not an end in itself to be profitably pursued by exploiting land where that means degrading it.'[30]

Murray's contribution to conservation cannot be precisely quantified. A large part of his influence was through the NGO sector, and has now been subsumed into wider currents of thinking and management of wild land.

As Robert Aitken explained: 'The impact of his writing and activity in SCAC and other bodies has been absorbed into the collective approach to conservation of wild land and landscape. At a very high level you could say it's similar to how nobody reads Rousseau or Walter Scott nowadays but their influence pervades our attitude to romantic landscapes; or a closer recent parallel, the influence of Fraser Darling on ecological thinking about the Highlands. FFD and WHM [Frank Fraser Darling and W.H. Murray] are only occasionally directly cited or even acknowledged – their major writings are at least 40 years in the past – but they've helped build the platform of perception from which many people see the Highlands.'[31]

Richard Balharry[32] told me that he thought Murray had made an 'indelible impression'.

It has been said that Murray lacked political cunning, that he could have been more assertive as a chairman and that he did not know how to handle the media. Some might say this is to his credit. The point is, that when someone was needed, he was the one whom others pushed forward, and he was the one who did not dodge the responsibility.

He lent his quiet authority and the tremendous respect in which he was held to a cause he believed in.

From the mid 60s to the mid 80s, at no time was he serving on less than three conservation bodies at any one time, and sometimes more.[33] In this same period he produced four major guidebooks, which called for a considerable amount of research, a collection of short stories and a biography – another work demanding many months of research. On top of this, he wrote numerous shorter pieces for magazines and journals, including many on topics related to conservation (see Appendix 2: Bibliography of Murray's published work). Under such a heavy load, his determination, dedication and stamina was impressive – his self-sacrifice, too, for his workload made it increasingly difficult to get away into the hills.

To quote Robin Campbell: 'This was a long and gruelling period of voluntary work, entailing heroically many taxing journeys from his remote heronry at Lochgoilhead, endured without complaint or adequate recompense.'[34]

Murray has been called a second John Muir,[35] a statement meant as the highest accolade one could bestow on a wild land conservationist. He was not a second anybody, he was a first Bill Murray, who acted in his own way and according to his own deeply felt beliefs. Their lives overlapped by one year and certainly there are parallels between the two, as writers, philosophers, and conservation campaigners, but true comparisons are difficult to make. Muir lived in a different century, on a different continent with different social conditions and environmental laws. Muir lived in a land that set up national parks 112 years earlier than Scotland did and which valued him in a way that Scotland has not valued Murray, giving his name to a long-distance trail, a mountain, a glacier, several schools and colleges and issuing a commemorative John Muir postage stamp. Perhaps it is not too late to follow this example.

Robert Aitken summed up Murray's contribution to Scottish mountain conservation: 'Bill Murray stands alongside James Bryce[36] and Frank Fraser Darling[37] in the pantheon of Scottish conservation. He made a major contribution to protection of Highland landscape through his writing, through his work in voluntary and official bodies, but also through the inspiration he provided by his writing and his example. This may yet prove to be his greatest legacy to Scotland.'[38]

NOTES

1. In his Glencoe climbing guidebook Murray did, however, deliberately refrain from making his descriptions too detailed, only pointing out the general line of a route, leaving climbers to solve the problem for themselves.
2. *The Evidence of Things Not Seen*, page 311.
3. Percy Unna (1878–1950), was educated at Eton and Cambridge and became a civil engineer. During World War I he served in the Royal Navy and in World War II he helped design the Mulberry Harbours used after D-Day. He was a keen mountaineer and became president of SMC in the 1930s. Using his inherited wealth he became the chief benefactor of the NTS. It was largely his money which bought Glencoe for the NTS in 1935. Over the remainder of his life he made considerable anonymous donations to the NTS to ensure the upkeep of these estates and to enable the purchase of further properties, including Kintail, Glen Shiel and Loch Duich. Towards the end of his life he set up the Mountain Country Trust which enabled the NTS to buy Ben Lawers, Goatfell and the Torridon estate.
4. For details of Stormonth Darling see Footnote 2 in Chapter Twenty-Three.
5. A case was made for 'granny stoppers' at the start of any path – a bit left unimproved in order to deter the non-serious walker, but this idea was soon dropped.
6. Rennie McOwan is a journalist, writer, broadcaster and lecturer who specialises in outdoor and Scottish cultural topics. He has a particular interest in Percy Unna and has done a great deal of research into his life. This conversation with Rennie was over the telephone, 4th May 2010.
7. In an article 'A Great Lover of the Hills,' *The Scots Magazine*, January 2010.
8. Much has changed since then. In later years, NTS gave a higher priority to preservation and had renewed respect for the Unna Rules – if not for the exact wording, at least for the spirit and intention of them.
9. The formation of the CCS resulted from The Countryside in 1970 Conference which was convened to look at the forthcoming decade of the 1970s and to anticipate and plan to meet the problems which lay ahead. Bob Grieve (whom Murray later came to know quite well) and Tom Weir played an important part within the Conference's Scottish Study Group. The CCS came to an end in 1992 when it was combined with the Nature Conservancy Council for Scotland to become Scottish Natural Heritage.
10. *The Evidence of Things Not Seen*, page 312.
11. *Ibid.*
12. A small island off the west coast of Mull, location of the famous Fingal's Cave.
13. Extracted from Aitkens's obituary of Murray in SMCJ, 1996. A slightly altered version of this obituary was also produced in pamphlet form for the Scottish Countryside Activities Council under the title of 'W.II. Murray: Mountain Conservationist'.
14. McQuarrie told me this when we met at his house in Helensburgh in April 2010.
15. John Foster CBE was a Director of CCS for 17 years. He was also Vice-president of the Scottish Campaign for National Parks.
16. In a letter to me dated 12th October 2010.

17. *W.H. Murray: Mountain Conservationist* by Robert Aitken, SCAC, 1996.
18. The path leads to Loch Coruisk in south-west Skye, in the heart of the Cuillin, one of the most beautiful and remote parts of Skye.
19. It was this failure to stop the plan going ahead which led to the formation of the Mountaineering Council of Scotland, in order to provide an effective lobbying organisation for mountaineers.
20. The Scottish Ski Club, a member organisation of SCAC, did not sign up to the protest.
21. Public Inquiry Precognition on behalf of SCAC, 1981.
22. *W.H. Murray, Mountain Conservationist* by Robert Aitken, SCAC, 1996.
23. *Ibid.*
24. 'Wild Scotland – A Priceless Asset in Danger' in *The Scots Magazine*, November 1967.
25. Public Inquiry Precognition on behalf of SCAC, 1981.
26. The John Muir Trust takes its name and inspiration from John Muir (see footnote 35), the pioneering, Scots-born American conservationist who was passionate about the wild. The Trust was founded to safeguard the future of wild lands against development and to promote awareness and recognition of the value of such places. It achieves this through ownership of land and through partnerships with other land owners.
27. Since the time when Murray was active in these organisations the NTS, SNH (which took over from CCS) and JMT are now closer to Murray's way of thinking.
28. Dr John Morton Boyd CBE (1925–1998) was a Scottish zoologist, writer and conservationist. He was a pioneer of nature conservation in Scotland.
29. 'The Uses of Freedom' by Ed Douglas, JMT Journal, autumn 2010.
30. In his Foreword to *Scotland's Mountains* by Andy Wightman (Scottish Wildlife Countryside Link, 1996).
31. In an email to me, dated 19th February, 2010.
32. Richard Balharry MBE was formerly Area Manager for SNH and, before that, an officer of CCS. He is currently chairman of JMT.
33. President SMC 1962–1964; NTS Mountain Adviser 1963–1982; President Scottish Area of the Ramblers' Association 1966–1984; CCS Commissioner 1968–1980; Chairman of SCAC 1968–1982; President of MCofS 1972–1975; Vice-president of the Alpine Club 1971–1972; on Council of Friends of Loch Lomond 1978–1988; Trustee of JMT 1984–1986; Patron of Scottish Council of National Parks 1990–1996.
34. Murray's obituary in *The Alpine Journal*, 1996.
35. John Muir (1838–1914) was a Scottish-born American naturalist, author, and early advocate of preservation of wilderness in the United States. His letters, essays, and books telling of his adventures in nature, especially in the Sierra Nevada mountains of California, have been read by millions. His activism helped to preserve the Yosemite Valley, Sequoia National Park and other wilderness areas. The Sierra Club, which he founded, is now one of the most important conservation organisations in the United States. One of the best known hiking trails in the US, the John Muir Trail, was named in his honour. Other places named in his honour are Muir Woods National Monument, Muir Beach, John

Muir College, Mount Muir, Camp Muir and Muir Glacier. In his later life, Muir devoted most of his time to the preservation of the Western forests. He petitioned the US Congress for the National Park Bill that was passed in 1890, establishing both Yosemite and Sequoia National Parks.

36. Viscount James Bryce (1838–1922) was a liberal politician and historian. He was MP for Aberdeen South. He campaigned in the 1880s for the right to freedom to roam in the Scottish countryside and for greater access to the Scottish mountains.

37. Frank Fraser Darling (1903–1979) was an English ecologist, ornithologist, farmer, conservationist and author of many books on natural history and human ecology. For most of his adult life he lived in Scotland. His best known book is *The Natural History of the Highlands and Islands* (1947). His 1969 Reith Lectures, 'Wilderness and Plenty', made an important contribution to the growing debate on man's responsibility for the natural environment.

38. *W.H. Murray, Mountain Conservationist* by Robert Aitken, SCAC, 1996.

CHAPTER TWENTY-FIVE

GREATER SCOPE FOR THE IMAGINATION

In the space of six years Murray had four novels published: *Five Frontiers* (1959), *The Spurs of Troodos* (1960), *Maelstrom* (1962), and *Dark Rose the Phoenix* (1965). They were all in the category of action adventures, involving either mountaineering or sailing and sometimes both.

Mountaineering fiction,[1] a sub-genre of action adventure, was well underway by the time Murray turned his thoughts to it. There was, for example, *Running Water* (1907) by A.E.W. Mason, *Secret Mission* (1942) by Frank Smythe, *First on the Rope* (1949) by Roger Frison-Roche, *Corpse at Camp Two* (1955) by Showell Styles (under the name of Glyn Carr). Under his own name, Showell Styles brought out *The Lost Glacier*, followed by *Kami the Sherpa*, both in 1957. Also published that year were *Far, Far the Mountain Peak* by John Masters and *The Gods are Angry* by Wilfred Noyce. This batch of mountaineering novels in the mid and late fifties may well have prompted Murray to follow suit.

An author's first novel is the one most likely to be autobiographical, partly because there is some kind of compulsion to get something of oneself onto paper, and partly because the advice most frequently given to new authors is to stick to what you know. In *Five Frontiers*, Murray's first novel, the hero, John Taunt, is roughly Murray's age, a mountaineer who is also keen on sailing and who lives in a cottage on the shores of Loch Goil, as did Murray. John Taunt's yacht is named *Fiona* – the name of Murray's girlfriend at the time he was writing this novel. The action in the first half of the book is set in the areas of the west coast of Scotland where Murray sailed such as Crinan, Loch Craignish, Mull, Ardnamurchan, Rum and the Small Isles. After an interlude in France and the Maritime Alps, the action shifts to the area of the Himalayas which Murray first spotted from the higher

slopes of Panch Chuli when on the 1950 Scottish Himalayan Expedition – the Api area of West Nepal, bordering Tibet, which Murray
then explored in 1953 with John Tyson. Figuring in the novel are
many of the places Murray knew at first hand, including the Seti
and Kali gorges and the Marmar Pass and villages such as Tinkar,
Taklakot and Barechina. Very much part of the story are the Dotial
and Bhotia porters who, in real life, had won Murray's respect.

Maureen, a young woman, approaches John Taunt to ask for help.
Her fiancé has been climbing in the Himalayas and had come across
a shady group of people up to no good. Suspecting that they mean
him harm he has managed to get a message to her, telling her that if
she does not hear from him he is in trouble and needs Taunt's help.
Savock, the evil mastermind, a man of Russian origin and also a good
climber, is assembling a super-weapon with which to threaten the
world. Taunt and Maureen and other climbing and sailing friends
try to discover what is going on and to find the missing fiancé. In the
process, Taunt and Maureen fall in love. Yuile, the fiancé, is rescued
from captivity near the Tibetan (Chinese) border, but is later killed
in an avalanche. After chases, escapes and plenty of adventure and
cutting of rope bridges, the baddies are thwarted and the black diary
and briefcase containing the plans captured, to be later handed over
to the British government. Savock, who is responsible for killing one
of Taunt's Nepali porters, is beheaded with a kukri in revenge.

If Murray used locations he knew for *Five Frontiers*, he also put
something of himself into the character of John Taunt. When Taunt
says, 'Happiness falls to men who learn to live in every moment of the
present; unhappiness to men who dwell in the past or fear the future,'
he is speaking for Murray. Taunt, like Murray, is a firm believer in
Providence.[2] Taunt refers to it several times, as for example: 'Nothing
has impressed me more than this hard fact, that scheme as best we
may our fate is never more than fractionally within our own control,
and that this fact is a great mercy, since we are not all-foreseeing' –
words which closely echo Murray's views.

Considering that the novel was written only a few years away from
the start of the permissive, swinging sixties, it is sexually naive. No
impure thoughts cross Taunt's mind and any idea that he and Maureen (who 'had character rather than looks') might sleep together
before marriage is out of the question. One of Taunt's team expresses

the opinion that a mountaineer should not think of women until he is 50. Murray himself fell a bit short of that, marrying when he was 47, but the general feeling that women could interfere with your climbing is there in the mind of both the author and his character. Bridget Jensen, who as a teenager and in her early twenties used to crew on the same yacht as Murray,[3] recounts how he gave her and the female skipper any bits in his early drafts to read that contained love scenes or female dialogue or thoughts. Bridget says that usually he was laughably off the mark concerning how women's minds worked and his initial efforts at describing love were rather stilted.[4] There might have been a dash of Murray in Monet (a minor goody in the story) who was fit, vigorous and attractive to women, Murray writes: 'Monet, however did not fall for women: not for any of them. He was gay, polite, considerate – and there his interest ended. Mountains were his all.'

For most writers of fiction an important source of material is their own life experiences, not lifted straight into the fiction, but used as a starting point for some parallel idea, or modified, adapted or extended to suit the needs of the story. We can see Murray doing this in *Five Frontiers*. For example, when he digs out the concussed porter after an avalanche, he is using the experience of helping the concussed Michael Ward when they were swept into a crevasse in the Alps. Or, in describing the effects of imprisonment by the Chinese on David Yuile, Murray is drawing on his observation of what being in a German POW camp could do to people:

'We found him a very different man from the Yuile I remembered ... after two months with the Chinese his body had gone down like a punctured balloon. He was bony and thin, the skin flaky, the finger-nails ridged. He reminded me of a cat that had been caught in a gin trap, when all the gloss goes out of the fur; so with Yuile that same bleak look: the once shiny fair hair had become dry, dull, staring; the eyes, once bold and clear, now cloudy and wild. He looked past me when he spoke, not at me. His spirit had come near to breaking ...'

Just occasionally, Murray gets carried away by the sailing details or the magnificence of the mountain scenery and now and then it reads more like a tourist guide than a novel, but on the whole his restraint is admirable. He resists the temptation to show off his undoubted descriptive powers, knowing that the needs of the story must come first and that any 'purple passages' slow down the pace and are self-indulgent.

Murray's appreciation of mountains at night has been noted previously, so in the short description below, giving us Taunt's reaction to the Tibetan sky at night, his restraint is commendable: 'I think it to be worth travelling all the way from the British Isles just to see this night sky over Tibet. It gives one a new angle on the universe. The sky is white with stars. The nearer ones hang in three-dimensional solidity, like lamps. The Milky Way rolls across the heavens like a sunlit cumulus cloud.'

One of the notable aspects *of Five Frontiers* is Murray's obvious love of the sea and his ability to write about it every bit as vividly as he writes about the mountains. For ten years or more before turning to writing fiction he had been exploring the Scottish west coast and islands by sea as well as on foot. For three or four weeks every summer he would join friends in crewing on a 52-foot ketch, *Sybil of Cumae*, owned and skippered by an eccentric lady known as 'Jimmy' Edwards. This yacht won the Tobermoray race on several occasions, but not, apparently, when Bill Murray was crewing. 'He was a bit of a handicap,' one of the crew told me. 'Always in a dream about something else and not concentrating on the race.' Murray said that he liked the sense of space the sea gave. 'It was akin to mountaintops and gave me physical involvement with the elements, with water and wind. I liked the tension of racing and learned the difference between the weekend sailor and the real sailor.'[5]

Some of the passages in *Five Frontiers* make one wonder why he didn't write more about the sea. The excitement of the big seas clearly thrilled him, as in this passage:

'The moment we rounded the long eastern arm of Sanday we met the swell – an intimidating mid-ocean swell, which towered above the ship, and then miraculously passed beneath, leaving us almost breathless with alternating alarm and relief, for the change to exposure after long lying in shelter was too sudden for the nerves. ... Thereafter the experience of mounting these gigantic waves, then of lurching down, down into the broad trough, which like a mountain valley cut us off from all the surrounding world save for a patch of grey sky, until again we mounted up, up to the next great rolling crest, gave us two of life's most exhilarating hours.'

Or as in this one:

'She would run on the very top of some giant wave for several minutes on end, her bow often projecting over the edge as though over a mountain-cliff with empty space below. Then down she would come into the trough, subsiding smoothly. During the upward lift and the long run on top, the sensation we had was of flying, on and on, as though never coming down, soaring and swooping, gliding at high, fantastic speeds, airborne.'

Towards the end of the novel, Taunt and his group are faced with an agonising decision. They are in the mountains. Nungia, the Dotial porter, has been shot by Savock and is dying. A storm is gathering and the danger of an avalanche increasing by the minute. Should they leave him to die alone or risk their lives by staying with him? This is one of the most intense and gripping scenes in the book. One wonders if Murray knew of a dilemma like this in real life. He makes no mention in his other books of being faced with such a decision himself. He may well, though, have asked himself what he would do should such a situation arise. In the novel, Taunt stays with Nungia while the others retreat off the mountain.

Five Frontiers was published by Dent in the UK and, under the name of *Appointment in Tibet*, by Putnam & Sons in the USA. With the history of American westward expansion, frontier towns and so forth, possibly the word 'frontier' in the title would have given a wrong impression of the book to American readers. In 1961 a paperback version was brought out by Consul.

The book was widely and favourably reviewed as the following extracts show:

'It is better in detail than Buchan, just as good on plot.' *Oxford Mail.*

'As the title implies, the reader is kept on the move; the chase is exciting; there is a sharp battle of wits, hair-breadth escapes and last-minute rescues. Best of all is the changing scene, which Mr Murray describes so freshly that the hills and the sea seem a majestic background for the struggle between the agents of Communism and freedom.' *Scotsman*

'The author is an experienced mountaineer, and sailing and climbing give an air of actuality to his excellent adventure story. ... Mr Murray has a real talent for bringing alive the world of action.' *Evening Standard*

'The skilful intrigue of Oppenheim with the broad vistas of Rider Haggard and Buchan.' *Nottingham Evening Post*

'Wholesome, colourful, readable adventure.' *Books and Bookmen*

'The novel makes reading fit to rival that of *Prester John* and *The Thirty-nine Steps*.' *Rochdale Observer*

'Mr Murray expertly manages to blend the right amount of excitement with some very fine descriptive writing.' *New Zealand Herald*, Auckland

'A thriller in the Buchan tradition ... ingenious, well constructed and excitingly told.' *Manchester Evening Chronicle*

It seems strange that, nowhere in his writings, does Murray mention that his sister, Margaret, also wrote fiction – children's fiction – and that her first novel was published in the same year as *Five Frontiers*, Murray's first novel.[6]

In Murray's next novel, *The Spurs of Troodos*, John Taunt is now married to Maureen. 'They find themselves' as the blurb on the jacket says, 'committed to quit their beloved Scotland in order to undertake another battle of wits against the arch-enemy, Savock, whom they had believed to be dead. They know him to be dedicated to the destruction of freedom in the Western world, and to be capable of every evil to that end. Working as a team, with the help of the British and Italian Secret Services, they are flung into a series of violent hazards in which the utmost demands are made on courage and quick-witted reactions to sudden danger ... The protagonists move from Paris to Rome, and finally to Cyprus, where are added the dangers from Eoka ... The final scenes of search, chase and capture on the shores of the Mediterranean and among the spurs of Troodos are tense and powerful.'

In the part which is set in Italy, some of the action takes place around Chieti where Murray was first imprisoned during the war. Taunt tells us, 'I wanted to stop to admire the Gran Sasso, a sky-cleaving peak to the north.' This is the peak which Murray had looked at so longingly from behind barbed wire and which had helped turn his thoughts towards writing *Mountaineering in Scotland*.

In the early years of the war the 2nd Battalion of the Highland Light Infantry, in which Murray was a young officer, was briefly switched from North Africa to Cyprus. Their principal duties were coastal patrols to forestall German attempts to land men and supplies from U-boats. This is mirrored in the novel, for much of the action in *The Spurs of Troodos* is to do with Taunt and his team taking small boats along the Cyprus coast, in and out of deserted coves and beaches, to watch for Savock's attempt to land his deadly weapon from a ship under the cover of dark.

During their time in Cyprus the HLI occupied the great fort on the sea front and Murray's company was billeted in Othello's Tower, the site of Shakespeare's play. In the novel, John and Maureen Taunt are given accommodation by the British Army in this same tower. The plot involves much traversing of rough mountain country, either to spy on the enemy or to evade them. In writing of this, Taunt, that is to say Murray, demonstrates a soldier's eye for the lie of the land, the cover it can give and the vantage points it provides. Again, Murray shows us his love of sailing. This time, instead of being in larger yachts, the sailing is in small dinghies like the one Murray owned and kept in his boathouse at Lochwood on the shores of Loch Goil.

Through Taunt, Murray expresses his delight in dinghy sailing: 'I found it most delightful to feel once again the tremble of the tiller and the forward surge of a small boat with sails filled; the dinghy bears the same relation to a yacht as motor-bike to car, or pony to cart-horse: more quick and lively, and much more exhilarating to handle, for one feels in closer union with the machine, which one *rides* [Murray's italics].'

As with his previous novel, Murray gives us some beautiful turns of phrase and some lyrical passages without overdoing it, without falling into the mistake of distracting us from the story by saying,

'Look at me, don't I write well!' He describes, for instance, a mountain road 'that twists like wounded vipers;' and white village houses
which were 'gleaming like pebbles on a beach over a dark green sea
of rolling forest'.

Action adventure novels, by their nature, do not focus overmuch on
personal feelings or relationships, so that, even by the end of a second
book in which John Taunt is the main character, we do not know him
all that well. Most of Murray's friends said the same about him – that
they had known him for years, yet did not really know him. One thing
we do learn about Taunt is that he favours the direct, bold approach.
'In boldness there is magic,' he thinks, echoing the now famous lines
from Murray's book, *The Scottish Himalayan Expedition*:

> 'Whatever you can do, or dream you can, begin it.
> Boldness has genius, power and magic in it!'[7]

Had Murray known just how famous that passage from the expedition book was to become he probably would not have put this
thought into Taunt's mind, for to know that it comes from outside
the carefully created bubble of make-believe bursts that bubble and
shatters the reader's suspension of disbelief.

For *Maelstrom* (1962), Murray found a fresh set of characters and
a new publisher, Secker & Warburg. The most likely reason for this
change to another publisher was that his editor at Dent was E.F.
Bozman and by 1962 Bozman would have been aged 67 and had
probably retired. Authors tend to go with specific editors as much as
they go with a particular publisher. Different editors have their own
lists of authors, their own favourites and likes and dislikes. Murray
needed to find an editor who appreciated his kind of writing.

A yacht is found abandoned off the north coast of Ireland. Its
owner, John Menzies, his wife, daughter and crew, have all vanished.
This is of particular interest to a number of people: to Graham John,
for Menzies was a friend and Graham John was shortly to have joined
the yacht; to young Hamish Martin, for he is in love with Menzies'
daughter, Thea; to MI5 and the CIA, for Menzies is one of the President's top scientific advisors.

Kirsten Strunk, Menzies' first wife, with whom he had kept on
friendliest terms, had emigrated to South Africa after the disappear-

ance and presumed death five months earlier of her second husband in a blizzard on Ben Nevis. Then Strunk dramatically reappears.

The mystery deepens when Hamish discovers Strunk has received a letter from his wife postmarked not South Africa but Braemar, and when two men from the CIA reveal what they know of the Strunks' past, the hunt is up. The chase takes Hamish, and his friend, Donald Garrick, who provides his yacht, in among the sounds, the lochs, the harbours of Scotland's west coast, by car across the breadth of the country, to the snow blizzards of the Cairngorm mountains and finally to the dreaded Strait of Corrievreckan. The title, 'Maelstrom' has a double meaning which embraces both the terrifying Corrievreckan whirlpool and the emotional flood in Graham John's past life which has swept him into his personal maelstrom. 'The "lost scientist" theme can have produced few better thrillers than Mr Murray's *Maelstrom*,' said the *Birmingham Post*.

Graham John, like John Taunt of the previous two novels, is a keen sailor with a belief in providence. A strange feature of the book is that Graham John, throughout, is referred to by his surname, and John Menzies by his forename, thus confusingly giving us two main characters in the book called John. The chapter entitled 'Resurrection' is an interesting example of the way Murray used material. Strunk turns up weak and bewildered at the door of the CIC hut at the foot of Ben Nevis. When he is able to speak he describes how he set out to climb Tower Ridge, but found much more snow on the upper part than he had anticipated and then encountered a howling gale in the Tower Gap which caused him to fall. Apart from the fall, this is a close re-enactment of Murray's winter ascent of Tower Ridge as described in *Mountaineering in Scotland*.[8] Strunk thinks he has fallen only the previous evening, but in fact (in the story) has been missing for several months and has been lying in a snow-drift in a state of suspended animation until a few hours ago. Strunk's story has a much shorter time lapse between the fall and regaining consciousness, otherwise it exactly matches the article 'Leighton Johnstone's Resurrection' that Murray wrote for the 1990 SMCJ. Apparently, Murray was wont to recount this story after a few whiskies. It was never easy to tell with Murray when, if at all, he had crossed the line between sobriety and alcoholic euphoria, so nobody was ever sure whether he believed this story or whether it was one big leg-pull.[9]

Dark Rose the Phoenix (1965) was Murray's last novel. The heads of the British, American, and French Secret Services have resigned and teamed up to form a private organisation whose object is to track down international crime. Their headquarters are Paris, where they are confronted almost at once with the kidnapping of the Englishman's wife. Simultaneously they learn that a junior minister is being blackmailed. Both crimes are the work of a gang of international crooks masquerading as a charitable organisation which purports to give confidential advice to people in trouble. The head of this gang is the notorious Schlinkel, Jew exterminator and close colleague of Eichmann. Schlinkel has mysteriously vanished. A shuttered house in Paris, a visit to the Rhineland, a chase by car and plane through France, lead up to a final battle of wits in the wild mountains of Andorra.

In Chapter Fourteen of this biography attention was drawn to the close similarity between the reaction of Ross (one of the three goodies in the novel) and the Nazi, Schlinkel, and Murray's account of his harrowing experience with the Gestapo while he was POW. It was noted in Chapter Fourteen that this is the first time Murray is known to have opened up, in writing at least, about his POW experience. Schlinkel, the former Gestapo man, is shown to have some good in him, to have reformed and is ultimately forgiven by Ross and allowed to live. Perhaps Ross' forgiveness is also Murray's and his final emergence from the long, dark shadow of the war. The rather obscure title could also be signalling this, for the phoenix is associated with resurrection, triumph over adversity and that which rises from the ashes.

John Buchan's fictional character, Richard Hannay, was one of Murray's childhood heroes. Critics and reviewers have pointed out that Murray's novels are in the John Buchan tradition[10] and follow Buchanesque themes: Scottish settings, kidnapping, mysterious vanishings, hostages, an evil mastermind bent on world dominance, cryptic messages, the action taking place in wild and lonely places, resourceful well-connected men who are usually middle-aged, have an interest in theology and philosophy and operate independently to put things right. Both authors used similar symbols for manliness and moral worth: pipe-smoking, the firm handshake, the steady gaze, the firm set of the jaw, immersion in cold water, and hard exercise – the harder the better, with exhaustion scoring extra points.

Murray's women are more active, whereas Buchan's tend to play a passive role, but both authors favoured slim, boyish, fit women.[11] Buchan was a huge admirer of the writing of Sir Walter Scott, whose Romantic influence led Buchan towards adventure stories where coincidences abound and plots are on the borders of probability. The same could be said of Murray's plots, particularly his use of the overheard conversation – the goodies often being in the right place at the right time to hear the one important conversation or exactly the information they need to know.

In the following decade Murray amassed a huge store of historical knowledge when writing his Scottish 'guidebooks'. However, he did not make use of this to produce any historical novels. Nor, after completing a biography of Rob Roy did he emulate Buchan who, after writing a biography of Montrose, used the research for his novel, *Witch Wood*. By then, Murray had moved away from novels, concluding that, as much as he enjoyed that form of writing, the monetary return for the amount of time put into them did not make economic sense.

Reviews at the time of publication were generally favourable and the comparisons with Buchan flattering. It is only with the passing of time that Murray's novels have come to be regarded as not quite making it into the 'A List'. Partly this is because his style of writing has gone out of fashion, seeming rather stiff for modern tastes, and partly because moral codes have changed considerably, leaving Murray's chaste heroes and heroines behind. Even before Murray's first novel was published, Ian Fleming and James Bond had burst upon the scene (*Casino Royale*, 1953). Murray's books drew upon an older pre-war model, whereas writers like Ian Fleming, Hammond Innes (*Campbell's Kingdom*, 1952) or fellow Scottish writer, Alastair Maclean (*The Guns of Navarone*, 1957) were more in tune with their post-war readers. One might also make the point that Murray's fiction suffered by comparison with his non-fiction, that his success in the latter was a very hard act to follow.

In the fiction section of her classic bibliography of mountain literature[12] Jill Neate says of Elizabeth Coxhead's *One Green Bottle* (1951)[13] that it is 'still a leading contender as the finest climbing novel ever written'. Whereas other authors receive a few words of praise such as 'fascinating', 'most charming' or 'thrilling', Murray's novels are given only a brief description of plot, with no accolades.

In 'Murray's Way,' the chapter on Bill Murray in *Weir's Way* (1981), Tom Weir tells us that, in Murray's opinion, unless you hit the jackpot, the return for writing fiction in Britain did not justify the effort. You had to have American sales as well. In this same chapter by Weir, Murray is reported as saying, 'Of my six thrillers, two were not worth writing from the financial aspect.' Either Weir made a mistake in noting down what Murray said, or there are two novels by Murray unaccounted for. It is just possible that two other novels were written which were never published. Murray said he preferred fiction to any other form of writing because it gave 'greater scope for the imagination'.[14]

Whatever posterity might say about his novels, they do tell us two things about him: he was a versatile writer, able to write articles, essays, full-length non-fiction and fiction all to publishable standard; and he was not afraid to branch out into a new form of writing, his exploratory instinct applying not only to mountainous areas but also to the world of writing and the realms of creativity.

NOTES

1. By the term 'mountaineering fiction' I mean fiction in which mountaineering is central to the story rather than it simply being set in a mountain landscape.
2. Murray's belief in Providence is covered in Chapters Eight and Twelve.
3. Bridget, who was then in her late teens, told me that, sometimes, a whole day's sailing could go by without Murray addressing a single word to her.
4. It seems, too, that Murray's knowledge of sailing was not quite as extensive as John Taunt's. 'Skipper' Jimmy Edwards supplied sailing notes for him to use in this novel.
5. *The Evidence of Things Not Seen*, page 284.
6. Margaret Hesketh MacAlpine wrote *The Hand in the Bag* (1959); *Dougal and the Wee Folk* (1961); *The Black Gull of Corrie Lochan* (1964); *Aura and the Storm Child* (1965).
7. This quote is discussed more fully in Chapter Twenty.
8. Chapter Ten of this biography also deals with this ascent.
9. In a footnote to Murray's 1990 SMCJ article on Leighton Johnstone, the editor added: 'Incredulous readers might care to be reminded of a similar miraculous escape. Some twelve years later, in January 1943, Brian Kellett fell from the Tower Gap while soloing the Secondary Tower Ridge and shot down the entire length of the West Chimney (now called Glover's Chimney), landing in snow at its foot. He, too, survived, managing to walk to the CIC Hut unaided. Apparently, when telling this tale, Murray, who spoke very slowly, could take up to forty minutes over it.'
10. As well as writing novels, John Buchan, Lord Tweedsmuir (1875–1940) was

a published historian and biographer, a lawyer, editor, war correspondent, Governor-General of Canada, MP and director of a successful publishing house. He was born and raised in Fife. He retained his Scottish connections and was a member of the SMC. He wrote nearly 30 novels, including the six which featured Richard Hannay and three which centred on Sir Edward Leithen. Murray quotes Buchan in *Mountaineering in Scotland*, page 209 (incorrectly as it happens).

11. Before reading too much into this we should remember that, in the 1920s and 30s, when Murray's taste in women was being formed, 'flappers', with their slim, flat-chested look were all the rage. This preference is also found in his collection of short stories, *The Real Mackay*, where Shuna, the earl's wife, is described admiringly as 'flat in the stomach and lithe as a tiger' – tiger also being a word sometimes used to describe the young Anne Clark who later became his wife.

12. *Mountaineering Literature: a bibliography of material published in English*, Cicerone Press, 1987.

13. *One Green Bottle*, unlike the novels listed in the opening paragraph of this chapter, is not an adventure thriller, being much more about personal growth, emotions and relationships. Unusually, for a mountaineering novel of that period, it was written by a woman.

14. Notes taken by Tom Weir for his chapter on Murray in *Weir's Way*, National Library of Scotland, Weir Collection.

CHAPTER TWENTY-SIX

FACT AND AFFECTION

In an eight-year period, between the ages of 52 and 60, Murray's three guidebooks were published. These were: *The Hebrides* (Heinemann, 1966), *The Companion Guide to the West Highlands of Scotland* (Collins, 1968), and *The Islands of Western Scotland* (Eyre Methuen, 1973). In all three cases he was approached by the publishers and invited to write them. Through his two classics of mountain literature and through *Highland Landscape* – the report he wrote based on his survey for the NTS – his reputation as one of the foremost writers about the wilder parts of Scotland was already established.

The blurb on the dust-jacket of *The Hebrides* has this to say about Murray: 'He is a Scot who has not only a passionate love for his native land and an extraordinary knowledge and understanding of it but is a mountaineer, a sailor, an ornithologist, a keen botanist and a geologist and a novelist as well. It is his skill as a writer which enables him to give such graphic descriptions of the Islands, whose beauty and grandeur has so often baffled descriptions by those without the power of words.'

Murray was now committed to making his living through writing and he was of the opinion that, whereas more people borrowed novels (he had written four novels at this point) from libraries than bought them, the reverse was true of non-fiction.

Murray's guidebooks should be considered in the light of his passionate belief that the landscape of the Highlands and Islands needed to be protected and in the context of the work he did to conserve it. He accepted these commissions because he saw tourism as a way of boosting the Scottish economy and thought that his books might help attract tourists to Scotland. At the same time he was beginning to appreciate the problems which an excess of visitors could bring and the dilemma that writers about unspoilt places so often face – does

writing about them help to preserve them, or does it contribute to
their destruction? In the final chapter of his autobiography he reflects
that 'today [the mid 1990s] one only has to write of an unspoilt area
to put it in danger. This was not always so.'[1]

The guidebooks Murray undertook to write dealt, for the most
part, with places already on the tourist maps. When, however, he was
approached, in the mid 1960s, by David Brower, the Director of the
Sierra Club,[2] to write a book on the wild lands of Scotland – remote
areas not on the tourist routes – he declined. Brower wanted descriptive
writing at its best and high quality, full-page colour photographs.
The idea was that readers, their eyes opened to the natural beauty of
their own land, would want to preserve it. Murray liked the idea and
was tempted. In the end he declined the offer because, 'I knew now
that the practical effect would not be what David Brower hoped, for
Scotland's wild lands, unlike those of the USA, were unprotected.
The better the book the more tourists would come to see the wild
lands portrayed. Quite involuntarily, numbers would destroy them
by erosion.'[3]

The Hebrides was regarded at the time as being one of the most
comprehensive books about the Hebrides ever written. It was certainly
a labour of love. Elsewhere, Murray recounts how, more than
a quarter of a century before the publication of The Hebrides, he
climbed to the summit of Sgurr Alasdair in the Cuilllin of Skye.

It was a cloudless morning in June and, for the first time, he saw
the Hebrides whole, as an archipelago fringing the Atlantic. It was a
clear day and the sea was a more brilliant blue than ever seen on the
Mediterranean. 'I looked forty miles across the channel of the Minch
to the long, lilac spine of the outer isles ... a realm of several hundred
islands lay awaiting discovery. I felt, in anticipation at least, some of
that exploratory excitement that the first Scandinavians and Scots
must have felt more than 1,500 years ago before me, and the Bronze
Age and Neolithic seamen still earlier.'[4]

Murray was not only highly motivated for this task, but already
well informed. In addition to being a mountaineer he was also a keen
sailor, so that he knew the Scottish west coast and its islands both
from the sea and from the land. Much of his research in the field
was done while camping – surely no better way to get intimate with
a landscape. He recounts (page 73) how he and his wife camped on

Scarba for several days, on a grassy patch amongst the rocks by the shores of the Gulf of Corryvreckan, directly opposite where the infamous whirlpool develops, so that they could observe its behaviour close to.

Murray knew the facts and the details, but more than that he felt the spirit and atmosphere of the Hebrides. 'A great deal of the fascination of the Hebrides,' he writes, 'lies in that edge of the world atmosphere: they are the last lands, the gateways – beyond them nothing is known (one feels). Thus they appear as the symbols of the frontier; appear thus to the islanders themselves, to whom Tir nan Og, the Land of the Ever-young, has always lain west across the horizon.' He delights in the extraordinary quality of light with the air 'luminous in a way rarely known to the mainland.'[5]

A review of *The Hebrides* in the *Irish Times* stated: 'He [Murray] clearly loves the Hebrides, but, what is more important, knows them extremely well – indeed in extraordinary detail ... It is refreshing to come across a book about these remarkable 500 and more islands in which the flesh of affection is supported by the hard bones and skeleton of verified fact.'[6]

Murray did not speak Gaelic, but he was certainly interested in the language and had sufficient knowledge of it to take other writers of guidebooks to task for using modern Gaelic to derive meanings from place names, rather than the classical, and now obsolete, Gaelic, which often revealed different, but correct meanings behind the names. It is part of Murray's attraction as a writer of such books that he can move so smoothly from precision to vividness, from the minutiae of the Gaelic language, to describing 'a machair drenched in dew and loudly abounding in larks at half-past three in the morning', or the colours of the Lewis hills as being like 'the soft hues of a pigeon's neck' – practical and informative on one page, poetic and sublime on the next.

The second of Murray's guide books, *The Companion Guide to the West Highlands of Scotland*, covering the seaboard from Kintyre to Cape Wrath, came six years later in 1968. Murray had, in fact, completed the book two years earlier, and found the delays at Collins (the publishers) extremely frustrating. Second and third editions followed in 1969 and a fourth edition a year later. Murray's survey of the Highland landscape which he had done for the NTS seven years earlier gave him a good start, with all but three of the 21 areas he selected for their outstanding beauty in his report falling within the scope of his new book.

As its title suggests, the book was one of a series of companion guides which covered selected areas of the UK and Europe. The aim of these guides was to provide a companion, in the person of the author, who knew intimately the places and people about which he or she wrote and was able to communicate this knowledge and affection to their readers. This was a commission and a remit which suited Bill Murray down to the ground, for this is no cold and formal compendium of information, but a book which allowed Murray to admire the beauty of a sunset, to wax lyrical about the play of light on a loch, to vent his anger against those who have despoiled the landscape and express, in a forthright manner, his own opinions. It is a book which is delightfully different from the glossy sales pitch which emanates from local and national tourist boards or is found on internet sites. Forty-five years after its publication, despite much of the information regarding roads, ferries, access, hotels, tourist development, occupations and land use being out of date, it is a book one can still read for pleasure.

In *The Companion Guide to the West Highlands of Scotland* Murray does not pull his punches if he thinks official bodies or individuals are despoiling the environment. 'Loch Maree is world famous for its beauty. It seems all the greater crime that its approach in lower Glen Docherty should be marred by hydro-electric pylons and telephone wires, of which the latter are the worst offenders.' (page 293) He has quite a number of scathing comments about the Forestry Commission 'whose official eyes seem unable to rise above the limits set by material profit and loss'.

When he thought it was called for he could be quite blunt: 'This point is the only one (in my own experience) where the few people inhabiting made it plain, without being hostile, that visitors were not welcome. The attitude so violates the known character of the Highlander that I must suppose it due to very strict instruction from the English estate-owner.' (Page 248) It is difficult to imagine today's super-cautious, bland and offence-free guidebooks, saying, 'the centre of Inellan near the pier suffers from a congestion of small ugly houses, for which the only cure is demolition.'

In the opening chapter, 'The Seaboard of the Gael', Murray provides a brief overview of each of the areas covered in the book. Each
one is described with love and with an amazing ability to see the
wider picture as if he were an eagle hovering high overhead; and, as
one might expect of someone who has explored and charted remote
and unmapped regions of the Himalayas, he has a strong feeling for
the lie of the land and its overall physical structure.

Typical of Murray's style in this book is his personal modesty.
He is often describing mountains on which he made his fame as a
climber and where he did daring first ascents. Yet there is no mention
of this. All the evidence leads one to conclude that he was not even
remotely tempted to boast about his own exploits. On the other hand,
as licensed by the publishers, he does not hesitate to give his opinion.
Nor is he inhibited from slipping in the occasional piece of quiet
humour. Above all, what distinguishes Murray's guide books from
most others is that they can be read as literature and provide a feast
of fine phrases, metaphors and descriptive passages. Here is just a tiny
sample of the delights to be found in *The Companion Guide to the
West Highlands of Scotland*:

'The Kyle's shore is beautifully scalloped by small bays haunted by
eider-duck.'

'Historic and prehistoric relics abound like mice in August corn.'

'No west coast passage is so splendidly endowed with islands as the
Sound of Luing. They swarm up it like bees on a branch.'

He can give us an eye-witness account of the unloading of the
herring boats in Mallaig harbour – a sight no longer seen a decade
later. Then he can move from that kind of reporting to lyrical passages
which capture the beauty and atmosphere of the landscape.

The General Editor of the *Companion Guides* was Vincent Cronin,[7]
son of the famous novelist, A.J. Cronin. Much of the editing for *The
Companion Guide to the West Highlands of Scotland* was done with
Philip Ziegler.[8] In all, the book went through eight editions – the last
one in 1985 – achieving both more editions and higher sales figures

than any other book in the *Companion Guide* series. There was a large number of revisions for each edition to bring it up to date with ferry and rail times, new roads etc. In a letter to Ziegler in 1973, Murray wrote: 'I have been astonished at the number of letters I continue to receive from readers saying that they have appreciated the dead-accuracy of the Companion Guide in both its descriptive and factual information.'[9]

Angus Wilson for the *Observer* in 1981 said: 'He has written the most expert and stimulating book on the West Highlands of modern times and one for which any visitor will be grateful.'

The third guide, *The Islands of Western Scotland*, which appeared in 1973, with several reprints in later years, was a different kind of book from the previous two. Instead of covering the area region by region, he devoted a chapter to each of the main topics or themes. There are chapters on Physical Description; Rock and Water; Climate and Life; Sea and Wild-life; Architecture of Church and Castle; Celtic Arts of the Hebrides; and several chapters on man's occupation of the land, covering the distant and the recent past.

In his Introduction (page 20), Murray points out that many books and papers had dealt in recent centuries with the geology, ecology, pre-history, the political and social history, economy and Gaelic culture of the Hebrides, but none had brought these six aspects together in one volume. 'If I wanted such a book,' he stated, 'it seemed that I would have to write it myself. I did want, for I believed that the Hebrides could be properly understood only in the round.'

This is a much more detailed and in-depth look at the Hebrides than his first book about them. In researching it he read more than three hundred books and papers and consulted a wide range of experts in the specialist disciplines that form the core of each chapter. His thorough research and unflagging curiosity and interest in all aspects of the Hebrides has made this one of the best guides to the Inner and Outer Hebrides ever written.

Thirty-three years later Ian Jack, writing for the *Guardian* in July 2006 about wind farms in the Hebrides, testifies to this: 'What great natural resource do the Outer Hebrides have? They have wind. "The climatic feature of the Hebrides, the outstanding feature, is wind, strong and persistent," wrote W.H. Murray in *The Islands of Western Scotland*, first published in 1973 and still the best guide to the region's history, geography and natural life. "If you ask an outer isleman for a weather forecast, he will not, like the mainlander, answer dry, wet or sunny, but quote you a figure from the Beaufort Scale, say Force 3 or Force 10. He listens to the shipping forecast. Wind is what matters here."'

As in *The Hebrides* and *The Companion Guide to the West Highlands of Scotland* Murray shows his remarkable ability to see the bigger picture and provide a masterly overview in time and space of these islands, and then move to a clear account of how the Gulf Stream works, the precise details of the construction of a black house, or the finer points of Ogham's alphabet. Because Murray took a thematic approach to the book it does not have quite the same sense of place as his other two guides. The prose, on the whole, is slightly more functional with fewer opportunities for his powers of description and evocation of landscape to emerge.

Despite this, there are still many jewels such as this one: 'I have been to Toe Head isthmus in Harris when it was wholly under daisies; it blazed like a snowfield, and half an hour later flushed pink as the cups closed in response to a cloud and a sharpening wind. In July, the Berneray and South Uist machairs are a rolling sea of buttercup, clover and daisy, each massing separately in the wide troughs but merging on the green billows. The wind is charged with clover scent. This can be strong enough on Tiree to carry seaward to an approaching steamer. When the cows are first turned on to well-flowered machair, they can soon have scented breath and their milk a flower-sweet taste.' (Page 84)

John Randall, Chairman of The Islands Book Trust, in a piece written specially for this biography, expressed his appreciation of *The Islands of Western Scotland* by saying: 'There has been no shortage of books written about the Hebrides over the centuries, many of them it has to be said superficial or partial, but W.H. Murray's 'The Islands of Western Scotland', first published in 1973, stands out as one of the very best. It is good for two main reasons: (i) the geographical scope of the book takes in both the Inner and Outer Hebrides, which enables the history of particular islands to be placed in a wider context, and for the forces shaping the whole region to be identified; and (ii) it considers the physical features of the landscape, breathtakingly beautiful by any standards, alongside the human and cultural history of the islands, including an assessment of current economic and social changes and future policy.

'In these respects, the book brings to mind earlier classics such as Martin Martin's 'A Description of the Western Islands of Scotland' (1703) which also had an ambitious and far-reaching agenda, combining detailed observation and insights into past and present customs with prescriptions for economic policy. As knowledge has advanced, and specialisation has developed, it has become increasingly rare for authors to attempt such a synthesis – we seem caught between the innumerable publications about the detail of particular islands, or about one dimension of their interest, written by specialists or local historians, on the one hand; and the most generalised, superficial, and frequently inaccurate, journalistic overviews written mainly for the tourist industry, on the other ... Overall, W.H. Murray's book is one of those rare works which is simultaneously instructive and thought-provoking, detailed and wide-ranging, serious yet entertaining, and worthy of the deepest study and reflection by both the Hebridean and the visitor to this remarkable region.' (The full text of John Randall's comments on *The Islands of Western Scotland* book can be found in online Appendix H)

Two further guide books followed – *The Scottish Highlands* (1976) and *Scotland's Mountains* (1987), the latter being an enlarged and updated version of the earlier book. Both were commissioned and published by the Scottish Mountaineering Trust, the publishing branch of The Scottish Mountaineering Club. Neither is in quite the same category as his previous three guides, being intended as companion readers to the SMT's eight district guide books which cover the main mountain areas of Scotland with the aim of providing essential details to climbers and hill walkers.

In these two books Murray picks out some of the best of the routes described in the district guides and also gives background information for use with them. There are chapters on geology, plant and animal life, and on the activities of man in the Highlands. In *The Scottish Highlands* he has a chapter on the development of mountaineering in Scotland – the first comprehensive account to appear in a book. Fifty pages of appendices supply a wealth of practical facts such as a list of the Munros, a list of mountaineering clubs, a glossary of names and their meanings.

Had Murray been a less thorough and conscientious man he might have been tempted to simply draw on what, by then, was a near-encyclopaedic knowledge of the Highlands and Islands without additional research, and to use the same descriptions as before. However, as the acknowledgements and bibliography show, he consulted the most recent publications of the day and the current experts and took account of their new findings; and in the text of these two books he can still produce fresh ways of describing the land he loved so well. Of this second book, Robert Aitken wrote in a review: 'As a piece of writing the book is a work of high craftsmanship. Overall, no writer could have done a better job to this limiting specification.'[10]

NOTES

1. *The Evidence of Things Not Seen*, page 317.
2. The Sierra Club was founded by John Muir in 1892 to conserve American wild land.
3. *The Evidence of Things Not Seen*, page 317.
4. From his Introduction to *The Islands of Western Scotland*, page 17.
5. *The Hebrides*, page 3.
6. This review was quoted on the jacket of the 1969 edition of *The Hebrides*, but the exact date or the author cannot be traced.
7. Vincent Cronin is known for his biographies of Louis XIV, Louis XVI, Marie Antoinette, Catherine the Great, and Napoleon.
8. Philip Ziegler (born 1929) is one of Britain's most distinguished biographers and historians. His works include biographies of Diana Cooper, Lord Melbourne, Mountbatten, Harold Wilson, Osbert Sitwell and Edward Heath.
9. Letter in Collins archives, Bishopbriggs, Glasgow.
10. SMCJ, 1988. Later, in an email to me (March 2012), Aitken expanded on what he meant by 'limiting specification'. He felt that it was an old-fashioned conception of a guidebook in a field that was rapidly giving way to more locally focused and user-friendly guides.

CHAPTER TWENTY-SEVEN

INTEGRITY, BETRAYAL AND BAD ADVICE

Murray's book, *Rob Roy MacGregor: His Life and Times*, was first published in 1982 by Richard Drew Publishing Ltd, and republished by Canongate Press in 1993. Rob Roy had already figured in quite a number of books, most famously in Sir Walter Scott's novel, *Rob Roy* (1817).[1] Although Rob Roy was not the main character in the novel, he captured readers' imaginations. Scott, whose works were read much more widely then than now, showed Rob Roy as a likeable rogue, but a rogue nonetheless. Rob Roy was a legend, even in his own lifetime – a legend reinforced by the publication of *Highland Rogue* in 1723 (once attributed to Daniel Defoe, but now thought not to be his work). Rob Roy's appeal was that of an ordinary man defying oppressive authority and getting away with it. This image of the man was further reinforced by the Walt Disney film, *Rob Roy: The Highland Rogue* (1953), starring Richard Todd, Glynis Johns and James Robertson Justice.

The story, generally accepted at the time Murray began his biography, was that, for their unruly behaviour, the entire Gregor clan had been outlawed in 1603 (no church marriages, burials, communion etc and no protection under the law) and survived almost two hundred years as outlaws. Within this context, Rob Roy MacGregor (1671–1734) established himself as a great swordsman and soldier. Paul H. Scott described him as 'a strange mixture of the brigand, the political guerrilla, of Robin Hood and Che Guevara.' (see footnotes 12 & 13) At the age of 18 he fought alongside his father against William of Orange. He discovered there was more money in 'protecting' cattle for pay than in rustling them. The legend of Rob Roy grew out of his feud with the Duke of Montrose. He had borrowed money from the Duke and failed to return it. Montrose charged him with embezzlement and had him outlawed.[2] Rob Roy retaliated by rustling

Montrose's cattle. Despite being hounded by Montrose, Rob Roy rallied the MacGregors in the Jacobite cause and, in 1715, led them in battle against the English.

Murray set out to find the real, historical Rob Roy MacGregor,[3] to sort fact from fiction, and sift the truth from the legend. To this end he consulted the estate papers of Argyll, Atholl, Breadalbane, Buchanan, MacGregor, Montrose and others, the Privy Council, Estates of Parliament and local governments, the historical MSS held by the Scottish Records Office, War Office and the National Library, and the social histories of that period.

The bibliography testifies to the assiduousness of his research, with six full pages listing documents consulted: estate papers, eye-witness accounts, official reports, historical manuscripts, eighteenth-century newspapers, early prints and maps. His general strategy was to consult sources as near to the events as possible. Less than one third of his sources consist of works written in the twentieth century.

The result of all this research was 'a book that gave me peculiar satisfaction in that justice to a man could be seen to be done. At last I had discovered the real Rob Roy, hitherto a villain of Scottish folklore ... I revealed – created – a character wholly different from that cast up on hearsay by his earlier traducers – a man of integrity and that of heroic proportion.'[4]

The journalist Jack Webster agreed with Murray, saying that he had 'changed the perception of Rob Roy from unprincipled rogue and brigand to a man of integrity.'[5]

In a letter to Bob Aitken he wrote:

'RR is a different character from Walter Scott's imaginings. He did almost no work on the subject, + his defamation is outrageous. Neither he nor others of the early 19thC had any real conception of life in the Highlands + didn't bother to find out. Men like Prebble have got at facts, but have been unable to interpret them in their land context + social history.'[6]

An impressive aspect of *Rob Roy MacGregor: His Life and Times* is Murray's knowledge of the way of life of the Highlanders in the seventeenth and eighteenth centuries, even down to such details as how to make *bland*, an alcoholic drink, or an emergency food called *sowens*. His feel for time and place comes through strongly, backed by his own intimate knowledge of the glens and hills inhabited by Rob Roy and his empathy with a fellow hill-man.

Murray was at pains to lay to rest the idea that Rob Roy was a cattle thief or involved in a protection racket such as we understand that term today. He explained that reiving (aka cattle-lifting) was a time-honoured custom in the Highland and Border counties. It was regarded as an adventurous sport, providing valuable training for hard campaigning. It was expected of every chief when he came of age that he should prove his ability by leading a cattle raid. Harsh conditions, with heavy losses of stock, hit different districts year by year. Reiving was a form of insurance in so much as, in hard times, you could lift cattle from a clan which was enjoying temporary abundance (and in the expectation that they would do the same to you). Murray pointed out that, in the Highlands, cattle-lifting was not equated with crime or dishonesty. Those who saw it as such were applying Lowland moral standards to a specific aspect of Highland society governed by a different ethic. In general, Murray claimed, standards of honesty were higher in the Highlands than in the Lowlands.

In similar vein, Murray explained the origin of the word 'blackmail': The word 'mail' meant rent. Black, which referred to the black cattle typical of the Highlands at the time (the red Highland cattle that we know today were bred later), was the rent paid to clan chieftains for guarding the mountain passes against marauding cattle raiders. This blackmail was legal provided it was conducted by the authorised Watch – and the MacGregors of Glengyle had been granted such powers. Indeed no other Watch was so greatly valued as preventers and protectors as the MacGregors led by Rob Roy.

Murray's declaration that Walter Scott's defamation of Rob Roy MacGregor was outrageous seems rather exaggerated in view of the fact that Scott was writing fiction and the fictional character was portrayed as having achieved fame for his kindness to and sympathy for the poor and oppressed. A bit of controversy, of course, always helps to sell a book, but a more likely reason why Murray defended Rob Roy so fiercely is that he identified with the subject of his biography. It is said that every good portrait of a person is also a portrait of the painter. The artist recognises in his/her subject those characteristics and emotions, pains and joys which they have

in common. Consequently, perhaps subconsciously, these are emphasised in the painting. To some extent this is true also of biography,
although the biographer tries to balance empathy with objectivity.
In Murray's case the former weighed heavier in the balance. He and
Rob Roy were both soldiers and mountaineers, both knew the same
countryside intimately, both put a high value on freedom, both were
outsiders, both had extraordinary resolution in adversity; and, so
Murray thought, both lived by a code in which personal integrity was
foremost. It is clear that Murray identified strongly with him and, in
certain passages, Murray is writing about himself as well as Rob Roy.

Describing Rob Roy's skills in patrolling the mountain passes and
intercepting cattle raiders, Murray says: 'He had to learn how to lead
a raid; how to conduct ten to thirty men a full hundred miles each
way as the crow flies, or thrice that across country; how to provision
them on the way yet direct them in small groups on to converging
or diverging routes, selected so that no advance warning might reach
the victim or alert the clans occupying the land traversed, where to
rendezvous for the final reconnaissance ...'[7]

There are strong echoes here of Murray's descriptions of going out
on patrol in the Western Desert. Again, one feels he is speaking as
much for himself as he is for Rob Roy when he writes: 'The greater
part of a soldier's life is spent waiting for something to happen. He
never positively forms the question, "Will I be alive tonight?" Men
before battle are protected by a fire-curtain, which the mind drops to
cut off fearful imaginings. But they lurk in the background and try to
filter through in disguise.'[8]

Murray quotes the lines said to have been scratched by Montrose
on the window of his jail and says it was a philosophy shared with
Clan Gregor:

> 'He either fears his fate too much,
> Or his deserts are small,
> That puts it not unto the touch,
> To win or lose it all.'[9]

This is the same philosophy that Murray encapsulated in the lines
he quoted in *The Scottish Himalayan Expedition* – that 'boldness has
genius'. The following words could be some biographer describing

Murray: 'His life's lasting value came of his fight to keep personal integrity,'[10] or this: 'He showed time and again a remarkable ability to live in the present moment, and enjoy of life what there was to enjoy.'[11]

This close identification with Rob Roy could have led Murray into projecting onto him qualities and characteristics which were not there, or not there to quite the same extent that Murray wanted to find – in particular, integrity and honour.

Naturally enough, this new interpretation of Rob Roy's life and times was favourably reviewed by the Clan MacGregor newsletter and website and received an enthusiastic reception from others glad of a refurbished Scottish hero and a tale of a charismatic character involved in daring acts and amazing escapes. The general dearth of rave reviews, however, is reflected on the back cover of the Canongate 1993 reissue. There is not a single quote from any of the reviews at the time of the first publication – only 'Some press opinions on previous books by W.H. Murray'.

Paul H. Scott,[12] reviewing the book for the *Scotsman*,[13] questioned the academic rigour of Murray's book: 'He tells us confidently about details of his subject where his only source is his imagination, or, at best, informed guess.'

Paul Scott accused Murray of being uncritical about his sources, citing Murray's reliance on H.G. Graham's notoriously unreliable book, *Social Life of Scotland in the Eighteenth Century*. Referring to Murray's rather surprising hostility to Sir Walter Scott, Paul Scott the reviewer goes on to say: 'Curiously, it is the novelist who is scrupulous about the evidence and the author of the *Life and Times* who is full of uncritical enthusiasm.'

The Scottish Historical Review similarly questioned Murray's objectivity and expressed the opinion that he had given excessive credence to some sources, while ignoring others.

Murray's lack of academic training told against him in his approach to this book. Probably without knowing it, he was 'cherry picking' the facts which suited the image of Rob Roy he wanted to create. As quoted previously, in describing what he felt he had achieved, he says: 'I revealed – created – a character …'

Murray does not mean here that he invented a new character for Roby Roy, but these words tell us something of his approach. His usual method of work with his guidebooks had been to consult the sources, write his own version and then run it past an expert. Either he didn't do this with *Rob Roy MacGregor*, or he was ill advised.

In 2004 a new biography of Rob Roy was published – *The Hunt for Rob Roy: The Man and the Myths* by David Stevenson, Professor Emeritus of Scottish History at the University of St Andrews. This book showed many of Murray's findings to be wrong.

The following passage gets to the heart of what Stevenson's research unearthed: 'There is no way of presenting a Rob Roy based on evidence rather than wish-fulfilment that does not admit that he was a man who carefully planned to defraud those he owed money to, and that he gave and sold intelligence about Jacobites to their enemies. Any assessment of the man which does not accept the reality of these events is make-belief.'[14]

As the blurb on the back of the book tells us: 'The picture of a man wronged and oppressed, forced into outlawry, has to be modified by the evidence that he was only outlawed after undertaking a careful plan to swindle his creditors; the supposed warrior leader never fought in a battle; and the reputed great duellist avoided violence whenever possible and is only known to have fought one duel – which he lost.'

In his Preface, Stevenson says: 'Astonishingly, it was not until 1982 that the first biography of Rob based on systematic use of historical evidence appeared. W.H. Murray's *Rob Roy MacGregor: His Life and Times* was a huge advance on anything previously available. However, as a work of history, it is seriously flawed. Murray was a noted writer on mountaineering in Scotland, and deeply loved the Highlands, but he lacked experience as a historian. The book is fascinating and evocative to read, but once it is examined closely it begins to unravel. Murray is too close to his subject, and though he accepts some criticisms of Rob, basically he argues the case for the defence, at times in defiance of the evidence.'

The very different findings of Stevenson and Murray were not simply a matter of the former being a trained historian with an objective approach and the latter being less experienced in handling such material and more subjective. In the 20 years or more that separated the two biographies there had been huge progress in archive management, in cataloguing public and private manuscripts and in making them much more accessible to researchers, not least the revolution brought about by placing catalogues online. Stevenson gives Murray part credit for the renewal of interest in Rob Roy which stimulated the Scottish Record Office (as the National Archives of Scotland were then called) into compiling *The Real Rob Roy: A Guide to the Sources in the Scottish Record Office* (1995).This was a goldmine for historians and, as Stevenson says, 'an essential starting place for a new hunt for Rob' – a source which had not been available to Murray.

Murray must have been disappointed at the reaction, from some quarters, to his book. With the passage of time, however, we can see that despite its faults it made a contribution to the serious study of the historical Rob Roy. It was the first full-length book on Rob Roy in a hundred years. It revived interest in the man and opened the way to further studies of the real Rob Roy rather than the legend. Murray's book showed the importance of seeing the man in the context of his time, his landscape and his Highland culture.

This aspect of the book was certainly appreciated by Iverach McDonald, for many years foreign editor and associate editor of *The Times*, who wrote to Murray saying: 'May I say how much I enjoyed and admired your *Rob Roy MacGregor* – a wholly admirable work. No book has given a clearer or more convincing picture of everyday life and the deeper forces at work in the Central and Southern Highlands of the early 18th Century. You bring out the structure of the clans, the organisation of the Watches, the rules of blackmail, the old unwritten codes in war and peace. No one has better demonstrated exactly what the patronage of a great nobleman meant to Rob Roy and others of his degree or how deep were the divisions within Clan Campbell or how utterly separate were the two worlds north and south of the Highland line.'[15]

Murray's book raised questions that demanded answers and his research unearthed or gained access to a range of documents that had not been seen before; and, as Stevenson generously pointed out, it played a part in stimulating a comprehensive cataloguing of relevant material.

In 1995 MGM released their blockbuster film *Rob Roy*, starring Liam Neeson as Rob Roy.[16] Through his publisher, Jamie Byng of Canongatge, Murray was aware of this film and its contents while it was still being made. Murray and his wife thought that the film's version of Rob Roy as a man of integrity, as an upright Highland chieftain protecting those in his care from unscrupulous noblemen had been lifted more or less straight from his book. They felt cheated and aggrieved and sought legal advice about payment for subsidiary rights.

In *The Evidence of Things Not Seen* the words of Alan Sharp, the screenwriter, are used to back up their case. He is quoted as saying in a newspaper article,[17] 'The painting of Rob Roy, cleaned and revealed by Murray, was the one I wished to portray.' And again as saying, 'I tried to model the character of Rob Roy on Murray's *Rob Roy*.' However, either Bill Murray as writer or Anne Murray as editor, seem to have overlooked Sharp's statement in the same article, 'I believe we all copy one another to some extent, but I've never felt I was taking someone else's work, more that I had a sense of being in tandem with them. Murray had written a biography covering Rob Roy's life. My film is about one year in his life and, from the point of view of material in his book which became part of my film, I don't think there was too much that he was owed.'

The main legal point on Murray's side was 'Unjustified Enrichment' – someone else profiting from work he had done. The main point against him was the complex matter of intellectual property rights and the general tendency of the law to rule that there is no copyright on ideas or on historical facts. The possibility of suing bogged down in legal entanglements and the whole matter gradually dwindled to nothing. The producer of the film, Peter Broughan, offered Murray £1,000 for a TV option on his book. However, Murray thought that the contract was confining and, on advice, he didn't sign it.

Murray's health was declining and he probably had neither the inclination nor the energy to pursue the matter. Indeed, he was only one year away from his death. What energy he had he would have wanted to put towards something that was far more important to him – the writing of his last book.

NOTES

1. The story of Scott's novel, *Rob Roy* starts prior to the first Jacobite rising of 1715. It follows the adventures of Francis Osbaldistone, the son of a rich London merchant. Francis is banished from his father's house and sent to live with his uncle in the north of England. Here he meets his uncle's six oafish sons,

including the evil Rashleigh. He also meets Diana Vernon and romance is in the bud. Rashleigh has designs both on Francis' considerable fortune and on Diana. Francis and Diana, accompanied by Bailie Nicol Jarvie of Glasgow, set out to find Rob Roy – a person known for his hatred of injustice – to ask for his help. They witness a clash between the clansmen and the Royalist 'redcoats' and Rob Roy's daring escape. Between them Francis, Rob Roy and Diana unmask and thwart Rashleigh's villainy.

2. Being outlawed as an individual was more rigorously enforced than the outlawing of the entire clan was.

3. Perhaps a halfway-house between the positions of Walter Scott and Murray would be Nigel Tranter who wrote his three novels comprising the MacGregor trilogy between 1957 and 1962, and also produced a non-fiction book about Rob Roy – *Outlaw of the Highlands* (1965). In discussing Rob Roy in *The Evidence of Things Not Seen*, Murray makes no mention of Tranter, nor does he list any of his books in his bibliography for *Rob Roy MacGregor*. The fact that the trilogy was fiction and that Murray used primary sources as much as he could might partly explain this.

4. *The Evidence of Things Not Seen,* page 302.

5. The *Herald,* March 13th, 1995.

6. Letter dated 1st August 1978. It took another three and a half years before the book was published. This is a little slow but not all that unusual. The typing, the corrections, the final changes, the seeking of permission to quote or use material, the hunt for suitable illustrations, the whole editing stage involving the preparation of the text, the indexing, preparing the bibliography, etc all take time, as do the printing, proof reading and the final publishing processes.

7. *Rob Roy MacGregor,* page 72.

8. *Ibid,* page 93.

9. *Ibid,* page 38.

10. *Ibid,* page 11.

11. *Ibid,* page 164.

12. Paul Henderson Scott is a distinguished Scottish author and scholar, a retired diplomat and a central figure in Scottish cultural life,

13. 'Highland Hero' in the *Scotsman,* 4th December, 1982.

14. *The Hunt for Rob Roy,* page 292.

15. An extract from this letter is reproduced in *The Evidence of Things Not Seen*, page 302.

16. Also starring in the film were Jessica Lange and John Hurt. Producer: Peter Broughan; Director: Michael Caton-Jones; Script writer: Alan Sharp. The estimated budget for the film was $28 million. Most of the film locations were in or around Glen Nevis.

17. The (Glasgow) *Herald*, 13th March, 1995, in an article by Jack Webster, with the rather inflammatory headline of 'Rob Roy the rogue would have had more scruples than this'.

CHAPTER TWENTY-EIGHT

HE REMAINS ELUSIVE STILL

Tom Weir tells us in *Weir's Way* (page 170) that he suggested to Murray it was time he wrote his autobiography since he had so much to say that nobody had heard yet. 'But the humorous glint in his blue eyes showed me he didn't take me seriously.'

This interview probably took place in 1979 or 1980. At that time, Murray was still fully engaged in completing his biography of Rob Roy and may not have been thinking of any other book but that one. Maybe seeds were sown that would later germinate.

In 1988 Robert Aitken and Peter Hodgkiss broached the idea to Murray of a published collection of his articles and shorter works. Murray rejected the suggestion, saying that he would prefer to write something new – perhaps the prison camps of which he had told only a fraction.[1] Then, in March 1994, shortly after his eighty-first birthday, he wrote to Aitken stating that he had in fact started writing 'a last book'. This was what was to eventually become *The Evidence of Things Not Seen*.

Either while Murray was planning and researching for this book, or possibly just after he had begun writing it, Weir sent him a draft copy of *Weir's World*, asking for his comments. In his reply, Murray advised him to ask himself what were the important things he had learned from his life. That Murray was asking himself the same question in relation to his own book is clear from the title he first gave it: 'To Live and Learn'.

The psychologist Susan Engel suggests[2] five motives for autobiography: *persuasion* – using your life story to promote a cause or some strongly held belief or point of view; *disguise* – to cover over some part of your real life or to reinvent yourself; *transcendence* – to use the autobiography as a way of freeing yourself from your problems, to rise above the feuds and quarrels of your life, and as a healing process by expressing hitherto suppressed fear and anger; *self-justification*; and *an invitation to intimacy* – the thrill of sharing secrets, the relief of casting off your habitual mask or shell. Readers of Murray's autobiography may well discern in it elements of Engel's five motivations, although most would agree that disguise was not in Murray's nature and that reticence was more typical of him than intimacy.

Murray used his autobiography, to some extent, to persuade his readers about the need to preserve Scotland's wild land, about the rightness of the Unna Rules and about the importance of a spiritual dimension to one's life. When discussing his motives for writing *Mountaineering in Scotland* he said he wanted to share his experiences with his readers. He was, in effect, saying, 'Look, this is what gave *me* joy,' and he is doing the same in *The Evidence of Things Not Seen*.

Writing this book must have been therapeutic for Murray. At the point in his life when he was writing it (or assembling it from previous things he had written) he had come to terms with his war experiences and his POW years. Nonetheless, going over these things again and laying them out on the page and 'coming out' about them, could be seen as a final act in the healing process. Murray was fairly certain that his life was nearing its end, and using this, his last book, as a way of understanding its meaning, its patterns and the lessons learned must also have been a kind of transcendence. Behind some of the motives mentioned by Engel there could also have been a pressing need to make some money.

The Evidence of Things Not Seen is sometimes described as a quasi-autobiography. This is because autobiographies normally give a full account of the whole of the person's life, whereas Murray does not do this, ignoring some parts, or only giving a sketchy account of them. In some respects it is more like a memoir, focusing heavily on certain aspects of his life and particular periods in it.

Murray died in March 1996, two years after starting on this, his final book, and before he had finished it. His normal working habit was to go through three drafts before he was satisfied with what he had written. In this case, he left an incomplete first draft. Murray's wife, Anne, states in an Epilogue to *The Evidence of Things Not Seen* that it was basically finished. She must have meant that the basic building blocks were in place. However, even some of these appear not to have been there. Unless large sections of the book were cut out by her at an early stage, it would have been a fairly thin book, nearly one hundred pages shorter than the final version, which was 'beefed up' with additional material after his death.

Anne Murray took on the task of editing and completing the book 'as he would have wished and as we discussed'.[3] She was closer to him than anyone else and the person most likely to know what his plans and intentions had been. On the other hand, it is a common phenomenon that one's deceased spouse suddenly achieves sainthood after death. There might possibly have been an element of this in her strong opposition to any suggestions about changing the original text.

The MS was sent first to the SMC whose editor at the time was Donald Bennet. His editorial suggestions were not to Anne Murray's liking and the MS was withdrawn. In April 1998 Peter Hodgkiss at Ernest Press[4] wrote to her:-

'Dear Mrs Murray,

Bob Aitken has suggested that I should write and let you know of our interest in a possible involvement with the publishing of your late husband's autobiography. Like many of my generation, I have great respect for Bill's writing, a respect deepened when I had some experience with him in mountaineering politics and when in 1986 he wrote a marvellous foreword to our reissue of Benny Humble's *The Cuillin of Skye*.

I would be delighted if the Ernest Press were to be considered as publisher for Bill's book and can assure you that we would apply the highest standards of production to printing and binding.'

After seeing the manuscript, Hodgkiss wrote again six weeks later:-

'... After removing the three or four small sections of text which are potentially litigious and making some other minor amendments, we could publish Bill's MS as it stands. And it would sell just on the basis of Bill's name. However, I would not want to do that since much of the text would not stand beside most of his other writing.'[5]

Hodgkiss then refers to the high quality of the Foreword which Murray had written for The *Cuillin of Skye* and goes on to say:

'There are sections of the current MS that so little compare to the finished quality of that foreword that I can think of them only as a draft. Other sections, notably the 'Api' account have that finished quality, and this contrast within the MS would not be missed by reviewers. Accordingly, while I repeat my offer to publish, I ask that we be given a free hand in editing the MS and in adding an unobtrusive linking commentary. Any textual adjustment would be made with Bill's other books as tutors, so that his style would be maintained. There are some surprising blanks in the MS, particularly concerning mountain politics and in word pictures of his contemporaries – in the latter case Bill showed great skill in painting a personality portrait that was rounded and properly critical and yet without a hint of malice.'

Anne Murray rejected this suggestion and, reluctantly, Hodgkiss gave up any plans to publish the book. Seven years later (in October 2005), Hodgkiss commented on Murray's autobiography in an email to Michael Cocker:

'Dear Mike,
    If anyone should have been concerned about the preservation of British mountain heritage, and more so the lack of it, it was Bill Murray. But, partly due to a misplaced modesty, he left a sanitised and incomplete autobiography and may have agreed with his wife that his diaries and correspondence should be destroyed after his death (I don't know their fate but will try to find out.). He expressed doubt about the value of his autobiography and it was only the urging of friends that got him started, and then only at the stage when his fatal illness began.'

Anne Murray then showed the MS to Ken Wilson at Bâton Wicks who agreed to publish it. Undoubtedly there was conflict over editorial control. Wilson, however, gallantly maintains that all was sweetness and light between them and that she was extremely supportive and helpful in the editorial process.[6]

Murray's book, now called *The Evidence of Things Not Seen*, was published in hardback in 2002, nearly six years after his death. This new title was chosen by Ken Wilson and is a reference to the title of the penultimate chapter of *Mountaineering in Scotland*. With appendices and a Foreword by Hamish MacInnes it is 348 pages long. It contains nine sections: Early Years; Pre-War Climbing in Scotland; Fortunes of War; Incarceration; The Post-War World; First Expeditions to the Himalaya; Exploring the Api Massif; Everest and the Muztagh Tower; Concerns Closer to Home; a chapter about Ben Humble and one entitled the Cragsmen of Lewis. There are 26 pages of photographs, some in colour, and also another 17 half-page or quarter-page photographs amongst the text. The majority of the photographs are from the Murray collection, John Tyson and Douglas Scott, with others by Tom Weir, Archie MacAlpine, Ken Wilson, Hamish MacInnes and Ben Humble.

The cover photograph was a studio portrait taken by J. Stephens Orr.[7] Murray had expressed a fondness for this photograph which had been taken years earlier and had been used, half a century before, on the inside cover of Murray's *The Story of Everest*. Wilson set out to track it down. The story, often told by Wilson, is that he visited the family of the now deceased Orr in Millport on Great Cumbrae island. Orr's daughter-in-law took him to a big cupboard stuffed full with old negatives and glass plates. The chances of finding the right one seemed slim. The very first glass plate Wilson picked up was the one of Murray. The photograph shows an aesthetic-looking Murray with the hood of his cagoule over his head, very much like a monk's cowl. Murray's mysticism and his intention, at one time, to enter a monastery are strongly suggested in the photograph.

The differences between the MS as it was when Murray died and the version which his widow showed to Hodgkiss at Ernest Press two years later under the title of 'To Live and Learn', are likely to remain unknown. What is known, or partly known,[8] is how that version differs from the version published by Ken Wilson at Diadem in 2002 as *The Evidence of Things Not Seen*. The coverage of Murray's pre-war winter climbing was considered to be scant and incomplete. To better capture the flavour of this, the whole chapter on the Garrick Shelf climb from *Mountaineering in Scotland* was inserted. Several pages have been cut concerning the retelling by Murray of an Arab legend. There has been a considerable expansion (from one chapter to six) of the section which deals with the 1950 Scottish Himalayan Expedition. Two new chapters, one about Ben Humble and one about the cragsmen of Lewis, have been added.[9] Much of the section about publishers and the state of publishing has been removed from the main text and put in an appendix; and the details about Murray's final illness and time in hospital have been reduced to a shorter version.

What is immediately noticeable is that over one third of the final version is devoted to Himalayan exploration. When the script was first shown to Wilson, Murray's Himalayan years were under-represented. It is possible that Murray planned to put in more of this later. Wilson has explained on several occasions to different people that he had originally intended to reprint Murray's *The Scottish Himalayan Expedition* and had obtained permission to do so. When Murray died, it seemed neater to work an abridged version of it into his autobiography. Thirty-six pages on the Api/Nampa expedition of 1953 were already there in the original version. Murray commented that he could easily have sold a second expedition book based on this venture, but that he had wanted to write about other things. It looks as though he was compensating for the book that never was by giving the expedition a lengthy write-up in his autobiography.

Those who are steeped in Murray's works, or who have read, within a comparatively short time, everything of his that has appeared in print, will know the extent to which long passages have been lifted straight out of his other writings and put, unaltered, into *The Evidence of Things Not Seen*. This applies not only to the Himalayan sections in the book and the Garrick Shelf adventure, but also to much of the rest of the book. For example, Murray's account of his introduction to mountains and mountaineering in *The Evidence of Things Not Seen* had already appeared in several publications.[10] Murray's accident in the Alps is lifted from earlier writing, as is his description of his encounter with the German tank commander[11] and much of the section entitled 'Incarceration'.[12] The text of MacAlpine's obituary has been grafted into the book, and Murray's description of his first meeting with Jimmy Bell is, word for word, the same as in *Mountaineering in Scotland*. This is just a sample of the cut and paste method by which a large proportion of *The Evidence of Things Not Seen* was assembled.

Whether or not Wilson was aware of the extent to which recycled material was being used is not certain. If he was, he may not have been overly concerned because his aim was to put as much as possible of the Murray oeuvre into accessible print and to ensure his place in mountaineering history, much as he had done in his big Diadem collections of the works of Shipton and Tilman.

It is just possible that Murray, feeling old and tired, conscious of the need to publish something that would generate money to help provide for Anne when he was gone, and aware that time was running out, decided to take the quickest and easiest way by using material he already had. A more likely explanation is that, in his first draft, Murray was blocking in the areas of his life he wanted to cover, intending to come back to them and rewrite them. As we noted earlier in this chapter, Murray was not keen on a book which was simply a collection of his previous writing. He took a pride in his work and would not have wanted to regurgitate old writing. We see this, for example, in his guidebooks where he could easily have repeated much of what he had already written, but he did not. The only occasions he plagiarised himself were when he was producing what he considered 'pot boilers' – that is to say, things written mainly to raise cash or to satisfy a demand from a magazine editor whom he didn't want to disappoint, but lacked the time to write something new. *The Evidence of Things Not Seen* he felt in his bones was going to be his last work and it would not have been in either of these categories.

Referring to his pre-war climbing days, Murray says: 'The particular advantage I now have in looking back on them is that great age comes like a hilltop in time, from which early years appear in true perspective.'[13] This thought was relevant to the whole book and he would have wanted to put a different perspective on what he had previously written.

Wilson rightly estimated that the majority of readers would not recognise the origins of the text; and both he and Mrs Murray might well have thought that Bill Murray expressed himself so well that his original words could not be bettered. In addition, they may have felt that, beyond a certain point, it was artistically unethical to alter his words without his agreement.

It is difficult to estimate the extent to which the posthumous editorial process changed the original direction and intent of the book. As we have seen, Murray's original title for this book was 'To Live and Learn' and his intention was to lay out the important lessons he had learned during his life. In a brief note at the front of the book, signed and dated 1995, Murray says, 'In selected incidents I have traced a long life to give one man's impression of his world.' This Murray does in an unobtrusive way, although it seems fairly obvious that Wilson steered the book towards appealing mainly to mountaineers. The photographs are 99 per cent orientated towards mountaineering; the Foreword is by a mountaineer rather than by a well-known conservationist or literary figure; and the new title he chose contains the subtitle 'A Mountaineer's Tale'. In terms of being a hard-nosed publisher and doing what was needed to ensure respectable sales figures, Wilson was probably correct.

The Evidence of Things Not Seen received mixed reviews. Only a few were unreservedly enthusiastic and there is a feeling about some of them that they were kinder than they might have been out of respect for a recently deceased and much admired man. 'His talent flared in glory one final time,' wrote David Rose.[14] 'It will round up a fine life well told,' said Ken Crocket.[15] There was general agreement that the earlier sections of the book were the best – particularly the vivid depictions of desert warfare and his engrossing account of life in POW camps.

The book won the Banff Prize 2002 (Mountain Literature category). 'This is a big, quiet book that resonates far beyond the clamour of ego and conquest,' commented Dermot Somers, Irish mountaineer and member of the 2002 Banff Book Festival jury. The *Canadian Alpine Journal* described it as 'a very engaging portrait of a time and a man'. It won an award from the United States Education Department and was shortlisted for the Boardman/Tasker Prize.

Dave Hewitt, writing for *The Angry Corrie*,[16] contributed one of the longest, most thoughtful and penetrating of all the reviews. Here are some extracts from 'Evidently maybe: The Evidence of Things Not Seen':

'What Bill Murray's failure to see his last work published meant in literary terms can be seen in the extent to which the eventual book is something of a jumble: there is the feel of an anthology, or an externally edited "reader" ... Were the book to stop at the end of the war years, then it would without doubt be a fine piece of work. Indeed, were the narrative shortfall to be covered by adding more depth and detail on Murray's friends and climbing colleagues (along the lines of the one-off chapter on Ben Humble near the actual book's end), then it could well have been tinged with greatness.'

But the book didn't end there and Hewitt goes on to say that the abridged chapters on the Himalayas lacked life and any real engagement with either his companions or the people met along the way. 'Perhaps most telling of all, there is Murray's unwillingness or inability to fully portray himself ... Understatement, self-deprecation, formal modesty – call it what you will – is a common trait amongst intelligent, articulate Scots, and can be endearing if encountered in the flesh. But it doesn't make for good autobiography and Murray, too humble for his own good, risks coming across as remote, clinical, even cold.'

Another reviewer, Nick Kempe, had this to say: 'For me, while his widow Anne Murray has obviously put tremendous effort into editing the book, which is beautifully produced, it still comes across as unfinished . . . it feels to me there are significant gaps . . . there is almost no description of the Everest reconnaissance expedition for example and the later chapters on the Cragsmen of Lewis and Ben Humble, while very interesting as essays, are not placed within any autobiographical context.'[17]

Also seeming out of place are the pages – both in the main body of the text and in an appendix – which deal with Murray's disagreement with the makers of the film *Rob Roy* regarding payment for using his book, *Rob Roy MacGregor*; and his comments in Appendix V about the practicalities of publishing. In both cases there is a disgruntled, complaining tone which seem untypical of Murray. One wonders if these sections would have survived another draft had he lived.

Most reviewers agreed that *The Evidence of Things Not Seen* still had the feel of being in draft form. There was consensus that Murray was too modest and there wasn't enough about himself. Like most of his friends, even those who had known him for years, readers of his autobiography find they hardly know the man. There is a certain irony in the fact that, after several years of researching for a biography of Rob Roy MacGregor, Murray observed ruefully that 'the man in his intimate life remains elusive still.'[18]

To some Murray connoisseurs the book was a disappointment. They were hoping for a final glorious swansong and this wasn't it. Perhaps he had left it too late and it would have been a better book if he had started ten years sooner. In the same letter quoted at the beginning of this chapter, Murray tells his friend of his declining powers – that he had slowed down mentally, his vocabulary was failing and finding the right word was much less easy.

Many will agree with Hewitt, who in his review concludes: 'On balance this book seems likely to leave his reputation in much the same place. We're 50 years on from *Mountaineering in Scotland* and *Undiscovered Scotland,* and in a further 50 years Murray will still be remembered for those books and not for this.'

NOTES

1. Murray wrote this in a letter to Aitken, dated 14th November 1988. Murray had previously written about his POW experiences in *Mountain Magazine* (May 1979), then later that same year in the *Scotsman.* The earlier article was included by Jim Perrin in his anthology *Mirrors in the Cliff* (1983).
2. In *Context is Everything: The Nature of Memory, Constructing Versions of Our Past* (Palgrave, 2000).
3. In an introductory note to *The Evidence of Things Not Seen*, page 13, written by Anne Murray.
4. Ernest Press was a small Glasgow-based publishing house, started in 1985 by Peter Hodgkiss. It operated until his death in 2010. Ernest Press specialised in mountaineering books, mountain biking guides and outdoor literature. In an obituary for Hodgkiss in the *Independent* (6th February 2010), Stephen Goodwin said that Hodgkiss had extended the scope and ambition of climbing literature and that 'Hodgkiss was a romantic who published out of a love of mountains and the climbing game, and a belief that if the writing was of quality then that book deserved to be in print.' Peter was a keen climber, secretary of the Glasgow JMCS and SMC member who knew Murray. He had a major hand in the design and production of the Munros and Corbetts guides for the SMT (the publishing branch of the SMC) and in redesigning the SMC's guidebooks.
5. Copies of these two letters are in the possession of Hodgkiss' widow, Joy.
6. Email to the author, 20th September 2011.
7. J. Stephens Orr was a Glasgow-based photographer, operating between 1930 and 1975. He specialised in portraits of well-known international and Scottish personalities. Amongst the people he photographed were Paul Robeson, Marc Chagall, Richard Burton, Jaques Tati and Stanley Baxter. In the 1950s, when Tom Weir and Douglas Scott set up a photographic business together, Orr let them use his darkroom.
8. This information comes from notes made by Hodgkiss and from what Aitken remembers of discussions he had, at that time, with Hodgkiss about the manuscript.
9. The Humble chapter is a slightly amended version of Murray's Foreword to the reissue of Humble's *The Cuillin of Skye* (1968). The chapter on the cragsmen of Lewis is drawn from Murray's article 'Stac of Handa: first crossing' in SMCJ. 1994.
10. This account had already appeared In *Undiscovered Scotland* (pages 1–3); in

Chapter 1 of 'The High Tops' in *Wildlife in Scotland* (1979); and in 'Present Moments,' *Alpine Journal*, 1981.

11. The Alpine accident had previously appeared in *Undiscovered Scotland* and in *The Alpine Journal*. Murray's capture in North Africa is recounted in *Undiscovered Scotland* and an article in *Mountain* magazine.

12. These chapters are transposed from Murray's article 'The Genesis of a Mountain Classic' in the *Scotsman* (2nd June 1979), which is identical to the article which appeared in *Mountain Magazine* in the same month under the title of 'To Write a Book'.

13. *The Evidence of Things Not Seen*, page 24.

14. *Observer*, Sunday 23rd June, 2002.

15. On the website ScotlandOnline.

16. *The Angry Corrie* is a fanzine for hillwalkers in Scotland, first published in 1991. It was also published on the internet until 2008. The editor, throughout, has been Dave Hewitt.

17. In *The Scottish Mountaineer* (the journal of the Mountaineering Council of Scotland), December 2002.

18. In the Foreword to *Rob Roy MacGregor*, page 9.

CHAPTER TWENTY-NINE

A SUPREME CRAFTSMAN AT WORK

Whatever he did, Murray liked to do it well. Whether it was fashion-ing delicate holds in thin, steep ice, navigating through the desert at night, or rigging his sailing dinghy, he applied himself to learning the craft, to mastering the skills. No aspect of his life better illustrates this than his painstaking and thorough approach to writing. He would edit, redraft, polish and polish again in the application of the writer's craft to his work.

In Chapter Eighteen some of the influences upon Murray's writ-ing were considered, particularly upon *Mountaineering in Scotland*. Amongst these influences was Robert Louis Stevenson. In his *Essays in the Art of Writing* (1905), Stevenson emphasises the importance of an apt choice and contrast in the words employed; and the finding or making of a pattern, which he says is 'the motive and end of all art'. Variety of rhythm and of length in a sentence are essential, he says, in order to achieve 'a perpetually fresh variety of movement' and 'a larger and more lawless melody than in verse'. Stevenson advises that a natural style is not necessarily the most effective and speaks of a 'designed reversal' in which 'the derangement of the phrases from their (so-called) natural order is luminous for the mind'. He also expands on the power of repeating vowel and consonant sounds and of 'one liquid or labial melting away into another'. Using these concordances, he says, 'is the final art in literature'. Murray applied all of this advice to his own writing.

On the matter of finding pattern, Murray often brings his essays back to where they started, but with an added twist. Two instances of this would be Chapter III and Chapter VI in *Mountaineering in Scotland*. In the former, he begins his essay with his friends gathered around the breakfast table in the SMC hut on Ben Nevis. They are wondering what route to do that day. Murray reads the hut log book and thinks that the accounts of the climbs done are far too succinct and tell nothing of the drama involved. They then go off and have a dramatic adventure on Slav route in very wet conditions. In the final paragraph they are back in the hut and Mackenzie (having goaded Murray by denying that it could be considered at all wet) records the climb in the log book with the cryptic words: 'Slav route – wet.'

Chapter VI starts with the words: 'I have no wish to embroil myself in that well-tried topic of the debating chamber: "To travel hopefully is a better thing than to arrive"; but let me say, non-committally, that whether these words be true or not of the spires of El Dorado, they are not infrequently true of Ben Nevis in summer.' He, Scott and MacAlpine then have a magnificent day of climbing on Rubicon Wall. The chapter ends with the paragraph: 'Was this, our El Dorado, a better thing than our hopeful pilgrimage? I experienced something of both that day – and still I cannot answer. I think the question is such a vexed one because it is not, in the first place, legitimate. The goal and way are one; they co-inhere; they are not to be separated.'[1]

In the passing, let us pause to consider Murray's craftsmanship in his choice of 'not infrequently' in the last part of this paragraph, rather than 'frequently'. It is more than just a matter of shade of meaning – he employs this term because it matches and balances 'non-committally' and because the double negative helps create the tone he wants in this passage of light-hearted, tongue-in-the-cheek, slightly over-the-top pedantry.

Yet another example of finding or making patterns can be seen in Chapter XVIII of *Undiscovered Scotland* – 'Ben Nevis by the North-east Buttress'. Murray begins by saying, 'No man will ever know Ben Nevis,' and develops the theme that the mountain is particularly prone to unpredictable weather and that conditions can vary enormously from day to day. He then illustrates the changeability of the mountain, its weather and its moods by recounting a winter ascent of the north-east buttress with Douglas Laidlaw. The day before the climb, while they are still in Fort William, Murray suggests to Laidlaw that a visit to the Nevis bar before setting out might be a good idea, to which Laidlaw jokingly responds, 'In the Nevis bar you get the uplift first and the headache after. On the Nevis cliffs the pains first and the joys after.'

With difficulty, after losing the line of the narrow path, they make their way in gathering dark and strong wind to the CIC hut. This passage is like a mini-enactment, a prophecy or forerunner of their climb on the following day, in which a narrow ridge, losing the way, strong wind and being caught out in the dark all happen again, but on a bigger and more serious scale. On their way up to the hut, the hurricane tears a rent in the clouds and 'the moon shone full upon the two-mile range of cliffs ... and picked out great ridges and buttresses and many a spectral tower, all whitened with new snow'.

The next day, well into the climb and with darkness having descended upon them, Murray switches on his torch. 'How different everything looked! ... numberless frost-cressets sparkled, the snow shone [note Stevenson's 'power of repeating consonant sounds']' – a passage which echoes the appearance of the moon the previous night, when they were on the path.

Murray ends this essay or chapter by repeating the phrase with which he began it: 'No man will ever know Ben Nevis.' And then he gives a twist to what had seemed a joking comment in the bar: 'On the other hand Nevis will always help him to know himself. There is no end to such knowledge. Likewise there is no end to the joy of getting it.'

Unless deliberately looking for it, readers may be unaware of the craftsmanship involved in a chapter like this, only that it has cohesion and unity, that there is something satisfying about it beyond being simply an adventure tale, and that it possesses a quality which makes the whole bigger than the sum of its parts. That the craftsmanship is unobtrusive and does not stand up and demand to be noticed is as it should be, for there is an art to concealing art and this is yet another skill displayed by Murray. One of the great merits of *Mountaineering in Scotland* is that, not only does each individual chapter have coherence and pattern, but so does the collection of essays as a whole.

Robert Aitken, in an unpublished paper on *Mountaineering in Scotland*, states: 'The book is essentially symphonic in structure. One of Bill Murray's masterly innovations was to resolve the problems of the necessarily episodic nature of Scottish climbing, based usually on weekend or single day-trips ... This is a problem which has bedevilled most books on mountaineering outwith the expedition format, which has its own problems of predictability. To give this a thematic developmental structure to provide coherence and lead the reader on without being intrusive, he introduces his higher theme which might be very simply stated as a leitmotiv of personal development in the apprehension and comprehension of mountain beauty.'

This quest starts in the opening chapter, amongst the Cuillin of Skye, when he says, 'here, for the first time, broke upon me the unmistakable intimation of a last reality underlying mountain beauty.' Throughout the book this intimation becomes stronger and stronger, culminating in 'Rocks and Realities' which is the most comprehensive summary of Murray's beliefs to be found in any of his writings.

This same chapter will serve to demonstrate Murray's application of several of Stevenson's precepts. Murray wrote: 'In heather there is much to admire; of its season, I have no good to say' – a line which exemplifies the derangement of a phrase for effect, as advocated by Stevenson. In normal or natural speech one is more likely to say something like: 'There is much to admire in heather, but I have nothing good to say about its season'. Much more arresting is the order in which Murray has arranged his words. Apart from the deliberate derangement which captures the attention, this sentence is highly effective because it is perfectly balanced, the semi-colon in the middle acting like a fulcrum for its two equally weighted halves. It is also effective because Murray understood that the beginning or the end of a sentence is where a word makes the most impact, so that is where you put the key words.[2] Thus 'heather ... admire' is a much stronger sentence than losing these two words in the middle of the sentence.

On the next page there is a fine example of using to good effect the repetition of sounds: 'by wandering the plateau and wooing the waters, we come fully to know these mountains and win the high reward of intimacy.' – the w sound in wandering, wooing, waters, win and reward give this sentence a flow which suggests wind and water and raises it above the ordinary.

Stevenson extols the virtues of variety of length and rhythm in prose. Take almost any Murray paragraph at random and we can see him putting this advice to work. In the middle paragraph on page 235 of this same chapter, for instance, the word count for each sentence is: 30, 9, 11, 41, 14, 28, 17, 5 – mixing long and short sentences, but never too predictably. Murray does here what he quite often does, which is to lead us into the heart of the paragraph with a fairly long sentence (but punctuated with one or more semi-colons) and then end it with a short, punchy line.

Murray's professionalism and pride in his work is evident in everything he wrote, but let us take just one example from *The Companion Guide to the West Highlands of Scotland*. Readers of guidebooks are frequently served up with some fairly plodding, functional prose, concerned only with giving the facts, but not in this one.

Take, for example, this opening paragraph from the chapter on Assynt (page 331): 'More visitors are drawn to Sutherland by the rocky desert of Assynt than by any other landscape feature of a county that stretches from the North Sea to the Atlantic. If one has the good fortune first to see Assynt by sailing into Enard Bay, its magic will at a glance be made apparent, especially if one comes late in the day, when Lochinver's white houses at the back of the sea-loch glow in a light mellowing the great stacks behind – the Quinag, Canisp, Suilven, and the peaks of Coigach, all set widely apart and each lifting its head like some petrified monster from the gneiss billows rolling in from the coast. The scene has a fantastic quality, hard to equal in the length of the seaboard.'

Apart from the opening and closing statements, this paragraph is one long sentence – the kind of thing that would have had a teacher of yesteryear reaching for the red pencil. But, of course, it is deliberate. The words come in waves, separated by commas, as if we are on a boat, being wafted into the bay, the stress and rhythm dipping and rising, dipping and rising. Then Murray cleverly makes the land itself a continuation of these waves, with 'gneiss billows rolling in from the coast'.

Stevenson mentions the effective use of 'one liquid labial melting into another' (his very words illustrating the point). Murray employs this literary device here with 'mellow', 'billow', 'rolling' and the soft, fluid sounds of the 'qu' in 'quality' and 'equal', all of which builds up the picture he wants to create in our minds of gentle, evening light and of a magical feel to the place.

Another aspect of Murray's craftsmanship is the way he deliberately shifts the focus from far to near or vice versa, moving both from distant objects to close-up, and from a broad abstract idea to a specific example and back again, as if his pen was a zoom lens. An illustration of this can be found in 'On the Rannoch Wall in Winter' (Chapter IV in *Mountaineering in Scotland*). Murray starts by discussing, in general terms, the harmony and tension between

1 The Cobbler, the first mountain Murray ever climbed, and where
he and Ben Humble once completed sixteen routes in one day.

2 The Buachaille Etive Mor, Murray's favourite mountain where he climbed
more frequently than anywhere else.

3 From left to right: Bill Mackenzie, Archie MacAlpine and Bill Murray on the summit of Ben Nevis, July 1937 after the third ascent of Rubicon Wall.

4 Final part of the Jericho Wall pitch of Clachaig Gully, Glencoe. Murray and his party made the first ascent in 1938. In this photo, taken 72 years later, Mike Cocker is leading.

5 Murray heading for SC Gully, Stob Coire
Nan Lochain, Glencoe, in 1939.

6 Alasdair Cain, Graham Moss and Mark Diggins approaching Tower Gap
in the 1994 film *The Edge* which was a recreation of the 1939 winter ascent of
Tower Ridge made my Murray, Bell and Laidlaw.

7 Murray, aged 37. Taken on the 1950 Scottish Himalayan Expedition.

8 Murray at the entrance to the Githri Gorge on the 1950 Scottish Himalayan Expedition. One of many fine shots taken by Douglas Scott who later became a professional photographer.

10 1950 Scottish Himalayan Expedition. Centre row from left to right: Scott, Murray, MacKinnon. The six porters are the Dotials who stayed with them throughout the four and a half months of the expedition.

9 Camp at the base of the Panch Chuli, 1950 Scottish Himalayan Expedition.

11 Lochwood on the shores of Loch Goil, which Murray bought in 1947 and lived there for the remaining 48 years of his life.

12 Murray (left) at a meeting of the CCS, Battleby House Conference Centre, Perthshire, in 1974. He is talking to Sir John Verney, at that time a Forestry Commissioner and Chairman of the Countryside Commission's English Committee.

13 Photo taken after presentation of Honorary Degrees by University of Strathclyde in 1991. Front (l to r): Prof. Ian Macleod, Murray, Sir Graham Hills (Vice-Chancellor); back: Peter West, unknown, unknown, and Dougie Donnelly the TV broadcaster who was also receiving an award that day.

15 Left to right: Murray, Scott and Weir in their later years.

16 Cover of first edition of
Mountaineering in Scotland,
published in 1947.

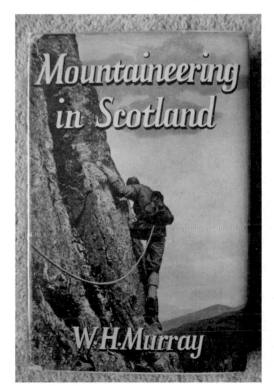

14 Murray with the adapted
slater's hammer which he used
on his pre-war ice climbs.

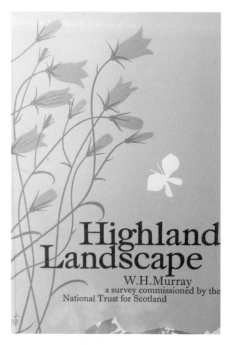

17 Murray's *Highland Landscape*, published in 1962, continues to influence country planning reports regarding the delineation and preservation of areas of natural beauty.

18 Murray, aged 80, in his study at Lochwood, reading from his manuscript of *Mountaineering in Scotland*.

the horizontal and the vertical, and then narrows it down to the contrast between the near-vertical Rannoch Wall and the almost flat Rannoch Moor. He then progresses and broadens this theme again by saying: 'For in true peace there are ever present and reconciled two logically irreconcilable elements – stillness and motion, rest and love,[3] silence and song. Whenever there is a union of the pairs of opposites so perfect that Reason Confounded cries: "Two distinct, divisions none!"[4] there too is an exceeding and eternal beauty.'

He does much the same in Chapter VIII of *Undiscovered Scotland* when describing a climb on Leac Mhor (on the north side of Loch Linnhe). He is standing on a ledge, half-way up the cliff and has been admiring the sun lighting up the hillsides: '… only a little earlier I was warming myself at the flame of that same glow in a solitary blade of grass and fern-frond, in one shoot of heather and a stone of quartz. The sweep of hill in front of me contained these little material things by the million, not one of them visible in its own form or beauty, but uniting to clothe the mountain, building a new beauty of feature.'

Murray was also influenced by Aldous Huxley, and with this in mind, an observation made by Phil Bartlett could be relevant to this near-far method which was part of Murray's literary craftsmanship: 'In discussing landscape painting, Huxley holds that though the inclusion of the human dimension may make a scene classically beautiful, it will certainly prevent it being visionary. To Huxley, visionary landscape can never mean 'the middle distance'; it can only mean the distant view or the close-up. The reason is that only these exorcise human involvement, leaving an emptiness and silence in which the mind can breathe.'[5]

Before leaving Leac Mhor and Chapter VIII of *Undiscovered Scotland*, let us consider the following sentence: 'We were poised in space, muscle and nerve tense, amid acres of arching rock.' Not only is the alliterative use of the 'a's and the 'c's effective in lifting the prose, but three successive sentences prior to this line start with a capital O (On, One, Our). No other letter in the alphabet has quite the same bulging, arching shape and mass which captures the character of Leac Mhor. This may or may not have been consciously thought out by Murray, but there are some things which come instinctively if a writer is experienced, has a feel for the tone, weight and colour of words and is able to get into the flow of the piece. Murray possessed all these attributes.

An article by Murray about his 1939 winter ascent of Tower Ridge on Ben Nevis was published in the 1946 spring issue of *Open Air in Scotland* magazine a year before an account of the same ascent appeared as Chapter XIV of *Mountaineering in Scotland*.[6] The two accounts are substantially the same, but there are some differences and it is instructive to look at these.

The *Open Air in Scotland* version states that they gathered at the CIC hut on Saturday 19th December. In 1939 the 19th of December was the Tuesday after the weekend in question. The correct date of Saturday 16th December is given in the *Mountaineering in Scotland*, showing that, of the two versions, this was the more finished and checked account.[7] Some of the differences might be put down to the needs of a magazine article as opposed to the needs of a book, the former having a more specialised readership, and strict rules regarding length. The input and influence of the respective editors at *Open Air in Scotland* and Dent would also have been of a different nature. However, these kinds of considerations apart, there are textual alterations which appear to have been made for no other reason than to better achieve perfection of style, precision of meaning, and a truer expression of what he really wanted to say. It is to the examination of these craft-related alterations that we now turn.

The opening paragraph alone amply demonstrates the degree to which Murray put his text under the microscope and closely studied it with a critical editorial eye. Here is the opening paragraph from *Open Air in Scotland*: 'It is notable how frequently the red-letter days of one's mountaineering come as a complete surprise. If I may express the matter in social terms, it is most often when one visits a mountain in expectation of no more than a light snack, that the too generous hostess confronts her unwary guest with a banquet, comprising many a morsel as tough as her victim can chew. One such December day I spent with Dr J.H. Bell and Douglas Laidlaw on Ben Nevis.'

Here is the final version as it appeared in *Mountaineering in Scotland*: 'It is noteworthy how often the red-letter days of our mountaineering come as a complete surprise. One such December day I spent with Dr J.H. Bell and Douglas Laidlaw on Ben Nevis.'

Murray has changed 'notable' to 'noteworthy' – a subtle shift of meaning from being something than claims your attention to something that is actively worth noting. 'Frequently' has become 'often'.

Possibly Murray had the rhythm of the sentence in mind here. Having increased the sentence by one syllable in making his notable/noteworthy alteration, he now restores the balance by finding a word one syllable shorter than before. In the *Open Air in Scotland* version he says 'one's mountaineering' and in *Mountaineering in Scotland*, 'our mountaineering', making the text slightly less aloof, including the reader in 'our', drawing us in. He cuts out the whole of the middle bit, probably judging that it was overstating the case and that images of banquets were not appropriate when setting the scene for the hard battle ahead on Tower Ridge. The last line is unchanged – and no wonder, for it is a fine, ringing, firecracker of a sentence with its hard 'ds' in December, day, Dr and Douglas. In its 17 words this sentence contains no less than ten capital letters, lending it swagger and boldness. This is craftsmanship of the highest order.

Similar changes occur throughout, including, for example, something as small as changing 'sun and wind' to 'wind and sun'.[8]

The true art of writing, Murray said,[9] 'is finding words to express what you really mean, so that you can balance on that knife-edge between two realities and let both speak.' Murray is referring to both the material and the subjective reality and the meaning between the lines. In the same article he applauds, 'a direct simplicity of expression, which is very hard to get, but which is the hall-mark of good writing. It goes to the heart of the matter.' He was modest about his ability to reach his own exacting standard, claiming that most writers, himself included, seldom managed to get it absolutely right. This kind of humility is part of the ingredients of his success and yet another of those knife-edge balancing acts that writers must perform – the confidence and self-belief to recognise that they have something worth saying and the ability to say it, combined with the humility to learn from others and to know that painstaking polishing and redrafting are required.

'Who can confidently say what ignites a certain combination of words, causing them to explode in the mind?' wrote E.B. White.[10] 'Who knows why certain notes in music are capable of stirring the listener deeply, though the same notes, slightly rearranged are impotent? These are high mysteries.' Undoubtedly, Murray had the gift of igniting his sentences, his paragraphs and his essays. His craftsmanship alone cannot account for this. Craftsmanship has to be applied to something worth crafting. No matter how well you express something, it has to be worth saying. Murray did have something worth saying about mountains and landscape beauty and about the personal inscapes which they evoked. To the communication of this he brought not only craftsmanship, but discipline, natural talent, humour, an alert and observant eye, sensitivity, intensity, vision and a passion for his subject.

NOTES

1. This same theme is developed in Stevenson's essay 'El Dorado' and in this essay he uses the phrase, 'the spires of El Dorado'.
2. This is a point made by Strunk in his *The Elements of Style*, which Murray is quite likely to have read. The first edition (1918) sold over two million copies. A revised edition came out in 1935 when Murray was already interested in writing. 'How to write' books were not so common then and, although it was an American publication, Murray may well have obtained a copy of this highly respected and classic little book.
3. To contrast rest with love indicates that Murray must have viewed love as turbulent and unsettling – very much the view of a young man and a bachelor, which, of course, he was then.
4. This is a quotation from Shakespeare's poem 'The Phoenix and the Turtle', an allegorical poem about the death of love. 'Turtle' here means turtle dove. This poem has been called the first great published metaphysical poem. One interpretation of it is that it is an elucidation of the relationship between truth and beauty. If Murray was aware of this, and it is more than likely that he was, it demonstrates the subtlety and depth of his sub-text.
5. *The Undiscovered Country* by Phil Bartlett, page 75.
6. This ascent is the subject of Chapter Ten, 'A red-letter day,' in this biography.
7. This disparity in dates also shows that Murray's remarkable ability for almost perfect recall while writing *Mountaineering in Scotland* did sometimes let him down.
8. Halfway through the *Open Air in Scotland* article, Murray describes the snow as having 'the pile and sheen of ermine'. This phrase is not in the *Mountaineering in Scotland* Tower Ridge chapter. Instead, it appears in Chapter IX, 'The North Buttress of Buachaille In Winter' (page 75). Murray was obviously proud of this phrase and must have succumbed to the temptation to give it an outing in print before *Mountaineering in Scotland* was published.
9. 'Writing and Climbing' in *Climber and Rambler* magazine, November 1984.
10. E.B. White in the third (1979) edition of *The Elements of Style*, which he updated and added an extra chapter at the end.

CHAPTER THIRTY

AT PLAY IN THE FIELDS OF FACT

Taking Murray's body of non-fiction writing as a whole, we find a number of contradictions, inconsistencies, inaccuracies, embellishments, recourse to fiction and other departures from strict fact. This is fairly normal for most non-fiction writers. Sometimes it is unwitting, sometimes it is deliberate. In either category, the frequency of these occasions in Murray's writing is well within the bounds of what would be considered normal for those particular genres. Nonetheless, examining some of these occasions and the reasons for them will shed further light on Murray's non-fiction writing.

Let it be said at the outset that no non-fiction account of events contains the whole truth. All such accounts are selective, picking out what the author sees as the salient, memorable or most interesting facts and rejecting others as being irrelevant, too trivial, inconvenient or unflattering. Therefore, by the same token, all such accounts are subjective. Indeed, there is a school of thought which declares that there is no absolute truth unless it be the sum total of multiple points of view, interpretations, perspectives and angles. We see this, for example, in the way Murray's account of the winter ascent of Tower Ridge differs in detail and emphasis from Bell's, his companion on that day;[1] or how Murray and Mackenzie write about their Observatory Ridge climb in very different ways.[2] This is illustrated on a larger scale in his *Rob Roy MacGregor: His Life and Times* where, probably at a subconscious level, empathy overruled objectivity, leading him to find what he wanted to find in the mass of evidence he had gathered.

In Chapter Five we observed that there was a discrepancy in statements by Murray regarding when he started climbing. Michael Cocker, who has been most assiduous in checking and cross-checking the dates and other details of Murray's pre-war climbs, is of the opinion that the weight of evidence points to Murray having started climbing in 1935, although Murray, both in *Undiscovered Scotland* (page 1) and in *The Evidence of Things Not Seen* (page 21) suggests that it was a year earlier in 1934.[3] However, in his SMC application and in MacAlpine's obituary[4] Murray states that it was April 1935. Cocker points out[5] that when compiling these two formal records Murray is unequivocal about the date, but when producing narrative he occasionally altered events. The reasons for this discrepancy are a matter for conjecture. Cocker's conclusion is that, 'when writing about this at different periods in his life he rather loosely interchanged the year that he started hill walking with the one when he first became interested in the idea of mountain climbing.' It may well be that Murray considered a matter of dates such as this to be of minor importance, being more interested in the broad sweep of things and in telling the story of his quest to find oneness with Beauty.

Cocker and others[6] have also wondered if there was a fictional element in Chapter XXI, 'Cairngorm Blizzard', in *Mountaineering in Scotland*. He says in his Chronology: 'Exactly when this event took place remains a mystery, as does the identity of Murray's chance companion Mortimer. The absence of any reference to this expedition in Murray's SMC application, a document that in all other respects appears to be a complete record, has to make one wonder if this event ever took place in the way it is described and if the account in *Mountaineering in Scotland* is largely fiction. The only other explanation is that Murray accidentally missed this expedition out when completing the application, but with the detailed chronicling of many other quite ordinary excursions this seems unlikely ... It is worth noting that Murray's account in *Mountaineering in Scotland* bears some similarity to an incident on Ben Macdui that occurred in May 1934, when three hill-walkers were caught in whiteout near the summit and lost their way with tragic consequences. This received considerable attention in the press at the time and Murray would almost certainly have been aware of it.'

The provenance of Chapter XX, 'Castle Buttress', in *Undiscovered Scotland* has also been questioned. Murray recounts how, one January (no year is specified), he and Laidlaw found unstable snow there and turned back before reaching the top. Cocker points out in his Chronology that the Castle had been the scene of one fatality and several narrow escapes in the past due to avalanches. There is no record of a

January ascent of the Castle by Murray and Laidlaw in the CIC hut log or in Murray's SMC application. Both the 'Cairngorm Blizzard' and the 'Castle Buttress' chapters were probably constructed around real experiences, then presented in a page-turning way in order to make points about mountain safety as effectively as possible. The purpose of the first was to warn against being caught unprepared in unseasonable and unexpected winter conditions; and of the second to show readers by example that there are times when even climbers of high ability consider it prudent to retreat if the avalanche risk is too great.

Similarly, there is no record of Murray having climbed the North-East Buttress of Ben Nevis with Laidlaw in the month of March as described in Chapter XVIII of *Undiscovered Scotland*. Cocker again:

'While many writers alter events slightly to make a better story, with such a wealth of experiences to draw on it is curious that Murray chose to stray into the realm of fiction. Laidlaw was killed in the Second World War when his plane was shot down over Germany and Murray was dismayed at his loss and it's possible that the two chapters – 'Castle Buttress' and 'Ben Nevis by the North-East Buttress' – were written in the form of idealised days to honour his memory.'

These two chapters and the Cairngorm Blizzard chapter bear some of the hallmarks of a 'composite account' – a device sometimes employed by writers of non-fiction. When there aren't enough interesting or exciting bits in any one of several adventures in the same place (or somewhere very similar), all the best bits are extracted and put into one semi-fictional composite account. Everything that is described did happen, but not all on the same trip.

'The Six Days' Challenge' (Chapter XIII of *Undiscovered Scotland*) is a variation on the composite account. It opens with MacAlpine declaring that writers expurgate their diaries to make their friends seem better than they are. Murray replies that, on the contrary, diaries are usually written when enthusiasm is fresh, with the result that friends are portrayed in a positive way. MacAlpine challenges Murray to take three lucky dips from his diaries and see whether his friends are shown in a good or a bad light. Murray pleads for a sample of six and this is granted.

As recounted in the chapter, Murray then opens his diaries at random and reads from them, followed by a discussion after each one of how his friends fared. Clearly this is a fictional device to link six accounts, none of which would have been long enough to make a chapter on its own, but which Murray deemed worthy of inclusion in the book. These six supposed extracts seem rather too literary and well polished to be the actual diary entries. Although MacAlpine may have once made a comment similar to the one outlined above, these would have been neither the exact words, nor the context in which they were actually uttered.

Invented dialogue is fairly normal in non-fiction, especially as a means of injecting humour. Authors are granted a comic licence and a little invention and embellishment is allowed for the sake of some light relief. That witty quip on the page, made in the face of danger, is quite likely to have been thought up later. Possibly it was what the author wished he'd said at the time, but didn't; or it might be something one of his companions came out with in the pub as they relived their adventure over a pint of beer. It seems highly likely that quite a number of the conversations between Murray and his friends, which Murray records in his various books, are of this kind.

Direct dialogue, in particular, seldom faithfully follows the original words. Most people are simply not that fluent. The author needs to tidy away the hesitancies, the repetitions, the sentences which trail off into nothing or switch halfway through to a different train of thought, and perhaps there are expletives to be expunged. Dialogue is also a user-friendly way for authors to impart information and, to this end, words are put into people's mouths.

The dialogue which took place in the North African desert between the German tank commander and the captured Murray is one of the most quoted passages from The *Evidence of Things Not Seen*. Some 40 or so years earlier Murray had described the same scene in *Undiscovered Scotland* (page 7). The two versions are not quite the same. Probably, neither version is exactly as it really happened. In the earlier version Murray and the tank commander talk about mountains they knew in Scotland and the Alps, and then Murray's captor finds some food for him. In the later version they talk about the mountains while they are eating. The German produces beer and they drink a toast to 'mountains'. This is Murray's earlier version:

'"Here's to mountains," he said, "and to mountaineers – to all of them everywhere." He took a pull at the bottle and passed it to me. I drank too. I felt moved to reply.

I said: "There are three good things you get out of mountains. You meet men and you meet battle and beauty. But the men are true, and the battle's the only kind that's worth fighting, and the beauty is Life."'

Here is the same moment in *The Evidence of Things Not Seen* (page 80):

'We shared the beer and toasted "mountains". Suddenly aware of the brotherhood that implied he added, "and mountaineers".

"Mountains give us some good things," I suggested. "Such as friends worth having, battles worth fighting and beauty worth seeing."'

The difference is more than just Murray's memory of the occasion having altered slightly over the years. In the second version Murray's words are more carefully crafted to give them greater rhythm and impact. It is unlikely that, stressed and in a state of shock, Murray was quite so eloquent in real life. In both versions there is the deliberate use of the rhetorical trick of speaking in threes.[7] The word 'brotherhood' is used in *The Evidence of Things Not Seen* version because, in the context of a chapter about his war experience, Murray wants to emphasise this aspect of the encounter and the common bond that mountains create between mountaineers, irrespective of other divisions.

We have noted in previous chapters three other departures from the exact facts: The matter of Murray's ankle injury prior to his winter ascent of Observatory Ridge (see Footnote 2 in Chapter One of this biography); the rather misleading suggestion that the first draft of *Mountaineering in Scotland* was written on toilet paper; and the somewhat dubious story of Leighton Johnstone's resurrection as told by Murray in SMCJ, 1990.

There is also an unwitting mistake of a slightly different nature: Murray's erroneous statement that the aeroplane carrying Herbert Buck home from POW camp crashed and Buck was killed. This was most likely a misunderstanding on Murray's part, although it must be said that Murray's version does make a more dramatic ending than the truth of what really happened. It was a version which supported his strong belief that Providence was looking after him, and a poignant ending to a significant phase of his life, with the Teacher, having performed his role in the Great Story, now departing the stage. It was a version that fitted how Murray would have wanted to see things and this might unconsciously have made him ready to accept it.

One final example of a discrepancy – one which might or might not be deliberate – is Murray's statement in *Mountaineering in Scotland* (page 199) that between 1935 and 1945 he climbed the Buachaille 79 times. But his own all-inclusive application form for SMC membership shows the total for that period to be 63.[8]

Editors can also depart from the strict truth. In an online review of *The Evidence of Things Not Seen* Ken Crocket praises the selection of photographs, but says: 'I have to state here that Ken Wilson has doctored the one taken by me, on a winter ascent of Crowberry Gully (he confessed to me to give him credit!) [this is Crocket saying this]. In order to make it more appropriate to the pre-crampon ascents in the 1930s, Wilson has edited out the crampons worn by the climber in the photograph.'[9]

In the same book there is a photograph of Murray and Bell standing outside the CIC hut, conferring about their plans for the day.[10] Laidlaw was in the original photograph but has been cut out – a harmless piece of editing maybe, but not the whole truth. Considering the strong bond between Murray and Laidlaw, the former would surely have objected. By the time Ken Wilson selected and edited the photographs, Murray was dead. Further editorial licence is exercised in quoting a letter from prison camp by Murray to his sister.[11] Passages have been cropped out of the letter, but these omissions are not indicated by dotted lines, giving the impression that this was the whole letter as Murray wrote it, whereas the full letter has a rather different tone to it; and the letter is wrongly dated.

Provided four main conditions are respected, it is usually considered acceptable practice for authors of certain kinds of non-fiction to rearrange the order of events, bend a few facts or embellish them a little. The 'rules' are: Firstly, elements of fiction are out of place if the accuracy of the piece is of prime importance as, for example, in official reports, news items, guidebooks, biographies or other instances where readers place their trust in and depend on the author's absolute adherence to the truth. Murray is impeccably accurate in his reports and guidebooks. Secondly, that no false claims are made regarding achievements or happenings that might falsely enhance or harm the reputations of those involved. Murray's motives are miles away from this.

It is also generally accepted that there should be no deliberate intention to mislead, only to improve a story, tidy it up, make it more entertaining or reach a wider, more universal truth than the awkward facts can convey. The author might be trying to make an educational point or striving for an emotional or spiritual truth or trying to make honest sense of his feelings, rather than simply to record what really took place. In describing his struggles to write *Mountaineering in Scotland*, Murray said, 'I would try for truth only.'[12] The context of this statement makes it clear that he meant the wider truth about mountains in their totality, how they demonstrated the oneness of things and their significance as a route to enlightenment.

Bruce Chatwin[13] occasionally changed details and fictionalised people, places and events in his non-fiction books. His biographer argued that 'He tells not half a truth, but a truth and a half.'[14] There are times in Murray's books, particularly when he writes about Beauty or the oneness of all things, when we feel that he is reaching for a wider perspective, the bigger picture, or some kind of higher truth beyond earthly facts. In a letter to Aitken (previously referred to in Chapter Twenty-Eight), in which Murray says he has started writing the semi-autobiographical book which was eventually published as *The Evidence of Things Not Seen,* he tells his friend that, 'memory has become slightly (not badly) erratic. Probably this means I shouldn't be writing at all. But in compensation, the causes, the motives, and consequences of acts and events are clearer.'

The final condition is that only a small proportion of the text contains departures from the real facts – otherwise it ceases to be non-fiction and becomes some other category of writing such as fantasy, allegory, docu-drama, faction, infotainment and other hybrids of literature that inhabit the boundaries between fact and fiction. In some cases, if fiction is masquerading as fact on a large scale, it could be regarded as fraud.

Murray's accounts of his mountaineering days in Scotland and the Himalayas and of other parts of his life are non-fiction, but they are also stories. They are crafted works of literature and memoirs. It is the nature of story-telling, particularly if the stories are repeated again and again, for them to evolve. The repetition might only be in the author's own mind. Nonetheless such stories will change, become more streamlined, develop a pattern that perhaps was not originally there, find ways to heighten the tension, and generally trade veracity for the needs of a good story. How big this trade-off has been in Murray's case it is hard to say but, inevitably, there will have been one.

Likewise, any form of creative writing has a life of its own. It has its own internal logic and momentum, its own rhythms and patterns and dynamic. It is fairly usual, under these circumstances, for authors to begin with an idea of what they want to say and to find, at the end, that they have departed from the plan. All art forms, in fact, develop their own dynamic. Take for example a painter depicting a battle, an historic event. The artist has in front of him a photograph of the scene and has also done a fair amount of research. His intention is to put on canvas a truthful depiction of the event. A fallen figure lies in the foreground of the photograph. The artist moves one arm in order to lead the eye into his picture. On his canvas a bush blooms with red flowers where there were no flowers, so as to make an ironic parallel with the red exploding shells. Clouds appear in a cloudless sky to echo the billowing smoke and bring greater unity to the painting . . . and so the painting grows, telling its own truth.

A memoir is the creation of a mind remembering. Murray regarded memory as some sort of filing cabinet or depository for information and images: 'The mind forgets nothing. It holds all experience in the minutest detail.'[15] Research since then has shown that memory is not so much a storehouse of fixed information as a selective, suggestible, blank-filling, teller of evolving stories. The psychologist Tali Sharot, a leading researcher into the psychology of optimism, thinks that the core function of the memory system could be to imagine the future – to prepare us for what is yet to come. 'The system is not designed to perfectly replay past events, it is designed to flexibly construct future scenarios in our minds. As a result, memory also ends up being a reconstructive process, and occasionally, details are deleted and others inserted.'[16]

Murray himself makes the point that, with the passing of time, perspectives change. Memories of pain fade and those of joy remain: 'But when it comes to recollection, after some decent interval, what a different tale is often told! The pains have gone, as if they had never been, or certainly not lasted. Whereas the day as a whole lasts in the mind. Are pains unimportant? We joke about them. But we had not felt like joking at the time. So where is the truth?'[17]

Intense imagination, provided it is well informed, is one path to recreating how things were. There is an interesting interview in *The Writer's Chronicle* (November 2010) with the American journalist, Faye Rapaport DesPres, entitled 'Authenticity and Imagination in Memoir'.

In it she says: 'In my memoir I needed to re-imagine my childhood in order to understand it. ... You have to be able to imagine that past and the person you once were ... I visualized/imagined the story as I went along, and I kept following what I saw. The fact that the story was taken from real events, people and situations was incidental. In truth, the known events and situations were my biggest obstacles to navigate. The difference between crafting a memoir as a literary work and writing it just the way you remember it depends on the permission the writer gives himself/herself to imagine and rearrange the chronology of events. We do this, not to cheat or write a more interesting story, but to better understand what it is we are trying to say.'

The following anecdote illustrates a number of things about the nature of memory, about how inaccuracies might occur and about how Murray could sometimes have a fairly relaxed attitude to factual mistakes. When Robin Smith and Jimmy Marshall climbed Point 5 Gully on Ben Nevis, Murray sent each of them a note of congratulation. 'Nothing in Scottish climbing has stirred me so much since 1937,' he wrote. Uncertain which event in 1937 Murray had in mind, Smith's biographer, Jimmy Cruickshank, contacted Murray for clarification. 'Murray confessed that he did not know either! ... adding that a wayward pen might have put 1937 instead of 1957, when Patey, MacInnes and Nicol made a memorable first ascent of Zero Gully in five hours. "I must have meant Zero in '57, but it's anyone's guess. The slip of the pen might have occurred from a mental cast-back to Garrick's Shelf ... One of life's mysteries," he chortled.'[18]

There are many levels of accuracy. There are memories that the writer can verify empirically. There are memories for which the evidence is irrecoverable. There are hazy memories, then conjecture, then informed imagination. How much Murray's subconscious mind, his memory and his imagination altered events, we will never know.

Everything we know about Murray tells us he was a man of integrity who would not consciously have given himself permission to imagine and rearrange events beyond the accepted 'rules'. There is certainly no suggestion of deliberate deception, only of a craftsman applying well-established techniques to his non-fiction work to enhance its power.

The divisions between fact and fiction are porous, the boundaries blurred. Authors draw the line for themselves[19] between what they feel comfortable doing and what they don't, between what, in their judgement, is professional conduct and what isn't. In Murray's case, he was well within the bounds of what any unofficial code of conduct might consider good practice. Examining where these boundaries lay for Murray might cause us to look at his writing in a different light, but in no way should it diminish our enjoyment of his books or our respect for him.

NOTES

1. Murray's account is given in Chapter XIV of *Mountaineering in Scotland*. Bell's account is found in his climbing diaries in the Bell Collection in the National Library of Scotland, Edinburgh.
2. See Chapter XI of *Mountaineering in Scotland* for Murray's version and SMCJ 1935 for Mackenzie's.
3. Murray also suggests 1934 in his article 'Present Moments', (*Alpine Journal*, 1981), and in his chapter 'High Tops' in *Wildlife in Scotland* (Macmillan, 1979).
4. SMCJ, 1995.
5. In Michael Cocker's Chronology of Murray's pre-war climbs, online Appendix K.
6. Others have expressed this opinion verbally, but Cocker is the first to say it in print in his Chronology.
7. Storytellers and politicians know the power of threes – for example: Faith, hope and charity; The butcher, the baker, the candlestick-maker; Location, location, location.
8. Thanks are due again to Michael Cocker for this information.
9. This photograph appears in black and white on page 45 of *The Evidence of Things Not Seen*.
10. To be found amongst the pages of photographs following page 64.
11. Letter dated 24th September, 1944, shown on page 96 of *The Evidence of Things Not Seen*.
12. *Ibid*, page 100.
13. Bruce Chatwin (1940–89), English novelist and travel writer. Three of his best known books are: *The Viceroy of Ouidah* (1980), *On the Black Hill* (1982), *The Songlines* (1987).
14. *Bruce Chatwin* by Nicholas Shakespeare, Harvill Press, 1999.

15. *The Evidence of Things Not Seen,* page 88.
16. Tali Sharot writing in the *Observer,* Ist January 2012, about her book, *The Optimism Bias* (Robinson, 2012).
17. *The Evidence of Things Not Seen,* page 343.
18. *High Endeavours: The Life and Legend of Robin Smith* (2005) by J. Cruickshank, page 148. Rather ironically, in telling this anecdote about Murray he muddled the facts, stating that, during the war, Murray was in a Japanese prison camp.
19. There are, of course, other parameters besides the author's own judgment, such as the laws of libel and fraud, and official censorship.

CHAPTER THIRTY-ONE

THE PEN THAT BRINGS THE SCENE TO LIFE

An author has to be moved by more than a need to earn his living, Murray believed. 'Will, heart and mind have to act as one. All obstacles fall to that triad.'[1] In previous chapters, which have looked at his main literary works, we have seen how this triad has lifted his books above the ordinary.

Murray wrote his first drafts longhand, using pen and paper until they became almost illegible with corrections He would then bang out a fresh version on his old manual typewriter. Murray said that his chief pleasure in writing was sharing with others what he had seen and experienced.[2] He enjoyed the craft of writing, comparing it to climbing: 'In climbing there is an elation just in practice of the craft when all is going well. You make the moves surely and swiftly with rhythm. When you are climbing well you know it. The same goes for writing.'[3]

Fiction was what he enjoyed writing most, since it gave greater scope for the imagination than non-fiction, which he thought was more tiring to write and involved a great deal more research. Journalism he found the least satisfactory. He recognised, however, that unless you were lucky enough to write a best-seller or sign a contract for the film rights, novels did not bring in the income that other forms of writing did.

Murray's writing passed through several phases. In his mid-twenties and thirties he focused on writing his mountaineering articles or essays, based on his own Scottish climbing experiences. His first published article was in the SMCJ of 1937 – 'Defeat: a December Night on the Crowberry Ridge'. This was followed by other, similar articles both in the SMCJ and *Open Air in Scotland,* until the latter folded in 1948.[4] Later, he hardly wrote anything for the SMCJ, except the obituaries of his deceased friends. When he began writing for a living after the war he could not afford to write unpaid for the SMCJ, and he was also concerned about their copyright policy. Ever on the watch to ensure that he did not stray from the path of right living and right thought, he worried, too, that it might be a form of vanity on his part to write, not for a living, but for the sake of seeing himself in print.

After his first two books – *Mountaineering in Scotland* (1947) and *Undiscovered Scotland* (1951) – he wrote virtually nothing for the rest of his life that elaborated, in a personal way, about his own Scottish climbing. Perhaps he realised he could never reach the same level of intensity again and that anything which tried to follow his two classics would be an anti-climax. His decision to write for a living also had a bearing on this. He did not want to mix the pleasure of mountaineering with the business of writing. Following the successful publication of *The Scottish Himalayan Expedition* (1951), he could easily have sold a second expedition book about his exploration of the Api region of the Himalayas. However, he chose not to write such a book, just as he turned a deaf ear to friends and admirers who wanted a third volume of memoirs about days spent in his beloved Scottish mountains.

Instead, after three years of Himalayan exploration, he returned to his house on the shores of Loch Goil and tried his hand at writing stage plays. He had read, and now studied, the works of Ibsen, Barrie, Shaw, Somerset Maugham, James Bridie, Tennessee Williams, Terence Rattigan, Arthur Miller and others. The producer at the Citizens Theatre, Glasgow, encouraged him and allowed him to attend rehearsals so that he could learn the practicalities of a stage production. In three years he wrote two plays: the first, *The Game of Love*, about the early years of St Francis of Assisi;[5] the second, *William Wallace*, about one of the main leaders of the Scottish Wars of Independence in the late thirteenth to early fourteenth centuries.[6] Although these plays were praised by a well-known agent and by an Edinburgh theatre director, they were never performed, being perceived as having too big a cast and too many scene changes, and also as having the potential to offend religious sensibilities.

After this foray into the world of drama, Murray, in his mid forties and early fifties, turned his attention to writing his four novels. Then came his three books on the landscape and natural history of the

Scottish Highlands and islands, often referred to as his guidebooks, although the research, craftsmanship and love which he put into them went well beyond the normal guidebook.

In his sixties he struggled to make room for his writing which was being crowded out by the number of conservation campaigns and committees which claimed his time and energy. The records show that, between the publication of *The Islands of Western Scotland* (1973) and *Rob Roy MacGregor: His Life and Times* (1982), there was a nine-year gap without any major publication. However, this gap is not as great as it looks. Murray finished *Rob Roy* in 1978, but there was then a three and a half year delay before publication. Allowing for three or four years of research and writing, the gap between finishing the previous book and starting on this one was minimal. So, despite the demands on his time, there was no arid period in his writing as might at first appear.

A bibliography of Murray's published work is provided in Appendix 2. It can be seen from this that he wrote a great deal more than has been discussed so far in this biography. What is immediately obvious is not only his huge output, but his versatility as a writer. Novels, short stories, essays, articles and non-fiction books all flowed from his pen; and within the latter category were guidebooks, memoirs and biography. As well as writing 15 full-length books,[7] he produced several shorter books and pamphlets, including his extremely useful *Rock Climbs in Glencoe and Ardgour* and his influential *Highland Landscape*. Another two of his shorter works are:

The Real Mackay (Heinemann, 1969) – a collection of a dozen humorous short stories about West Highland life. In May 1967 Murray wrote to Bob Aitken saying: 'My west seaboard book[8] was finished last Xmas and I've written nothing since. I'm beginning to feel conscience-stricken at my idle life, but for the present can't think of a (profitable) subject on which I want to write.' *The Real Mackay* was the book he finally hit upon to write. The stories take an affectionate look at the lives of the laird, his tenants and the crofters, their romances, rivalries and cunning schemes to get rich. Murray heard them told in pubs and from Bob Grieve, a great raconteur. Grieve, the first chairman of the Highlands and Islands Development Board, picked up these stories on his travels. They tend to be slightly over-the-top, and to present the characters with a touch of caricature about them.

Most of the characters are Gaelic speakers and Murray represents this with an inverted construction as in 'Great was the love Sir John Drumgast had for his money' or 'Not a bite would he eat for his lunch'. At times, the humour seems a bit forced. Murray's humour was at its best when it was dry, ironic, and pithy, arising naturally from situations of adversity and centred round his sharp observations of his friends. His attempts at being funny to order and in fictional form are not so successful, seeming laboured at times.

The Curling Companion (Richard Drew, 1981) – The book contains short chapters on the history of the game, the rise of the curling clubs, some of the greatest matches, curling abroad, curling today, and the rules of the game. Murray knew next to nothing about curling when he was asked to write the book. He joked that, if could write about vertical ice, he should be able to write about horizontal ice. The curling expert, Bob Cowan of Glasgow, told him all he needed to know, a fact fully and handsomely acknowledged by Murray. As the publisher's blurb says: 'To conjure up an authentic account and to evoke the atmosphere of curling and conditions under which it has been played from its origins to its present day calls for a master storyteller who understands fully the social and historical background of Scotland and its people. Dr W.H. Murray, already justly famous for his books about the countryside and the outdoor life, is just such an author.'

In addition to the shorter books and pamphlets, Murray wrote ten forewords, introductions or individual chapters for other people's books. He also wrote nearly 40 articles for magazines and journals such as SMCJ, *Open Air in Scotland, The Alpine Journal, The Himalayan Journal, Blackwood's Magazine* and *The Scots Magazine*. On top of this he penned pieces for several different newspapers and the newsletters of the various organisations to which he belonged, such as the John Muir Trust or Friends of Loch Lomond. He regularly reviewed books for some of these publications and also wrote numerous letters to them on matters related to conservation.

Murray also worked for his publisher, Dent, as a jobbing editor, correcting and tidying up other authors' manuscripts. In some cases this amounted to a major revamp, as with Philip Temple's[9] *Narwok!* (1962) and Nea Morin's[10] autobiography, *A Woman's Reach* (1968). Some of the basic work for Dent and the shorter reviews were, in fact, done by Anne Murray.

Most professional authors aim to sell their work more than once to different magazines or overseas publishers,[11] or, in the name of economy of effort, to use the same material, even the same wording, in different books and articles of their own. Murray was no different in this respect, so that, although his output was prolific, running into hundreds of thousands of words, some of it was repetition.

In his review of *Scotland's Mountains* in the SMCJ of 1988, Robert Aitken wrote: 'One had hoped that the Scottish Mountaineering Club, recognising its obligations to the wider climbing fraternity and to posterity, would on the proud occasion of its centenary have eschewed a series of self-congratulatory beanfeasts and a cauld-kale collation from the Journal in favour of commissioning a true work of art from its Old Master. Is it yet too late?'

That same year Peter Hodgkiss, of Ernest Press in Glasgow, and Bob Aitken put up £1,000 each to finance a collection of Murray's writing. They wanted to reprint the best of his articles on climbing and conservation. They also wanted him to write some new retro-spective evaluative essays on topics like the row over the leadership of the 1953 Everest Expedition, mountaineering literature, or more of his excellent pen portraits of friends. Murray refused outright, saying he wasn't interested in re-hashing old material or picking over old bones. It is possible he thought that anything new he wrote wouldn't rise to the same heights as his earlier work. From Murray's point of view, it seems, it was too late.

In his novels Murray wrote so well about sailing that it raises the question, why didn't he write about sailing more than he did? The answer is guesswork, but it could have been that he abhorred any kind of 'humbug'. Compared to those who did write for the sailing magazines, his experience and technical knowledge were not in the same league and he might have felt he hadn't earned the right to do so. Being familiar with Wordsworth's lines:-

> 'Two voices are there; one is of the sea,
> One of the mountains; each a mighty Voice,'[12]

he may have concluded that each was such a huge and challenging subject that to write about just one of them, fully and in depth, was a lifetime's task.

A similar question arises about Murray and poetry. His prose has often been described as poetic and yet he was never drawn to write poetry. In his opinion the true art of writing lay in being able to convey both the material facts and the subjective reality beneath them and to bring out the meaning between the lines. 'The true art is to balance on that knife-edge between the two realities and let them both speak. Poetry is a prime example of this. But prose can also be made to walk this bright edge.'[13] Since his skill enabled him to occasionally walk the bright edge in prose, he may not have felt the need to turn to poetry. It was also his opinion that much poetry, of the kind that was less than great, was about the sound and play of words for their own sake and this he did not want. What he aimed for was the true essence of an experience which came from the heart, not words which pleased merely by their clever arrangement.

Scotland's Splendour,[14] a lavishly illustrated coffee-table book, for which Murray wrote one section, contains a Publisher's Preface which states: 'Pictures capture the visual splendour at one moment of time, but it is the pen that brings the scene to life when the writer knows his subject and his craft so well that he can put you there beside him.'

This is exactly what Murray achieved again and again in his writing. It was with good reason that his insights and his powerful prose were in demand to add extra quality to books that were not his own, or to state the case for various conservation causes. It was with good reason that his work was represented in no less than five anthologies of mountain or outdoor writing. At his best, his writing is sublime. Robert Aitken, speaking from a wide knowledge of mountain literature, gave it as his opinion that Murray is 'the finest writer about mountains and mountaineering we may ever have in Scotland'.[15]

In discussing Thoreau,[16] Frank Stewart in his *A Natural History of Nature Writing* says: 'He gave us a vision of nature as an inner as well as an outer phenomenon – a conceptual wildness as important as the outer one.'[17] Stewart was discussing American writers, but Murray has done the same for the Scottish Highland landscape and its wildland areas.

Robin Campbell called Murray's first two books the *Iliad* and *Odyssey* of Scottish mountain writing. What was truly remarkable about Murray's writing, Campbell said, was 'a rare and peculiar talent for capturing mountain landscape in a way that compellingly exposed its character and beauty.'[18]

Praise for Murray and evaluation of his writing has sometimes tended to have a Scottish dimension and context to it. It is time to re-evaluate his work in a British, European and worldwide context. In this author's opinion, in the fields of mountaineering literature, wilderness writing and landscape description,[19] he would hold his own with the best.

NOTES

1. *The Evidence of Things Not Seen,* page 305. Murray is echoing here what he said about making his decision not to enter monastic life but to become a writer (page 133): 'I had set my course, and mind and heart and will were at last one.'
2. *Ibid,* page 307.
3. *Ibid.* Murray is using here the text of a speech he gave to the British Mountaineering Council in 1984.
4. See note 19 in Chapter Seven.
5. Note 19 in Chapter Fourteen further explains the affinity which Murray felt with St Francis of Assisi (known in his lifetime as Francesco Bernadone).
6. Sir William Wallace was a Scottish knight and landowner, who was one of the main leaders of the Scottish Wars of Independence. He was captured in 1305 and handed over to King Edward I of England, who had him hanged, drawn, and quartered for high treason.
7. These 15 books in the order in which they were written, are: *Mountaineering in Scotland, Undiscovered Scotland, The Scottish Himalayan Expedition, The Story of Everest, Five Frontiers, The Spurs of Troodos, Maelstrom, Dark Rose the Phoenix, The Hebrides, The Companion Guide to the West Highlands of Scotland, The Islands of Western Scotland, The Scottish Highlands, Rob Roy MacGregor, Scotland's Mountains* and *The Evidence of Things Not Seen* (unfinished).
8. By 'my west seaboard book' Murray means *The Companion Guide to the West Highlands of Scotland* which was published the following year.
9. Philip Temple was born in England in 1939, but then moved to New Zealand. He is an award winning author of novels, children's stories and non-fiction books, dealing mostly with outdoor and environmental themes. One of his earlier books was *Narwok!*, describing a mountaineering expedition to New Guinea.
10. Nea Morin (1905–1986) was a British mountaineer. She climbed in the Alps in the 1920s and was a member of the Ladies Alpine Club. She climbed often with other women and advocated the *cordée féminine*, climbing only with women on a rope. Her autobiography, *A Woman's Reach* (1968), describes her climbing and the achievements of other women in the mountains.
11. Articles are sold as 'First British Serial Rights', or, if being sold for the second time in Britain as 'Second British Serial Rights', or as 'First North American Serial Rights' etc, their commercial value usually dropping each time they are

sold in the same country. It is not unusual for authors to sell their work three or four times over.

12. 'The Sea and the Mountains, Each a Mighty Voice' in *Poetical Works of William Wordsworth* (1896).

13. *The Evidence of Things Not Seen*, page 307.

14. *Scotland's Splendour* (Collins, 1961) is divided into seven sections, each dealing with a region of Scotland and each written by a well-known author such as Seton Gordon and Tom Weir. Murray's section was on 'The West'. In it he says, 'Granted sun, the West Highlands are the most colourful country on earth.'

15. In a review of *Scotland's Mountains*, SMCJ, 1988.

16. Henry David Thoreau (1817–1862) was an American author, poet, philosopher, abolitionist, naturalist, tax resister, development critic, surveyor, historian, and leading transcendentalist. He is best known for his book *Walden*. His books, articles, essays, journals, and poetry total over 20 volumes. Among his lasting contributions were his writings on natural history and philosophy, where he anticipated the methods and findings of ecology and environmental history.

17. *A Natural History of Nature Writing*, Island Press, Washington DC, 1995.

18. Obituary of W.H. Murray, *Alpine Journal*, 1997.

19. Aspects of Murray's work would also qualify for discussion and comparison amongst wider categories of literature such as travel writing, environmental literature, nature writing and eco-literature, or in sub-genres such as Paradise Discourse.

CHAPTER THIRTY-TWO

A GAME OF TWO HALVES

Although Murray could not know it at the time, when he returned from his last Himalayan expedition he was just a couple of years short of the half-way point in his life. It was as if, with some rather lax time-keeping on the referee's part, the years up to his phase of Himalayan exploration were the first half of the game; the period 1950–53 (the Himalayan interlude) was the half-time break, and the rest of his life after that was the second half.

The years between 1937, when he began to be counted amongst the best Scottish climbers of that era, and 1953, when he returned from his last Himalayan expedition, might seem to be the period when Murray's star was highest and brightest in the firmament. These were the years in which he excelled as a mountaineer and explorer; and the years in which he wrote *Mountaineering in Scotland* and *Undiscovered Scotland*, the two books for which he was to become most famous; and *The Story of Everest* which, of all his books, made him the most money.

The second half of his life did not hold the same adventure, glamour or public acclaim, despite the various honours and awards he received in later life: the Mungo Park Medal of the Royal Scottish Geographical Society (1953), for mountain exploration; OBE (1966) for services to mountaineering; an Honorary Doctorate from the University of Stirling (1975) and a D.Litt. from the University of Strathclyde (1991). The main text of *The Evidence of Things Not Seen* totals 304 pages, of which only 18 deal with the second half of Murray's life. The conservation work to which he gave so much of his time was unspectacular, being largely concerned with committee meetings, dry reports and officialdom. Yet, it is his endeavours in this field which probably have impacted for the good upon the lives of a greater number of people than anything else he did.

'Pleasant as it was roaming the Himalaya, I couldn't do this forever. I had to work to live.'[1] So, as he entered middle-age, he settled down at Lochwood, his cottage on the shores of Loch Goil, to write for a living. Murray's Himalayan days did, in fact, receive an extension. Between 1969 and 1974 he led four trekking trips to the Himalayas organised by Mountain Travel Nepal, one of the first of its kind, which had recently been set up by Colonel Jimmy Roberts.[2] He also led one for Thomas Cook & Sons to Everest Base Camp. These were 30-day treks going up to 18,000 feet and covering as much as 300 miles. In a letter he wrote of his 1974 trip that 'it was the best I've ever had it – small party, all climbers, very good company, perfect weather, no troubles. It saved my sanity, getting away from the everlasting rain.'[3]

One might be tempted to think that this shy, reserved, often mono-syllabic man (at least with those he didn't know well) was not cut out to be a tour guide. Those who were in his groups would disagree. They report that he was unfailingly charming, informative and attentive. In Scotland, Murray advocated that wild areas should be preserved in their natural state as far as possible and that people should not be assisted in their invasion of them by roads, bridges and mechanised transport. Whether having a guide came under the term 'assisted' is a moot point. Possibly he thought the pressure of population in the remote Himalayas was not the same as in crowded Britain; or that the kind of tours he was leading on foot, and involving clients who were already mountaineers likely to appreciate and respect the mountain wilderness, were exempt from his strictures. It seems he could not resist returning and this was the only way he could afford to do it. The Himalayan magic cast a spell on him, beckoning him back, but he learned that the magic can only be won on initiatives taken by oneself, not by others.

Another apparent contradiction to Murray's usual stance is that, in this same period, he acted as a guide and lecturer on National Trust cruises to areas like Torridon, where parties of non-climbers would sail in luxury to remote places and then be led into the mountains. These cruises had a high educational content and were under responsible leadership. In Murray's opinion, the benefits of creating and encouraging an informed and caring body of supporters for wilderness areas outweighed the damage done by tramping feet.

Mary Mackenzie, wife of Bill Mackenzie, later said[4] that in about

1958 Murray went with her and her husband to the Swiss Alps and
that he was having personal problems and seemed out of sorts and
in very low spirits. The reasons for this are not known. It might have
been some sort of mid-life crisis. At the time, he was working on
his novel, *Five Frontiers*. It could be simply that he had hit a sticky
patch with it. A cause of his low spirits might have been that, around
this time, Fiona Graham[5] ended their fairly long-term relationship. It
would also have been close to the time that he first met Anne Clark
and was captivated by her. Perhaps he was struggling with the choice
between marriage and the loss of freedom it might entail, or the intrusion upon his time to write, or even upon his intensely private life.
Perhaps, too, was the thought that now was when he should finally
give up serious climbing.

As Phil Bartlett says in his book, when discussing climbers' reactions to near-death experiences in the mountains and whether it is
blasphemy to wilfully jeopardise one's life: 'The first time it happens:
no, that's not blasphemy. The second or third time? Perhaps not. But
the hundredth ... ?'[6] Or it may have been that Murray was having
money problems and was finding that earning a living as a writer
was not easy.

By now, Murray had been overtaken by the next generation of
young climbers who raised standards to new heights. He was beginning to acquire the status of one of the 'Last of the Grand Old Masters'
as wittily caricatured in Tom Patey's song:

> 'I'm the last of the Grand Old Masters
> The Tigers of Yesterday
> When the March of Progress passed us
> We were left to Fade Away.'[7]

A couple of months before his forty-seventh birthday, he married
Anne Clark. The following year saw the start of an active engagement
in protecting the Highland landscape – work which he threw himself
into for the next three decades, doing most of it on a voluntary basis
or for minimal expenses. Service to others and forgetfulness of self
had been a guiding principle for most of his adult life. Now he followed it as never before, sacrificing precious time in the mountains,
writing time and time for enjoying home life.

As he approached 70 his respiratory problems, which had been with him for years, had worsened and he hardly ever set foot on a mountainside. His seventies were marked by increasing ill health, the inevitable processes of ageing and a gradual withdrawal from public life with a succession of resignations from the various committees and organisations on which he served. Married to someone who is herself a very private person, and living in an isolated cottage, Murray did become something of a recluse in later life and his tendency to privacy even more pronounced.

It was during this final phase of his life that *Scotland's Mountains* (1987) was published. This book demonstrated that, although Murray might have been ageing physically and withdrawing socially, he retained his mental energy. He understood the saying, 'whom the gods love die young' to mean that the gods love those who are young in mind whatever their age, who see the world afresh every day and still know that feeling of awe and wonder. Murray was one such person.

As a student of Hindu philosophy and religion, Murray was aware of the four stages of life as laid down in the Ramayana: One – the celibate student, a stage which usually lasted until about the age of 25. During this stage, a young man is expected to leave home and study under a guru. Two – the married family man and householder. Three – the hermit in a retreat. He leaves home and lives in a hut in the forest, leading a life of meditation and contemplation and also becomes a teacher in order to share his experiences with others. Four – the final stage, seldom reached, in which a man becomes a wandering ascetic, focused entirely on God. Murray would have aspired to a great deal of this. Indeed these four 'ashramas' are reflected in his life, but not quite as the orthodox texts would have it.

Given Murray's shyness, the middle-class sexual inhibitions of the pre-war years, his moral code and self-discipline and the fact that he was climbing so intensively every weekend that there was little time for anything else, it is quite possible that the celibate student phase lasted beyond the stipulated 25 years. This was then followed by the enforced celibacy of the POW camps. His guru was Herbert Buck, under whom he studied the Perennial Philosophy. In Murray's case, stages two and three were reversed – he did not marry until he was 47, although he did become a householder fairly soon after the war. Lochwood, a remote cottage situated between forested mountain slopes and a loch, almost qualifies as a hermit's retreat and the stipulated hut in the forest; here he did lead a life of meditation and contemplation and, through his writing, he did become a teacher. The final phase, the wandering ascetic, is detectable in Murray from early on. He could become like that when climbing – in the stillness of a moonlit night on a Scottish peak, or striding over Rannoch Moor, alone except for his dog, or in the vastness of the Himalayan ranges, focused on his search for Beauty. He was like that when writing, lost to the world around him, wandering over time and space, his mind on the oneness of things.

The influence of the Buddhist Eightfold Noble Path, which Murray had studied, can also be discerned in Murray's life. Indeed, it is almost a summary of the kind of man Murray tried to be in his personal and public life – right understanding, right thought, right speech, right action, right livelihood, right effort, right mindfulness, right concentration.

In the second half of Murray's life there were five constants – his house in which he lived for nearly half a century; his continued pilgrimage towards the metaphorical sunlit summit where he might glimpse true Beauty and Unity; his marriage; his love for the Highland landscape, its mountains and lochs; and his writing.

Lochwood, his cottage on the shores of Loch Goil – the first of these constant factors – he bought in 1947 and lived there for the rest of his life. This was where he wrote all his books except *Mountaineering in Scotland*. At first, he was away from Lochwood more than he was there, what with his work on the Glencoe guidebook, his Scottish climbing trips and his Himalayan expeditions. Of the post-expedition years, when he became more settled, he said: 'I enjoyed being back at Lochwood, its sounds and silence, its wildlife. In season the colour and smell of this place could put a spell on me.'[8]

Azaleas, cherry trees and rare rhododendrons brought enchantment as did the rockeries on different levels and the strands of oak, holly, birch and sycamore. Two rocky outcrops kept Murray in trim for climbing and provided a challenge to visitors, and a boathouse enabled him to work on his sailing dinghy during the winter. Inside his house there was a comfortable muddle of assorted furniture, with plenty of loaded book cases and mountain pictures on the walls.

It did have its drawbacks, though. The house was over one hundred years old and had been neglected. There were two and a half acres of garden which had run wild in his absence. He confided to friends that he thought Lochwood would give him time, free from interruption, to write, but that it hadn't worked out that way. Not only did the house, grounds and various sheds demand constant upkeep, but he hadn't realised that solitude is sometimes easier to find in a city where neighbours are not so welcoming and sociable as in a rural community. He also complained of a lack of stimulation, the high rainfall, the newspapers being a day late and the difficulty of travelling from there to committee meetings or to the big libraries in Glasgow and Edinburgh. The spell cast by Lochwood was too strong, however, despite the disadvantages, he never seriously entertained the thought of leaving it.

Murray wrote rather less about his beliefs and philosophy in the second half of his life than had come bursting out of him in *Mountaineering in Scotland* and the articles he wrote for SMCJ immediately after the war. This was not an indication of a waning faith or flagging enthusiasm but a sober realisation that most people were not interested. His philosophy was individual and personal and he was not in the business of gaining converts. It was not until he came to write his final book, when he felt his life was drawing to an end that he put in writing, for public consumption, a fairly intimate account of the influence of Herbert Buck and the Perennial Philosophy upon him. That he chose to do so, from so many other things in his life he could have written about, shows the importance it held for him. Writing of his quest for spiritual growth he said that 'all the energies of a lifetime'[9] are wanted to reach the spiritual heights and he quoted T.S. Elliot's 'We shall not cease from exploration'.[10] Murray did not cease from his quest and he continued meditating and taking instruction all his life, striving for personal and spiritual growth.

Perhaps some part of him still wanted to be a monk. A photograph in *Weir's World*, taken by Tom Weir during the Scottish Himalayan expedition, gives credence to this. It shows Murray sitting draped in a long white robe, looking very monk-like. Another photograph, taken at Namche on the Everest Reconnaissance Expedition, shows Murray clad in the robes of a Buddhist monk. The photograph on the cover of *The Evidence of Things Not Seen*, one of Murray's favourite photos, shows him with the hood of his jacket over his head, in the manner of a monk's cowl. This was not a shot taken in the mountains, but in a studio and was deliberately composed that way.

In Murray's original version of *The Evidence of Things Not Seen* (then with the title of 'To Live and Learn') there is an Arab parable which he transposed from sand and desert to snow and mountain to make it more personal. The lone climber meets a man near the summit who says, 'I am He whom you long denied.' And the man invites the climber to look back at his footsteps in the snow, unrolling his life like a trail. The climber sees two sets of footprints running side by side, showing how they have travelled together. Whenever there has been a crisis in the climber's life the double tracks change to single. The climber takes this to mean that he has been abandoned at these times. The single footsteps, he discovers, belong to the other traveller and are where the latter carried him in his arms.[11] It is clear from this that Murray's belief that some force, which he called Providence, was looking after him was undiminished in his later years as was his quest to reach the spiritual summit.

For the last 36 years of Murray's life he was married to Anne (neé Clark). She was a physiotherapist, based in Dundee, a nature lover committed to conservation, a poet and a prominent member of the Ladies Scottish Climbing Club. She also belonged to the Grampian Climbing Club and the Carn Dearg, the latter priding itself on its toughness.

Murray described how they met: 'Coming down from the tops in the gloaming of a winter's day I turned to look back. Someone was running lightly down the last slopes out of the day's ebb. It was a woman, hair seemingly on fire. It blazed brighter than the flare of the sinking sun behind her. I stared. Who was this? We spoke briefly but soon had to go our separate ways.'[12]

He made a point of seeking her out, climbing with her and getting to know her, 'a tall slim redhead with eyes that could glint like peaty pools in sunlight or be deep and unfathomable.'[13] Their wedding, in December 1960, was a quiet affair, attended by close friends only – the Mackenzies, the Dunns and the MacAlpines. Anne was 20 years younger than her husband and was sometimes taken for his daughter. By all accounts it was a happy and successful marriage, if somewhat unusual and eccentric. Both were intensely private and independent people who tended to lead separate lives, doing their own thing. Anne used to say that Bill spent a lot of time inside his own head and that she often had no idea what was going on in there. Murray's mother had been living with him at Lochwood and continued to do so after his marriage. How the strong-willed older woman and the fiery new addition to the household co-existed is a matter on which Murray was silent.

In 1991 Anne was involved in a bad car crash. She fell asleep at the wheel while returning from the mountains and hit a tree. Amongst her many injuries was her nose which was completely destroyed and had to be reconstructed. Although the surgeons did a good job, they replaced her long nose with a short one, considerably altering her appearance.

The fourth strand running through the second half of Murray's life was his intense involvement with the Highlands and Islands of Scotland and his strong desire to protect and preserve their wilder, remoter parts. This took the form of both a physical involvement through his mountaineering, sailing and his field research for his guidebooks and his NTS report, *Highland Landscape*; and a mental, creative, spiritual and ethical involvement through his writing and his huge commitment to conservation work as described in a previous chapter.

Murray expressed the thrill he obtained from sailing mainly through his fiction. For him, sailing, particularly dinghy racing, provided the same kind of nervous tension as rock-climbing. He had thought of acquiring a five-ton yacht in order to combine sailing and exploration of some of the less accessible parts of the Scottish west coast. However, he concluded there would be too many problems about leaving a yacht unattended (unexpected storms, dragging anchors etc) while he disappeared into the hills; and problems of having to wait for the tide.

As the number of days in the hills grew less for Murray, the SMC continued to provide social occasions with its annual dinners and anniversary events where Murray could meet up with his former climbing companions. The SMC was and is an all-male club, which was how Murray preferred it. Women could attend events as invited guests if they were mountaineers in their own right, rather than simply a friend or partner of a member. These events could be a strange mix

of formality – grace before the meal, a toast to the reigning monarch
– and great humour, with the club enjoying poking fun at itself, or
the whole room roaring out the chorus to the club song:

> 'Oh my big hobnailers! Oh my big hobnailers!
> How they speak of mountain peak,
> And lengthy stride o'er moorland wide!
> Oh my big hobnailers! Oh my big hobnailers!
> Memories raise of joyous days
> Upon the mountainside!'

Murray was on the committee and served as Vice-president, then
as president from 1962–1964. Robin Campbell told me that he
thought that, while Murray had been a competent and conscientious
president, he had not been an outstanding one. 'You have to hit the
ground running to make much impression in a two-year term of
office,' Campbell said, adding that Murray had been extremely tied
up with his conservation work both before and during that time.

When Murray returned from his Api expedition in the Himalayas
in 1953, it was with the purpose of settling down as a professional
writer, which he did to good effect, producing another 16 books.
Since several chapters have already discussed his literary output, no
more will be said here except that his love of writing had begun in his
childhood and remained with him till his death. It was, indeed, the
most constant factor in his life. He chose to be a writer rather than a
banker, knowing that he was opting for a life on a low and unsteady
income compared to one of relative affluence and economic security.
Although a natural ascetic, when faced with the choice of becoming
a writer or a monk, the former won the day. It even took precedence
over mountaineering.

Allied to, and perhaps inseparable from, his love of writing was his
love of reading. From his schooldays onwards he was an avid reader.
In this he was encouraged by his sister who was studying English
Literature and Philosophy at university. His POW years provided
ample opportunity and leisure for intensive reading. Literary allusions
abound in his books. Some are deliberate, but others are probably
unconscious, such was the extent to which he became steeped in and
absorbed the classics of literature.

These five strands running through the second half of Murray's life could be said to emanate from two overriding loves – his love of the wilderness and his love of exploration. Scottish mountain tops are wilderness areas, even if their lower slopes have been partly tamed and it was here that Murray felt most alive, free and in his proper element. The remoter parts of Britain were the subject of the majority of his non-fiction books and the preservation of these areas was the aim of much of his committee work. His novels, too, were largely set in wild country. Lochwood's surroundings of mountain, loch and woodland was what made him buy it; and it was her free, wild spirit that attracted him to Anne. In Murray's quest to be part of the oneness of all things and to glimpse true Beauty, it was in the wilderness he felt closest to achieving it.

His love of exploration took him to the mountains and to tracts of little-known country, but it extended also to exploring his talents, exploring different kinds of writing and taking his thoughts and his mysticism into realms that few have charted.

We have looked at Murray's life in terms of different phases, constant themes or threads and motivating forces. It can also be viewed in terms of key moments and turning points. As in all our lives, some of these are obvious at the time, others only become apparent later. It has been said that our lives are the sum total of the choices we make. Certainly outside influences and events beyond our control play a part, but so do the decisions we make in response to them.

Some of these key moments and life-changing decisions were: Overhearing by chance a conversation about the wonders of being on a mountain-top and deciding to experience this for himself; the coming of war, which, of course, hugely affected the whole nation; his decision not to jump into a recently created shell hole – the story of his life would have ended there if he had; his decision, while in POW camp, to start writing *Mountaineering in Scotland*; and his meeting with Herbert Buck at a point when he was wide open to Buck's teachings. After the war, his decision not to enter the monastic life, to leave banking and become a full-time writer were all turning points, as was the manner in which he found Lochwood[14] and bought it, and his meeting with Anne and marriage to her. Being commissioned by the NTS to research and write *Highland Landscape* was another key moment for Murray. It opened his eyes to the perils confronting many of Scotland's most beautiful and remote places and led to over three decades of involvement in conservation causes.

In 1995, the year before Murray died, a short poem about him appeared in the SMCJ, the final verse of which was:

'This morning our eyes met through an hotel window
as I strode to the mountains and I saw reflections,
reflections on comrades lost in war, reflections on past glories
and above all reflections on the physical limitations of age.'[15]

Whether Murray reflected often on these things is hard to say. He must have done on occasions and it would have been with serenity. More typical of him would be to enjoy the present moment or look forward to exploring the future. Old age did bring its limitations. Murray never complained, but accepted them philosophically. He approached the final phase of his life as would an explorer in undiscovered country where, with the certainty of death as his companion, life was appreciated afresh from a grander, more sweeping viewpoint.

NOTES

1. *The Evidence of Things Not Seen*, page 283.
2. Colonel Roberts was a retired British Army Gurkha officer, whom Murray had thought might have been in the running to lead the 1953 Everest expedition.
3. In a letter to Bob Aitken, January 1975.
4. In a letter to Michael Cocker, dated 2nd September 2003.
5. Murray used to crew for Fiona Graham, who kept a 10-foot dinghy on Loch Fyne. She admired Murray's books, especially their mystical aspect. When in hospital after a skiing accident, she compiled the basic list of Scottish mountains between the heights of 2,000–2,500 feet, still known today as 'Grahams'. She later married and became Mrs Talbot. While on a walking holiday, aged 62, she was raped and murdered at Bridge of Orchy by her landlord's son. 1993
6. *The Undiscovered Country*, page 146.
7. The full text can be found on Patey's *One Man's Mountains*. NOT ORCHY, INVERINATE
8. *The Evidence of Things Not Seen*, page 283.
9. *Ibid*, page 102.
10. *The Four Quartets*.
11. This information is taken from notes left by Peter Hodgkiss and from Robert Aitken's memory of comments made to him by the latter.
12. *The Evidence of Things Not Seen*, page 285.
13. *Ibid*, page 286.
14. Murray recounts in *The Evidence of Things Not Seen* (page 136) how, when

the estate agent was temporarily absent from the room, he glanced at his ledger and saw this house which had not been one the agent had thought worthy of mentioning.

15. 'Reflections' by Charles Orr, written 4th December, 1994, Alexandra Hotel, Fort William.

CHAPTER THIRTY-THREE

TO LIVE AND LEARN

'To Live and Learn' was the original title of *The Evidence of Things Not Seen*. Murray had in mind that he would review the big lessons of his life – not facts and knowledge, but the development of his guiding values and beliefs. What Murray identified these as being tells us a great deal about him. In presenting these lessons here, extracted from the book as a whole, and laid out in condensed form, an impression might be gained that Murray's autobiography is a thinly disguised, finger-wagging moral lecture. This is far from the truth. The book is no missionary tract, but a brave and honest account of certain aspects of his life and adventures and his development as a human being.

One thing Murray learned – more a fact of life than a guiding principle – was that one's beliefs and values contain contra-currents; that life is often like walking a tightrope between two opposites. Murray was an intensely private man and yet, through his books, he exposed his inmost thoughts and beliefs to thousands of strangers. He wrote about the joys of living in the present moment, in the now, yet for a large part of each day he was absent from the everyday world, lost in deep meditation, or living inside his own mind, in the past or in a world of fiction. He wanted something akin to a monastic life and, at the same time, was compelled by his concern for the wilderness to engage in the practicalities of committees, campaigns and the politics of conservation.

Perhaps his greatest dilemma, the one that most explorers have to face, is the tendency to destroy the thing we love. By exploring the wilderness we destroy its most desirable quality – that it is unexplored, mysterious and unknown. Murray played an important role in spotting the route to the summit of Everest by which the first successful ascent was made; and he would have liked to have been picked for the 1953 expedition. At the same time, he expressed the opinion that success on Everest was the worst thing that could happen to the mountain and to mountaineering.[1]

By writing about the wilderness we attract people to it, so that, inevitably, its pristine state is spoiled. After *Undiscovered Scotland,* Murray wrote no more books specifically about the Scottish mountains, even turning down a lucrative offer from the Sierra Club to write a book for them on the Scottish Highlands. His reason was that he feared he would do more harm than good, and that, by extolling their attractions, the beautiful and remote places he loved would cease to be the way that he described them and become tamed and overused. His natural instinct to share his love of mountains with others conflicted with an equally strong desire to preserve them as they were.

Murray relied on his two classics to bring in much-needed income. He was in the difficult position of wanting his books to sell well, but not wanting too many people to read about the remote places he loved so much.[2] When, in 1979, Ken Wilson suggested that *Mountaineering in Scotland* and *Undiscovered Scotland* be combined into one volume, in order to boost the sales of both books, he agreed. By then the situation had changed. It was obvious that the growing invasion of the countryside from the cities could not be stopped and was irreversible, and that only government decisions at high level could bring about the desired conservation measures. Political will being geared to votes and popularity, the more people who knew how important it was to preserve Scotland's precious wildlife and wild land, the more guardians they would have. As the Sierra Club maxim states: 'Wilderness will be preserved in proportion to the number of people who know its value at first hand.'

In his conservation work Murray faced a related dilemma – how to balance freedom to enjoy the wilderness with the need to preserve it. In this case, the conflict was more between him and the policies of the NTS, CCS and government departments. He was clear in his own mind that preservation was the priority, but he had to face accusations of selfishness and of being undemocratic.

As with many people, one of Murray's greatest teachers in life was adversity – adversity encountered in the mountains, in battle and in the POW camps, the kind of adversity which challenged and tested him and his companions to their utmost. In the mountains he learned to respect the resilience, courage and hidden reserves of his fellow climbers. Mackenzie's performance on their ascent of Observatory Ridge in winter inspired him to write: 'Each time I look back dispassionately on that performance, my respect for the human animal increases. He has powers within him of which he knows too little.'[3]

The POW camps, likewise, increased his admiration for how the men around him behaved under stress: 'Two important things I learned were never to judge men by their outward appearance, or by casual talk. Both can be utterly misleading. Nearly all have high qualities or real merits, hidden until educed by circumstances or friendship.'[4]

He learned something similar from the Himalayan people he met and whom he observed in dangerous or taxing situations at high altitude: 'Humankind had manifold diversity and a potential for good too rarely realised. I deeply respected these hill people of Nepal and India.'[5]

The appalling conditions of the prison camps taught him that 'Mankind cannot live above a bestial state without ideals. They alone make life worth living.'[6] After encountering the Gestapo he was in no doubt that ideals must be acted upon and that the war of last resort should never be shirked. Destructive evils can only be ended when action is taken on ideals, never by compromise with evil itself. But ideals must be informed and guided by love and wisdom. Hitler, Murray concluded, probably had high moral standards in his early days, but without these two qualities they became corrupted.

Murray's values were far from materialistic. His experience of war and its carnage had taught him that, compared to loss of life, money and property were unimportant – provided that one was still young, unattached and in good health.[7] Later in life, when he was older, married and with a house to maintain, money did become a worry, but never important to the extent that it determined what he did for a living or deterred him from throwing himself into hours of unpaid work for causes he believed in.

Murray's love of exploration was a main thread and motivating force throughout his life. Perhaps it was not a lesson learned, but something deep inside him from the start. 'It is indeed for striving and exploring and discovering that we all are made,' he wrote.[8] What life taught him was to listen to this instinct and act upon it, whether it was committing himself to a Himalayan expedition, launching into a new kind of writing, or setting out on the steep and difficult path of meditation, study and mental discipline that would lead him nearer to the sunlit summit which lay above the clouds of unknowing.

In his spiritual, mental and physical explorations Murray was aided by other lessons learned, such as the value of commitment and that 'all obstacles are imposters, and none impossible'[9] and that 'dreams are more potent than reason: that if you can dream a thing you can attain it too, as often as not ... Dreams are for action.'[10] He came to know the importance of single-mindedness 'that can cut a swathe where blunt instruments fail'.[11] He learned, too, to trust in Providence, not worry about the future and live in the present moment.[12] Himalayan travel, with its variety and uncertainties, reinforced these messages and helped him to accept with serenity whatever life threw at him.

Murray especially loved Scotland's wild and remote places. One of the greatest lessons they taught him was that they existed in their own right and were not there purely for our recreation and profit.

His attitude to the mountains was shaped by men like Geoffrey Winthrop Young and Tom Longstaff from a previous generation of mountaineers; and by near-contemporaries such as Bill Tilman and Eric Shipton. For them, mountaineering was not about peak-bagging, conquest and boosting one's personal ego and reputation, but about enjoying the total environment and experience of the wilderness, about exploration and adventure with friends. These people and the mountains themselves taught him that the true joys of mountaineering are spiritual.

Murray saw Longstaff as a wonderful example of how men who live true to their life's purpose stay young in heart. 'A man's goal in life is his self-fulfilment,' Murray stated.[13] Ever since meeting his mentor, Herbert Buck, in prison camp, Murray had known that his own life's purpose and self-fulfilment lay in achieving oneness with Reality (or Beauty or Truth), however fleeting such glimpses might be. He found that, through mystical training, meditation and forgetfulness of self, this was a goal that could be attained, not just in the afterlife, but in this life, and he came to believe that our real selves are our spiritual selves.

In the last chapter of *Mountaineering in Scotland* (page 243) Murray set out the biggest, most important, most exciting discovery of his life: 'From our promontory we look up to the cloud of unknowing that wraps the last height, and from its radiance we know the summit is in sunlight. The way and the goal are before us. To one of exploratory instinct action is irresistible, and he takes to himself the axe of single-mindedness and the compass of his love for beauty. His further ascent is severe, more adventurous than any physical one, dangerous if the route be lost, and the issue sometimes in doubt. In his every upward step is a joy surpassing all that mountains offer. Such a man has understood the schooling of life, and is destined to its fullness.'

As he said in a letter to his sister, to refuse this ascent is to deny the lessons of life.

NOTES

1. In an interview with Rennie McOwan for *The Scots Magazine* (December 2001) he said he felt the same in later years when the first moon landing took place.
2. I asked the environmentalist Sir John Lister-Kaye for his views on this same dilemma. This was his reply: 'This troubled Gavin Maxwell hugely. He was well and painfully aware that *Ring of Bright Water* had wrecked the idyll of Sandaig for him forever. And I agree with the principle. But, and it is a very big but, the evidence that ecotourism is helping us to hang on to a few last wild places and their wildlife is mounting every day. I work in Africa a lot and I am in no doubt that without it there would be virtually nothing left. So, on balance, I think I'm in favour of writers sharing their special places.' (Letter to me dated 25th May, 2010)
3. *Mountaineering in Scotland*, page 109.
4. *The Evidence of Things Not Seen*, page 101.
5. *Ibid*, page 211.
6. *Ibid*, page 108.
7. *Ibid*, page 129.
8. *The Story of Everest*, page 186.
9. *The Evidence of Things Not Seen*, page 273.
10. *Ibid*, page 278.
11. *Ibid*, page 319.
12. 'Present Moments' is the title of an article by Murray in the *Alpine Journal*, 1991.
13. *Undiscovered Scotland*, page 218.

CHAPTER THIRTY-FOUR

WAYS OF SEEING WITH THE HEART

In October 1991 Murray went down with an obscure viral infection and the doctors thought he was dying. After a lengthy stay in hospital Murray recovered and went home to Lochwood, but his heart had been weakened.

Then, at Easter 1995, he fell while repairing the roof of his house. A hospital examination revealed an aortic aneurysm. A second examination showed the need for an operation – one which the surgeon thought would present no problems to a man of Murray's fitness. However, there were post-operation complications and an infection and Murray suffered a cardiac arrest, resulting in another prolonged stay in the Vale of Leven Hospital, near Dumbarton.

During that stay in hospital, Donald McIntyre visited him:

'He had little strength to speak but he told me he was going to die, indeed the doctors thought this very likely. Bill looked on death, and indeed on every eventuality, with quite extraordinary composure. He knew no fear. As an experienced mystic he was confident that through death he would arrive at a higher level of perception and adoration.'[1]

Ken Crocket recounts how later, in the winter of 1995, he also went to visit Murray there:

'He said he was going for a walk, and would I like to come along. I was intrigued and not a little worried. "Won't the hospital staff be unhappy?" I asked. "They've given up," he replied. We left the ward and went along the corridor. It was on the top floor of the hospital. At the end of the corridor were more stairs, which led to the roof. There was not only a very cold wind coming down the stairs, there was in fact a thin dusting of spindrift. Bill started walking up and down the short flight of stairs for exercise. It would help a faster recovery he said. He was then in his 84th year, in his pyjamas covered by a dressing gown, and not in bed with the other patients, most younger and happy to snooze the hours by under bedcovers. It was the last time I saw him.'[2]

Again Murray recovered and went home. After only a few weeks of enjoying home life, he had a relapse and had to return to hospital. He died two days later, on the 19th March 1996, the day after his eighty-third birthday.

In the last lines of his autobiography, Murray summed up his life:

'I have found my way through the years, not always easily, and certainly not affluently, but I have had riches and there has always been a thread to follow. I am aware now of not being young. Time may be limited. But the past was a good age to live in. I was lucky to view the world earlier when more was unspoiled, untouched. Looking back over a wide landscape, cloud shadows racing over the mountains, sun, wind. I know that I have known beauty.'[3]

Murray was cremated at Cardross Crematorium. His funeral was a quiet affair, attended by friends and family. Anne Murray has never said what happened to his ashes. One would like to think that they were thrown to the winds at the summit of the Cobbler where he first saw range upon range of Scottish mountains stretching away into the distance and realised what a lifetime of exploration lay before him; or perhaps taken to his favourite mountain, the Buachaille Etive Mor. It could be that they are quietly fertilising the azaleas, rhododendrons and plum trees at Lochwood.

Almost every national broadsheet newspaper in the UK carried an obituary notice of Murray, most of them a full page. The newsletters and journals of mountaineering and conservation organisations, likewise, honoured him. The SMCJ carried an unprecedented ten pages of obituaries of him. Recorded below is but a small sample of what was written about Murray at the time of his death:

'William Hutchinson Murray, who has died aged 83, will be remembered for as long as literate mountaineers survive to appreciate his work on what are generally accepted as the two finest books ever written about our British hills. ... His literary legacy will continue to inform and enhance the activities and mountains he loved for as long as there are people of open heart and mind.' (Jim Perrin, the *Guardian*, 25th March 1996)

'Bill Murray was a gentle knight of the mountains (although he would have winced to hear anyone say that). His quiet, modest manner and the fact that his mountaineering exploits took place before TV spectaculars and outdoor programmes became commonplace, contributed to his not being as well known to the general public as he should have been. He was in fact the most widely respected mountaineer in Scotland since the Second World War and his books now have the status of outdoor classics. Murray was also an outstanding conservationist and his pioneering work had a profound effect on modern protection measures and on the debate as a whole. ... Bill was a man of clear-cut opinions and those were based on years of experience, but he offered them with kindliness and in a pleasant fashion.' (Rennie McOwan, *Scotsman*, 23rd March 1996)

'With the passing of Bill Murray, Scottish mountaineering and its literature has lost one of its central and most important figures. His book, *Mountaineering in Scotland*, provided the inspiration for a whole generation of climbers, and his influence on the Scottish mountain scene can hardly be overestimated ... He was, in the best sense of the word, a humble man, straightforward, acutely perceptive and totally without malice or deception.' (Roger Smith, *Scotsman*, 23rd March 1996)

The comprehensive tributes to Murray made by Robert Aitken (SMCJ, 1996) and Robin Campbell (*Alpine Journal*, 1997) have been quoted extensively in previous chapters. The full texts of both obituaries are given in online Appendix I. In his final paragraph Aitken said:

'In our age of flexible morality and uncertain conviction, Bill Murray came closer than anyone I have known to the model of a man *sans peur et sans reproche*. On casual acquaintance he could appear distant, but to those to whom he extended his friendship he showed absolute loyalty, infinite kindness, and touches of wicked humour. We who had the privilege of knowing and working with him over the many years strive to emulate and to carry forward the quietly passionate commitment of this most humane of mountain conservationists.'

And in his final paragraph Robin Campbell said: 'We flounder in the wake of a loss which seems irreplaceable.'

An 'In Memorium' of a different kind is the W.H. Murray Literary Prize, suggested by Tom Weir and set up by the SMC two years after Murray's death.[4]

Well after Murray's death a tribute to him reached me in the form of a letter. It expressed in writing the same sentiments that many others had said to me:

'I only knew Bill in his later years as a fellow member who always attended the annual SMC dinner. He was a tall, slim, charming man always keen to talk on any aspect of climbing and mountaineering. He was a great advocate of the Scottish hills, encouraging people to enjoy them but also to look after them. He was genuinely held in high regard, not only by his fellow SMC members, but by climbers and hill folk in general.' (Greg Strange, 20th April 2010)

We can be sure that, just as Murray made his mark during his lifetime, his life and work will have meanings for future generations. What these meanings will be we cannot foresee with certainty, for 'Books shed meanings as trees their leaves, year after year, in their slow growth and maturation.'[5]

In the matter of mountain ethics, Murray, as a young tiger in the 1930s, was regarded by the Scottish mountaineering establishment of the day as a rebel. Later, he himself was seen as an establishment figure, not in favour of some of the latest innovations. However, it may not be too long before the pendulum starts to swing back again and Murray's writings could become a catalyst for all those who are disenchanted with the artificiality of modern climbing, the 'theme park approach', and the way it has distanced itself from the natural environment. Sport climbing[6] – which enables basically poor climbers to climb badly at a high standard – has gained in popularity. Cliffs of great natural beauty have been disfigured by bolting[7] and other artificial aids. Munro-baggers follow well-trodden paths (causing erosion) to their designated peak, ignoring more interesting or beautiful mountains of lesser height. Bouldering,[8] often conducted within a few yards of a road, and indoor climbing are no longer a means to an end, but an end in themselves. 'Mountaineering' grows ever closer to becoming an over-guided, low-level or indoor sport.

There is merit in all these activities and enjoyment to be had from them, but maybe there will come a time, if it has not come already, when a voice is needed to remind us what we are in danger of losing. Such a voice would speak to us of the thrills and challenges of traditional (relatively unaided) climbing; of the adventure and beauty to be found amongst mountains of all sorts and in all weathers, and not just on selected and well-protected, well bolted routes.[9] It would speak of the joys to be obtained from mountaineering that have nothing to do with fame, reputation, competition, money or ego. If such a voice were needed, there could be none better than Murray's.

Murray may yet make his mark in the new environmental ethics, in the developing field of eco-philosophy and the moves to bridge the gap between nature and the environmentally damaging Old Testament religions which proclaimed that 'Man shall have dominion over everything that moves on this earth', and 'shall have sovereignty over the animals'.[10] Phil Bartlett, in *The Undiscovered Country* (page 115), makes this perceptive comment:

> 'In mountains one often feels oneself to be part of a greater whole. In worship in the presence of the sacred, yet western theology does not dovetail well with this. Popular Christian thought has generally put "God highest, man below God, and nature a poor third". It still has no bulk of substantial theological thought with which to buttress the mountain aesthetic. And the inevitable result is that the love of mountains begets all sorts of vague mystical philosophies, well sprinkled with notions of pantheism and nature worship, rather than a serious and codified mountain ethic.'

More than most mountain writers, Murray has advanced the discussion of mountain mysticism. He did much to provide the missing 'substantial theological thought with which to bolster the mountain aesthetic'. Not everyone will agree with his interpretation of the mystical experience, but he has penetrated the clouds of unknowing and vagueness and shown that there is a link to be made to an established body of philosophical and mystical thought.

Murray's contemporary, the American eco-theologian, Thomas Berry,[11] was convinced that our environmental problems are primarily issues of the spirit. He used the phrase 'spiritual intelligence' in the context of reconnecting with the natural world as a way for Man to find his true meaning. That kind of intelligence was, and is likely to remain, a rare commodity. Murray had it.

Murray has been likened to John Muir. He can also be likened to Thoreau.[12] Frank Stewart tells us in *A Natural History of Nature Writing* (1995) that Thoreau and the nature writers after him have: 'continued to transform our perception of what we find irreplaceably beautiful, rapturous, and essential in nature – that which is *in us* as well as in the nonhuman world.' Stewart, in the same book, also says that these writers have 'made the world larger and richer by giving us ways of seeing with our hearts and imaginations as well as with our eyes.'[13] All this is true of Murray. Philip Hamerton once said that 'land belongs to it its owners, but landscape belongs to him who beholds it.'[14] In this sense, Murray gave us the Scottish landscape, because he taught us how to see it. In doing so, he delivered it into our care.

Murray reminds us, more persuasively than most, that we are part of the wilderness and not separate from it. Only by embracing this truth will wilderness survive. In a letter to Aitken he strongly agreed with Aldo Leopold[15] who said that recreational development was not a matter of building roads into lovely places but of building receptivity into the human mind. This is what Murray's books do and will continue to do.

The American mountaineer, environmentalist and academic, Jeffrey Mathes McCarthy, puts climbing narratives into three categories:[16] conquest, caretaking and connection. Conquest narratives are about domination, putting a flag on a peak, naming a route, national pride, or earning bragging rights. Caretaking stories show sympathy for and appreciation of the natural world and concern to preserve it so that we may continue to experience it. Although not as damaging as conquest narratives, they do treat the environment as a human resource, there to be used for our convenience. In connection narratives the writer is not an outsider, but part of the natural world. There is a heightened awareness of the mountains, nature and wilderness and a sense of unity and harmony with them. Mathes places Murray in this third category of writing. This category, he says, which connects with the wilderness and teaches that we are part of it, is essential to its survival, just as wilderness is essential to our survival.

As Thoreau said in *Walden*, 'In wilderness is the survival of the world'; and as Jay Griffiths said, 'The human mind developed in wilderness and needs it still.'[17] The majority of the so-called 'civilised' world has lost touch with nature, the wilderness and wildness, is alienated from its roots and cut off from the means of fulfilling deep psychological needs. In the face of mounting ecological and environmental disaster the world desperately needs writers of Murray's calibre and wisdom who can reconnect us with the natural world. He reconnects us by showing us, rather than telling us. He takes us with him to the places he loves and speaks to us from the heart.

NOTES

1. From Professor McIntyre's funeral address, March 1996.
2. From 'A Mountaineer's Tale' – a review of *The Evidence of Things Not Seen* by Ken Crocket on the website ScotlandOnline, posted 8th August, 2002, six years after Murray's death. Murray would have been 82 at the time of the incident described.
3. *The Evidence of Things Not Seen*, page 320.
4. The prize, a cheque for £250, is for the best article sent to the SMC journal editor that year. The material has to be original and not been published elsewhere
5. Tim Robinson in his introduction to J.M. Synge's *The Aran Islands* (1907). I am indebted to Robert Aitken for drawing my attention to this quote.
6. See Glossary.
7. See Glossary.
8. See Glossary.
9. Pat Littlejohn in 'The Great Alpine Theme Park' (AJ 1997), identifies three kinds of 'bolters': The Greedy New Router; The Misguided Philanthropist (safety and accessibility for all); and The Ruthless Professional (able to take clients up with fixed ropes). Murray would have regarded all three kinds with horror.
10. *Genesis* 1.28.
11. Thomas Berry (1914–2009) was a Roman Catholic priest who advocated eco-spirituality. He wrote several influential books, including *The Great Work: Our Way into the Future (*1999) and *The Dream of the Earth* (2006).
12. The American author, poet, philosopher and naturalist, Henry David Thoreau (1817–1862). He is best known for his book *Walden* (1854), a reflection upon simple living in natural surroundings.

13. From A *Natural History of Nature Writing* by Frank Stewart. Copyright © 1995 Frank Stewart. Reproduced by permission of Island Press, Washington, DC.

14. Philip Gilbert Hamerton (1834–1894) was an English artist and art critic who settled in the Scottish Highlands. Author of *Imagination in Landscape Painting*.

15. Letter dated 24th May, 1971. Aldo Leopold (1887–1948) was an American author, scientist, ecologist, forester, and environmentalist, best known for his book *A Sand County Almanac* (1949). He was influential in the development of modern environmental ethics. He held that: 'a land ethic changes the role of Homo Sapiens from conqueror of the land-community to plain member and citizen of it. It implies respect for his fellow-members, and also respect for the community as such.'

16. McCarthy develops this theme both in his book *Contact: Mountain Climbing and Environmental Thinking* (2008), and in an essay, 'Why Climbing Matters' in the journal, *Interdisciplinary Studies in Literature and Environment* (summer, 2008).

17. *Wild* (2006), page 180. Richard Louv had much the same message when he coined the phrase 'nature deficit disorder'. (see the Bibliography)

THE NINE DECADES OF MURRAY'S LIFE

The events and names listed for each decade are far from being a complete picture of that period, nor are they in strict order, many of the items overlapping. They are provided only to represent the decade and give the general feel of those times and provide a backdrop to Murray's life.

1913–1919

Amundsen and Scott race to the South Pole (1912); Henry Ford introduces assembly line and mass production of cars; first crossword puzzle; Shackleton's epic journey in Antarctica; Art Nouveau; World War I; the influenza pandemic; Russian Revolution; League of Nations; Ethel Merman; Al Jolson; Jerome Kern; Adele and Fred Astaire; Easter Rising in Ireland; Panama Canal opened; Rudyard Kipling; H.G. Wells; G.K. Chesterton.

1913: Born in Liverpool on 18th March
1915: Father killed at Gallipoli; moves with mother and sister to Glasgow
1918–24: Attends The Glasgow Academy's Preparatory School

1920s

Prohibition in USA; invention of TV; first solo flight across Atlantic; Wall Street crash; the General Depression; the General Strike; Albert Einstein; Sigmund Freud; Virginia Woolf; D.H. Lawrence; James Joyce; Charlie Chaplain; Rudolph Valentino; Marlene Dietrich; Wally Hammond; Jack Dempsey; Louis Armstrong; Duke Ellington; Lewis Grassic Gibbon; 10 per cent of Scottish population emigrate during this decade.

1924–28: Attends The Glasgow Academy
1928–32: Trainee banker at Union Bank of Scotland

1930s

Empire State Building completed; first claimed sighting of the Loch Ness monster; first combine harvesters in UK; rise of Third Reich and Nazi Party in Germany; Hitler becomes Chancellor of Germany; Berlin Olympics; Jesse Owens; death of George V; abdication of Edward VIII; Art Deco; Disney's 'Snow White and the Seven Dwarfs'; 'The Wizard of Oz'; 'Gone with the Wind'; first: ball point pen, jet engine, cats-eyes on roads, helicopters and frozen foods; Humphrey Bogart; Laurel & Hardy; Tolkien; Donald Bradman; Joe Louis; Graham Greene; Evelyn Waugh; George Orwell; Scottish National Party; coronation of George VI.

1933: Becomes qualified member of Institute of Bankers and continues to work at Union Bank of Scotland in Glasgow
1935: Climbs the Cobbler, his first mountain; joins JMCS
1936: Teams up with Mackenzie, Dunn and MacAlpine
1937: Garrick Shelf climb; traverse of the Cuillin ridge; his first published article in SMCJ
1938: Becomes Secretary of Glasgow JMCS; Observatory Ridge in winter; first ascent of Clachaig Gully; started climbing with Bell; first Alpine trip (Arolla)
1939: Deep Cut Chimney; Parallel Buttress; war declared with Germany; Tower Ridge in winter

1940s

World War II in Europe, North Africa and Asia; Churchill, Roosevelt and Stalin; Rommel, Montgomery and Eisenhower; the Holocaust; radar; jet planes; ballistic missiles; the atom bomb; Nuremberg trials; United Nations; huge numbers of refugees; new nations of Israel, India, Pakistan & Communist China; the Cold War; Bing Crosby, Jane Russell, Frank Sinatra, Glenn Miller, Stanley Matthews, George Orwell; Gandhi assassinated; Ernest Hemingway; Arthur Miller; Rita Hayworth; Abbott & Costello; Danny Kaye; Thor Heyerdahl & Kon-tiki; Sugar Ray Robinson; Benny Goodman; the Welfare State & the National Health Service; London Olympics, Emil Zatopek.

1940: Registered for military service
1941: Called up for war service; last climb on the Buachaille before entering army; his mother in Clydebank blitz, but unharmed; joins HLI as 2nd Lieutenant
1942: Posted to North Africa, Cyprus, Iraq and North Africa again; Western Desert campaign; promoted to Captain; captured at Mersa Matruh
1942–45: Prisoner of War in Chieti, Italy (1942), Moosberg, Bavaria & Mahrisch Trubau, Czechoslovakia (1943), then Brunswick, Saxony (1944); starts writing *Mountaineering in Scotland*; introduced to Perennial Philosophy and meditation by Herbert Buck

1945: Release from POW camp; brief time in Wales, Adjutant in RE in
Vale of Leven; joins SMC

1946: Demobbed from army; returns to Glasgow and the Union Bank;
short spell at Buckfast Abbey; begins work on Glencoe guidebook;
climbs Twisting Gully

1947: *Mountaineering in Scotland* published; resigns from Union Bank;
buys Lochwood on the shores of Loch Goil; involved in serious
accident in Dauphiné Alps and suffers fractured skull

1948: On SMC Committee (till 1951); in Alps (Scheidegg) with AC/SMC

1949: Glencoe guidebook published; in Alps (Chamonix area)

1950s

*Korean War; conflict in Malaya; Sputnik & the space race; Harold Macmil-
lan says 'you've never had it so good'; McCarthy witch hunt for communists
in America; rock'n roll; Elvis Presley; Buddy Holliday; Suez crisis; apartheid
in South Africa; death of George VI; coronation of Queen Elizabeth II;
Everest climbed; Roger Bannister runs 4-minute mile; colour TV; Doris
Day; James Dean; Grace Kelly; Cary Grant; Dean Martin; Marilyn Monroe;
Maria Callas; Jackson Pollock; Castro in Cuba; link made between smoking
and cancer; Mau Mau in Kenya; Martin Luther King; first passenger jets;
European Common Market; Vietnam War begins.*

1950: Scottish Himalayan Expedition

1951: *Undiscovered Scotland* published; *The Scottish Himalayan Expedition* published; deputy leader of Everest Reconnaissance Expedition
& exploration in adjacent areas; Mungo Park Medal from RSGS

1952: Working on *The Story of Everest* and on house and garden at
Lochwood; various lectures on Everest reconnaissance

1953: Becomes Hon. President of Perth JMCS (until 1957); *The Story of
Everest* published; in Api region of Himalayas with John Tyson;
several revisions/updates of *The Story of Everest*

1954: For the next three years he tries his hand at writing stage drama; *The
Highlands in Colour* published

1955: Made Vice-president of SMC (until 1957)

1957: Turns to writing fiction and starts working on his first novel

1959: *Five Frontiers* published

1960s

*John F. Kennedy becomes President of USA; Cuban missile crisis; Vietnam
war in full swing; Yuri Gagarin the first man in outer space; Martin Luther
King killed; Malcolm X and Black Power; Profumo scandal; Che Guevara
killed; death of Marilyn Monroe; the Beatles; flower power; the mini-skirt;*

Women's Liberation Movement; Cultural Revolution in China & the Red Guard; James Bond; Bob Dylan; Rolling Stones; Jimi Hendrix; Rudolph Nureyev; England win World Cup Football for the first time; Sir Francis Chichester sails solo around the world; Aberfan disaster in Wales; Torrey Canyon oil tanker disaster; the contraceptive pill; Apollo Mission tragedy; first video recorders; the Troubles escalate in Northern Ireland; increasing use of computers; Neil Armstrong and Buzz Aldrin the first men on the Moon; beginning of North Sea oil boom.

1960: *The Spurs of Troodos* published; marries Anne B. Clark
1961: Field work for *Highland Landscape*
1962: Becomes President of SMC (until 1964); *Highland Landscape* published; *Maelstrom* published; Philip Temple's *Narwok!* published (rewritten for Dent by Murray)
1963: Becomes Mountain Adviser for NTS (until 1982)
1964: *The Craft of Climbing* (jointly authored with J.E.B.Wright) published
1965: *Dark Rose the Phoenix* published; fieldwork for *Companion Guide to the West Highlands*
1966: Field work continues; becomes President of the Scottish Branch of the Ramblers' Association (until 1984); awarded OBE
1967: Working on *Companion Guide to the West Highlands* and on Nea Morin's *A Woman's Reach*
1968: Becomes a Commissioner for CCS (until 1980) and Chairman of SCAC (until 1982); *Companion Guide to the West Highlands* published
1968: His first Everest trek, leading a group for Col. Roberts' trekking company
1969: *The Real Mackay* published

1970s

North Sea oil boom in full swing; Britain joins the European Common Market; murder of Israeli athletes at Munich Olympics; decimal currency; pocket calculators; Nixon & the Watergate scandal; Beatles break up; Margaret Thatcher first woman PM of Britain; IRA bombings; Vietnam war comes to an end; civil war in Rhodesia/Zimbabwe; Ayatollah Khomeini takes control in Iran; Idi Amin in Uganda; Wonderwoman and Superman; men wear flares; Mary Peters; Sebastian Coe; Martina Navratilova; Marlon Brando, Woody Allan; Mohammad Ali; Elvis Presley dies; Pol Pot and the killing fields in Cambodia; hippies, punk rock and skinheads; Twiggy; Abba; Rod Stewart; Mick Jagger; David Bowie; Barbra Streisand; David Hockney; Andy Warhol.

1970: Heavily engaged throughout the 70s with conservation issues (issues related to North Sea oil, the Grampian Way and other long-distance routes, bulldozed tracks etc.)

1971: Vice-president of Alpine Club (until 1972); *Scotland's Splendour* published

1972: President of MCof S (until 1975)

1973: *The Islands of Western Scotland: The Inner and Outer Hebrides* published; another Himalayan trek as guide

1974: A month's trek as guide in Annapurna and Dhaulagiri area

1975: Receives honorary doctorate from the University of Stirling; working on *The Scottish Highlands*

1976: *The Scottish Highlands* published; *Beautiful Scotland* published; researching for his biography of Rob Roy; nominated as President of Alpine Club but declines because of pressure of work

1978: On council of Friends of Loch Lomond (until 1988); finishes first draft of *Rob Roy MacGregor*

1979: Combined volume of *Mountaineering in Scotland* and *Undiscovered Scotland* published

1980s

USA boycott Moscow Olympics; John Lennon assassinated; Mount St Helena erupts; IRA bomb fails to kill Margaret Thatcher and her Cabinet; Royal wedding of Prince Charles and Princess Diana; racehorse Shergar kidnapped; AIDS pandemic; personal computers; Falklands War; famine in Ethiopia; Lockerbie air disaster; Chernobyl nuclear accident; fatwa on Salman Rushdie; Hungarian uprising; Tiananman Square massacre; arrival of political correctness & gay rights; Steven Spielberg; Michael Jackson; Madonna; Prince; Bon Jovi; Bruce Willis; the Brat Pack, Eddie Murphy; Arnold Schwarzenegger; 'Dynasty' and 'Dallas' soap operas; Real Madrid; Ian Botham; Mike Tyson; Boris Becker; Stefi Graf; Gary Lineker; cabbage patch dolls; padded shoulders & power dressing.

1980: Retires from CCS

1981: *The Curling Companion* published

1982: Retires from SCAC and NTS; *Rob Roy MacGregor: his life and times* published; takes on advisory role with Scottish Wild Land Group

1903: Retires as President of Ramblers (Scotland)

1984: Big renovations at Lochwood; becomes Founding Trustee of JMT (until 1986)

1985: Judging on panel of Boardman Tasker Literary Prize

1987: *Scotland's Mountains* published

1988: Retires from Council of Friends of Loch Lomond
1989: Made SMC Honorary President

1990–1996

Dawn of the information age, internet, emails etc; Rawandan genocide; Hubble space telescope launched; Nelson Mandela freed; the Gulf War; the Chechen War; conflict in Bosnia, Croatia, Kosovo, and Serbia; collapse of the Soviet Union; South Africa repeals apartheid laws; IRA truce; official end to the Cold War; reunification of Germany; mad cow disease; channel tunnel opens; David Beckham; Eric Cantona; Paul Gascoigne; Pete Sampras; Roger Federer; Shane Warne; Tiger Woods; Liam Neeson; Jack Nicholson; the Spice Girls; Oasis; John Thaw.

1990: Becomes Patron of Scottish Council for National Parks; dangerously ill in hospital
1991: Anne has serious road accident; D.Litt from the University of Strathclyde
1992: Attends his last SMC dinner
1993: Starts writing his autobiography
1995: Falls while repairing the roof of his house; hospital reveals an underlying heart problem – surgery and complications
1996: A relapse and dies in hospital, 19th March

BIBLIOGRAPHY OF MURRAY'S PUBLISHED WORK

This bibliography was compiled by Robert Aitken, with some additions by Mike Cocker. For inclusion in this Appendix it has been slightly abridged. Unless stated otherwise, the publishers are located in London.

1. Books and pamphlets

1947 *Mountaineering in Scotland* Dent
and 1962 new edition: Dent
1966 paperback edition: Dent (Aldine)
1979 combined with *Undiscovered Scotland:* Diadem (later Bâton Wicks)

1949 *Rock Climbs: Glencoe and Ardgour* Edinburgh: SMC

1951 *Undiscovered Scotland* Dent
and 1954
1979 combined with *Mountaineering in Scotland* Diadem

1951 *The Scottish Himalayan Expedition* Dent

1953 *The Story of Everest* Dent
and 1953 four revisions
1954 one revision
and *L'histoire de l'Everest 1921–53*
Paris: Payot, 1953

1954 *The Highlands in Colour* (photos by W.S.Thomson)
Edinburgh: Oliver & Boyd

1959 *Five Frontiers* Dent

1960 *The Spurs of Troodos* Dent

1962 *Maelstrom* Secker & Warburg

1962 *Highland Landscape* Aberdeen UP for the National Trust for Scotland

1963 *Glencoe, Blackmount and Lochaber*: NTS (NTS Regional Guide No 1)

1964 (with J E.B. Wright) *The Craft of Climbing* Kaye

1965 *Dark Rose the Phoenix* Secker & Warburg

1966 *The Hebrides* Heinemann

1967 *Winter Climbing in Scotland* Glasgow: JMCS

1968 *The Companion Guide to the West Highlands:* Collins seven
editions to 1977; 1991 new edition by HarperCollins

1969 *The Real Mackay: a comedy in twelve chapters* Heinemann
1973 *The Islands of Western Scotland: the Inner and Outer Hebrides* Eyre & Methuen
1976 *The Scottish Highlands* Edinburgh: Scottish Mountaineering Trust
1976 *Beautiful Scotland* Batsford
1981 *The Curling Companion,* Glasgow: Richard Drew (and paperback) 1982 (revised) Toronto: Collins
1982 *Rob Roy MacGregor: his life and times* Glasgow: Richard Drew Publishing (and paperback). And in 1993, Edinburgh: Canongate Press Ltd
1987 *Scotland's Mountains* Scottish Mountaineering Trust

2a. W.H. Murray contributions to collections and to others' books

1950 'Ben Nevis' in Eileen Molony (ed.) *Portraits of Mountains* Dennis Dobson
1956 'British Mountains' in James Ramsey Ullman *The Age of Mountaineering* Collins
1961 'Foreword' in Leonard Moules *Some Want it Tough* Christian Literature Crusade
1961 'The West' in *Scotland's Splendour* Glasgow: Collins reprinted 1965, 1968
1968 'Reconnaissance 1951' [Everest] in Malcolm Milne (ed.) *The Book of Modern Mountaineering* Barker
1970 'Introduction' in John Hunt, *The Ascent of Everest* Heron Books
1979 'The High Tops' in Fred Holliday (ed.) *Wildlife of Scotland* Macmillan
1981 'Foreword' in Roger Smith (ed.) *Walking in Scotland* Edinburgh: Spurbooks/Ramblers' Association (Scottish Area)
1986 'Foreword' in B.H. Humble *The Cuillin of Skye* [second, facsimile ed. with biographical foreword by W.H.M.] Glasgow: Ernest Press
1996 'Foreword' in Andy Wightman *Scotland's Mountains: an agenda for Sustainable Development* Perth: Scottish Wildlife & Countryside Link

2b. Anthologised items

1964 'The top of Tower Ridge, Ben Nevis, in winter' [part of Ch. XIV from *Mountaineering in Scotland*] in Wilfrid Noyce (ed.) *The Climber's Fireside Book* Heinemann
1966 'Moonlight' [Ch.VI from *Undiscovered Scotland*] in Michael Ward (ed.) *The Mountaineer's Companion* Eyre & Spottiswoode
1981 'New Year on Ben Nevis' [Ch XVII from *Mountaineering in Scotland*] in Roger Smith (ed.) *The Winding Trail*

1983 'Prisoner of war' [from *Mountain* 67, 1979] in Jim Perrin (ed.) *Mirrors in the Cliffs* Diadem Books

1997 'Mountains', from 1947 *Mountaineering* in British Mountaineering Council, *The First Fifty Years of the British Mountaineering Council* edited by Geoff Milburn with Derek Walker and Ken Wilson, Manchester: BMC

3. Scottish Mountaineering Club Journal articles and notes

1937 'Defeat: a December night on the Crowberry Ridge' *Scottish Mountaineering Club Journal* 21 (128)

1938 'The Great Gully of Sgurr nam Fiannaidh, Glencoe' *Scottish Mountaineering Club Journal* 21 (129)

1940 'Nights up There – II. Hogmanay on Ben Nevis' *Scottish Mountaineering Club Journal* 22

1941 'The Last Day on Buachaille' *Scottish Mountaineering Club Journal* 23 (132)-

1946 'The Evidence of Things Not Seen' Scottish Mountaineering Club Journal 23 (137)

1947 'The Great Gully of Garbh Bheinn' *Scottish Mountaineering Club Journal* 23 (138)
'New Routes in Glencoe' *Scottish Mountaineering Club Journal* 23 (138)

1948 'The Approach Route to Beauty' *Scottish Mountaineering Club Journal* 24 (139)

1951 'The Scottish Himalayan Expedition' *Scottish Mountaineering Club Journal* 24 (142)

1962 'Highland Landscape' (letter to the Editor), *Scottish Mountaineering Club Journal* XXVII (153)

1963 'The Country of the Blind' *Scottish Mountaineering Club Journal* XXVII (154)

1964 'The Last Twenty-five Years' *Scottish Mountaineering Club Journal* XXVIII (155)

1965 'In Memoriam: Tom Longstaff' *Scottish Mountaineering Club Journal* XXVIII (156)

1969 'Wilderness Areas' (letter to the Editor), *Scottish Mountaineering Club Journal* XXIX (160)

1075 'JMCS Jubilee, 1925–75: The Glasgow Section: 1935–1940' *Scottish Mountaineering Club Journal* XXX (166)

1976 'J.H.B. Bell as climber' [obituary] *Scottish Mountaineering Club Journal* XXXI (167)

1979 'The CIC Hut Jubilee: The 1930's' *Scottish Mountaineering Club Journal* XXXI (170)

1981 'In Memoriam: Nancy Girvan' *Scottish Mountaineering Club Journal* XXXII (172)

1987 'In Memoriam: John Hartog' *Scottish Mountaineering Club Journal* XXXIII (178)

1990 'Leighton Johnstone's "Resurrection"' *Scottish Mountaineering Club Journal* XXXIV (181)
'In Memoriam: A. Ian L. Maitland, FRCS' *Scottish Mountaineering Club Journal* XXXIV (181)

1993 'Peculiarities of the High Climber' *Scottish Mountaineering Club Journal* XXXV (184)

1994 'Stac of Handa: first crossing' *Scottish Mountaineering Club Journal* XXXV (185)

1995 'In Memoriam: Alastair Lorimer Cram MC j.1930' [j = date joined SMC] *Scottish Mountaineering Club Journal* XXXV (186)
'In Memoriam: Archie MacAlpine j.1945' *Scottish Mountaineering Club Journal* XXXV (186)

4. Articles in other publications

1946 'Tower Ridge', *Open Air in Scotland*[2] spring
'First Ascent', *Open Air in Scotland*[3] summer

1947 'The Moonlit Ridge' *Open Air in Scotland*[7] autumn/winter

1948 'The Bristling Buttress' *Open Air in Scotland*[9] summer
'Mountain Training: in Switzerland' *Open Air in Scotland*[10] winter

1949 'Mountains' *Mountaineering*

1950 'The Castle Buttress of Ben Nevis' *Blackwood's Magazine* 267 (1616) June

1951 'Scottish Garwhal and Kumaon Expedition' *Alpine Journal* LVIII (282)

1952 'The Scottish Kumaon Expedition' *Himalayan Journal 1951–52*
'The Reconnaissance of Mount Everest, 1951', *Alpine Journal* LVIII (285)

1954 'The Exploration of Api' *Blackwood's Magazine* 275 (1662) April

1962 'Changed Face of the Highlands' *Guardian* 24th May

1964 'Survival in Storm' *Scots Magazine* December

1967 'Glen Affric's Magic Window' *Guardian* 25th February p. 8

1968 'Wild Scotland – a priceless asset in danger' *Scots Magazine*: New Series 88[5] February

1973 'A Traveller's Tale' *Mountain Life* 8, June

1975 'Mountaineering: 50 years of Progress' [JMCS Jubilee] *Scottish Field* CXXII (874) October

1976 'As I see it: keep it open and free' *Scots Magazine*: New Series 104[6] March

1979 'To Write a Book' *Mountain* 67 June
1979 'Genesis of a Mountain Classic' *The Weekend Scotsman* 2nd June
1984 'Writing & Climbing' *Climber & Rambler* XXIII[11] November
1985 'A Question of Intent' *The John Muir Trust Newsletter* 1 August
1984 '1984: Newspeak in the Hills' *Wild Land News* 3 Spring
1984 'Scotland: The 1930s' *Mountain 98*
1987 'My Cairngorms' in *Cairngorms at the Crossroads* Edinburgh: Scottish Wild Land Group.
1989 'The Cairngorms' *Save the Cairngorms Campaign, Bulletin No. 2,* February
1991 'Present Moments' *Alpine Journal* 86
1992 'The Old Loch Lomond Road' *Friends of Loch Lomond Newsletter* autumn

5. Reviews

1949 SMC *Guide to the Island of Skye* (eds Steeple, Barlow, MacRobert and Bell)
Alpine Journal LVII (278)
1953 *The Ascent of Everest* by John Hunt
Scottish Geographical Magazine 69
1954 SMC Guide to the Northern Highlands (ed. E.W. Hodge)
Alpine Journal LIX (289)
1957 *White Fury* by R. Lambert and C. Kogan
Alpine Journal LXI (294)
1958 *Prisoner in Red Tibet* by Sydney Wignall
Alpine Journal LXIII (296)
1965 *Red Peak* by C.G.M. Slesser
Scottish Geographical Magazine 81[2]
1966 *Mountain Conquest* by Eric Shipton
Alpine Journal LXXI (313)
1967 *The Mountaineer's Companion* by Michael Ward
Alpine Journal LXXII (314)
1990 *The Cairngorms Scene – and Unseen –* Sydney Scroggie
Scottish Mountaineering Club Journal XXIV (181)
1991 *The Northwest Highlands* by Donald Bennet and Tom Strang
Scottish Mountaineering Club Journal XXIV (182)
One Step in the Clouds, an omnibus of mountain fiction compiled by Audrey Salked and Rosie Smith
Scottish Mountaineering Club Journal XXIV (182)

FULL TEXT OF PERCY UNNA'S LETTER TO THE NTS

Letter from P.J.H. Unna, Esq, President, Scottish Mountaineering Club, to the Chairman and Council of the National Trust for Scotland, dated 23rd November 1937.

DEAR SIRS, As the movement initiated by a group of members of the Scottish Mountaineering Club to acquire Dalness Forest and hand it over to the National Trust for Scotland, to be held for the use of the nation, so that the public may have unrestricted access at all times, has now materialised; as subscriptions to that end were invited not only from the members of the Scottish Mountaineering Club, but also from the members of all the other mountaineering clubs in Great Britain; and as the fund so subscribed enables the forest to be handed over free of cost to the Trust, together with a surplus to be used as an endowment fund – it is considered desirable that what are believed to be the views of the subscribers as to the future of the estate should be expressed in writing, and recorded in the Minutes of the Trust. This is all the more necessary, as in the attached circular which was issued for the purpose of inviting these subscriptions it was stated that the land 'would be held on behalf of the public and preserved for their use,' and 'that the Trust' would 'be asked to undertake that the land be maintained in its primitive condition for all time with unrestricted access to the public.' The views in question are:

That 'Primitive' means not less primitive than the existing state.

That sheep farming and cattle grazing may continue, but that deer stalking must cease, and no sport of any kind be carried on, or sporting rights be sold or let; any use of the property for sport being wholly incompatible with the intention that the public should have unrestricted access and use. It is understood, however, that deer may have to be shot, as that may be necessary to keep down numbers and so prevent damage, but for that purpose alone.

That the word 'unrestricted' does not exclude regulations, but implies that regulations if any, should be limited to such as may in future be found absolutely necessary, and be in sympathy with the views expressed herein.

That the hills should not be made easier or safer to climb.

That no facilities should be introduced for mechanical transport; that paths should not be extended or improved; and that new paths should not be made.

That no directional or other signs, whether signposts, paint marks, cairns or of any other kind whatsoever, should be allowed: with the exception of such signs as may be necessary to indicate that the land is the property of the Trust, and to give effect to the requirement in the Provisional Order of 1935 that by-laws must be exhibited.

That should a demand spring up for hotels or hostels, it is possible that it may have to be satisfied to a limited extent. If so, they should only be built alongside public roads, and should be subject to control by the Trust; and it is suggested that no hotels or hostels should be built in Glencoe itself, or on any other part of the property, except, perhaps, in the lower reaches of the Trust property in Glen Etive. It is hoped that the Trust may be able to come to an understanding with neighbouring proprietors as to corresponding restrictions being maintained in regard to land near to that held by the Trust.

That no other facilities should be afforded for obtaining lodging, shelter, food or drink; and especially, that no shelter of any kind be built on the hills.

It is hoped that the design of any buildings which may be necessary will be carefully considered by the Trust; and that, where possible, trees will be planted in their vicinity.

In conclusion, it is suggested that the whole question of the management of the Trust properties in Glen Etive and Glencoe should receive special attention, in view of the possibility that the policy adopted by the National Trust for Scotland in the present instance may create a precedent for similar areas in other mountainous districts, not only in Scotland, but also in England and Wales.

Yours faithfully, P. J. H. Unna.

GLOSSARY OF CLIMBING TERMS & ACRONYMS

Abseil: A controlled slide down a doubled rope. The rope is retrieved, sometimes with difficulty, by pulling one end.

Aid, Artificial Aid, Artificial Climbing: Where the climber pulls directly on a bolt, chock, ice screw, piton or sling rather than climbing the rock.

AJ: Alpine Journal

Belay: Tying the Leader or the Second to the rock face while the other climbs a Pitch.

Bolt: Expansion bolt with a hole into which a Karabiner can be clipped, inserted into bare rock by drilling a small hole.

Bouldering: a style of rock climbing done without a rope and normally limited to very short climbs over a bouldering mat, so that a fall will not result in serious injury. It is typically practised on large natural boulders or artificial boulders in gyms.

Carabiner: a metal alloy snaplink, sometimes called a 'crab' or spelt Karabiner

CCS: Countryside Commission for Scotland

Chock: Wedge or hexagonal-shaped piece of metal, with a wire or rope loop to which a Karabiner can be attached. Inserted into a crack to provide a belay or running belay. Chocks are removed by the Second and do not damage the rock.

Col: The lowest point on a mountain ridge between two peaks.

Combined Tactics: Where the leader uses the Second for aid, typically using his knee, shoulder or head as a foothold.

Cornice: Windblown overhang of snow.

Corrie: A steep bowl-shaped hollow occurring at the upper end of a valley, usually associated with glacial activity. Also known as a cwm.

Crevasse: a large crack or fissure which has opened up in a glacier, usually because of the slow downward movement of the glacier.

Crux: The hardest section of a climb.

Cwm: See corrie.

Exposure: The increasing sense of height as a climb is ascended. More pronounced on steep and open rock faces. The feeling of exposure can be very debilitating.

Free Climbing: Climbing the rock without direct aid from a bolt, chock, ice screw, piton or sling, although all of these may be used to provide running belays. See **Aid**.

Glissade: To slide down snow standing up.

Ice Screw: A hollow cylinder of metal which is screwed into ice to provide a belay or running belay.

JMCS: Junior Mountaineering Club of Scotland

JMT: John Muir Trust

Leader: Person who goes first when climbing a route.

Leading through: A term for doing alternate leads.

MC of S: Mountaineering Council of Scotland

NTS: National Trust for Scotland

Peg or piton: Metal spike with an eye that is usually left permanently in place when hammered into a crack.

Pitch: The distance between consecutive stances (ledges where climbers can anchor themselves, and belay their climbing partners). Climbs may be single-pitch or multi-pitch.

Runner: A method of placing something on or in the rock through which the rope can run in the middle of a pitch to reduce the length of a fall.

Run out: The length of rope that has been run out between the leader and his/her second.

SCAC: Scottish Countryside Activities Council

Second: The second person to climb a pitch. On a vertical pitch, the second is protected by a rope from above and so is much safer than the leader. On a traverse, both climbers are exposed to a potential fall.

Sling: A loop of rope or tape with a karabiner attached which can be put over a flake of rock or threaded behind a natural chockstone to provide a belay or running belay.

SMC: Scottish Mountaineering Club

SMCJ: Scottish Mountaineering Club Journal

SNH: Scottish Natural Heritage

Sport-Climbing: Specially prepared routes with bolts pre-placed every few metres. Relatively rare in Britain but common on the continent.

Step cutting: Using an ice axe to cut holds in snow.

Top-Rope: Climbing with a rope from above.

Traditional climbing: traditional climbing, or 'trad' climbing, as it's popularly known, is how climbing was always done until fairly recently.

Verglas: A thin coating of ice on rock.

ONLINE APPENDICES TO THE SUNLIT SUMMIT

These appendices can be found both on the author's website: www.robinlloyd-jones.com and on the website of Sandstone Press: www.sandstonepress.com.

A   A note on how climbs are graded in Britain – the grading systems for rock climbing and for winter snow and ice climbing.

B   The Campaign in the Western Desert 1940-42 – covering the period of Rommel's main victories and Murray's capture.

C   About Captain Herbert Buck – including his activities behind enemy lines and his daring escape.

D   Mountains and mysticism – a look at the possible causes of mystical experiences in mountains.

E   Further notes on the Perennial Philosophy, mysticism and meditation – as relevant to Murray's beliefs and the kind of meditation he practised.

F   Full text of Murray's 1975 Presidential Address to the Mountaineering Council of Scotland – includes his views on access, preservation, mountain rescue and outdoor education.

G   Recipients of the Mungo Park Medal – an interesting list of explorers and adventurers.

H   Full text of John Randall's Appreciation of The Islands of Western Scotland – John Randall, Chairman of the Islands Book Trust, discusses Murray's book in the context of other books about the Western Isles.

I   Full text of the obituaries of W.H. Murray by (i) Robert Aitken; (ii) Robin Campbell – these two obituaries are the most comprehensive of the many obituaries which appeared.

J   An anthology of Murray's special places – a list of places mentioned by Murray in his books, articles and other writings as having especially impressed him in some way.

K   A Chronology of Murray's Climbs 1935-45 by Michael Cocker – tells us when, where and with whom and provides a well-informed commentary. This is an on-going work which will be updated from time to time.

BIBLIOGRAPHY

Abram, David. 1966. *The Spell of the Sensuous*. New York: Vintage.

Alvarez, A. 2003. *Feeding the Rat*. London: Bloomsbury.

Aitken, Robert. 1996. *National Parks for Scotland, A Paper for Scottish Wildlife and Countryside Link*. Edinburgh: NTS.

Aitken, Robert. 1984. *Scottish Mountain Footpaths, A reconnaissance review of their condition*. Countryside Commission for Scotland. Perth: CCS.

Anderson J.R.L. 1970. *The Ulysses Factor*. London: Hodder and Stoughton.

Baker, Ernest. A. 1923. *The Highlands with Rope and Rucksack*. London: Witherby.

Bates, Robert H. 2000. *Mystery, Beauty and Danger: The Literature of the Mountains and Mountain Climbing published in English before 1946*. Portsmouth, New Hampshire: Peter Randall.

Bartlett, Phil. 1993. *The Undiscovered Country: The Reasons we Climb*. Glasgow: Ernest Press.

Bell, J.H.B. 1950. *A Progress in Mountaineering*. Edinburgh: Oliver & Boyd.

Blackshaw, A. 1965. *Mountaineering*. London: Penguin.

Boardman, P. 1978. *The Shining Mountain*. London: Hodder & Stoughton.

Borthwick, A. 1939. *Always a Little Further*. London: Faber & Faber.

Bozman, E.F. and Bell, J.H.B.. 1940. *British Hills and Mountains*. London: Batsford.

Brady, Emily. 2003. *Aesthetics of the Natural Environment*. Edinburgh: Edinburgh University Press.

Brooker, W.D. 1988. *A Century of Scottish Mountaineering*. Edinburgh: Scottish Mountaineering Trust.

Callicott, J. Baird and Michael Nelson. 1998. *The Great New Wilderness Debate*. Atlanta.

Carrit E.F. 1931. *Philosophies of Beauty*. Oxford: Oxford University Press.

Carson, Rachel. 1956. *The Sense of Wonder*. New York: Harper & Row.

Chevalier, T. (ed.) 1997. *The Encyclopedia of Essayists*. Chicago University Press.

Clark, R.W. 1953. *The Victorian Mountaineers*. London: Batsford.

Clark, R.W. and Pyatt E.C. 1957. *Mountaineering in Britain*. London: Phoenix House.

Coleridge, E.H., (ed.) 1912. *The Poems of Samuel Taylor Coleridge*. Oxford: Oxford University Press.

Conway, M. 1905. *The Alps from End to End*. London: Constable.

Conway, M. 1920. *Mountain Memories: A Pilgrimage of Romance*. London: Cassell.

Countryside Commission for Scotland. 1974. *A Park System for Scotland*. Perth: CCS.

Countryside Commission for Scotland. *The Mountain Areas of Scotland, Conservation and Management*. Perth: CCS.

Countryside Commission for Scotland. 1978. *Scotland's Scenic Heritage*. Perth: CCS.

Craig, David. 1987. *Native Stones*. London: Secker & Warburg.

Csikszentmihalyi, Mihaly. 1990. *Flow: The Psychology of Optimal Experience*. New York: Harper and Row.

Engel, Susan. 1999. *Context is Everything: The Nature of Memory, Constructing Versions of Our Past*. New Jersey: W.H. Freeman & Co.

Fleck, Richard F. (ed.) 1984. *John Muir: Mountaineering essays*. Salt Lake City. Gibbs M. Smith.

Folio Society. 1991. *Coleridge among the Lakes & Mountains: from his Notebooks, Letters and Poems 1794–1804*. London: Hudson Folio.

Fox, Michael, W. 1980. *One Earth, One Mind*. New York: Coward, McCann & Geoghegan.

Garrett, Richard. 1988. *P.O.W.: The Uncivil Race of War*. Newton Abbot: David & Charles.

Gempel, Ann. 2011. *E.R. Zenthon, His Life and Work*: privately published in Loughborough.

Gifford, Terry. 2006. *Reconnecting with John Muir*. University of Georgia Press.

Gillies, Midge. 2011. *The Barbed-Wire University*. London. Aurum Press.

Graham, Stephen. 1927. *The Gentle Art of Tramping*. London: Robert Holden.

Griffiths, Jay. 2006. *Wild: An Elemental Journey*. London: Penguin.

Griggs, E. L. 1956. *Collected Letters of Samuel Taylor* Coleridge. Oxford: Clarendon Press.

Guss, David. 2013. *Almost Home: A biography of Alastair Cram*. unpublished manuscript

Hankinson, Alan. 1995. *Geoffrey Winthrop Young: poet, mountaineer, educator*. London: Hodder & Stoughton.

Hillary, Edmund. 1955. *High Adventure*. London: Hodder & Stoughton.

Holmes, Richard. 1982. *Coleridge*. Oxford University Press.

Homes, Steven. 1999. *The Young John Muir: An Environmental Biography*. Madison: University of Wisconsin Press.

Humble, Ben. 1968 edition. *The Cuillins of Skye*. Edinburgh: Canongate.

Humble, Roy. M. 1995. *The Voice of the Hills: The Story of Ben Humble MBE*. Edinburgh: The Pentland Press.

Hunt, J. 1953. *The Ascent of Everest*. London: Hodder & Stoughton.

Hunter, J. 1995. *On the Other Side of Sorrow: Nature and People in the Scottish Highlands*. Edinburgh: Mainstream.

Huxley, Aldous. 1946. *The Perennial Philosophy*. London: Chatto & Windus.

Jameson, Dale (ed.). 2003. A Companion to Environmental Philosophy. Oxford: Blackwell.

Kaplan, Stephen. 1992. *Environmental Preferences in a Knowledge-Seeking, Knowledge-Using Organism*. Oxford University Press.

Lambert, Robert. A. 2001. *Contested Mountains: Nature, Development and Environment in the Cairngorms Region of Scotland 1880–1989*. Cambridge: Whitehorse Press.

Laski, Marghanita. 1961. *Ecstasy: a Study of Some Secular and Religious Experiences*. London: Crescent Press.

Leopold, Aldo. 1949. *A Sand County Almanac*. New York. Reprint OUP, 1989.

Longstaff, T. 1950. *This is my Voyage*. London: John Murray.

Louv, Richard. 2011. *The Nature Principle: Human Restoration and the End of Nature-Deficit Disorder*. Chapell Hill NC: Algonquin Press.

Lunn, A. 1957. *A Century of Mountaineering 1857–1957*. London: George Allen & Unwin.

Macfarlane, Robert. 2003. *Mountains of the Mind: A History of a Fascination*. London: Granta Books.

Macfarlane, Robert. 2007. *The Wild Places*. London: Granta Books.

MacLeod, Ian. 1997. *The Glasgow Academy*. Glasgow: The Glasgow Academicals' War Memorial Trust.

McCarthy, Jeffrey Mathes (ed.) 2008. *Contact*. Reno: Nevada University Press.

McKibben, Bill. 1990. *The End of Nature*. London: Viking.

McNeish, Cameron & Else, Richard. 1994. *The Edge. 100 Years of Scottish Mountaineering*. London: BBC Publications.

Mitchell, Richard G. 1983. *Mountain Experience: the Psychology and Sociology of Adventure*. University of Chicago Press.

Mollison, D. 1994. *Sharing the Land*. Musselburgh: John Muir Trust.

Mummery, A.F. 1895. *My Climbs in the Alps and Caucasus*. London: Fisher Unwin.

Neate, Jill. 1986. *Mountaineering Literature*. Milnthorpe, Cumbria: Cicerone Press.

Nicolson, Marjorie. 1959. *Mountain Gloom and Mountain Glory: The Development of the Aesthetics of the Infinite*. Republished 1997. University of Washington Press.

Parham, John (ed.) 2002. *The Environmental Tradition in English Literature*, Aldershot: Ashgate.

Patey, T. 1971. *One Man's Mountains*. London: Victor Gallancz.

Perrin, J. (ed.) 1983. *Mirrors in the Cliffs*. London: Diadem Books.

Perrin, J. 2006. *The Climbing Essays*. Glasgow: The In Pinn.

Rackham, Oliver. 1986. The *History of the Countryside, the classic history of Britain's landscape, flora and fauna*. London: Dent.

Raeburn, H. 1920. *Mountaineering Art*. London: Fisher Unwin.

Rollings, Charles. 2007. *Prisoner of War*. London: Ebury Press.

Scottish National Parks Committee, Scottish Wild Life Conservation Committee. 1949. *Nature Reserves in Scotland*. Edinburgh.

Scott, Walter. Reprinted 1995. *Rob Roy*. Hertfordshire: Wordsworth Classics.

Scottish Wildlife and Countryside Link. 1997. *Protecting Scotland's Finest Landscapes, A Call for Action on National Parks for Scotland.*

Shepard, Paul. 1967. *Man in the Landscape: A Historic View of Esthetics of Nature*. New York: Alfred Knopf.

Shipton, E. 1951. *The Mount Everest Reconnaissance Expedition*. London: Hodder & Stoughton.

Shipton, E. 1969. *That Untravelled World*. London: Hodder & Stoughton.

Simpson, J. 1988. *Touching the Void*. London: Jonathan Cape.

Smout, T.C. 2000. *Nature Contested – Environmental History in Scotland and Northern England since 1600*. Edinburgh: Edinburgh University Press.

Snyder, Gary. 1990. *The Practice of the Wild*. San Francisco: North Point Press.

Steele, P. 1998. *Eric Shipton: Everest and Beyond*. London: Constable.

Stevenson, David. 2004. *The Hunt for Rob Roy*. Edinburgh: Birlinn.

Strunk, William & White, E.B. 1979. *The Elements of Style*. New York: Macmillan.

Tasker, J. 1982. *Savage Arena*. London: Methuen.

Thompson, Simon. 2010. *Unjustifiable Risk? The Story of British Climbing*. Cumbria: Cicerone Press.

Thomson, I.D.S. 1993. *The Black Cloud*. Glasgow: Ernest Press.

Thomson, W.S. 1954. *The Highlands in Colour*. London: Oliver and Boyd.

Tudor, Malcolm. 2000. *British Prisoners of War in Italy: Paths of Freedom*. Newtown, Powys: Emilia Publishing.

Underhill, Evelyn. 1992. *Heaven a Dance: An Evelyn Underhill Anthology*. London: Triangle.

Underhill, Evelyn. 2003. *The Cloud of Unknowing*. London: Dover.

Underhill, Evelyn. 1911. *Mysticism*. London: Methuen.

Unsworth, W. 1968. *Because it is there*. London: Victor Gollancz.

Wall, Derek. 1994. *Green History: A Reader in Environmental History, Philosophy and Politics*. London: Routledge.

Ward, Michael. 1972. *In This Short Span: A Mountaineering Memoir*. London: Victor Gollancz.

Weir, Tom. 1953. *East of Katmandu*. London: Oliver & Boyd.

Weir, Tom. 1983. *Weir's Way*. St Albans: Granada.

Weir, Tom. 1994. *Weir's World*. Edinburgh: Canongate Books.

Wells, C. 2001. *A Brief History of British Mountaineering*. Penrith: The Mountain Heritage Trust.

™Wheeler, Michael (ed.) 1995. *Ruskin and Environment*. New York: St Martin's Press.

Wightman, Andy. 1996. *Scotland's Mountains, An Agenda for Sustainable Development*. Perth: Scottish Wildlife and Countryside Link.

Williams, Raymond. 1973. *The Country and the City*. New York: Oxford University Press.

Wilson, K. 1978. *The Games Climbers Play*. London: Diadem Books.

Whymper, E. 1871. *Scrambles Amongst the Alps*. London: John Murray.

Young G.W. 1927. *On High Hills*, 1927. London: Methuen.

Young G. W. 1936. *Collected Poems*. London: Methuen.

In addition to the books listed above, I have consulted the following newspapers, magazines and journals:

Alpine Journal, American Journal of Psychiatry, American Journal of Psychology, Blackwood's Magazine, British Medical Journal, Climber & Rambler, Climbing Club Journal, Countryside Commission for Scotland (various booklets & reports), *Friends of Loch Lomond Newsletter, Geographical Journal, Guardian*, (Glasgow) *Herald, Himalayan Journal, Independent, Interdisciplinary Studies in Literature and Environment* (journal of ASLE), *Irish Times, John Muir Trust Newsletter, Journal of the Fell and Rock Club, Journal of the Mountaineering Council of Scotland, Mountain Magazine*, National Trust for Scotland (various publications), *Open Air in Scotland, Royal Scottish Geographical Magazine, Scottish Mountaineering Club Journal, The Scots Magazine, Scotsman, The Times*.

I have also consulted a wide range of websites. Chief amongst these were: the websites of the organisations whose publications are given above, Amazon. co.uk, The Angry Corrie website, the BBC's 'People's War' website, The Glencoe Mountaineer, Imperial War Museum, the website of the National Ex-Prisoner of War Association, ScotlandOnline, Wikipedia and other online encyclopaedias.

INDEX